NORTHWEST
Reprints

Northwest Reprints

Series Editor: Robert J. Frank
Other titles in the series:

Narrative of a Journey
across the Rocky Mountains, to the Columbia River, and a Visit to the Sandwich Islands, Chili, &c., with a Scientific Appendix

by
John Kirk Townsend

Introduction and Annotation by
George A. Jobanek

Oregon State University Press
Corvallis

Publication of this book was made possible in part
by a contribution from

The Delmer Goode Fund

Oregon State University Press is grateful for this support

The paper in this book meets the guidelines for permanence and
durability of the Committee on Production Guidelines for Book
Longevity of the Council on Library Resources and the minimum
requirements of the American National Standard for Permanence of
Paper for Printed Library Materials Z39.48-1984.

Library of Congress Cataloging-in-Publication Data
Townsend, John Kirk, 1809-1851.
    Narrative of a Journey across the Rocky Mountains to the
Columbia River/by John Kirk Townsend ; introduction and
annotation by George A. Jobanek.—1st ed.
        p. cm.—(Northwest reprints)
    Originally published: Philadelphia : H. Perkins, 1839.
    ISBN 0-87071-525-9 (alk. paper)
    1. Northwest, Pacific—Description and travel. 2. Rocky
Mountains—Description and travel. 3. Hawaii—Description and
travel. 4. Townsend, John Kirk, 1809-1851—Journeys. 5. Overland
journeys to the Pacific. 6. Natural history—Northwest, Pacific.
7. Natural History—Rocky Mountains. 8. Natural History—
Hawaii. I. Title. II. Series.

    F880.T7 1999
    917.9504'3—dc21   99-047898

Oregon State University Press
101 Waldo Hall
Corvallis OR 97331-6407
541-737-3166 •fax 541-737-3170
http://osu.orst.edu/dept/press

Contents

Preface   xii

Introduction   xiii

Narrative of a Journey across the Rocky Mountains, to the Columbia River, and a Visit to the Sandwich Islands, Chili, &c., with a Scientific Appendix

Preface

In 1837, upon his return to Philadelphia, John Kirk Townsend began writing his account of his two years spent journeying to and residing in the Oregon country, his experiences in the Sandwich (Hawaiian) Islands, and his journey home via Chile and Cape Horn. A young man still his in his twenties, Townsend intended his travelogue for a small audience of family and friends. In 1839, the Philadelphia publishing firm of Henry Perkins published his book, complete with his "scientific appendix," in which he detailed the birds and mammals he found on his western travels.

The next year, in 1840, the London firm of Henry Colburn reissued the narrative, dividing it into two volumes and retitling it *Sporting Excursions in the Rocky Mountains, Including a Journey to the Columbia River, and a Visit to the Sandwich Islands, Chili, &c.* The publishers chose to delete some material (although the deletions are very minor), and introduced new paragraph breaks. From this time on, Townsend's *Narrative* would never again assume its original form.

Greatly truncated versions of Townsend's *Narrative* appeared in the mid and late 1800s, essentially telling just the story of the trip west. Reuben Gold Thwaites largely restored Townsend's *Narrative* in 1905 as part of his multi-volume Early Western Travels series. Thwaites removed, however, the chapters on Townsend's activities in the Hawaiian Islands, and his return home. Thwaites's abridgment was subsequently reprinted by Ye Galleon Press and by University of Nebraska Press, Bison Books.

This edition by Oregon State University Press is the first since 1839 to restore Townsend's text to its entirety. Townsend's engaging story, his encounters with remarkable and significant historical figures, his accomplishments and perils and scientific pursuits in a largely untraveled land, can again be read and enjoyed as they were originally written for his family and friends. Townsend spoke in his *Narrative* of the particular joy of the scientist in discovering something new, but we as readers can also experience "delight amounting to ecstasy" in this wonderful story of western exploration.

Introduction

If John K. Townsend is remembered at all today, it is as the diarist of a western journey. His *Narrative of a Journey Across the Rocky Mountains to the Columbia River* is an enchanting account of his trek to Oregon on Nathaniel Wyeth's 1834 expedition, his two years in Oregon, and his travels back to the east coast of the United States by way of Hawaii and Chile. Townsend's success as a diarist, however, has overshadowed his accomplishments as a naturalist. John K. Townsend journeyed west with a purpose, as a participant in the Second Great Age of American Discovery, as a scientific explorer in a new land.[1]

John Kirk Townsend was born in Philadelphia October 10, 1809.[2] The Quaker city was fertile ground in which to introduce a young man to the delights of science. Philadelphia enjoyed a reputation from colonial times as the "scientific capital of the country." Its prestigious institutions included the American Philosophical Society and the Academy of Natural Sciences, as well as Charles W. Peale's Museum, which popularized interest in natural history. Philadelphian institutions and scientists, and the atmosphere of "intellectual creativity" in which they existed, provided the scientific training for western explorers.[3]

John Townsend's family background perhaps predisposed him to intelligence and an interest in natural history. His parents were Charles, a watchmaker, and Priscilla (née Kirk), Quakers with long familial attachments in medicine and science.[4] Three of John's brothers were dentists and active in attempting to improve the profession. His brother Edward, in addition, was a noted philanthropist, interested in prison reform. His sister Hannah published (posthumously) *A History of England in Verse* (1852). His sister Mary wrote *Life in the Insect World: or, Conversations upon Insects Between an Aunt and Her Nieces* (1844), and by her intelligence and disposition inspired others to emulate her.[5]

Young John attended from 1819 the Friends' Boarding School at Westtown, Pennsylvania, where the entomologist Thomas Say had earlier boarded, and whose later alumni included the ornithologist John Cassin and the vertebrate paleontologist Edward Drinker Cope. The natural sciences were a focus of the Friends' School and it is perhaps during this period that John developed his skill at taxidermy and learned to prepare study skins of birds. With William Townsend, a cousin, and the doctor Ezra Michener, an older friend, John Townsend began a collection of the birds of West Chester County, hunting the woods, streamsides, and fields. Townsend proved as proficient with a shotgun as he was skilled in identification, and the collection he amassed with his companions was a nearly complete sampling of the local avifauna. John James Audubon, an acquaintance, remarked upon Townsend's "zeal for the study of ornithology and his fine eye."[6]

On May 11, 1833, while collecting with John Richards at New Garden, Pennsylvania, Townsend noticed a bird he did not know sitting on a fence rail. The bird was very shy and as Townsend maneuvered to get close enough to shoot it, it flew from tree to tree. Aware of its rarity, Townsend focused on securing it for his collection. "Anxiety to procure it," he admitted, "prevented my observing its habits more particularly." When at last he held its lifeless body in his hand, his initial observation was confirmed—this was a bird unlike any he had seen before. When John James Audubon stopped in Philadelphia on his way south, Townsend showed him the specimen and Audubon concurred that the bird was undescribed, a new species. Townsend prepared a manuscript, dated September 27, 1833, formally describing the species and naming it after Audubon, *Emberiza auduboni*, Audubon's Bunting. For some reason this manuscript was never published. Audubon, in the second volume of his *Ornithological Biography* (1834), named it *Emberiza townsendi*, honoring its collector. "I am happy in thus paying my tribute of respect to him for his great attainments in ornithology." Townsend mounted the specimen and gave it to Ezra Michener. The species was never seen again, and taxonomists to this day argue whether Townsend collected the last individual of a dying species or whether the specimen is a hybrid or aberrant individual. Elliott Coues described the Townsend's Bunting as "a species which died at its birth."[7]

While Townsend was collecting this unique specimen and earning a Doctor of Science degree, Nathaniel J. Wyeth was engaged in an expedition that would shortly change the course of Townsend's life. Wyeth was a Cambridge, Massachusetts ice merchant who dreamed of establishing a fur trading company on the western coast of the continent. In early 1832, he departed the east coast with a small band of men, which included his cousin, John Wyeth, a neighbor of the Harvard botanist and ornithologist Thomas Nuttall. Nathaniel Wyeth expected to meet a supply ship when he reached the Pacific, but upon arrival at Fort Vancouver he learned that his ship had been wrecked in the South Pacific. Wyeth made the acquaintance of John McLoughlin, the chief factor of the Hudson's Bay Company at Fort Vancouver, as well as of David Douglas, who was then collecting plants in Oregon for the Horticultural Society of London.[8]

In February, 1833, Wyeth left Fort Vancouver to return to Massachusetts. Along the way home he collected plants for his friend, Thomas Nuttall.[9] Wyeth returned not at all disheartened by the failure of his endeavor but eager to again set out for Oregon, this time to seek salmon and peddle trade goods. Nuttall, piqued by Wyeth's plant specimens, longed to join this second expedition and resigned his position at Harvard to be free to do so. Undoubtedly intending to devote most of his time on the expedition studying plants, Nuttall invited John Townsend along to collect and study the new species of birds they would certainly encounter.[10]

Wyeth was delighted that another naturalist would be on the expedition. In February 1834, he wrote to Nuttall advising the new man what to bring. "As he will probably have no servant I would not recommend to him to take many goods…. I do not see that he need provide anything before reaching St. Louis more than he has unless he carrys [sic] *implements of science,*"[11]

Townsend, twenty-four years old, was no doubt as excited about the expedition as Thomas Nuttall, eager to see new lands and new species.[12] Townsend visited both the American Philosophical Society and the Academy of Natural Sciences of Philadelphia, to which he had been elected a member the previous year, and requested funding, receiving from each one hundred twenty-five dollars.[13] In turn, he agreed to collect natural history specimens for both institutions. No doubt Samuel G. Morton, corresponding secretary of the Academy, pressed upon Townsend the importance of collecting Indian skulls; Morton needed these for his "craniographic" research.[14] On March 13, 1834, Townsend packed his guns, Nuttall's two-volume *Manual of Ornithology* and a treatise on North American birds by Charles L. Bonaparte, works which held little information on the scientifically poorly-explored West but standard references in the East, and joined Thomas Nuttall on the stage for Pittsburgh.[15] They were off on their western adventure.

On the stage to Pittsburgh, Townsend rode into another realm. Breaking his ties to family and region, he joined a growing stream of exploring naturalists seeking new vistas, new creatures, new ideas in new lands. As had Joseph Banks on the Cook expedition and Alexander

Von Humboldt in his travels through Amazonia, as had John James Audubon in his wanderings through the southeast and Thomas Nuttall, the man seated next to young John on the bouncing, jarring stage, had in Arkansas before him, Townsend became part of the second great age of discovery.[16] As a curious naturalist, he sought new species of birds and hoped to study plants and native inhabitants, rocks and gems. He was riding the coattails of commerce on the Wyeth expedition to Oregon, the first ornithologist, along with Thomas Nuttall, to visit the territory.[17]

The stage coach ride to Pittsburgh was an unpleasant beginning of the journey, three days and four nights of bad roads. "I have never tried constant riding in a stage for several successive days before," Townsend wrote to his sister, "and thee may believe me I never wish to try it again. The stage was packed full else our bones might have suffered still more, as it is, I think our pasengers generally feel tolerably sore all over." The road wound around precipitous cliffs and the stage at times came so close to pitching into the abyss that "several of our passengers (all men, too) could scarcely repress a cry." Upon arrival in Pittsburgh, Townsend found the city "a vile, vile place—I have been in it but an hour and am wholly and completely disgusted with it and wish to leave it as quick as I can." The houses were "all encrusted with a black filthy soot from the smoke of the villianous bituminous coal which is eternally hanging like a foul incubus over the place—the very visages of the inhabitants are begrimed with the same dirty material and as for handsome women I have not yet seen one that was decent, they look as though they have been dealing in charcoal." What a contrast to Philadelphia, Townsend's own "noble and delightful city."[18]

Thomas Nuttall arranged for a boat to take Townsend and himself down the Ohio River to Cincinnati. Townsend found crossing the border from Pennsylvania into Ohio emotionally difficult. "As we passed this line, and as the shores of my native state receded from my view a feeling of sadness came upon me. I stood upon the upper deck and watched the sandy boundary, until blotted out by the distance and then ret'ned to the cabin with feelings such as I never experienced before, I felt that I was leaving the scenes of my childhood, the spot which had witnessed all the happenings I ever knew, the home where all my affections centered. I was entering a land of strangers and would be compelled hereafter to mingle with those who would look upon me with indifference or treat me with neglect."[19]

Uneasy with this homesickness, Townsend and Nuttall were glad when they arrived in St. Louis March 24 to find Nathaniel Wyeth still there, waiting for trade goods and supplies shipped from Baltimore. Wyeth took the scientists in hand and helped them with their shopping for the journey ahead. He selected for each of them leather trousers, "an enormous over-coat made of *green flannel,* only think of that!," and a white wool hat, "with round crown, fitting tightly to the head, brims five inches wide, and almost hard enough to resist a rifle ball." John confided to his father that "we shall look very beautiful no doubt."[20]

While his family might be amused by John's humorous tale of outfitting for the journey, his descriptions of Indians must have startled them, esconced as they were in Philadelphia. A day after shopping with Wyeth, a group of Sauk Indians passed through on their way to Jefferson Barracks, the government fort. "They were dressed and decorated in the true primitive style; their heads shaved closely, and painted with alternate stripes of fiery red and deep black, leaving only the long scalping tuft, in which was interwoven a quantity of elk hair and eagle's feathers.... The faces and bodies of the men were, almost without an exception, fantastically painted, the predominant color being deep red, with occasionally a few stripes of dull clay white around the eyes and mouth."[21]

Since Wyeth was to be kept in St. Louis for at least a week waiting for his supplies, Townsend and Nuttall decided to walk to Independence. As in Pittsburgh earlier, Townsend was happy to be leaving. "I was glad to be rid of [St. Louis] as I think it without exception the most disagreeable, extortionate, and uncomfortable town that I have yet found. Every article that a traveler finds is necessary to purchase, the little services and attentions that he requires are charged for most exorbitantly and withal there is scarcely a grain of comfort to be found in the largest and acknowledged best Hotel in this place."[22]

Striking the prairies, free from town, Townsend and Nuttall were in their heaven. Pileated Woodpeckers were in every riverside grove of trees and Greater Prairie-Chickens warily stalked the tall prairie grasses. Ducks were "exceedingly abundant" in every stream and easy targets, "so that amongst them all we were living in clover as we travel along." Nuttall, however, refused to carry a gun and would not use Townsend's, so that it was up to John to procure their meals of game. When they arrived at a house, the naturalists shared their bounty with their hosts, providing a meal in payment for lodging. As they steadily walked westward to Independence, Sandhill Cranes and Passenger Pigeons were flying north to nesting grounds.[23]

Unfamiliar species awaited them every bit of the way. "N[uttall] is continually calling my attention to plants that are new and strange and I am frequently meeting with birds that I have not before seen." Near Boonville, Missouri, they encountered "vast numbers" of Carolina Parakeets, sunshine gleaming and flashing off the brilliant red, green, and yellow bodies. Townsend began collecting the parakeets but the experience was not enjoyable. "They seem entirely unsuspicious of danger, and after being fired at, only huddle closer together, as if to obtain protection from each other, and as their companions are falling around them, they curve down their necks, and look at them fluttering upon the ground, as though perfectly at a loss to account for so unusual an occurrence. It is a most inglorious sort of shooting; down right, cold-blooded murder."[24]

Nearly a week later, Townsend and Nuttall arrived in Independence. Wyeth fell immediately to organizing his supplies and trade goods, impressing Townsend with his management of the men and his consideration of their ideas and feelings. The trapper Milton Sublette, who had been associated with Nathaniel Wyeth on the first expedition, joined the party. Sublette, "a man of strong sense and observation and better acquainted with indian manners and habits than any other man in the country," proposed to take personal care of Townsend and "make a man" of him. Townsend himself was relieved to find letters from his family awaiting him in Independence. He readied a box of specimens for the Academy of Natural Sciences of Philadelphia. He confided to his father that he dreaded "to look forward to a long, long separation, without the possibility of having one word of the welfare of those dearest to me on earth."[25]

On April 28, the expedition left Independence, seventy men, two hundred fifty horses. The Baptist missionaries Jason Lee and his nephew Daniel trailed the party with their cattle. Townsend was caught up in the grandeur of the scene, and the joyful emotional release of the men. "I frequently sallied out from my station to look at and admire the appearance of the cavalcade, and as we rode out from the encampment, our horses prancing, and neighing, and pawing the ground, it was altogether so exciting that I could scarcely contain myself. Every man in the company seemed to feel a portion of the same kind of enthusiasm; uproarious bursts of merriment, and gay and lively songs, were constantly echoing along the line." As they rode through the prairie, the air pulsed black, and yellow, and red as blackbirds rose in clouds from the grasses and alighted on the horses' backs.[26]

As the expedition worked its way west, spring crept northward to meet them, and new birds were everywhere around Townsend. Their very abundance was astonishing. "There is a considerable variety, and many of them have not before been seen by naturalists." Along the Platte River, Long-billed Curlews probed the mud of shallow ponds, and Sandhill Cranes and Great Blue Herons stalked fish. Farther on, American Avocets flew crying away from the march of the horses. Violet-green Swallows skimmed low over the grasstops, hawking insects flushed out by the procession.[27]

The naturalists found it difficult to collect scientific specimens while on the march. Nuttall often traveled ahead to gather his plants before they would be crushed by the hooves of the horses. Both men placed their collections over their own personal comfort. "Already we have cast away all our useless and superfluous clothing, and have been content to mortify our natural pride, to make room for our specimens. Such things as spare waistcoats, shaving boxes, soap, and stockings, have been ejected from our trunks, and we are content to dress, as we live, in a style of primitive simplicity."[28]

Despite the press of the march, they spent each day in rapture.

> *In the morning, Mr. N. and myself were up before the
> dawn, strolling through the umbrageous forest, inhaling the
> fresh, bracing air, and making the echoes ring with the
> report of our gun, as the lovely tenants of the grove flew by
> dozens before us. I think I never before saw so great a variety
> of birds within the same space. All were beautiful, and
> many of them quite new to me; and after we had spent an
> hour amongst them, and my game bag was teeming with its
> precious freight, I was still loath to leave the place, lest I
> should not have procured specimens of the whole.*
>
> *None but a naturalist can appreciate a naturalist's
> feelings—his delight amounting to ecstacy—when a
> specimen such as he has never before seen, meets his eye, and
> the sorrow and grief which he feels when he is compelled to
> tear himself from a spot abounding with all that he has
> anxiously and unremittingly sought for.*[29]

Nuttall devoted himself to plants, and found a large number of new species, while Townsend studied the birds.[30] Near the Platte River of western Nebraska he became the first naturalist to collect the Chestnut-collared Longspur and the Lark Bunting. He discovered the Mountain Plover on the tableland along the Sweetwater River of Wyoming; nearby he found the Sage Thrasher. In Idaho, with an accurate aim of his gun, he introduced the Green-tailed Towhee to science. He compiled a long list of birds he observed on the trek from Independence to Oregon.[31]

Townsend performed other duties on the expedition besides just amassing his natural history collections. Every third night, he served as captain of the guard, posting his guards around the sleeping caravan and patrolling amongst them, checking to see that every man was awake and alert, watching that Indians not steal any of the expedition's supplies. Unfortunately for Townsend, Milton Sublette's promise to "make a man" out of him was voided when Sublette left the expedition with an injured leg.[32]

Townsend threw himself into the adventure of the western trek. He stalked buffalo with the expedition's hunters and downed one himself, an old bull too tough to eat. While hunting geese he stumbled upon a grizzly bear, "his savage eyes glaring with horrible malignity, his mouth wide open, and his tremendous paws raised as though ready to descend" upon him. Townsend backed away, fortunate that the bear had not attacked him at once, and, after a slow, backwards retreat of a hundred yards, turned and "flew, rather than ran," back to camp. At the Green River rendezvous, an amazed Townsend observed the behavior of the mountain men, and being an abstemious Quaker, was disgusted by the drunken debauchery occurring around him.[33]

Townsend was likewise astonished and repulsed by the chief hunter's method of slaking thirst. On a hunt with Jason Lee and Townsend, the hunter cut open a freshly-killed buffalo and exposed the stomach. Townsend and Lee watched the hunter "plunge his knife into the distended paunch, from which gushed the green and gelatinous juices, and insinuate his tin pan into the opening, and by depressing its edge, strain off the water which was mingled with its contents." Both Lee and Townsend rejected the offered cup of "cider." "It was too thick with the excrement the [sic?] please my fancy," Lee remarked to his diary. Only moments later, however, Townsend, urged by the hunter to taste the heart's blood, was overcome by his thirst, and "plunged [his] head into the reeking ventricles, and drank until forced to stop for breath." In "assimilating [himself] so nearly to the brutes," Townsend had traveled, in more than just a physical dimension, a considerable distance from Philadelphia.[34]

By the time Townsend arrived with the Wyeth expedition at Fort Vancouver in mid-September, nearly five months after leaving Independence, his exuberance was beginning to wane. Near the end of the journey, as he listened to the declarations of Captain Benjamin Bonneville regarding the appeal of the mountain man's way of life, Townsend realized he himself "had become somewhat weary of rough travelling and rough fare, and looked forward with no little pleasure to a large rest under a Christian roof, and a general participation in Christian living."[35]

Arrival in Oregon offered a respite from the hard travelling. On September 16, 1834, the expedition beached their canoes on the sand in front of Fort Vancouver and John McLoughlin extended a friendly hand to Wyeth, the naturalists, the missionaries, and the expedition's men. McLoughlin urged Townsend and Nuttall to stay in his house, and arranged for a servant to attend to their needs. The naturalists divided their time between the fort and Wyeth's supply ship, the *May Dacre*, moored off of Warrior's Point, at the northern end of Sauvie Island, at the juncture of the Columbia and the Willamette Rivers. There was so much activity on the ship and the island where Wyeth was building a trade fort, that Townsend remarked in a letter to his father that "it is difficult to fancy oneself in a howling wilderness inhabited only by the wild and improvident indian and his scarcely more free and fearless neighbors the bear and the wolf." Townsend turned down an offer by Wyeth to return eastward to meet some of Wyeth's fur trappers in the mountains. Instead he plunged into his investigation of the region's birdlife.[36]

Collecting principally on Sauvie Island and near Fort Vancouver, but also travelling to points as far away as Astoria, Fort Walla Walla and the Blue Mountains, and the Falls of the Willamette, Townsend enjoyed a thorough acquaintance with the local avifauna. As on the westward journey, most of the birds in Oregon were different than the birds Townsend knew so well in Philadelphia, though similar. The towhees were strikingly spotted with white on the back and scapulars. The Fox Sparrows were a rich chocolate brown. The swifts overhead were so like the eastern Chimney Swift that at first Townsend thought them to be that familiar species; upon collecting some, he realized they were unique, an undescribed species. He bestowed upon them the name of an Academy of Natural Sciences member who had contributed to his expedition fund. He named a new warbler, so reminiscent of the Mourning Warbler, after a new friend from Fort

Vancouver. Flocks of small birds moving through the riparian underbrush during migration might easily have included several previously unknown species; Townsend named five new warblers, two new chickadees, and several new woodpeckers and finches. During the nesting season, he and Nuttall collected nests, and Townsend compiled long lists of birds and mammals occurring in the area.[37]

In October, 1835, the Reverend Samuel Parker visited Fort Vancouver, on a tour representing the American Board of Commissioners for Foreign Missions. Parker asked Townsend to prepare for him a report of the birds of the Columbia River region. Parker included an abridged version of Townsend's report in his book recounting his western trip. Townsend's report reveals a thorough knowledge of the lower elevation species inhabiting the area.[38]

Townsend's relationship with the region's Indians was ambivalent. He alternately saw them as a threat, pitied them, or used their services to his advantage. He wished the Christian missionaries good luck "in humanizing this miserable debased people." Perhaps amused by his interest in birds, the Indians called Townsend the "bird chief." They served him as collectors, bringing him many specimens of birds and mammals. Once, while after a species of jackrabbit at Fort Walla Walla, Townsend organized a collecting party of a dozen Indians with bows and arrows. He offered payment for the rarer species of birds he could not easily procure himself. In return for their efforts, above the prices he paid for specimens, Townsend provided medical care for several children, once concocting a medicine from the bark of the Pacific dogwood to treat malaria. In a darker sense, the Indians themselves became the subjects of Townsend's collecting. Robbing burial canoes, he gathered skulls, perhaps for S. G. Morton's craniographic research, and once tried to abscond with the mummified body of a young woman. Among the living, he recorded vocabularies of numerous tribes all along the Columbia drainage.[39]

Nuttall and Townsend, while certainly friends who travelled together on occasion, also collected apart from each other. Shyer and less comfortable among society, Nuttall perhaps was not as attracted to the Fort Vancouver community than the sociable Townsend, although Nuttall did visit the Lees' mission at Champoeg Settlement. Townsend and Nuttall had spent the winter of 1834–1835 together in the Sandwich (Hawaiian) Islands, escaping the "wet and disagreeable winter" in Oregon. Nuttall sailed again to the Islands the following winter, and his decision not to return to Oregon disconcerted

Townsend, who felt deserted by his friend. Nuttall sailed with Townsend's bird specimens and ultimately into literature, encountering upon a San Diego beach his former student Richard Henry Dana, who later wrote of the odd encounter in *Two Years Before the Mast*.[40]

With Nuttall on the ship to the Sandwich Islands was Dr. Meredith Gairdner, the surgeon at Fort Vancouver and a man of some scientific persuasion himself. Gairdner was seeking relief from tuberculosis and in his absence John McLoughlin appointed Townsend as fort surgeon. Townsend held this post until Dr. William F. Tolmie arrived at the fort about six months later. Tolmie and Townsend became good friends and it is after Tolmie that Townsend named one of his new warblers.[41]

Townsend also served as magistrate of the first public trial in Oregon. A gunsmith employed at Wyeth's Fort William (his trading post on Sauvie Island) shot and killed the fort's tailor during an argument over a young Indian woman. After hearing the evidence, resulting from Townsend's investigation and interviews, the jury ruled the killing was justifiable homicide. Townsend noted that the slain tailor was a man whose "appetite for ardent spirits was of the inordinate kind," on one occasion even decanting the alcohol off of a collection Townsend had made of lizards and snakes.[42]

On November 30, 1836, John Townsend left Oregon. As when he crossed the Pennsylvania border on the western journey and was emotionally affected by the thoughts of loved ones he might never see again, so, too, he regretted that leaving the Oregon country meant final goodbyes to good friends and companions. He had a particularly difficult time leaving John McLoughlin:

> *Much as I desire again to see home, much as I long to embrace those to whom I am attached by the strongest ties, I have nevertheless felt something very like regret at leaving Vancouver and its kind and agreeable residents. I took leave of Doctor McLoughlin with feelings akin to those with which I should bid adieu to an affectionate parent; and to his fervent, "God bless you, sir, and may you have a happy meeting with your friends," I could only reply by a look of the sincerest gratitude. Words are inadequate to express my deep sense of the obligations which I feel under to this truly generous and excellent man, and I fear I can only repay them by the sincerity with which I shall always cherish the recollection of his prosperity and happiness.*[43]

The *Columbia* reached Maui on December 22, 1836, and spent the next three months cruising amongst the Islands. While in the Sandwich Islands, Townsend busied himself with natural history collecting, getting the island residents to bring him birds, fishes, and shells. He collected for a time with a Prussian naturalist named Deppe, and together they discovered, as Townsend had done in Oregon, species of birds unknown to science before them. "Our object has been to procure birds, plants &c," Townsend wrote, "and we have so far been very successful. I have already prepared about eighty birds which I procured here." At least one species that Townsend and Deppe collected, the Oahu Oo, is now extinct; indeed, their collections are the last record of the bird. Besides pursuing his collecting activities, Townsend also found time to visit with missionaries and merchants. He enjoyed an audience with the king, Kamehameha III, and was present when Kamehameha received a message that his sister's, Nahienaena, health had worsened. After she died, Townsend attended the funeral rites.[44]

The long journey home led from the Sandwich Islands to Tahiti and Chile. In Valparaiso, Townsend became very ill and spent several weeks recovering, attended to by a doctor from Philadelphia. In September, Townsend rounded Cape Horn. While in the southern waters, he collected a number of pelagic birds. On November 14, 1837, his ship returned him to Philadelphia and to his family. He had been gone six months on the long trek west, over two years in the western wilderness, and one year on the journey home. Twenty-four years old when he left, he was now twenty-eight, and his collection of birds was already creating a sensation.[45]

Nuttall took Townsend's collection of birds assembled at that time with him when he departed Oregon. The specimens arrived at the Academy of Natural Sciences in Philadelphia in June, 1836, and Nuttall arrived in Boston three months later. Audubon anxiously sought access to both the collection and the naturalist. At work on his monumental *Birds of America* and wanting to illustrate the western species, Audubon greatly desired to talk with Nuttall about his discoveries in the west and to see Townsend's specimens. Townsend's supporters in Philadelphia, however, felt that Townsend should be enabled to publish the results of his own field work. It was finally agreed that Audubon might purchase duplicates of Townsend's specimens and that he and Nuttall would prepare a paper, under Townsend's name, publishing the new species. Thus a year before John Townsend returned from his long sojourn, Samuel Morton read his paper at an Academy of Natural Sciences meeting.[46]

Audubon was delighted with Townsend's specimens and wrote about them to his friend John Bachman:

> *Now good friend open your Eyes! aye open them tight!! Nay place specks on your probosis if you chuse! Read aloud!! quite aloud!!!—I have purchased Ninety Three Bird Skins! Yes 93 Bird Skins!—Well what are they? Why nought less than 93 Bird Skins sent from the Rocky Mountains and the Columbia River by Nuttal & Townsend!—Cheap as Dirt too—only one hundred and Eighty Four Dollars for the whole of these, and hang me if you do not echo my saying so when you see them!!—Such beauties! such rarities! Such Novelties! Ah my Worthy Friend how we will laugh and talk over them!—*[47]

Audubon incorporated the species in *Birds of America*, drawing them while in Charleston at Bachman's home. He waited impatiently for Townsend's return from the west and the probability of additional specimens. When Townsend returned in November, 1837, Audubon, then in London, arranged through his friend Edward Harris to purchase as much of Townsend's collection as he could. These were sent to London directly to Audubon, after a delay that was perhaps a result of Townsend's unfavorable financial situation. Audubon painted these new birds for later installments of the *Birds of America*.[48]

About this time, Audubon grew very critical of Townsend, complaining to John Bachman privately that Townsend's correspondence about the birds contained so little information "that I cannot understand how he spent his whole days and years at Fort Vancouver." He later wrote, now back in the United States, that "I have seen a great deal of Townsend of late, and am sorry to say have lost much towards him, he has become or perhaps always was Lazy and careless in the extreme and hardly speaks of those *who have befriended him when in need* in sufficient words of gratitude." Audubon claimed that he had received very little that was new from Townsend.[49]

Certainly the latter assertion was not justified; of the 508 species Audubon included in the octavo edition of *Birds of America*, 74 were sent him by Townsend. Perhaps this criticism stems from two things. Townsend was critical of several statements in the fifth volume (1839) of Audubon's *Ornithological Biography*, the text to the folio plates of *Birds of America*. In marginal annotations to his personal copy,

Townsend pointed out where Audubon misused both his and Nuttall's notes. Furthermore, Townsend felt that Audubon had not properly acknowledged their contributions and observations.[50]

Perhaps more threatening to the competitive Audubon was that Townsend was writing a book. He published the *Narrative of a Journey Across the Rocky Mountains* in 1839, but began also the same year a projected work that would directly compete with Audubon (who seemed to feel that only he could describe or depict the western species). If Townsend's observations to Audubon were incomplete, it was perhaps because he intended to publish his own records in his own book. He envisioned his *Ornithology of the United States* as a multipart, illustrated compendium of the country's birds. While he was to write the text, French artists would draw the birds "from nature." One part appeared, but not until 1849, treating, in twelve pages and four plates, three species of vultures and one of caracara. The book could not compete, however, against Audubon's octavo edition of *Birds of America*, which appeared in the 1840s. No other part of Townsend's projected book was ever published.[51]

The western expedition was in a real sense the climax of Townsend's ornithological career. He served as a curator of the collection of the Academy of Natural Sciences and for the National Institution for the Promotion of Science in Washington, D.C., where he was instrumental in the growth and fine appearance of the ornithological collection. William Baird remarked that "Townsend can skin, stuff and sew up a bird, so as to make it look far superior to any I have ever seen, in five minutes." Townsend published articles relating to his western trip in the *Proceedings* of the National Institute and in the *Literary Record*, the organ of the Linnaean Association of Pennsylvania College, of which he was an officer. About this time, he married Miss Harriet Holmes, whose sister was the wife of William Baird, brother of the ornithologist Spencer Fullerton Baird. Townsend's personality and charm, courtesy and kindness, "his brilliant conversational powers, fortified with a vivacious intellect and a fund of knowledge covering almost all subjects" attracted people to him. Spencer Baird considered him among "the cleverest people of [his] acquaintance."[52]

Townsend could never overcome, though, disadvantageous financial difficulties. In 1843, he was discharged from his position at the National Institute, a result of a dispute between the Institute and Charles Wilkes, commander of the United States Exploring Expedition just completed. Instead, Townsend turned to dentistry, a career in which his brothers had achieved prominence. But his curatorial duties had already adversely affected his health. Although William Baird considered Townsend's blend of arsenical powder (used in preparing and preserving bird skins) as safe, Townsend was continually exposed to this cumulative poison. His brother-in-law recalled seeing him, while preparing specimens, enveloped in a cloud of arsenic dust. Townsend hoped to serve as naturalist on an expedition to Africa, but he was too sick. On February 6, 1851, as the ships sailed from port, bound for the dark continent, John Kirk Townsend lost the light of life and died, at only 41 years of age.[53]

John Townsend has never received the focus that he warrants. Historians, focusing on the westward movement, treat him as a diarist. Certainly his *Narrative* is an important document of that event, an engaging, personal record of the first trek along what would shortly become the principal route to the Oregon country. But this focus blurs his accomplishments as a scientist. Unfortunately, historians of science and natural history too often focus their attention on the more widely-travelled and renowned Thomas Nuttall, and treat Townsend as a peripheral character, as Nuttall's companion. They abandon Townsend in the Oregon wilderness, while Nuttall in their accounts sails away to Hawaii and California, later to be bound for home on Dana's *Pilgrim*.[54]

This has not always been true. Ornithologists of the late 1800s–early 1900s had the highest regard for Townsend's scientific accomplishments. Witmer Stone noted that Townsend's collection of western birds was the most important yet taken and formed the beginning of the collection of the Academy of Natural Sciences of Philadelphia, recently considered one of the principal ornithological collections in the United States. Stone thought Townsend "a genius," whom by competition with a talented and dominant Audubon and his own financial difficulties was "prevented from reaching his proper place in ornithological annals." Theodore S. Palmer also considered him "a brilliant young ornithologist who lived in advance of his time."[55]

A new evaluation of Townsend's life should assume a more general focus, addressing other aspects of his experiences and career, than has been done in the past. All of the aspects of his career can be related to how he interpreted the western environment, or allowed others to interpret the opening frontier. Townsend's scientific activities, his role in bringing culture to the west and in its settlement are the pieces of the frame that define his life.

Scientific exploration was a creative way of interpreting the environment. Townsend possessed all of the traits of the naturalist identified by William Goetzmann: "The passion for organized information, a genius for accurate and meaningful observation, the collector's instinct, an eye for novelty, and most of all a love for the primitive and exotic." His collections scientifically defined the new frontier for those scientists who could not experience it first hand. Townsend was the first ornithologist to convey to the east what the western avian mosaic was like. His *Narrative* and the papers he published in the Academy of Natural Science's *Journal* informed other scientists of the new world in this new land. Thomas Nuttall used Townsend's, as well as his own, observations in the second edition of his *Manual of Ornithology*, as did Audubon in both the folio and octavo editions of the *Birds of America* and the *Ornithological Biography*. The western records in Thomas Brewer's "North American Oölogy" are Townsend's. His bird specimens were an important source for Baird, Cassin, and Lawrence's epochal *Birds*. For over twenty years, Townsend's observations in Oregon were not matched.[56]

His studies also made the far west more understandable to the average citizen. The collections pointed out the great similarities of Oregon to the settled parts of the country. Many of the bird species were identical to those in the east, while others differed only slightly in form or coloration. This reinforced the idea that Oregon was not an alien land but a familiar one, a desirable destination for anyone seeking a new beginning.

In a broader sense, Townsend helped open the west to culture and commerce. As a literate Philadelphian, he filled a part in the cultural environment of Fort Vancouver and western Oregon in the 1830s. He was an early practicioner of medicine in the northwest. He served as magistrate of the first public trial in Oregon.[57]

The Wyeth expedition of 1834 was a remarkable venture that united commerce, religion, and science. Each played a significant part in an interpretation of the west that attracted newcomers to Oregon. Wyeth revealed the route to the Oregon country and suggested the financial possibilities on the west coast. The missionaries brought the white man's culture to the wilderness and in letters home drew a seductive picture of the attractions of Oregon. Townsend's bird report in Parker's *Journal of an Exploring Tour* reached a religious audience; his *Narrative* depicted the west in honest and appealing terms for a secular, east coast audience.[58]

Introduction

John Kirk Townsend was a member of what William Goetzmann has called the second great age of discovery. Townsend contributed to the scientific discovery of the region and in so doing facilitated its use and exploitation by those following him. Science, as represented by Townsend, joined hands with commerce and religion in opening the west. He served an equal part, with the businessman and the missionaries, in forging a new interpretation of the west, a new vision, that others could use in forming new ideas, new dreams, about this new land.

Acknowledgements

Several individuals at Oregon State University Press made this edition possible. I would especially like to thank Jeffrey Grass, Warren Slesinger, Jo Alexander, Amy Callahan, and Tami Hotard. Patti Fowler offered a critical reading of the introduction. As always, my family, Margaret Hadaway, Jessica Jobanek, and Andy Jobanek, provided their support and encouragement.

Chapter I

Arrival at St. Louis—Preparations for the journey—
Sâque Indians—Their appearance, dress, and
manners—Squaws—Commencement of a pedestrian
tour—Sandhill cranes—Prairie settlers—Their
hospitality—Wild pigeons, golden plovers, and prairie
hens—Mr. P. and his daughters—An abundant repast—
Simplicity of the prairie maidens—A deer and turkey
hunt—Loutre Lick hotel—Unwelcome bed-fellows—A
colored charon—Comfortable quarters—Young men of
the west—Reflections on leaving home—Loquacity of the
inhabitants—Gray squirrels—Boonville—Parroquets—
Embarkation in a steamboat—Large catfish—Accident
on board the boat—Arrival at Independence—
Description of the town—Procure a supply of horses—
Encampment of the Rocky Mountain company—
Character of the man—Preparation for departure—
Requisites of a leader—Backwoods familiarity—Milton
Sublette and his band—Rev. Jason Lee, the missionary—
A letter from home—Mormonites—Military discipline
and its consequences.

O n the evening of the 24th of March, 1834, Mr. Nuttall and
myself arrived at St. Louis, in the steamboat Boston from
Pittsburg.

On landing, we had the satisfaction to learn that Captam Wyeth
was already there, and on the afternoon of the next day we called
upon him, and consulted him in reference to the outfit which it would
be necessary to purchase for the journey. He accompanied us to a
store in the town, and selected a number of articles for us, among
which were several pairs of leathern pantaloons, enormous overcoats,
made of green blankets, and white wool hats, with round crowns,
fitting tightly to the head, brims five inches wide, and almost enough
to resist a rifle ball.[1]

The day following we saw about one hundred Indians of the Sâque tribe who had left their native forests for the purpose treating for the sale of some land at the Jefferson barracks. They were dressed and decorated in the true primitive style; their heads shaved closely, and painted with alternate stripes of fiery red and deep black, leaving only the long scalping tuft, in which was interwoven a quantity of elk hair and eagle's feathers. Each man was furnished with a good blanket, and some had an under dress of calico, but the greater number were entirely naked to the waist. The faces and bodies of the men were, almost without an exception, fantastically painted, the predominant color being deep red, with occasionally a few stripes of dull clay white around the eyes and mouth. I observed one whose body was smeared with light colored clay, interspersed with black streaks. They were unarmed, with the exception of tomahawks and knives. The chief of the band, (who is said to be Black Hawk's father-in-law[2]) was a large dignified looking man, of perhaps fifty-five years of age, distinguished from the rest, by his richer habiliments, a more profuse display of trinkets in his ears, (which were cut and gashed in a frightful manner to receive them,) and above all, by a huge necklace made of the claws of the grizzly bear. The squaws, of whom there were about twenty, were dressed very much like the men, and at a little distance could scarcely be distinguished from them. Among them was an old, superannuated crone, who, soon after her arrival, had been presented with a broken umbrella. The only use that she made of it was to wrench the plated ends from the whalebones, string them on a piece of wire, take her knife from her belt, with which she deliberately cut a slit of an inch in length along the upper rim of her ear, and insert them in it. I saw her soon after this operation had been performed; her cheeks were covered with blood, and she was standing with a vast deal of assumed dignity among her tawny sisters, who evidently envied her the possession of the worthless baubles.

28th.—Mr. N. and myself propose starting to-morrow on foot towards the upper settlements, a distance of about three hundred miles. We intend to pursue our journey leisurely, as we have plenty of time before us, and if we become tired, we can enter the stage which will probably overtake us.

29th.—This morning our Indians returned from the barracks, where I understand they transacted their business satisfactorily. I went on board the boat again to see them. I feel very much interested in them, as they are the first Indians I have ever seen who appear to be in a state of uncultivated nature, and who retain the savage garb and manners of their people. They had engaged the entire covered deck for their especial use, and were lolling about in groups, wrapped in their blankets. Some were occupied in conversation, others seemed more contemplative, and appeared to be thinking deeply, probably of the business which brought them amongst us. Here and there two might be seen playing a Spanish game with cards, and some were busily employed in rendering themselves more hideous with paint. To perform this operation, the dry paint is folded in a thin muslin or gauze cloth, tied tightly and beaten against the face, and a small looking-glass is held in the other hand to direct them where to apply it. Two middleaged squaws were frying beef, which they distributed around to the company in wooden bowls, and several half loaves of bread were circulating rapidly amongst them, by being tossed from one to another, each taking a huge bite of it. There were among the company, several younger females, but they were all so *hard favored* that I could not feel much sympathy with them, and was therefore not anxious to cultivate their acquaintance. There was another circumstance, too, that was not a very attractive one; I allude to the custom so universal amongst Indians, of seeking for vermin in each other's heads, and then *eating* them. The fair damsels were engaged in this way during most of the time that I remained on board, only suspending their delectable occupation to take their bites of bread as it passed them in rotation. The effect upon my person was what an Irishman would call the attraction of repulsion, as I found myself almost unconsciously edging away until I halted at a most respectable distance from the scene of slaughter.

At noon, Mr. N. and myself started on our pedestrian tour, Captain Wyeth offering to accompany us a few miles on the way. I was glad to get clear of St. Louis, as I felt many respects while there, and the bustle and restraint of a town was any thing but agreeable to me. We proceeded over a road generally good, a low dry prairie, mostly heavily timbered, the soil underlaid with horizontal strata of limestone, abounding in organic remains, shells, coralines, &c., and arrived in the evening at Florisant, where we spent the night. The next day Captain Wyeth left us for St. Louis, and my companion and myself proceeded on our route.[3] We observed great numbers of the brown, or sandhill crane, (*Grus canadensis*,) flying over us; some flocks were so high as to be entirely beyond the reach of vision, while their harsh, grating voices were very distinctly heard. We saw several flocks of the same cranes while ascending the Mississippi, several days since. At about noon, we crossed the river on a boat worked by horses, and stopped at a little town called St. Charles.

We find it necessary, both for our comfort and convenience, to travel very slowly, as our feet are already becoming tender, and that we may have an opportunity of observing the country, and collecting interesting specimens. Unfortunately for the pursuits of my companion, the plants (of which he finds a number that are rare and curious) are not yet in flower, and therefore of little use to him. The birds are in considerable numbers, among the principal of which is the large pileated woodpecker (*Picus pileatus*).

Mr. N. and myself are both in high spirits. We travel slowly, and without much fatigue, and when we arrive at a house, stop and rest, take a drink of milk, and chat with those we see. We have been uniformly well treated; the living is good, and very cheap, and at any house at which we stop the inhabitants are sure to welcome us to their hospitality and good cheer. They live comfortably, and without much labor; possess a fruitful and easily tilled soil, for which they pay the trifling sum of one dollar and a quarter per acre; they raise an abundance of good Indian corn, potatoes, and other vegetables; have excellent beef and pork, and, in short, every thing necessary for good, wholesome living.

31st.—*The road to-day was muddy and slippery, rendered so by a* heavy rain which fell last night. This morning, we observed large flocks of wild pigeons passing over, and on the bare prairies were thousands of golden plovers; the ground was often literally covered with them for acres. I killed a considerable number. They were very fat, and we made an excellent meal of them in the evening. The prairie hen, or pinnated grouse, is also very numerous, but in these situations is shy, and difficult to be procured.

Towards evening we were overtaken by a bluff, jolly looking man, on horseback, who, as is usual, stopped, and entered into conversation with us. I saw immediately that he was superior to those we had been accustomed to meet. He did not ply us with questions so eagerly as most, and when he heard that we were naturalists, and were travelling in that capacity, he seemed to take considerable interest in us. He invited us to stop at his house, which was only a mile beyond, and as night was almost upon us, we accepted the invitation with cheerfulness. Upon arriving at his mansion, our good host threw wide his hospitable doors, and then with a formal, and rather ultra-dignified politeness, making us a low bow, said, "Gentlemen, my name is P., and I am very happy of your company." We seated ourselves in a large, and well-furnished parlor. Mr. P. excused himself for a few minutes, and soon returned, bringing in three fine looking girls, whom he introduced as his daughters. I took a particular fancy to one of them, from a strong resemblance which she bore to one of my female friends at home. These girls were certainly very superior to most that I had seen in Missouri, although somewhat touched with the awkward bashfulness and prudery which generally characterizes the prairie maidens. They had lost their mother when young, and having no companions out of the domestic circle, and consequently no opportunity of aping the manners of the world, were perfect children of nature. Their father, however, had given them a good, plain education, and they had made some proficiency in needle work, as was evinced by numerous neatly worked *samplers* hanging in wooden frames around the room. Anon, supper was brought in. It consisted of pork chops, ham, eggs, Indian bread and butter, tea, coffee, milk, potatoes, *preserved ginger,* and though last, certainly not least in value, an enormous tin dish of plovers, (the contents of my game-bag,) *fricaseed*. Here was certainly a most abundant repast, and we did ample justice to it.

I endeavored to do the agreeable to the fair ones in the evening, and Mr. N. was monopolized by the father, who took a great interest in plants, and was evidently much gratified by the information my companion gave him on the subject.

The next morning when we rose, it was raining, and much had evidently fallen during the night, making the roads wet and muddy, and therefore unpleasant for pedestrians. I confess I was not sorry for this, for I felt myself very comfortably situated, and had no wish to take to the road. Mr. P. urged the propriety of our stopping at least another day, and the motion being seconded by his fair daughter, (my favorite,) it was irresistible.

On the following morning the sun was shining brightly, the air was fresh and elastic, and the roads tolerably dry, so that there was no longer any excuse for tarrying, and we prepared for our departure. Our good host, grasping our hands, said that he had been much pleased with our visit, and hoped to see us again, and when I bid good bye to the pretty Miss P., I told her that if I ever visited Missouri again, I would go many miles out of my way to see her and her sisters. Her reply was unsophisticated enough. "Do come again, and come in May or June, for then there are plenty of prairie hens, and you can shoot as many as you want, and you must stay a long while with us, and we'll have nice times; good bye; I'm so sorry you're going."

April 4th.—I rose this morning at daybreak, and left Mr. N. dreaming of weeds, in a little house at which we stopped last night, and in company with a long, lanky boy, (a son of the poor widow, our hostess,) set to moulding bullets in an old iron spoon, and preparing for deer hunting. The boy shouldered a rusty rifle, that looked almost antediluvian, and off we plodded to a thicket, two miles from the house. We soon saw about a dozen fine deer, and the boy, clapping his old fire-lock to his shoulder, brought down a beautiful doe at the distance of a full hundred yards. Away sprang the rest of the herd, and I crept round the thicket to meet them. They soon came up, and I fired my piece at a large buck, and wounded the poor creature in the leg; he went limping away, unable to overtake his companions; I felt very sorry, but consoled myself with the reflection that he would soon get well again.

We then gave up the pursuit, and turned our attention to the turkies, which were rather numerous in the thicket. They were shy, as usual, and, when started from their lurking places, ran away like deer, and hid themselves in the underwood. Occasionally, however, they would perch on the high limbs of the trees, and then we had some shots at them. In the course of an hour we killed four, and returned to the house, where, as I expected, Mr. N. was in a fever at my absence, and after a late, and very good breakfast, proceeded on our journey.

We find in this part of the country less timber in the same space than we have yet seen, and when a small belt appears, it is a great relief, as the monotony of a bare prairie becomes tiresome.

Towards evening we arrived at Loutre Lick. Here there is a place called a *Hotel.* A Hotel, forsooth! a pig-stye would be a more appropriate name. Every thing about it was most exceedingly filthy and disagreeable, but no better lodging was to be had, for it might not be proper to apply for accommodation at a private house in the immediate vicinity of a public one. They gave us a wretched supper, not half so good as we had been accustomed to, and we were fain to spend the evening in a comfortless, unfurnished, nasty barroom, that smelt intolerably of rum and whiskey, to listen to the profane conversation of three or four uncouth individuals, (among whom were the host and his brother,) and to hear long and disagreeably minute discussions upon horse-racing, gambling, and other vices equally unpleasant to us.

The host's brother had been to the Rocky Mountains, and soon learning our destination, gave us much unsought for advice regarding our method of journeying; painted in strong colors the many dangers and difficulties which we must encounter, and concluded by advising us to give up the expedition. My fast ebbing patience was completely exhausted. I told him that nothing that he could say would discourage us—that we went to that house in order to seek repose, and it was unfair to intrude conversation upon us unasked. The ruffian made some grumbling reply, and left us in quiet and undisturbed possession of our bench. We had a miserable time that night. The only spare bed in the house was so intolerably filthy that we dared not undress, and we had hardly closed our eyes before we were assailed by swarms of a vile insect, (the very name of which is offensive,) whose effluvia we had plainly perceived immediately as we entered the room. It is almost needless to say, that very early on the following morning, after paying our reckoning, and refusing the landlord's polite invitation to "*liquorize,*" we marched from the house, shook the dust from our feet, and went elsewhere to seek a breakfast.

Soon after leaving, we came to a deep and wide creek, and strained our lungs for half an hour in vain endeavors to waken a negro boy who lived in a hut on the opposite bank, and who, we were told, would ferry us over. He came out of his den at last, half naked and rubbing his eyes to see who had disturbed his slumbers so early in the *marning.* We told him to hurry over, or we'd endeavor to assist him, and he came at last, with a miserable leaky little skiff that wet our feet completely. We gave him a *pickayune* for his trouble, and went on. We soon came to a neat little secluded cottage in the very heart of a thick forest, where we found a fine looking young man, with an interesting wife, and a very pretty child about six months old. Upon being told that we wanted some breakfast, the woman tucked up her sleeves, gave the child to her husband, and went to work in good earnest. In a very short time a capital meal was smoking on the board, and while we were partaking of the good cheer, we found our vexation rapidly evaporating. We complimented the handsome young hostess, patted the chubby cheeks of the child, and were in a good humor with every body.

6th.—Soon after we started this morning, we were overtaken by a stage which was going to Fulton, seven miles distant, and as the roads were somewhat heavy, we concluded to make use of this convenience. The only passengers were three young men from the far west, who had been to the eastward purchasing goods, and were then travelling homeward. Two of them evidently possessed a large share of what is called *mother wit,* and so we had jokes without number. Some of them were not very refined, and perhaps did not suit the day very well, (it being the Sabbath,) yet none of them were really offensive, but seemed to proceed entirely from an exuberance of animal spirits.

In about an hour and a half we arrived at Fulton, a pretty little town, and saw the villagers in their holiday clothes parading along to church. The bell at that moment sounded, and the peal gave rise to many reflections. It might be long ere I should hear the sound of the "church-going bell" again. I was on my way to a far, far country, and I did not know that I should ever be permitted to revisit my own. I felt that I was leaving the scenes of my childhood; the spot which had witnessed all the happiness I ever knew, the home where all my affections were centered. I was entering a land of strangers, and would be compelled hereafter to mingle with those who might look upon me with indifference, or treat me with neglect.

These reflections were soon checked, however. We took a light lunch at the tavern where we stopped. I shouldered my gun, Mr. N. his stick and bundle, and off we trudged again, westward, ho! We soon lost sight of the prairie entirely, and our way lay through a country thickly covered with heavy timber, the roads very rough and stony, and we had frequently to ford the creeks on our route, the late freshets having carried away the bridges.

Our accommodation at the farm houses has generally been good and comfortable, and the inhabitants obliging, and anxious to please. They are, however, exceedingly inquisitive, propounding question after question, in such quick succession as scarcely to allow you breathing time between them. This kind of catechising was at first very annoying to us, but we have now become accustomed to it, and have hit upon an expedient to avoid it in a measure. The first question generally asked, is, "where do you come from, gentlemen?" We frame our answer somewhat in the style of Dr. Franklin. "We come from Pennsylvania; our names, Nuttall and Townsend; we are travelling to Independence on foot, for the purpose of seeing the country to advantage, and we intend to proceed from thence across the mountains to the Pacific.

Have you any mules to sell?" The last clause generally changes the conversation, and saves us trouble. To a stranger, and one not accustomed to the manners of the western people, this kind of interrogating seems to imply a lack of modesty and common decency, but it is certainly not so intended, each one appearing to think himself entitled to gain as much intelligence regarding the private affairs of a stranger, as a very free use of his lingual organ can procure for him.

We found the common gray squirrel very abundant in some places, particularly in the low bottoms along water courses; in some situations we saw them skipping on almost every tree. On last Christmas day, at a squirrel hunt in this neighborhood, about thirty persons killed the astonishing number of *twelve hundred,* between the rising and setting of the sun.

This may seem like useless barbarity, but it is justified by the consideration that all the crops of corn in the country are frequently destroyed by these animals. This extensive extermination is carried on every year, and yet it is said that their numbers do not appear to be much diminished.

About mid-day on the 7th, we passed through a small town called Columbia, and stopped in the evening at Rocheport, a little village on the Missouri river. We were anxious to find a steam-boat bound for Independence, as we feared we might linger too long upon the road to make the necessary preparations for our contemplated journey.

On the following day, we crossed the Missouri, opposite Rocheport, in a small skiff. The road here, for several miles, winds along the bank of the river, amid fine groves of sycamore and Athenian poplars, then stretches off for about three miles, and does not again approach it until you arrive at Boonville. It is by far the most hilly road that we have seen, and I was frequently reminded, while travelling on it, of our Chester county. We entered the town of Boonville early in the afternoon, and took lodgings in a very clean, and respectably kept hotel. I was much pleased with Boonville. It is the prettiest town I have seen in Missouri; situated on the bank of the river, on an elevated and beautiful spot, and overlooks a large extent of lovely country. The town contains two good hotels, (but no *grog shops,* properly so called,) several well-furnished stores, and five hundred inhabitants. It was laid out thirty years ago by the celebrated western pioneer, whose name it bears.

We saw here vast numbers of the beautiful parrot of this country, (the *Psittacus carolinensis.*)[4] They flew around us in flocks, keeping a constant and loud screaming, as though they would chide us for invading their territory; and the splendid green and red of their plumage glancing in the sunshine, as they whirled and circled within a few feet of us, had a most magnificent appearance. They seem entirely unsuspicious of danger, and after being fired at, only huddle closer together, as if to obtain protection from each other, and as their companions are falling around them, they curve down their necks, and look at them fluttering upon the ground, as though perfectly at a loss to account for so unusual an occurrence. It is a most inglorious sort of shooting; down right, cold-blooded murder.

On the afternoon of the 9th, a steamboat arrived, on board of which we were surprised and pleased to find Captain Wyeth, and our "*plunder.*" We embarked immediately, and soon after, were puffing along the Missouri, at the rate of seven miles an hour. When we stopped in the afternoon to "wood," we were gratified by a sight of one of the enormous catfish of this river and the Mississippi, weighing full sixty pounds. It is said, however, that they are sometimes caught of at least double this weight. They are excellent eating, coarser, but quite as good as the common small catfish of our rivers. There is nothing in the scenery of the river banks to interest the traveller particularly. The country is generally level and sandy, relieved only by an occasional hill, and some small rocky acclivities.

A shocking accident happened on board during this trip. A fine looking black boy (a slave of one of the deck passengers) was standing on the platform near the fly-wheel. The steam had just been stopped off, and the wheel was moving slowly by the impetus it had acquired. The poor boy unwittingly thrust his head between the spokes; a portion of the steam was at that moment let on, and his head and shoulders were torn to fragments. We buried him on shore the same day; the poor woman, his mistress, weeping and lamenting over him as for her own child. She told me she had brought him up from an infant; he had been as an affectionate son to her, and for years her only support.

March 20th [=April 20].—On the morning of the 14th, we arrived at Independence landing, and shortly afterwards, Mr. N. and myself walked to the town, three miles distant. The country here is very hilly and rocky, thickly covered with timber, and no prairie within several miles.

The site of the town is beautiful, and very well selected, standing on a high point of land, and overlooking the surrounding country, but the town itself is very indifferent; the houses, (about fifty,) are very much scattered, composed of logs and clay, and are low and inconvenient. There are six or eight stores here, two taverns, and a few tipling houses. As we did not fancy the town, nor the society that we saw there, we concluded to take up our residence at the house on the landing until the time of starting on our journey. We were very much disappointed in not being able to purchase any mules here, all the salable ones having been bought by the Santa Fee traders, several weeks since. Horses, also, are rather scarce, and are sold at higher prices than we had been taught to expect, the demand for them at this time being greater than usual. Mr. N. and myself have, however, been so fortunate as to find five excellent animals amongst the hundreds of wretched ones offered for sale, and have also engaged a man to attend to packing our loads, and perform the various duties of our camp.

The men of the party, to the number of about fifty, are encamped on the bank of the river, and their tents whiten the plain for the distance of half a mile. I have often enjoyed the view on a fine moonlight evening from the door of the house, or perched upon a high hill immediately over the spot. The beautiful white tents, with a light gleaming from each, the smouldering fires around them, the incessant hum of the men, and occasionally the lively notes of a bacchanalian song, softened and rendered sweeter by distance. I probably contemplate these and similar scenes with the more interest, as they exhibit the manner in which the next five months of my life are to be spent.

We have amongst our men, a great variety of dispositions. Some who have not been accustomed to the kind of life they are to lead in future, look forward to it with eager delight, and talk of stirring incidents and hair-breadth 'scapes. Others who are more experienced seem to be as easy and unconcerned about it as a citizen would be in contemplating a drive of a few miles into the country. Some have evidently been reared in the shade, and not accustomed to hardships, but the majority are strong, able-bodied men, and many are almost as rough as the grizzly bears, of their feats upon which they are fond of boasting.

During the day the captain keeps all his men employed in arranging and packing a vast variety of goods for carriage. In addition to the necessary clothing for the company, arms, ammunition, &c., there are thousands of trinkets of various kinds, beads, paint, bells, rings, and such trumpery, intended as presents for the Indians, a well as objects of trade with them. The bales are usually made to weigh about eighty pounds, of which a horse carries two.

I am very much pleased with the manner in which Captain W. manages his men. He appears admirably calculated to gain the good will, and ensure the obedience of such a company, and adopts the only possible mode of accomplishing his end. They are men who have been accustomed to act independently; they possess a strong and indomitable spirit which will never succumb to authority, and will only be conciliated by kindness and familiarity. I confess I admire this spirit. It is noble; it is free and characteristic, but for myself, I have not been accustomed to seeing it exercised, and when a rough fellow comes up without warning, and slaps me on the shoulder, with, "stranger what for a gun is that you carry?" I start, and am on the point of making an angry reply, but I remember where I am, check the feeling instantly, and submit the weapon to his inspection. Captain W. may frequently be seen sitting on the ground, surrounded by a knot of his independents, consulting them as to his present arrangements and future movements, and paying the utmost deference to the opinion of the least among them.

We were joined here by Mr. Milton Sublette, a trader and trapper of some ten or twelve years' standing. It is his intention to travel with us to the mountains, and we are very glad of his company, both on account of his intimate acquaintance with the country, and the accession to our band of about twenty trained hunters, "true as the steel of their tried blades," who have more than once followed their brave and sagacious leader over the very track which we intend to pursue. He appears to be a man of strong sense and courteous manners, and his men are enthusiastically attached to him.

Five missionaries, who intend to travel under our escort, have also just arrived. The principal of these is a Mr. Jason Lee, (a tall and powerful man, who looks as though he were well calculated to buffet difficulties in a wild country,) his nephew, Mr. Daniel Lee, and three younger men of respectable standing in society, who have arrayed themselves under the missionary banner, chiefly for the gratification of seeing a new country, and participating in strange adventures.[5]

My favorites, the birds, are very numerous in this vicinity, and I am therefore in my element. Parroquets are plentiful in the bottom lands, the two species of squirrel are abundant, and rabbits, turkies, and deer are often killed by our people.

I was truly rejoiced to receive yesterday a letter from my family. I went to the office immediately on my arrival here, confidently expecting to find one lying there for me; I was told there was none, and I could not believe it, or would not; I took all the letters in my hand, and examined each of them myself, and I suppose that during the process my expressions of disappointment were "loud and deep," as I observed the eyes of a number of persons in the store directed towards me with manifest curiosity and surprise. The obtuse creatures could not appreciate my feelings. I was most anxious to receive intelligence from home, as some of the members of the family were indisposed when I left, and in a few days more I should be traversing the uncultivated prairie and the dark forest, and perhaps never hear from my home again. The letter came at last, however, and was an inexpressible consolation to me.

The little town of Independence has within a few weeks been the scene of a brawl, which at one time threatened to be attended with serious consequences, but which was happily settled without bloodshed. It had been for a considerable time the stronghold of a sect of fanatics, called Mormons, or Mormonites, who, as their numbers increased, and they obtained power, showed an inclination to lord it over the less assuming inhabitants of the town. This was a source of irritation which they determined to rid themselves of in a summary manner, and accordingly the whole town rose, *en masse*, and the poor followers of the prophet were forcibly ejected from the community. They took refuge in the little town of Liberty, on the opposite side of the river, and the villagers here are now in a constant state of feverish alarm. Reports have been circulated that the Mormons are preparing to attack the town, and put the inhabitants to the sword, and they have therefore stationed sentries along the river for several miles, to prevent the landing of the enemy. The troops parade and study military tactics every day, and seem determined to repel, with spirit, the threatened invasion. The probability is, that the report respecting the attack, is, as John Bull says, "all humbug," and this training and marching has already been a source of no little annoyance to us, as the miserable little skeleton of a saddler who is engaged to work for our party, has neglected his business, and must go a soldiering in stead. A day or two ago, I tried to convince the little man that he was of no use to the army, for if a Mormon were to say *pooh* at him, it would blow him away beyond the reach of danger or of glory; but he thought not, and no doubt concluded that he was a "marvellous proper man," so we were put to great inconvenience waiting for our saddles.[6]

Chapter II

On the 28th of April, at 10 o'clock in the morning, our caravan, consisting of seventy men, and two hundred and fifty horses, began its march; Captain Wyeth and Milton Sublette took the lead, Mr. N. and myself rode beside them; then the men in double file, each leading, with a line, two horses heavily laden, and Captain Thing (Captain W.'s assistant) brought up the rear. The band of missionaries, with their horned cattle, rode along the flanks.[1]

I frequently sallied out from my station to look at and admire the appearance of the cavalcade, and as we rode out from the encampment, our horses prancing, and neighing, and pawing the ground, it was altogether so exciting that I could scarcely contain myself. Every man in the company seemed to feel a portion of the same kind of enthusiasm; uproarious bursts of merriment, and gay and lively songs, were constantly echoing along the line. We were certainly a most merry and happy company. What cared we for the future? We had reason to expect that ere long difficulties and dangers, in various shapes, would assail us, but no anticipation of reverses could check the happy exuberance of our spirits.

Our road lay over a vast rolling prairie, with occasional small spots of timber at the distance of several miles apart, and this will no doubt be the complexion of the track for some weeks.

In the afternoon we crossed the *Big Blue* river at a shallow ford. Here we saw a number of beautiful yellowheaded troopials, (*Icterus zanthrocephalus*) feeding upon the prairie in company with large flocks of black birds, and like these, they often alight upon the backs of our horses.[2]

29th.—A heavy rain fell all the morning, which had the effect of calming our transports in a great measure, and in the afternoon it was succeeded by a tremendous hail storm. During the rain, our party left the road, and proceeded about a hundred yards from it to a range of bushes, near a stream of water, for the purpose of encamping. We had just arrived here, and had not yet dismounted, when the hail storm commenced. It came on very suddenly, and the stones, as large as musket balls, dashing upon our horses, created such a panic among them, that they plunged, and kicked, and many of them threw their loads, and fled wildly over the plain. They were all overtaken, however, and as the storm was not of long duration, they were soon appeased, and *staked* for the night.

To stake or fasten a horse for the night, he is provided with a strong leathern halter, with an iron ring attached to the chin strap. To this ring, a rope of hemp or plaited leather, twenty-two feet in length, is attached, and the opposite end of the line made fast with several clove hitches around an oak or hickory pin, two and a half feet long. The top of this pin or stake is ringed with iron to prevent its being bruised, and it is then driven to the head in the ground. For greater security, hopples made of stout leather are buckled around the fore legs; and then, if the tackling is good, it is almost impossible for a horse to escape. Care is always taken to stake him in a spot where he may eat grass all night. The animals are placed sufficiently far apart to prevent them interfering with each other.

Camping out to-night is not so agreeable as it might be, in consequence of the ground being very wet and muddy, and our blankets (our only bedding) thoroughly soaked; but we expect to encounter greater difficulties than these ere long, and we do not murmur.

A description of the formation of our camp may, perhaps, not be amiss here. The party is divided into messes of eight men, and each mess is allowed a separate tent. The captain of a mess, (who is generally an "old hand," *i. e.* an experienced forester, hunter, or trapper,) receives each morning the rations of pork, flour, &c. for his people, and they choose one of their body as cook for the whole. Our camp now consists of nine messes, of which Captain W.'s forms one, although it only contains four persons besides the cook.

When we arrive in the evening at a suitable spot for an encampment, Captain W. rides round a space which he considers large enough to accommodate it, and directs where each mess shall pitch its tent. The men immediately unload their horses, and place their bales of goods in the direction indicated, and in such manner, as in case of need, to form a sort of fortification and defence. When all the messes are arranged in this way, the camp forms a hollow square, in the centre of which the horses are placed and staked firmly to the ground. The guard consists of from six to eight men, and is relieved three times each night, and so arranged that each gang may serve alternate nights. The captain of a guard (who is generally also the captain of a mess) collects his people at the appointed hour, and posts them around outside the camp in such situations that they may command a view of the environs, and be ready to give the alarm in case of danger.

The captain cries the hour regularly by a watch, and all's well, every fifteen minutes, and each man of the guard is required to repeat this call in rotation, which if any one should fail to do, it is fair to conclude that he is asleep, and he is then immediately visited and stirred up. In case of defection of this kind, our laws adjudge to the delinquent the hard sentence of walking three days. As yet none of our poor fellows have incurred this penalty, and the probability is, that it would not at this time be enforced, as we are yet in a country where little molestation is to be apprehended; but in the course of another week's travel, when thieving and ill-designing Indians will be outlying on our trail, it will be necessary that the strictest watch be kept, and, for the preservation of our persons and property, that our laws shall be rigidly enforced.

May 1st.—On rising this morning, and inquiring about our prospects of a breakfast, we discovered that the cook of our mess (a little, low-browed, ill-conditioned Yankee) had decamped in the night, and left our service to seek for a better. He probably thought the duties too hard for him, but as he was a miserable cook, we should not have much regretted his departure, had he not thought proper to take with him an excellent rifle, powder-horn, shot-pouch, and other matters that did not belong to him. It is only surprising that he did not select one of our best horses to carry him; but as he had the grace to take his departure on foot, and we have enough men without him, we can wish him God speed, and a fair run to the settlements.

We encamped this evening on a small branch of the Kanzas river. As we approached our stopping place, we were joined by a band of Kanzas Indians, (commonly called *Kaw* Indians.) They are encamped in a neighboring copse, where they have six lodges. This party is a small division of a portion of this tribe, who are constantly wandering; but although their journeys are sometimes pretty extensive, they seldom approach nearer to the settlements than they are at present. They are very friendly, are not so tawdrily decorated as those we saw below, and use little or no paint. This may, however, be accounted for by their not having the customary ornaments, &c., as their ears are filled with trinkets of various kinds, and are horribly gashed in the usual manner. The dress of most that we have seen, has consisted of ordinary woollen pantaloons received from the whites, and their only covering, from the waist up, is a blanket or buffalo robe. The head is shaved somewhat in the manner of the Sâques and Foxes, leaving the well known scalping tuft; but unlike the Indians just mentioned, the hair is allowed to grow upon the middle of the head, and extends backwards in longitudinal ridge to the occiput. It is here gathered into kind of queue, plaited, and suffered to hang down the back. There were amongst them several squaws, with young children tied to their backs, and a number of larger urchins ran about our camp wholly naked.

The whole of the following day we remained in camp, trading buffalo robes, *apishemeaus*, &c., of the Indians.[3] These people became at length somewhat troublesome to us who were not traders, by a very free exercise of their begging propensities. They appear to be exceedingly poor and needy, and take the liberty of asking unhesitatingly, and without apparent fear of refusal, for any articles that happen to take their fancy.

I have observed, that among the Indians now with us, none but the chief uses the pipe. He smokes the article called *kanikanik*,—a mixture of tobacco and the dried leaves of the poke plant, (*Phytolacca decandra*.) I was amused last evening by the old chief asking me in his impressive manner, (first by pointing with his finger towards the sunset, and then raising his hands high over his head,) if I was going to the mountains. On answering him in the affirmative, he depressed his hands, and passed them around his head in both directions, then turned quickly away from me, with a very solemn and significant ugh! He meant, doubtless, that my brain was turned; in plain language, that I was a fool. This may be attributed to his horror of the Blackfeet Indians, with whom a portion of his tribe was formerly at war. The poor Kaws are said to have suffered dreadfully in these savage conflicts, and were finally forced to abandon the country to their hereditary foes.

We were on the move early the next morning, and at noon arrived at the Kanzas river, a branch of the Missouri. This is a broad and not very deep stream, with the water dark and turbid, like that of the former. As we approached it, we saw a number of Indian lodges, made of saplings driven into the ground, bent over and tied at top, and covered with bark and buffalo skins. These lodges, or wigwams, are numerous on both sides of the river. As we passed them, the inhabitants, men, women, and children, flocked out to see us, and almost prevented our progress by their eager greetings. Our party stopped on the bank of the river, and the horses were unloaded and driven into the water. They swam beautifully, and with great regularity, and arrived safely on the opposite shore, where they were confined in a large lot, enclosed with a fence. After some difficulty, and considerable detention, we succeeded in procuring a large flat bottomed boat, embarked ourselves and goods in it, and landed on the opposite side near our horse pen, where we encamped. The lodges are numerous here, and there are also some good frame houses inhabited by a few white men and women, who subsist chiefly by raising cattle, which they drive to the settlements below. They, as well as the Indians, raise an abundance of good corn; potatoes and other vegetables are also plentiful, and they can therefore live sufficiently well.

The canoes used by the Indians are mostly made of buffalo skins, stretched, while recent, over a light frame work of wood, the seams sewed with sinews, and so closely, as to be wholly impervious to water. These light vessels are remarkably buoyant, and capable of sustaining very heavy burthens.

In the evening the principal Kanzas chief paid us a visit in our tent. He is a young man about twenty-five years of age, straight as a poplar, and with a noble countenance and bearing, but he appeared to me to be marvellously deficient in most of the requisites which go to make the character of a *real* Indian chief, at least of such Indian chiefs as we read of in our popular books. I begin to suspect, in truth, that these lofty and dignified attributes are more apt to exist in the fertile brain of the novelist, than in reality. Be this as it may, *our* chief is a very lively, laughing, and rather playful personage; perhaps he may put on his dignity, like a glove, when it suits his convenience.

We remained in camp the whole of next day, and traded with the Indians for a considerable number of robes, *apishemeaus*, and halter ropes of hide. Our fat bacon and tobacco were in great demand for these useful commodities.

The Kaws living here appear to be much more wealthy than those who joined our camp on the prairie below. They are in better condition, more richly dressed, cleaner, and more comfortable than their wandering brothers. The men have generally fine countenances, but all the women that I have seen are homely. I cannot admire them. Their dress consists, universally of deer skin leggings, belted around the loins, and over the upper part of the body a buffalo robe or blanket.

On the 20th in the morning, we packed our horses and rode out of the Kaw settlement, leaving the river immediately, and making a N. W. by W. course—and the next day came to another village of the same tribe, consisting of about thirty lodges, and situated in the midst of a beautiful level prairie.

The Indians stopped our caravan almost by force, and evinced so much anxiety to trade with us, that we could not well avoid gratifying them. We remained with them about two hours, and bought corn, moccasins and leggings in abundance. The lodges here are constructed very differently from those of the lower village. They are made of large and strong timbers, a ridge pole runs along the top, and the different pieces are fastened together by leathern thongs. The roofs,— which are single, making but one angle,—are of stout poplar bark, and form an excellent defence, both against rain and the rays of the sun, which must be intense during midsummer in this region. These prairies are often visited by heavy gales of wind, which would probably demolish the huts, were they built of frail materials like those below. We encamped in the evening on a small stream called Little Vermillion creek, where we found an abundance of excellent catfish, exactly similar to those of the Schuylkill river. Our people caught them in great numbers. Here we first saw the large ravens, (*Corvus corax.*) They hopped about the ground all around our camp; and as we left it, they came in, pell-mell, croaking, fighting, and scrambling for the few fragments that remained.

8th.—This morning Mr. Sublette left us to return to the, settlements. He has been suffering for a considerable time with a fungus in one of his legs, and it has become so much worse since we started, in consequence of irritation caused by riding, that he finds it impossible to proceed. His departure has thrown a gloom over the whole camp. We all admired him for his amiable qualities, and his kind and obliging disposition. For myself, I had become so much attached to him, that I feel quite melancholy about his leaving us.[4]*

The weather is now very warm, and there has been a dead calm all day, which renders travelling most uncomfortable. We have frequently been favored with fresh breezes, which make it very agreeable, but the moment these fail us we are almost suffocated with intense heat. Our rate of travelling is about twenty miles per day, which, in this warm weather, and with heavily packed horses, is as much as we can accomplish with comfort to ourselves and animals.

On the afternoon of the next day, we crossed a broad Indian trail, bearing northerly, supposed to be about five days old, and to have been made by a war party of Pawnees. We are now in the country traversed by these Indians, and are daily expecting to see them, but Captain W. seems very desirous to avoid them, on account of their well known thieving propensities, and quarrelsome disposition. These Indians go every year to the plains of the Platte, where they spend some weeks in hunting the buffalo, jerking their meat, and preparing their skins for robes; they then push on to the Black Hills, and look out for the parties of Blackfeet, which are also bound to the Platte river plains. When the opposing parties come in collision, (which frequently happens,) the most cruel and sanguinary conflicts ensue. In the evening, three of our men deserted. Like our quondam cook, they all took rifles, &c., that did not belong to them, and one of these happened to be a favorite piece of Captain W.'s, which had done him good service in his journey across this country two years ago. He was very much attached to the gun, and in spite of his calm and cool philosophy in all vexatious matters, he cannot altogether conceal his chagrin.

The little streams of this part of the country are fringed with a thick growth of pretty trees and bushes, and the buds are now swelling, and the leaves expanding, to "welcome back the spring." The birds, too, sing joyously amongst them, grosbeaks, thrushes, and buntings, a merry and musical band. I am particularly fond of sallying out early in the morning, and strolling around the camp. The light breeze just bends the tall tops of the grass on the boundless prairie, the birds are commencing their matin carollings, and all nature looks fresh and

---

* I have since learned that his limb was twice amputated; but notwithstanding this, the disease lingered in the system, and about a year ago, terminated his life.

beautiful. The horses of the camp are lying comfortably on their sides, and seem, by the glances which they give me in passing, to know that their hour of toil is approaching, and the patient kine are ruminating in happy unconsciousness.

11th.—We encountered some rather serious difficulties today in fording several wide and deep creeks, having muddy and miry bottoms. Many of our horses, (and particularly those that were packed,) fell into the water, and it was with the greatest difficulty and labor that they were extricated. Some of the scenes presented were rather ludicrous to those who were not actors in them. The floundering, kicking, and falling of horses in the heavy slough, man and beast rolling over together, and *squattering* amongst the black mud, and the wo-begone looks of horse, rider, and horse-furniture, often excited a smile, even while we pitied their begrimed and miserable plight. All these troubles are owing to our having lost the trail yesterday, and we have been travelling to-day as nearly in the proper course as our compass indicated, and hope soon to find it.

12th.—Our scouts came in this morning with the intelligence that they had found a large trail of white men, bearing N. W. We have no doubt that this is Wm. Sublette's party, and that it passed us last evening.[5] They must have travelled very rapidly to overtake us so soon, and no doubt had men ahead watching our motions. It seems rather unfriendly, perhaps, to run by us in this furtive way, without even stopping to say good morning, but Sublette is attached to a rival company, and all stratagems are deemed allowable when interest is concerned. It is a matter of some moment to be the first at the mountain rendezvous, in order to obtain the furs brought every summer by the trappers.

Last night, while I was serving on guard, I observed an unusual commotion among our band of horses, a wild neighing, snorting, and plunging, for which I was unable to account. I directed several of my men to go in and appease them, and endeavor to ascertain the cause. They had scarcely started, however, when about half of the band broke their fastenings, snapped the hopples on their legs, and went dashing right through the midst of the camp. Down went several of the tents, the rampart of goods was cleared in gallant style, and away went the frightened animals at full speed over the plain. The whole camp was instantly aroused. The horses that remained, were bridled as quickly as possible; we mounted them without saddles, and set off in hard pursuit after the fugitives. The night was pitch dark, but we needed no light to point out the way, as the clattering of hoofs ahead on the hard ground of the prairie, sounded like thunder. After riding half an hour, we overtook about forty of them, and surrounding them with difficulty, succeeded in driving them back, and securing them as before. Twenty men were then immediately despatched to scour the country, and bring in the remainder. This party was headed by Mr. Lee, our missionary, (who, with his usual promptitude, volunteered his services,) and they returned early this morning, bringing nearly sixty more. We find, however, upon counting the horses in our possession, that there are yet three missing.

While we were at breakfast, three Indians of the Otto tribe, came to our camp to see, and smoke with us. These were men of rather short stature, but strong and firmly built. Their countenances resemble in general expression those of the Kanzas, and their dresses are very similar. We are all of opinion, that it is to these Indians we owe our difficulties of last night, and we have no doubt that the three missing horses are now in their possession, but as we cannot prove it upon them, and cannot even converse with them, (having no interpreters,) we are compelled to submit to our loss in silence. Perhaps we should even be thankful that we have not lost more.

While these people were smoking the pipe of peace with us, after breakfast, I observed that Richardson, our chief hunter, (an experienced man in this country, of a tall and iron frame, and almost child-like simplicity of character, in fact an exact counterpart of *Hawk-eye* in his younger days,) stood aloof, and refused to sit in the circle, in which it was always the custom of the *old hands* to join.

Feeling some curiosity to ascertain the cause of this unusual diffidence, I occasionally allowed my eyes to wander to the spot where our sturdy hunter stood looking moodily upon us, as the calamet passed from hand to hand around the circle, and I thought I perceived him now and then cast a furtive glance at one of the Indians who sat opposite to me, and sometimes his countenance would assume an expression almost demoniacal, as though the most fierce and deadly passions were raging in his bosom. I felt certain that hereby hung a tale, and I watched for a corresponding expression, or at least a look of consciousness, in the face of my opposite neighbor, but expression there was none. His large features were settled in a tranquillity which nothing could disturb, and as he puffed the smoke in huge volumes from his mouth, and the fragrant vapor wreathed and curled around his head, he seemed the embodied spirit of meekness and taciturnity.

The camp moved soon after, and I lost no time in overhauling Richardson, and asking an explanation of his singular conduct.

"Why," said he, "that *Injen* that sat opposite to you, is my bitterest enemy. I was once going down alone from the rendezvous with letters for St. Louis, and when I arrived on the lower part of the Platte river, (just a short distance beyond us here,) I fell in with about a dozen Ottos. They were known to be a friendly tribe, and I therefore felt no fear of them. I dismounted from my horse and sat with them upon the ground. It was in the depth of winter; the ground was covered with snow, and the river was frozen solid. While I was thinking of nothing but my dinner, which I was then about preparing, four or five of the cowards jumped on me, mastered my rifle, and held my arms fast, while they took from me my knife and tomahawk, my flint and steel, and all my ammunition. They then loosed me, and told me to be off. I begged them, for the love of God, to give me my rifle and a few loads of ammunition, or I should starve before I could reach the settlements. No—I should have nothing, and if I did not start off immediately, they would throw me under the ice of the river. And," continued the excited hunter,—while he ground his teeth with bitter, and uncontrollable rage,—"that man that sat opposite to you was the chief of them. He recognised me, and knew very well the reason why I would not smoke with him. I tell you, sir, if ever I meet that man in any other situation than that in which I saw him this morning, I'll shoot him with as little hesitation as I would shoot a deer. Several years have passed since the perpetration of this outrage, but it is still as fresh in my memory as ever, and I again declare, that if ever an opportunity offers, I will kill that man." "But, Richardson, did they take your horse also?" "To be sure they did, and my blankets, and every thing I had, except my clothes." "But how did you subsist until you reached the settlements? You had a long journey before you." "Why, set to *trappin'* prairie squirrels with little nooses made out of the hairs of my head." I should remark that his hair was so long, that it fell in heavy masses on his shoulders. "But squirrels in winter, Richardson, I never heard of squirrels in winter." "Well but there was plenty of them, though; little white ones, that lived among the snow." "Well, really, this was an unpleasant sort of adventure enough, but let me suggest that you do very wrong to remember it with such blood-thirsty feelings." He shook his head with a dogged and determined air, and rode off as if anxious to escape a lecture.

A little sketch of our hunter may perhaps not be uninteresting, as he will figure somewhat in the following pages, being one of the principal persons of the party, the chief hunter, and a man upon whose sagacity and knowledge of the country we all in a great measure depended.

In height he is several inches over six feet, of a spare but remarkably strong and vigorous frame, and a countenance of almost infantile simplicity and openness. In disposition he is mild and affable, but when roused to indignation, his keen eyes glitter and flash, the muscles of his large mouth work convulsively, and he looks the very impersonation of the spirit of evil. He is implacable in anger, and bitter in revenge; never forgetting a kindness, but remembering an injury with equal tenacity. Such is the character of our hunter, and none who have known him as I have, will accuse me of delineating from fancy. His native place is Connecticut, which he left about twelve years ago, and has ever since been engaged in roaming through the boundless plains and rugged mountains of the west, often enduring the extremity of famine and fatigue, exposed to dangers and vicissitudes of every kind, all for the paltry, and often uncertain pittance of a Rocky Mountain hunter. He says he is now tired of this wandering and precarious life, and when he shall be enabled to save enough from his earnings to buy a farm in Connecticut, he intends to settle down a quiet tiller of the soil, and enjoy the sweets of domestic felicity. But this day will probably never arrive. Even should he succeed in realizing a little fortune, and the farm should be taken, the monotony and tameness of the scene will weary his free spirit; he will often sigh for a habitation on the broad prairie, or a ramble over the dreary mountains where his lot has so long been cast.

15th.—We saw to-day several large white wolves, and two herds of antelopes. The latter is one of the most beautiful animals I ever saw. When full grown, it is nearly as large as a deer. The horns are rather short, with a single prong near the top, and an abrupt backward curve at the summit like a hook. The ears are very delicate, almost as thin as paper, and hooked at the tip like the horns. The legs are remarkably light and beautifully formed, and as it bounds over the plain, it seems scarcely to touch the ground, so exceedingly light and agile are its motions. This animal is the *Antelope furcifer* of zoologists, and inhabits the western prairies of North America exclusively.[6] The ground here is strewn with great quantities of buffalo bones; the skulls of many of them in great perfection. I often thought of my friend Doctor M. and his *golgotha*, while we were kicking these fine specimens about the ground.[7] We are now travelling along the banks of the Blue river,—a small fork of the Kanzas. The grass is very luxuriant and good, and we have excellent and beautiful camps every night.

This morning a man was sent ahead to see W. Sublette's camp, and bear a message to him, who returned in the evening with the information that the company is only one day's journey beyond, and consists of about thirty-five men. We see his deserted camps every day, and, in some cases, the fires are not yet extinguished. It is sometimes amusing to see the wolves lurking like guilty things around these camps seeking for the fragments that may be left; as our party approaches, they sneak away with a mean, hang-dog air which often coaxes a whistling bullet out of the rifle of the wayfarer.

Chapter III

On the 18th of May we arrived at the Platte river. It is from one and a half to two miles in width, very shoal; large sand flats, and small, verdant islands appearing in every part. Wolves and antelopes were in great abundance here, and the latter were frequently killed by our men. We saw, also, the sandhill crane, great heron, *(Ardea heroidas,)* and the long-billed curlew, stalking about through the shallow water, and searching for their aquatic food.

The prairie is here as level as a race course, not the slightest undulation appearing throughout the whole extent of vision, in a north and westerly direction; but to the eastward of the river, and about eight miles from it, is seen a range of high bluffs or sand banks, stretching away to the south-east until they are lost in the far distance.

The ground here is in many places encrusted with an impure salt, which by the taste appears to be a combination of the sulphate and muriate of soda; there are also a number of little pools, of only a few inches in depth, scattered over the plain, the water of which is so bitter and pungent, that it seems to penetrate into the tongue, and almost to produce decortication of the mouth.

We are now within about three days' journey of the usual haunts of the buffalo, and our men (particularly the uninitiated) look forward to our arrival amongst them with considerable anxiety. They have listened to the garrulous hunter's details of "*approaching,*" and "*running,*" and "*quartering,*" until they fancy themselves the very actors in the scenes related, and are fretting and fuming with impatience to draw their maiden triggers upon the unoffending rangers of the plain.

The next morning, we perceived two men on horseback, at a great distance; and upon looking at them with our telescope, discovered them to be Indians, and that they were approaching us. When they arrived within three or four hundred yards, they halted, and appeared to wish to communicate with us, but feared to approach too nearly. Captain W. rode out alone and joined them, while the party proceeded slowly on its way. In about fifteen minutes he returned with the information that they were of the tribe called Grand Pawnees. They told him that a war party of their people, consisting of fifteen hundred warriors, was encamped about thirty miles below; and the captain inferred that these men had been sent to watch our motions, and ascertain our place of encampment; he was therefore careful to impress upon them that we intended to go but a few miles further, and pitch our tents upon a little stream near the main river. When we were satisfied that the messengers were out of sight of us, on their return to their camp, our whole caravan was urged into a brisk trot, and we determined to steal a march upon our neighbors. The little stream was soon passed, and we went on, and on, without slackening our pace, until 12 o'clock at night. We then called a halt on the bank of the river, made a hasty meal, threw ourselves down in our blankets, without pitching the tents, and slept soundly for three hours. We were then aroused, and off we went again, travelling steadily the whole day, making about thirty-five miles, and so got quite clear of the Grand Pawnees.

The antelopes are very numerous here. There is not half an hour during the day in which they are not seen, and they frequently permit the party to approach very near them. This afternoon, two beautiful does came bounding after us, bleating precisely like sheep. The men imitated the call, and they came up to within fifty yards of us, and stood still; two of the hunters fired, and both the poor creatures fell dead. We can now procure as many of these animals as we wish, but their flesh is not equal to common venison, and is frequently rejected by our people. A number are, however, slaughtered every day, from mere wantonness and love of killing, the greenhorns glorying in the sport, like our striplings of the city, in their annual murdering of robins and sparrows.

20th.—This afternoon, we came in sight of a large *gang* of the long-coveted buffalo. They were grazing on the opposite side of the Platte, quietly as domestic cattle, but as we neared them, the foremost *winded* us, and started back, and the whole herd followed in the wildest confusion, and were soon out of sight. There must have been many thousands of them. Towards evening, a large band of elk came towards us at full gallop, and passed very near the party. The appearance of these animals produced a singular effect upon our horses, all of which became restive, and about half the loose ones broke away, and scoured over the plain in full chase after the elk. Captain W. and several of his men went immediately in pursuit of them, and returned late at night, bringing the greater number. Two have, however, been lost irrecoverably. Our observed latitude, yesterday, was 40° 31´, and our computed distance from the Missouri settlements, about 360 miles.

The day following, we saw several small herds of buffalo on our side of the river. Two of our hunters started out after a huge bull that had separated himself from his companions, and gave him chase on fleet horses.

Away went the buffalo, and away went the men, hard as they could dash; now the hunters gained upon him, and pressed him hard; again the enormous creature had the advantage, plunging with all his might, his terrific horns often ploughing up the earth as he spurned it under him. Sometimes he would double, and rush so near the horses as almost to gore them with his horns, and in an instant would be off in a tangent, and throw his pursuers from the track. At length the poor animal came to bay, and made some unequivocal demonstrations of combat; raising and tossing his head furiously, and tearing up the ground with his feet. At this moment a shot was fired. The victim trembled like an aspen, and fell to his knees, but recovering himself in an instant, started again as fast as before. Again the determined hunters dashed after him, but the poor bull was nearly exhausted, he proceeded but a short distance and stopped again. The hunters approached, rode slowly by him, and shot two balls through his body with the most perfect coolness and precision. During the race,—the whole of which occurred in full view of the party,—the men seemed wild with the excitement which it occasioned; and when the animal fell, a shout rent the air, which startled the antelopes by dozens from the bluffs, and sent the wolves howling like demons from their lairs.

This is the most common mode of killing the buffalo, and is practised very generally by the travelling hunters; many are also destroyed by approaching them on foot, when, if the bushes are sufficiently dense, or the grass high enough to afford concealment, the hunter,—by keeping carefully to leeward of his game,—may sometimes approach so near as almost to touch the animal. If on a plain, without grass or bushes, it is necessary to be very circumspect; to approach so slowly as not to excite alarm, and, when observed by the animal, to imitate dexterously, the clumsy motions of a young bear, or assume the sneaking, prowling attitude of a wolf, in order to lull suspicion.

The Indians resort to another stratagem, which is, perhaps, even more successful. The skin of a calf is properly dressed, with the head and legs left attached to it. The Indian envelopes himself in this, and with his short bow and a brace of arrows, ambles off into the very midst of a herd. When he has selected such an animal as suits his fancy, he comes close alongside of it, and without noise, passes an arrow through its heart. One arrow is always sufficient, and it is generally delivered with such force, that at least half the shaft appears through the opposite side. The creature totters, and is about to fall, when the Indian glides around, and draws the arrow from the wound lest it should be broken. A single Indian is said to kill a great number of buffaloes in this way, before any alarm is communicated to the herd.

Towards evening, on rising a hill, we were suddenly greeted by a sight which seemed to astonish even the oldest amongst us. The whole plain, as far as the eye could discern, was covered by one enormous mass of buffalo. Our vision, at the very least computation, would certainly extend ten miles, and in the whole of this great space, including about eight miles in width from the bluffs to the river bank, there was apparently no vista in the incalculable multitude. It was truly a sight that would have excited even the dullest mind to enthusiasm. Our party rode up to within a few hundred yards of the edge of the herd, before any alarm was communicated; then the bulls,—which are always stationed around as sentinels,—began pawing the ground, and throwing the earth over their heads; in a few moments they started in a slow, clumsy canter; but as we neared them, they quickened their pace to an astonishingly rapid gallop, and in a few minutes were entirely beyond the reach of our guns, but were still so near that their enormous horns, and long shaggy beards, were very distinctly seen. Shortly after we encamped, our hunters brought in the choice parts of five that they had killed.

For the space of several days past, we have observed an inclination in five or six of our men to leave our service. Immediately as we encamp, we see them draw together in some secluded spot, and engage in close and earnest conversation. This has occurred several times, and as we are determined, if possible, to keep our horses, &c., for our own use, we have stationed a sentry near their tent, whose orders are peremptory to stop them at any hazard in case of an attempt on their part, to appropriate our horses. The men we are willing to lose, as they are of very little service, and we can do without them; but horses here are valuable, and we cannot afford to part with them without a sufficient compensation.

22d.—On walking into our tent last night at eleven o'clock, after the expiration of the first watch, (in which I had served as supernumerary, to prevent the desertion of the men,) and stooping to lay my gun in its usual situation near the head of my pallet, I was startled by seeing a pair of eyes, wild and bright as those of a tiger, gleaming from a dark corner of the lodge, and evidently directed upon me. My first impression, was that a wolf had been lurking around the camp, and had entered the tent in the prospect of finding meat. My gun was at my shoulder instinctively, my aim was directed between the eyes, and my finger pressed the trigger. At that moment a tall Indian sprang before me with a loud *wah!* seized the gun, and elevated the muzzle above my head; in another instant, a second Indian was by my side, and I saw his keen knife glitter as it left the scabbard. I had not time for thought, and was struggling with all my might with the first savage for the recovery of my weapon, when Captain W., and the other inmates of the tent were aroused, and the whole matter was explained, and set at rest in a moment. The Indians were chiefs of the tribe of Pawnee Loups, who had come with their young men to shoot buffalo: they had paid an evening visit to the captain, and as an act of courtesy had been invited to sleep in the tent. I had not known of their arrival, nor did I even suspect that Indians were in our neighborhood, so could not control the alarm which their sudden appearance occasioned me.

As I laid myself down, and drew my blanket around me, Captain W. touched me lightly with his finger, and pointed significantly to his own person, which I perceived,—by the fire light at the mouth of the tent,—to be garnished with his knife and pistols; I observed also that the muzzle of his rifle laid across his breast, and that the breech was firmly grasped by one of his legs. I took the hint; tightened my belt, drew my gun closely to my side, and composed myself to sleep. But the excitement of the scene through which I had just passed, effectually banished repose. I frequently directed my eyes towards the dark corner, and in the midst of the shapeless mass which occupied it, I could occasionally see the glittering orbs of our guest shining amidst the surrounding obscurity. At length fatigue conquered watchfulness, and I sank to sleep, dreaming of Indians, guns, daggers, and buffalo.

Upon rising the next morning, all had left the tent: the men were busied in cooking their morning meal; kettles were hanging upon the rude cranes, great ribs of meat were roasting before the fires, and loading the air with fragrance, and my dreams and midnight reveries, and apprehensions of evil, fled upon the wings of the bright morning, and nought remained but a feeling of surprise that the untoward events of the night should have disturbed my equanimity.

While these thoughts were passing in my mind, my eye suddenly encountered the two Indians. They were squatting upon the ground near one of the fires, and appeared to be surveying, with the keenness of morning appetite, the fine "*hump ribs*" which were roasting before them. The moment they perceived me, I received from them a quick glance of recognition: the taller one,—my opponent of the previous night,—rose to his feet, walked towards me, and gave me his hand with great cordiality; then pointed into the tent, made the motions of raising a gun to his shoulder, taking aim, and in short repeated the entire pantomime with great fidelity, and no little humor, laughing the whole time as though he thought it a capital joke. Poor fellow! it was near proving a dear joke for him, and I almost trembled as I recollected the eager haste with which I sought to take the life of a fellow creature. The Indian evidently felt no ill will towards me, and as a proof of it, proposed an exchange of knives, to which I willingly acceded. He deposited mine,—which had my name engraved upon the handle, in the sheath at his side, and walked away to his *hump ribs* with the air of a man who is conscious of having done a good action. As he left me, one of our old trappers took occasion to say, that in consequence of this little act of savage courtesy, the Indian became my firm friend; and that if I ever met him again, I should be entitled to share his hospitality, or claim his protection.

While the men were packing the horses, after breakfast, I was again engaged with my Indian friend. I took his bow and arrows in my hand, and remarked that the latter were smeared with blood throughout: upon my expressing surprise at this he told me, by signs, that they had passed through the body of the buffalo. I assumed a look of incredulity; the countenance of the savage brightened, and his peculiar and strange eyes actually flashed with eagerness, as he pointed to a dead antelope lying upon the ground about forty feet from us, and which one of the guard had shot near the camp in the morning. The animal lay upon its side with the breast towards us: the bow was drawn slightly, without any apparent effort, and the arrow flew through the body of the antelope, and skimmed to a great distance over the plain.

These Indians were the finest looking of any I have seen. Their persons were tall, straight, and finely formed; their noses slightly aqualine, and the whole countenance expressive of high and daring intrepidity. The face of the taller one was particularly admirable; and Gall or Spurzheim, at a single glance at his magnificent head, would have invested him with all the noblest qualities of the species.[1] I know not what a physiognomist would have said of his eyes, but they were certainly the most wonderful eyes I ever looked into; glittering and scintillating constantly, like the mirrorglasses in a lamp frame, and rolling and dancing in their orbits as though possessed of abstract volition.

The tribe to which these Indians belong, is a division of the great Pawnee nation. There are four of these divisions or tribes, known by the names of Grand Pawnees, Pawnee Loups, Pawnee Republicans, and Pawnee Picts. They are all independent of each other, governed exclusively by chiefs chosen from among their own people, and although they have always been on terms of intimacy and friendship, never intermarry, nor have other intercourse than that of trade, or a conjunction of their forces to attack the common enemy. In their dealings with the whites, they are arbitrary and overbearing, chaffering about the price of a horse, or a beaver skin, with true huckster-like eagerness and mendacity, and seizing with avidity every unfair advantage, which circumstances or their own craft may put in their power.

The buffalo still continue immensely numerous in every direction around, and our men kill great numbers, so that we are in truth living upon the fat of the land, and better feeding need no man wish. The savory buffalo hump has suffered no depreciation since the "man without a cross" vaunted of its good qualities to "the stranger;" and in this, as in many other particulars, we have realized the truth and fidelity of Cooper's admirable descriptions.

23d.—When we rose this morning, not a single buffalo, of the many thousands that yesterday strewed the plain, was to be seen. It seemed like magic. Where could they have gone? I asked myself this question again and again, but in vain. At length I applied to Richardson, who stated that they had gone to the bluffs, but for what reason he could not tell; he, however, had observed their tracks bearing towards the bluffs, and was certain that they would be found there. He and Sandsbury (another hunter) were then about starting on a hunt to supply the camp, and I concluded to accompany them; Mr. Lee, the missionary, also joined us, and we all rode off together. The party got under way about the same time, and proceeded along the bank of the river, while we struck off south to look for the buffalo. About one hour's brisk trotting carried us to the bluffs, and we entered amongst large conical hills of yellow clay, intermixed with strata of limestone, but without the slightest vegetation of any kind. On the plains which we had left, the grass was in great luxuriance, but here not a blade of it was to be seen, and yet, as Richardson had predicted, here were the buffalo. We had not ridden a mile before we entered upon a plain of sand of great extent, and observed ahead vast clouds of dust rising and circling in the air as though a tornado or a whirlwind were sweeping over the earth. "Ha!" said Richardson, "there they are; now let us take the wind of them, and you shall see some sport." We accordingly went around to leeward, and, upon approaching nearer, saw the huge animals rolling over and over in the sand with astonishing agility enveloping themselves by the exercise in a perfect atmosphere of dust; occasionally two of the bulls would spring from the ground and attack each other with amazing address and fury, retreating for ten or twelve feet, and then rushing suddenly forward, and dashing their enormous fronts together with a shock that seemed annihilating. In these rencontres, one of the combatants was often thrown back upon his haunches, and tumbled sprawling upon the ground; in which case, the victor, with true prize-fighting generosity, refrained from persecuting his fallen adversary, contenting himself with a hearty resumption of his rolling fit, and kicking up the dust with more than his former vigor, as if to celebrate his victory.

This appeared to be a good situation to approach and kill the buffalo, as, by reason of the plentiful distribution of the little clay hills, an opportunity would be afforded of successful concealment; we separated, therefore, each taking his own course. In a very few minutes I heard the crack of a rifle in the direction in which Richardson had gone, and immediately after saw the frightened animals flying from the spot. The sound reverberated among the hills, and as it died away the herd halted to watch and listen for its repetition. For myself, I strolled on for nearly an hour, leading my horse, and peering over every hill, in the hope of finding a buffalo within range, but not one could I see that was sufficiently near; and when I attempted the stealthy approach which I had seen Richardson practise with so much success, I felt compelled to acknowledge my utter insufficiency. I had determined to kill a buffalo, and as I had seen it several times done with so much apparent ease, I considered it a mere moonshine matter, and thought I could compass it without difficulty; but now I had attempted it, and was grievously mistaken in my estimate of the required skill. I had several times heard the guns of the hunters, and felt satisfied that we should not go to camp without meat, and was on the point of altering my course to join them, when, as I wound around the base of a little hill, I saw about twenty buffalo lying quietly on the ground within thirty yards of me. Now was my time. I took my picket from my saddle, and fastened my horse to the ground as quietly as possible, but with hands that almost failed to do their office, from my excessive eagerness and trembling anxiety. When this was completed, I crawled around the hill again, almost suspending my breath from fear of alarming my intended victims, until I came again in full view of the unsuspecting herd. There were so many fine animals that I was at a loss which to select; those nearest me appeared small and poor, and I therefore settled my aim upon a huge bull on the outside. just then I was attacked with the *"bull fever"* so dreadfully, that for several minutes I could not shoot. At length, however, I became firm and steady, and pulled my trigger at exactly the right instant. Up sprang the herd like lightning, and away they scoured, and my bull with them. I was vexed, angry, and discontented; I concluded that I could never kill a buffalo, and was about to mount my horse and ride off in despair, when I observed that one of the animals had stopped in the midst of his career. I rode towards him, and sure enough, there was my great bull trembling and swaying from side to side, and the clotted gore hanging like icicles from his nostrils. In a few minutes after, he fell heavily upon his side, and I dismounted and surveyed the unwieldy brute, as he panted and struggled in the death agony.

When the first ebullition of my triumph had subsided, I perceived that my prize was so excessively lean as to be worth nothing, and while I was exerting my whole strength in a vain endeavor to raise the head from the ground for the purpose of removing the tongue, the two hunters joined me, and laughed heartily at my achievement. Like all inexperienced hunters, I had been particular to select the largest bull in the gang, supposing it to be the best, (and it proved, as usual, the poorest,) while more than a dozen fat cows were nearer me, either of which I might have killed with as little trouble.

As I had supposed, my companions had killed several animals, but they had taken the meat of only one, and we had, therefore, to be diligent, or the camp might suffer for provisions. It was now past mid-day; the weather was very warm, and the atmosphere was charged with minute particles of sand, which produced a dryness and stiffness of the mouth and tongue, that was exceedingly painful and distressing. Water was now the desideratum, but where was it to be found? The arid country in which we then were, produced none, and the Platte was twelve or fourteen miles from us, and no buffalo in that direction, so that we could not afford time for so trifling a matter. I found that Mr. Lee was suffering as much as myself, although he had not spoken of it, and I perceived that Richardson was masticating a leaden bullet, to excite the salivary glands. Soon afterwards, a bull was killed, and we all assembled around the carcass to assist in the manipulations. The animal was first raised from his side where he had lain, and supported upon his knees, with his hoofs turned under him; a longitudinal incision was then made from the nape, or anterior base of the hump, and continued backward to the loins, and a large portion of the skin from each side removed; these pieces of skin were placed upon the ground, with the under surface uppermost, and the *fleeces,* or masses of meat, taken from along the back, were laid upon them. These fleeces, from a large animal, will weigh, perhaps, a hundred pounds each, and comprise the whole of the hump on each side of the vertical processes, (commonly called the *hump ribs,*) which are attached to the vertebra. The fleeces are considered the choice parts of the buffalo, and here, where the game is so abundant, nothing else is taken, if we except the tongue, and an occasional marrow bone.

This, it must be confessed, appears like a useless and unwarrantable waste of the goods of Providence; but when are men economical, unless compelled to be so by necessity? Here are more than a thousand pounds of delicious and savory flesh, which would delight the eyes and gladden the heart of any epicure in Christendom, left neglected where it fell, to feed the ravenous maw of the wild prairie wolf, and minister to the excesses of the unclean birds of the wilderness. But I have seen worse waste and havoc than this, and I feel my indignation rise at the recollection. I have seen dozens of buffalo slaughtered merely for the tongues, or for practice with the rifle; and I have also lived to see the very perpetrators of these deeds, lean and lank with famine, when the meanest and most worthless parts of the poor animals they had so inhumanly slaughtered, would have been received and eaten with humble thankfulness.

But to return to ourselves. We were all suffering from excessive thirst, and so intolerable had it at length become, that Mr. Lee and myself proposed a gallop over to the Platte river, in order to appease it; but Richardson advised us not to go, as he had just thought of a means of relieving us, which he immediately proceeded to put in practice. He tumbled our mangled buffalo over upon his side, and with his knife opened the body, so as to expose to view the great stomach, and still crawling and twisting entrails. The good missionary and myself stood gaping with astonishment, and no little loathing, as we saw our hunter plunge his knife into the distended paunch, from which gushed the green and gelatinous juices, and then insinuate his tin pan into the opening, and by depressing its edge, strain off the water which was mingled with its contents.

Richardson always valued himself upon his politeness, and the cup was therefore first offered to Mr. Lee and myself, but it is almost needless to say that we declined the proffer, and our features probably expressed the strong disgust which we felt, for our companion laughed heartily before he applied the cup to his own mouth. He then drank it to the dregs, smacking his lips, and drawing a long breath after it, with the satisfaction of a man taking his wine after dinner. Sansbury, the other hunter, was not slow in following the example set before him, and we, the audience, turned our backs upon the actors.

Before we left the spot, however, Richardson induced me to taste the blood which was still fluid in the heart, and immediately as it touched my lips, my burning thirst, aggravated by hunger, (for I had eaten nothing that day,) got the better of my abhorrence; I plunged my head into the reeking ventricles, and drank until forced to stop for breath. I felt somewhat ashamed of assimilating myself so nearly to the brutes, and turned my ensanguined countenance towards the missionary who stood by, but I saw no approval there: the good man was evidently attempting to control his risibility, and so I smiled to put him in countenance; the roar could no longer be restrained, and the missionary laughed until the tears rolled down his cheeks. I did not think, until afterwards, of the horrible ghastliness which must have characterized my smile at that particular moment.

When we arrived at the camp in the evening, and I enjoyed the luxury of a hearty draft of water, the effect upon my stomach was that of a powerful emetic: the blood was violently ejected without nausea, and I felt heartily glad to be rid of the disgusting encumbrance. I never drank blood from that day.[2]

Chapter IV

Change in the face of the country—Unpleasant
visitation—its effects—N. fork of the Platte—A day's
journey over the hills—Wormwood bushes, and poor
pasture—Marmots—Rattlesnake and gopher—
Naturalist's success and sacrifices—A sand storm—Wild
horses—Killing of a doe antelope—Bluffs of the Platte—
The chimney—"Zip Coon," the young antelope—Birds—
Feelings and cogitations of a naturalist—Arrival at
Laramie's fork—Departure of two "free trappers" on a
summer "hunt"—Black hills—Rough traveling—Red
butes—Sweet-water river, and Rock Independence—
Avocets—Wind river mountains—Rocky Mountain
sheep—Adventure of one of the men with a grizzly
bear—Rattlesnakes—Toilsome march, and arrival at
Sandy river—Suffering of the horses—Anticipated
delights of the rendezvous.

On the morning of the 24th of May we forded the Platte river, or rather its south fork, along which we had been travelling during the previous week. On the northern. side, we found the country totally different in its aspect. Instead of the extensive and apparently interminable green plains, the monotony of which had become so wearisome to the eye, here was a great sandy waste, without a single green thing to vary and enliven the dreary scene. It was a change, however, and we were therefore enjoying it, and remarking to each other how particularly agreeable it was, when we were suddenly assailed by vast swarms of most ferocious little black gnats; the whole atmosphere seemed crowded with them, and they dashed into our faces, assaulted our eyes, ears, nostrils, and mouths, as though they were determined to bar our passage through their territory. These little creatures were so exceedingly minute that, singly, they were scarcely visible; and yet their sting caused such excessive pain, that for the rest of the day our men and horses were rendered almost frantic, the former bitterly imprecating, and the latter stamping, and kicking, and rolling in the sand, in tremendous, yet vain, efforts to rid themselves of their pertinacious little foes. It was rather amusing to see the whole company with their handkerchiefs, shirts, and coats, thrown over their heads, stemming the animated torrent, and to hear the greenhorns cursing their tormenters, the country, and themselves, for their foolhardiness in venturing on the journey. When we encamped in the evening, we built fires at the mouths of the tents, the smoke from which kept our enemies at a distance, and we passed a night of tolerable comfort, after a day of most peculiar misery.

The next morning I observed that the faces of all the men were more or less swollen, some of them very severely, and poor Captain W. was totally blind for two days afterwards.

25th.—We made a noon camp to-day on the north branch or fork of the river, and in the afternoon travelled along the bank of the stream. In about an hour's march, we came to rocks, precipices, and cedar trees, and although we anticipated some difficulty and toil in the passage of the heights, we felt glad to exchange them for the vast and wearisome prairies we had left behind. Soon after we commenced the ascent, we struck into an Indian path very much worn, occasionally mounting over rugged masses of rock, and leaping wide fissures in the soil, and sometimes picking our way over the jutting crags, directly above the river. On the top of one of the stunted and broad spreading cedars, a bald eagle had built its enormous nest; and as we descended the mountain, we saw the callow young lying within it, while the anxious parents hovered over our heads, screaming their alarm.

In the evening we arrived upon the plain again; it was thickly covered with ragged and gnarled bushes of a species of wormwood, (*Artemesia*,) which perfumed the air, and at first was rather agreeable. The soil was poor and sandy, and the straggling blades of grass which found their way to the surface were brown and withered. Here was a poor prospect for our horses; a sad contrast indeed to the rich and luxuriant prairies we had left. On the edges of the little streams, however, we found some tolerable pasture, and we frequently stopped during the day to bait our poor animals in these pleasant places.

We observed here several species of small marmots, (*Arctomys*,) which burrowed in the sand, and were constantly skipping about the ground in front of our party.[1] The short rattlesnake of the prairies was also abundant, and no doubt derived its chief subsistence from foraging among its playful little neighbors. Shortly before we halted this evening, being a considerable distance in advance of the caravan, I observed a dead gopher, (*Diplostoma*,)—a small animal about the size of a rat, with large external cheek pouches, —lying upon the ground;[2] and near it a full grown rattlesnake, also dead. The gopher was yet warm and pliant, and had evidently been killed but a few minutes previously; the snake also gave evidence of very recent death, by a muscular twitching of the tail, which occurs in most serpents, soon after life is extinct. It was a matter of interest to me to ascertain the mode by which these animals were deprived of life. I therefore dismounted from my horse, and examined them carefully, but could perceive nothing to furnish even a clue. Neither of them had any external or perceptible wound. The snake had doubtless killed the quadruped, but what had killed the snake? There being no wound upon its body was sufficient proof that the gopher had not used his teeth, and in no other way could he cause death.

I was unable to solve the problem to my satisfaction, so I pocketed the animal to prepare its skin, and rode on to the camp.

The birds thus far have been very abundant. There is a considerable variety, and many of them have not before been seen by naturalists. As to the plants, there seems to be no end to them, and Mr. N. is finding dozens of new species daily. In the other branches of science, our success has not been so great, partly on account of the rapidity and steadiness with which we travel, but chiefly from the difficulty, and almost impossibility, of carrying the subjects. Already we have cast away all our useless and superfluous clothing, and have been content to mortify our natural pride, to make room for our specimens. Such things as spare waistcoats, shaving boxes, soap, and stockings, have been ejected from our trunks, and we are content to dress, as we live, in a style of primitive simplicity. In fact, the whole appearance of our party is sufficiently primitive; many of the men are dressed entirely in deerskins, without a single article of civilized manufacture about them; the old trappers and hunters wear their hair flowing on their shoulders, and their large grizzled beards would scarcely disgrace a Bedouin of the desert.

The next morning the whole camp was suddenly aroused by the falling of all the tents. A tremendous blast swept as from a funnel over the sandy plain, and in an instant precipitated our frail habitations like webs of gossamer. The men crawled out from under the ruins, rubbing their eyes, and, as usual, muttering imprecations against the country and all that therein was; it was unusually early for a start, but we did not choose to pitch the tents again, and to sleep without them here was next to impossible; so we took our breakfast in the open air, devouring our well sanded provisions as quickly as possible, and immediately took to the road.

During the whole day a most terrific gale was blowing directly in our faces, clouds of sand were driving and hurtling by us, often with such violence as nearly to stop our progress; and when we halted in the evening, we could scarcely recognise each other's faces beneath their odious mask of dust and dirt.

There have been no buffalo upon the plain to-day, all the game that we have seen, being a few elk and antelopes; but these of course we did not attempt to kill, as our whole and undivided attention was required to assist our progress.

28th.—We fell in with a new species of game to-day; —a large band of wild horses. They were very shy, scarcely permitting us to approach within rifle distance, and yet they kept within sight of us for some hours. Several of us gave them chase, in the hope of at least being able to approach sufficiently near to examine them closely, but we might as well have pursued the wind; they scoured away from us with astonishing velocity, their long manes and tails standing out almost horizontally, as they sprang along before us. Occasionally they would pause in their career, turn and look at us as we approached them, and then, with a neigh that rang loud and high above the clattering of the hoofs, dart their light heels into the air, and fly from us as before. We soon abandoned this wild chase, and contented ourselves with admiring their sleek beauty at a distance.

In the afternoon, I committed an act of cruelty and wantonness, which distressed and troubled me beyond measure, and which I have ever since recollected with sorrow and compunction. A beautiful doe antelope came running and bleating after us, as though she wished to overtake the party; she continued following us for nearly an hour, at times approaching within thirty of forty yards, and standing to gaze at us as we moved slowly on our way. I several times raised my gun to fire at her,—but my better nature as often gained the ascendency, and I at last rode into the midst of the party to escape the temptation. Still the doe followed us, and I finally fell into the rear, but without intending it, and again looked at her as she trotted behind us. At that moment, my evil genius and love of sport triumphed; I slid down from my horse, aimed at the poor antelope, and shot a ball through her side.

Under other circumstances, there would have been no cruelty in this; but here, where better meat was so abundant, and the camp was so plentifully supplied, it was unfeeling, heartless murder. It was under the influence of this too late impression, that I approached my poor victim. She was writhing in agony upon the ground, and exerting herself in vain efforts to draw her mangled body farther from her destroyer; and as I stood over her, and saw her cast her large, soft, black eyes upon me with an expression of the most touching sadness, while the great tears rolled over her face, I felt myself the meanest and most abhorrent thing in creation. But now a finishing blow would be mercy to her, and I threw my arm around her neck, averted my face, and drove my long knife through her bosom to the heart. I did not trust myself to look upon her afterwards, but mounted my horse, and galloped off to the party, with feelings such as I hope never to experience again. For several days the poor antelope haunted me, and I shall never forget its last look of pain and upbraiding.

The bluffs on the southern shore of the Platte, are, at this point, exceedingly rugged, and often quite picturesque; the formation appears to be simple clay, intermixed, occasionally, with a stratum of limestone, and one part of the bluff bears a striking and almost startling resemblance to a dilapidated feudal castle. There is also a kind of obelisk, standing at a considerable distance from the bluffs, on a wide plain, towering to the height of about two hundred feet, and tapering to a small point at the top. This pillar is known to the hunters and trappers who traverse these regions, by the name of the "*chimney.*" Here we diverged from the usual course, leaving the bank of the river, and entered a large and deep ravine between the enormous bluffs.*

The road was very uneven and difficult, winding from amongst innumerable mounds six to eight feet in height, the space between them frequently so narrow as scarcely to admit our horses, and some of the men rode for upwards of a mile kneeling upon their saddles. These mounds were of hard yellow clay, without a particle of rock of any kind, and along their bases, and in the narrow passages, flowers of every hue were growing. It was a most enchanting sight; even the men noticed it, and more than one of our matter-of-fact people exclaimed, *beautiful, beautiful!* Mr. N. was here in his glory. He rode

---

*These are called "Scott's Bluffs," so named from an unfortunate trader, who perished here from disease and hunger, many years ago. He was deserted by his companions; and the year following, his crumbling bones were found in this spot.

on ahead of the company, and cleared the passages with a trembling and eager hand, looking anxiously back at the approaching party, as though he feared it would come ere he had finished, and tread his lovely prizes under foot.

The distance through the ravine is about three miles. We then crossed several beautiful grassy knolls, and descending to the plain, struck the Platte again, and travelled along its bank. Here one of our men caught a young antelope, which he brought to the camp upon his saddle. It was a beautiful and most delicate little creature, and in a few days became so tame as to remain with the camp without being tied, and to drink, from a tin cup, the milk which our good missionaries spared from their own scanty meals. The men christened it *"Zip Coon,"* and it soon became familiar with its name, running to them when called, and exhibiting many evidences of affection and attachment. It became a great favorite with every one. A little pannier of willows was made for it, which was packed on the back of a mule, and when the camp moved in the mornings, little *Zip* ran to his station beside his long-eared hack, bleating with impatience until some one came to assist him in mounting.

On the afternoon of the 31st, we came to green trees and bushes again, and the sight of them was more cheering than can be conceived, except by persons who have travelled for weeks without beholding a green thing, save the grass under their feet. We encamped in the evening in a beautiful grove of cottonwood trees, along the edge of which ran the Platte, dotted as usual with numerous islands.

In the morning, Mr. N. and myself were up before the dawn, strolling through the umbrageous forest, inhaling the fresh, bracing air, and making the echoes ring with the report of our gun, as the lovely tenants of the grove flew by dozens before us. I think I never before saw so great a variety of birds within the same space. All were beautiful, and many of them quite new to me; and after we had spent an hour amongst them, and my game bag was teeming with its precious freight, I was still loath to leave the place, lest I should not have procured specimens of the whole.

None but a naturalist can appreciate a naturalist's feelings —his delight amounting to ecstacy —when a specimen such as he has never before seen, meets his eye, and the sorrow and grief which he feels when he is compelled to tear himself from a spot abounding with all that he has anxiously and unremittingly sought for.

This was peculiarly my case upon this occasion. We had been long travelling over a sterile and barren tract, where the lovely denizens of the forest could not exist, and I had been daily scanning the great extent of the desert, for some little oasis such as I had now found; here was my wish at length gratified, and yet the caravan would not halt for me; I must turn my back upon the *El Dorado* of my fond anticipations, and hurry forward over the dreary wilderness which lay beyond.

What valuable and highly interesting accessions to science might not be made by a party, composed exclusively of naturalists, on a journey through this rich and unexplored region! The botanist, the geologist, the mamalogist, the ornithologist, and the entomologist, would find a rich and almost inexhaustible field for the prosecution of their inquiries, and the result of such an expedition would be to add most materially to our knowledge of the wealth and resources of our country, to furnish us with new and important facts relative to its structure, organization, and natural productions, and to complete the fine native collections in our already extensive museums.

On the 1st of June, we arrived at Laramie's fork of the Platte, and crossed it without much difficulty.[3]

Here two of our " free trappers" left us for a summer "hunt" in the rugged Black Hills. These men joined our party at Independence, and have been travelling to this point with us for the benefit of our escort. Trading companies usually encourage these free trappers to join them, both for the strength which they add to the band, and that they may have the benefit of their generally good hunting qualities. Thus are both parties accommodated, and no obligation is felt on either side.

I confess I felt somewhat sad when I reflected upon the possible fate of the two adventurous men who had left us in the midst of a savage wilderness, to depend entirely upon their unassisted strength and hardihood, to procure the means of subsistence and repel the aggression of the Indian.

Their expedition will be fraught with stirring scenes, with peril and with strange adventure; but they think not of this, and they care not for it. They are only two of the many scores who annually subject themselves to the same difficulties and dangers; they see their friends return unscathed, and laden with rich and valuable furs, and if one or two should have perished by Indian rapacity, or fallen victims to their own daring and fool-hardy spirit, they mourn the loss of their brethren who have not returned, and are only the more anxious to pursue the same track in order to avenge them.

On the 2d, we struck a range of high and stony mountains, called the Black Hills. The general aspect here, was dreary and forbidding; the soil was intersected by deep and craggy fissures; rock jutted over rock, and precipice frowned over precipice in frightful, and apparently endless, succession. Soon after we commenced the ascent, we experienced a change in the temperature of the air; and towards mid-day, when we had arrived near the summit, our large blanket *capeaus*, —which in the morning had been discarded as uncomfortable, — were drawn tightly around us, and every man was shivering in his saddle as though he had an ague fit. The soil here is of a deep reddish or ferruginous hue, intermixed with green sand; and on the heights, pebbles of chalcedony and agate are abundant.

We crossed, in the afternoon, the last and steepest spur of this chain, winding around rough and stony precipices, and along the extreme verges of tremendous ravines, so dangerous looking that we were compelled to dismount and lead our horses.

On descending to the plain, we saw again the north fork of the Platte, and were glad of an opportunity of encamping. Our march to-day has been an unusually wearisome one, and many of our loose horses are bruised and lame.

7th.—The country has now become more level, but the prairie is barren and inhospitable looking to the last degree. The twisted, aromatic wormwood covers and extracts the strength from the burnt sand and soil. The grass is dry and brown, and our horses are suffering extremely for want of food. Occasionally, however, a spot of lovely green appears, and here we allow our poor jaded friends to halt, and roam without their riders, and their satisfaction and pleasure is expressed by many a joyous neigh, and many a heart-felt roll upon the verdant sward.

In the afternoon, we arrived at the "Red Butes," two or three brown-red cliffs, about two thousand feet in height. This is a remarkable point in the mountain route. One of these cliffs terminates a long, lofty, wooded ridge, which has bounded our southern view for the past two days. The summits of the cliffs are covered with patches of snow, and the contrast of the dazzling white and brick-red produces a very pretty effect.

The next day, we left the Platte river, and crossed a wide, sandy desert, dry and desolate; and on the 9th, encamped at noon on the banks of the Sweet-water. Here we found a large rounded mass of granite, about fifty feet high, called Rock Independence. Like the Red Butes, this rock is also a rather remarkable point in the route. On its smooth, perpendicular sides, we see carved the names of most of the mountain *bourgeois,* with the dates of their arrival. We observed those of the two Sublette's, Captains Bonneville, Serre, Fontinelle, &c., and after leaving our own, and taking a hearty, but hasty lunch in the shade of a rock, and a draught from the pure and limpid stream at its base, we pursued our journey.

The river is here very narrow, often only twelve or fifteen feet wide, shallow, and winding so much, that during our march, to-day, we crossed it several times, in order to pursue a straight course. The banks of the stream are clothed with the most luxuriant pasture, and our invaluable dumb friends appear perfectly happy.

We saw here great numbers of a beautiful brown and white avocet, (the *Recurvirostra americana* of ornithologists.) These fine birds were so tame as to allow a very near approach, running slowly before our party, and scarcely taking wing at the report of a gun. They frequent the marshy plains in the neighborhood of the river, and breed here.

On the 10th, about ninety miles to the west, we had a striking view of the Wind-river mountains. They are almost wholly of a dazzling whiteness, being covered thickly with snow, and the lofty peaks seem to blend themselves with the dark clouds which hang over them. This chain gives rise to the sources of the Missouri, the Colorado of the west, and Lewis' river of the Columbia, and is the highest land on the continent of North America.

We saw, to-day, a small flock of the hairy sheep of the Rocky Mountains, the big horn of the hunters, (*Ovis montana.*) We exerted ourselves in vain to shoot them. They darted from us, and hid themselves amongst the inaccessible cliffs, so that none but a chamois hunter might pretend to reach them. Richardson says that he has frequently killed them, but he admits that it is dangerous and wearisome sport; and when good beef is to be found upon the plains, men are not anxious to risk their necks for a meal of mutton.

In the afternoon, one of our men had a somewhat perilous adventure with a grizzly bear. He saw the animal crouching his huge frame in some willows which skirted the river, and approaching on horseback to within twenty yards, fired upon him. The bear was only slightly wounded by the shot, and with a fierce growl of angry malignity, rushed from his cover, and gave chase. The horse happened to be a slow one, and for the distance of half a mile, the race was hard contested; the bear frequently approaching so near the terrified animal as to snap at his heels, while the equally terrified rider, —who had lost his hat at the start, —used whip and spur with the most frantic diligence, frequently looking behind, from an influence which he could not resist, at his rugged and determined foe, and shrieking in an agony of fear, "shoot him, shoot him?" The man, who was one of the greenhorns, happened to be about a mile behind the main body, either from the indolence of his horse or his own carelessness; but as he approached the party in his desperate flight, and his lugubrious cries reached the ears of the men in front, about a dozen of them rode to his assistance, and soon succeeded in diverting the attention of his pertinacious foe. After he had received the contents of all the guns, he fell, and was soon dispatched. The man rode in among his fellows, pale and haggard from overwrought feelings, and was probably effectually cured of a propensity for meddling with grizzly bears.

A small striped rattlesnake is abundant on these plains: —it is a different species from our common one at home, but is equally malignant and venomous. The horses are often startled by them, and dart aside with intuitive fear when their note of warning is sounded in the path.[4]

12th.—The plains of the Sweet-water at this point— latitude 43° 6', longitude 110° 30', —are covered with little salt pools, the edges of which are encrusted with alkaline efflorescences, looking like borders of snow. The rocks in the vicinity are a loose, fine-grained sandstone, the strata nearly horizontal, and no organic remains have been discovered. We have still a view of the lofty Wind-river mountains on our right hand, and they have for some days served as a guide to determine our course. On the plain, we passed several huge rhomboidal masses of rock, standing alone, and looking, at a little distance, like houses with chimneys. The freaks of nature, as they are called, have often astonished us since we have been journeying in the wilderness. We have seen, modeled without art, representations of almost all the most stupendous works of man; and how do the loftiest and most perfect creations of his wisdom and ingenuity sink into insignificance by the comparison. Noble castles, with turrets, embrazures, and loop holes, with the drawbridge in front, and the moat surrounding it: behind, the humble cottages of the subservient peasantry, and all the varied concomitants of such a scene, are so strikingly evident to the view, that it requires but little stretch of fancy to imagine that a race of antediluvian giants may here have swayed their iron sceptre, and left behind the crumbling palace and the tower, to tell of their departed glory.

On the 14th, we left the Sweet-water, and proceeded in a south-westerly direction to Sandy river, a branch of the Colorado of the west. We arrived here at about 9 o'clock in the evening, after a hard and most toilsome march for both man and beast. We found no water on the route, and not a single blade of grass for our horses. Many of the poor animals stopped before night, and resolutely refused to proceed; and others with the remarkable sagacity, peculiar to them, left the track in defiance of those who drove and guided them, sought and found water, and spent the night in its vicinity. The band of missionaries, with their horses and horned cattle, halted by the way, and only about half the men of the party accompanied us to our encampment on Sandy. We were thus scattered along the route for several miles; and if a predatory band of Indians had then found us, we should have fallen an easy prey.

The next morning by about 10 o'clock all our men and horses had joined us, and, in spite of the fatigues of the previous day, we were all tolerably refreshed, and in good spirits. Towards noon we got under way, and proceeded seven or eight miles down the river to a spot where we found a little poor pasture for our horses. Here we remained until the next morning, to recruit. I found here a beautiful new species of mocking bird,* which I shot and prepared.[5] Birds are, however, generally scarce, and there is here very little of interest in any department of natural history. We are also beginning to suffer somewhat for food: buffalo are rarely seen, the antelopes are unusually shy, and the life of our little favorite, " Zip," has been several times menaced. I believe, however, that his keeper, from sheer fondness, would witness much greater suffering in the camp, ere he would consent to the sacrifice of his playful little friend.

16th.—We observed a hoar frost and some thin ice, this morning at sunrise; but at mid-day, the thermometer stood at 82°. We halted at noon, after making about fifteen miles, and dined. Saw large herds of buffalo on the plains of Sandy river, grazing in every direction on the short and dry grass. Domestic cattle would certainly starve here, and yet the bison exists, and even becomes fat; a striking instance of the wonderful adaptation of Providence.

---

*This is the mountain mocking bird, (*Orphus montanus*), described in the Appendix.

1 7th. —We had yesterday a cold rain, the first which has fallen in our track for several weeks. Our vicinity to the high mountains of Wind river will perhaps account for it. To-day at noon, the mercury stood at 92° in the shade, but there being a strong breeze, we did not suffer from heat.

Our course was still down the Sandy river, and we are now looking forward with no little pleasure to a rest of two or more weeks at the mountain rendezvous on the Colorado. Here we expect to meet all the mountain companies who left the States last spring, and also the trappers who come in from various parts, with the furs collected by them during the previous year. All will be mirth and jollity, no doubt, but the grand desideratum with some of us, is to allow our horses to rest their tired limbs and exhausted strength on the rich and verdant plains of the Siskadee. At our camp this evening, our poor horses were compelled to fast as heretofore, there being absolutely nothing for them to eat. Some of the famished animals attempted to allay their insatiable cravings, by cropping the dry and bitter tops of the wormwood with which the plain is strewed.

We look forward to brighter days for them ere long; soon shall they sport in the green pastures, and rest and plenty shall compensate for their toils and privations.

Chapter V

June 19th.—We arrived to-day on the Green river, Siskadee or
Colorado of the west,—a beautiful, clear, deep, and rapid stream,
which receives the waters of Sandy,—and encamped upon its
eastern bank. After making a hasty meal, as it was yet early in the day,
I sallied forth with my gun, and roamed about the neighborhood for
several hours in quest of birds. On returning, towards evening, I found
that the whole company had left the spot, the place being occupied
only by a few hungry wolves, ravens, and magpies, the invariable
gleaners of a forsaken camp.

I could not at first understand the meaning of all I saw. I thought
the desertion strange, and was preparing to make the best of it, when
a quick and joyful neigh sounded in the bushes near me, and I
recognized the voice of my favorite horse. I found him carefully tied,
with the saddle, &c., lying near him. I had not the least idea where the

company had gone, but I knew that on the rich, alluvial banks of the river, the trail of the horses would be distinct enough, and I determined to place my dependence, in a great measure, upon the sagacity of my excellent dumb friend, satisfied that he would take me the right course. I accordingly mounted, and off we went at a speed which I found some difficulty in restraining. About half an hour's hard riding brought us to the edge of a large branch of the stream, and I observed that the horses had here entered. I noticed other tracks lower down, but supposed them to have been made by the wanderings of the loose animals. Here then seemed the proper fording place, and with some little hesitation, I allowed my nag to enter the water; we had proceeded but a few yards, however, when down he went off a steep bank, far beyond his depth. This was somewhat disconcerting; but there was but one thing to be done, so I turned my horse's head against the swift current, and we went snorting and blowing for the opposite shore. We arrived at length, though in a sadly wet and damaged state, and in a few minutes after, came in view of the new camp.

Captain W. explained to me that he had heard of good pasture here, and had concluded to move immediately, on account of the horses; he informed me, also, that he had crossed the stream about fifty yards below the point where I had entered, and had found an excellent ford. I did not regret my adventure, however, and was congratulating myself upon my good fortune in arriving so seasonably, when, upon looking to my saddle, I discovered that my coat was missing. I had felt uncomfortably warm when I mounted, and had removed the coat and attached it carelessly to the saddle; the rapidity of the current had disengaged it, and it was lost forever. The coat itself was not of much consequence after the hard service it had seen, but it contained the second volume of my journal, a pocket compass, and other articles of essential value to me. I would gladly have relinquished every thing the garment held, if I could have recovered the book; and although I returned to the river, and searched assiduously until night, and offered large rewards to the men, it could not be found.

The journal commenced with our arrival at the Black Hills, and contained some observations upon the natural productions of the country, which to me, at least, were of some importance; as well as descriptions of several new species of birds, and notes regarding their habits, &c., which cannot be replaced.

I would advise all tourists, who journey by land, never to carry their itineraries upon their persons; or if they do, let them be attached by a cord to the neck, and worn under the clothing. A convenient and safe plan would probably be, to have the book deposited in a close pocket of leather, made on the inner side of the saddle-wing; it would thus be always at hand, and if a deep stream were to be passed the trouble of drying the leaves would not be a very serious matter.

In consequence of remaining several hours in wet clothes, after being heated by exercise, I rose the next morning with so much pain, and stiffness of the joints, that I could scarcely move. But notwithstanding this, I was compelled to mount my horse with the others, and to ride steadily and rapidly for eight hours. I suffered intensely during this ride; every step of my horse seemed to increase it, and induced constant sickness and retching.

When we halted, I was so completely exhausted, as to require assistance in dismounting, and shortly after, sank into a state of insensibility from which I did not recover for several hours. Then a violent fever commenced, alternating for two whole days, with sickness and pain. I think I never was more unwell in my life; and if I had been at home, lying on a feather bed instead of the cold ground, I should probably have fancied myself an invalid for weeks.*

22d.—We are now lying at the rendezvous.[1] W. Sublette, Captains Serre, Fitzpatrick, and other leaders, with their companies, are encamped about a mile from us, on the same plain, and our own camp is crowded with a heterogeneous assemblage of visitors. The principal of these are Indians, of the Nez Percé, Banneck and Shoshoné tribes, who come with the furs and peltries which they have been collecting at the risk of their lives during the past winter and spring, to trade for ammunition, trinkets, and " fire water." There is, in addition to these, a great variety of personages amongst us; most of them calling themselves white men, French-Canadians, half-breeds, &c., their color nearly as dark, and their manners wholly as wild, as the Indians with whom they constantly associate. These people, with their obstreperous mirth, their whooping, and howling, and quarrelling, added to the mounted Indians, who are constantly dashing into and through our camp, yelling like fiends, the barking and baying of savage wolf-dogs, and the incessant cracking of rifles and carbines, render our camp a perfect bedlam. A more unpleasant situation for an invalid could scarcely

---

*I am indebted to the kindness of my companion and friend, Professor Nuttall, for supplying, in great measure, the deficiency caused by the loss of my journal.

be conceived. I am confined closely to the tent with illness, and am compelled all day to listen to the hiccoughing jargon of drunken traders, the *sacré* and *foutre* of Frenchmen run wild, and the swearing and screaming of our own men, who are scarcely less savage than the rest, being heated by the detestable liquor which circulates freely among them.

It is very much to be regretted that at times like the present, there should be a positive necessity to allow the men as much rum as they can drink, but this course has been sanctioned and practised by all leaders of parties who have hitherto visited these regions, and reform cannot be thought of now. The principal liquor in use here is alcohol diluted with water. It is sold to the men at *three dollars* the pint! Tobacco, of very inferior quality, such as could be purchased in Philadelphia at about ten cents per pound, here brings two dollars! and everything else in proportion. There is no coin in circulation, and these articles are therefore paid for by the independent mountain-men, in beaver skins, buffalo robes, &c.; and those who are hired to the companies, have them charged against their wages.

I was somewhat amused to-day by observing one of our newly hired men enter the tent, and order, with the air of a man who knew he would not be refused, *twenty dollars' worth of rum, and ten dollars worth of sugar,* to treat two of his companions who were about leaving the rendezvous!

30th.—Our camp here is a most lovely one in every respect, and as several days have elapsed since we came, and I am convalescent, I can roam about the country a little and enjoy it. The pasture is rich and very abundant, and it does our hearts good to witness the satisfaction and comfort of our poor jaded horses. Our tents are pitched in a pretty little valley or indentation in the plain, surrounded on all sides by low bluffs of yellow clay. Near us flows the clear deep water of the Siskadee, and beyond, on every side, is a wide and level prairie, interrupted only by some gigantic peaks of mountains and conical *butes* in the distance. The river, here, contains a great number of large trout, some grayling, and a small narrow-mouthed white fish, resembling a herring. They are all frequently taken with the hook, and, the trout particularly, afford excellent sport to the lovers of angling. Old Izaac Walton would be in his glory here, and the precautionary measures which he so strongly recommends in approaching a trout stream, he would not need to practise, as the fish is not shy, and bites quickly and eagerly at a grasshopper or minnow.

Buffalo, antelopes, and elk are abundant in the vicinity, and we are therefore living well. We have seen also another kind of game, a beautiful bird, the size of a half grown turkey, called the cock of the plains, *(Tetrao urophasianus.)*[2] We first met with this noble bird on the plains, about two days' journey east of Green river, in flocks, or *packs,* of fifteen or twenty, and so exceedingly tame as to allow an approach to within a few feet, running before our horses like domestic fowls, and not unfrequently hopping under their bellies, while the men amused themselves by striking out their feathers with their riding whips. When we first saw them, the temptation to shoot was irresistible; the guns were cracking all around us, and the poor grouse falling in every direction; but what was our disappointment, when, upon roasting them nicely before the fire, we found them so strong and bitter as not to be eatable. From this time the cock of the plains was allowed to roam free and unmolested, and as he has failed to please our palates, we are content to admire the beauty of his plumage, and the grace and spirit of his attitudes.

July 2d.—We bade adieu to the rendezvous this morning; packed up our moveables, and journied along the bank of the river. Our horses are very much recruited by the long rest and good pasture which they have enjoyed, and, like their masters, are in excellent spirits.

During our stay at the rendezvous, many of us looked anxiously for letters from our families, which we expected by the later caravans, but we were all disappointed. For myself, I have received but one, since I left my home, but this has been my solace through many a long and dreary journey. Many a time, while pacing my solitary round as night-guard in the wilderness, have I sat myself down, and stirring up the dying embers of the camp fire, taken the precious little memento from my bosom, undrawn the string of the leathern sack which contained it, and poured over the dear characters, till my eyes would swim with sweet, but sad recollections, then kissing the inanimate paper, return it to its sanctuary, tighten up my pistol belt, shoulder my gun, and with a quivering voice, swelling the "*all's well*" upon the night breeze, resume my slow and noiseless tramp around my sleeping companions.

Many of our men have left us, and joined the returning companies, but we have had an accession to our party of about thirty Indians; Flat-heads, Nez Percés, &c., with their wives, children, and dogs. Without these our camp would be small; they will probably travel with us until we arrive on Snake river, and pass over the country where the most danger is to be apprehended from their enemies, the Black-feet.

Some of the women in this party, particularly those of the Nez Percé nation, are rather handsome, and their persons are decked off in truly savage taste. Their dresses of deer skin are profusely ornamented with beads and porcupine quills; huge strings of beads are hung around their necks, and their saddles are garnished with dozens of little hawk's bells, which jingle and make music for them as they travel along. Several of these women have little children tied to their backs, sewed up papoose fashion, only the head being seen; as they jolt along the road, we not unfrequently hear their voices ringing loud and shrill above the music of the bells. Other little fellows who have ceased to require the maternal contributions, are tied securely on other horses, and all their care seems to be to sleep, which they do most pertinaciously in spite of jolting, noise, and clamor. There is among this party, a Blackfoot chief,—a renegado from his tribe, who sometime since killed the principal chief of his nation, and was in consequence under the necessity of absconding. He has now joined the party of his hereditary foes, and is prepared to fight against his own people and kindred. He is a fine, warlike looking fellow, and although he takes part in all the war-songs, and sham-battles of his adopted brothers, and whoops, and howls as loud as the best of them, yet it is plain to perceive that he is distrusted and disliked. All men, whether, civilized or savage, honorable, or otherwise, detest and scorn a traitor!

We were joined at the rendezvous by a Captain Stewart, an English gentleman of noble family, who is travelling for amusement, and in search of adventure.[3] He has already been a year in the mountains, and is now desirous of visiting the lower country, from which he may probably take passage to England by sea. Another Englishman, a young man, named Ashworth, also attached himself to our party, for the same purpose.[4]

Our course lay along the bank of Ham's fork, through a hilly and stony, but not a rocky country; the willow flourished on the margin of the stream, and occasionally the eye was relieved, on scanning the plain, by a p:retty clump of cottonwood or poplar trees. The cock of the plains is very abundant here, and our pretty little summer yellow bird, (*Sylvia aestiva*,) one of our most common birds at home, is our constant companion.[5] How natural sounds his little monotonous stave, and how it seems to carry us back to the dear scenes which we have exchanged for the wild and pathless wilderness!

4th.—We left Ham's fork this morning, —now diminished to a little purling brook,—and passed across the hills in a north-westerly direction for about twenty miles, when we struck Muddy creek. This is a branch of Bear river, which empties into the Salt lake, or "lake Bonneville," as it has been lately named, for what reason I know not. Our camp here, is a beautiful and most delightful one. A large plain, like a meadow, of rich, waving grass, with a lovely little stream running through the midst, high hills, capped with shapely cedars on two sides, and on the others an immense plain, with snow clad mountains in the distance. This being a memorable day, the liquor kegs were opened, and the men allowed an abundance. We, therefore, soon had a renewal of the coarse and brutal scenes of the rendezvous. Some of the bacchanals called for a volley in honor of the day, and in obedience to the order, some twenty or thirty " happy " ones reeled into line with their muzzles directed to every point of the compass, and when the word "fire" was given, we who were not "happy" had to lie flat upon the ground to avoid the bullets which were careering through the camp.

In this little stream, the trout are more abundant than we have yet seen them. One of our *sober* men took, this afternoon, upwards of thirty pounds. These fish would probably average fifteen or sixteen inches in length, and weigh three-quarters of a pound; occasionally, however, a much larger one is seen.

5th.—We travelled about twenty miles this day, over country abounding in lofty hills, and early in the afternoon arrived on Bear river, and encamped. This is a fine stream of about one hundred and fifty feet in width, with a moveable sandy bottom. The grass is dry and poor, the willow abounds along the banks, and at a distance marks the course of the stream, which meanders through an alluvial plain of four to six miles in width. At the distance of about one hundred miles from this point, the Bear river enters the Salt lake, a large body of salt water, without outlet, in which there is so large an island as to afford streams of fresh water for goats and other animals living upon it.

On the next day we crossed the river, which we immediately left, to avoid a great bend, and passed over some lofty ranges of hills and through rugged and stony valleys between them; the wind was blowing a gale right ahead, and clouds of dust were flying in our faces, so that at the end of the day, our countenances were disguised as they were on the plains of the Platte. The march today has been a most laborious and fatiguing one both for man and beast; we have travelled steadily from morning till night, not stopping at noon; our poor horses' feet are becoming very much worn and sore, and when at length we struck Bear river again and encamped, the wearied animals refused to eat, stretching themselves upon the ground and falling asleep from very exhaustion.

Trout, grayling, and a kind of char are very abundant here —the first very large. The next day we travelled but twelve miles, it being impossible to urge our worn-out horses farther. Near our camp this evening we found some large gooseberries and currants, and made a hearty meal upon them. They were to us peculiarly delicious. We have lately been living entirely upon dried buffalo, without vegetables or bread; even this is now failing us, and we are upon short allowance. Game is very scarce, our hunters cannot find any, and our Indians have killed but two buffalo for several days. Of this small stock they would not spare us a mouthful, so it is probable we shall soon be hungry.

The alluvial plain here presents many unequivocal evidences of volcanic action, being thickly covered with masses of lava, and high walls and regular columns of basalt appear in many places. The surrounding country is composed, as usual, of high hills and narrow, stony valleys between them; the hills are thickly covered with a growth of small cedars, but on the plain, nothing flourishes but the everlasting wormwood, or *sage* as it is here called.

Our encampment on the 8th, was near what are called the "White-clay pits," still on Bear river. The soil is soft chalk, white and tenacious; and in the vicinity are several springs of strong supercarbonated water, which bubble up with all the activity of artificial fountains. The taste was very agreeable and refreshing, resembling Saratoga water, but not so saline. The whole plain to the hills, is covered with little mounds formed of calcareous sinter, having depressions on their summits, from which once issued streams of water. The extent of these eruptions, at some former period, must have been very great. At about half a mile distant, is an eruptive thermal spring of the temperature of 90°, and near this is an opening in the earth from which a stream of gas issues without water.

In a thicket of common red cedars, near our camp, I found, and procured several specimens of two beautiful and rare birds which I had never before seen—the Lewis' woodpecker and Clark's crow, (*Picus torquatus* and *Corvus columbianus*.)[6]

We remained the whole of the following day in camp to recruit our horses, and a good opportunity was thus afforded me of inspecting all the curiosities of this wonderful region, and of procuring some rare and valuable specimens of birds. Three of our hunters sallied forth in pursuit of several buffalo whose tracks had been observed by some of the men, and we were overjoyed to see them return in the evening loaded with the meat and marrow bones of two animals which they had killed.

We saw here the whooping crane, and white pelican, numerous; and in the small streams near the bases of the hills, the common canvass-back duck, shoveller, and black duck, *(Anas obscura)* were feeding their young.

We were this evening visited by Mr. Thomas McKay, an Indian trader of some note in the mountains. He is a step-son of Dr. McLaughlin, the chief factor at Fort Vancouver, on the Columbia, and the leader of a party of Canadians and Indians, now on a hunt in the vicinity.[7] This party is at present in our rear, and Mr. McKay has come ahead in order to join us, and keep us company until we reach Portneuf river, where we intend building a fort.

10th.—We were moving early this morning: our horses were very much recruited, and seemed as eager as their masters to travel on. It is astonishing how soon a horse revives, and overcomes the lassitude consequent upon fatigue, when he is allowed a day's rest upon tolerable pasture. Towards noon, however, after encountering the rough lava-strewn plain for a few hours, they became sufficiently sobered to desist from all unnecessary curvetting and prancing, and settled down into a very matter-of-fact trudge, better suited to the country and to the work which they have yet to do.

Soon after we left, we crossed one of the high and stony hills by which our late camp is surrounded; then making a gentle descent, we came to a beautiful and very fertile plain. This is, however, very different from the general face of the country; in a short time, after passing over the rich prairie, the same dry aridity and depauperation prevailed, which is almost universal west of the mountains. On the wide plain, we observed large sunken spots, some of them of great extent, surrounded by walls of lava, indicating the existence, at some very ancient date, of active craters. These eruptions have probably been antediluvian, or have existed at a period long anterior to the present order of creation. On the side of the hills are high walls of lava and basaltic dykes, and many large and dark caves are formed by the juxtaposition of the enormous masses.

Early in the afternoon we passed a large party of white men, encamped on the lava plain near one of the small streams. Horses were tethered all around, and men were lolling about playing games of cards, and loitering through the camp, as though at a loss for employment. We soon ascertained it to be Captain Bonneville's company resting after the fatigues of a long march. Mr. Wyeth and Captain Stewart visited the lodge of the "bald chief," and our party proceeded on its march. The difficulties of the route seemed to increase as we progressed, until at length we found ourselves wedged in among huge blocks of lava and columns of basalt, and were forced, most reluctantly, to retrace our steps for several miles, over the impediments which we had hoped we were leaving forever behind us. We had nearly reached Bonneville's camp again, when Captains Wyeth and Stewart joined us, and we struck into another path which proved more tolerable. Wyeth gave us a rather amusing account of his visit to the worthy captain. He and Captain Stewart were received very kindly by the veteran, and every delicacy that the lodge afforded was brought forth to do them honor. Among the rest, was some *metheglin* or diluted alcohol sweetened with honey, which the good host had concocted; this dainty beverage was set before them, and the thirsty guests were not slow in taking advantage of the invitation so obligingly given. Draught after draught of the precious liquor disappeared down the throats of the visitors, until the anxious, but still complaisant captain, began to grow uneasy.

"I beg you will help yourselves, gentlemen," said the host, with a smile which he intended to express the utmost urbanity, but which, in spite of himself, had a certain ghastliness about it.

"Thank you, sir, we will do so freely," replied the two worthies, and away went the metheglin as before.

Cup after cup was drained, until the hollow sound of the keg indicated that its contents were nearly exhausted, when the company rose, and thanking the kind host for his noble entertainment, were bowed out of the tent with all the polite formality which the accomplished captain knows so well how to assume.

Towards evening, we struck Blackfoot river, a small, sluggish, stagnant stream, heading with the waters of a rapid rivulet passed yesterday, which empties into the Bear river. This stream passes in a north-westerly direction through a valley of about six miles in width, covered with quagmires, through which we had great difficulty in making our way. As we approached our encampment, near a small grove of willows, on the margin of the river, a tremendous grizzly bear rushed out upon us. Our horses ran wildly in every direction, snorting with terror, and became nearly unmanageable. Several balls were instantly fired into him, but they only seemed to increase his fury. After spending a moment in rending each wound, (their invariable practice,) he selected the person who happened to be nearest, and darted after him, but before he proceeded far, he was sure to be stopped again by a ball from another quarter. In this way he was driven about amongst us for perhaps fifteen minutes, at times so near some of the horses, that he received several severe kicks from them. One of the pack horses was fairly fastened upon by the terrific claws of the brute, and in the terrified animal's efforts to escape the dreaded gripe, the pack and saddle were broken to pieces and disengaged. One of our mules also lent him a kick in the head while pursuing it up an adjacent hill, which sent him rolling to the bottom. Here he was finally brought to a stand.

The poor animal was so completely surrounded by enemies that he became bewildered. He raised himself upon his hind feet, standing almost erect, his mouth partly open, and from his protruding tongue the blood fell fast in drops. While in this position, he received about six more balls, each of which made him reel. At last, as in complete desperation, he dashed into the water, and swam several yards with astonishing strength and agility, the guns cracking at him constantly; but he was not to proceed far. Just then, Richardson, who had been absent, rode up, and fixing his deadly aim upon him, fired a ball into the back of his head, which killed him instantly. The strength of four men was required to drag the ferocious brute from the water, and upon examining his body, he was found completely riddled; there did not appear to be four inches of his shaggy person, from the hips upward, that had not received a ball. There must have been at least thirty shots made at him, and probably few missed him; yet such was his tenacity of life, that I have no doubt he would have succeeded in crossing the river, but for the last shot in the brain. He would probably weigh, at the least, six hundred pounds, and was about the height of an ordinary steer. The spread of the foot, laterally, was ten inches, and the claws measured seven inches in length. This animal was remarkably lean; when in good condition, he would, doubtless, much exceed in weight the estimate I have given. Richardson, and two other hunters, in company, killed two in the course of the afternoon, and saw several others.

This evening, our pet antelope, poor little " Zip Koon," met with a serious accident. The mule on which he rode, got her feet fastened in some lava blocks, and, in the struggle to extricate herself, fell violently on the pointed fragments. One of the delicate legs of our favorite was broken, and he was otherwise so bruised and hurt, that, from sheer mercy, we ordered him killed. We had hoped to be able to take him to the fort which we intend building on the Portneuf river, where he could have been comfortably cared for. This is the only pet we have had in the camp, which continued with us for more than a few days. We have sometimes taken young grizzly bears, but these little fellows, even when not larger than puppies, are so cross and snappish, that it is dangerous to handle them, and we could never become attached to any animal so ungentle, and therefore young "*Ephraim,*" (to give him his mountain cognomen,) generally meets with but little mercy from us when his evil genius throws him in our way. The young buffalo calf is also very often taken, and if removed from the mother, and out of sight of the herd, he will follow the camp as steadily as a dog; but his propensity for keeping close to the horse's heels often gets him into trouble, as he meets with more kicks than caresses from them. He is considered an interloper, and treated accordingly. The bull calf of a month or two old, is sometimes rather difficult to manage; he shows no inclination to follow the camp like the younger ones, and requires to be dragged along by main force. At such times, he watches for a good opportunity, and before his captor is aware of what is going on, he receives a *butt* from the clumsy head of the intractable little brute, which, in most cases, lays him sprawling upon the ground.

I had an adventure of this sort a few days before we arrived at the rendezvous. I captured a large bull calf, and with considerable difficulty, managed to drag him into the camp, by means of a rope noosed around his neck, and made fast to the high pommel of my saddle. Here I attached him firmly by a cord to a stake driven into the ground, and considered him secure. In a few minutes, however, he succeeded in breaking his fastenings, and away he scoured out of the camp. I lost no time in giving chase, and although I fell flat into a ditch, and afforded no little amusement to our people thereby, I soon overtook him, and was about seizing the stranded rope, which was still around his neck, when, to my surprise, the little animal showed fight; he came at me with all his force, and dashing his head into my breast, bore me to the ground in a twinkling. I, however, finally succeeded in recapturing him, and led and pushed him back into the camp; but I could make nothing of him; his stubbornness would neither yield to severity or kindness, and the next morning I loosed him and let him go.

11th.—On ascending a hill this morning, Captain Wyeth, who was at the head of the company, suddenly espied an Indian stealing cautiously along the summit, and evidently endeavoring to conceal himself. Captain W. directed the attention of McKay to the crouching figure, who, the moment he caught a glimpse of him, exclaimed, in tones of joyful astonishment, "a Blackfoot, by—!" and clapping spurs to his horse, tore up the hill with the most frantic eagerness, with his rifle poised in his hand ready for a shot. The Indian disappeared over the hill like a lightning flash, and in another second, McKay was also out of sight, and we could hear the rapid clatter of his horse's hoofs, in hot pursuit after the fugitive. Several of the men, with myself, followed after at a rapid gait, with, however, a very different object. Mine was simply curiosity, mingled with some anxiety, lest the wily Indian should lead our impetuous friend into an ambushment, and his life thus fall a sacrifice to his temerity. When we arrived at the hill-top, McKay was gone, but we saw the track of his horse passing down the side of it, and we traced him into a dense thicket about a quarter of a mile distant. Several of our hardy fellows entered this thicket, and beat about for some time in various directions, but nothing could they see either of McKay or the Indian. In the mean time, the party passed on, and my apprehensions were fast settling into a certainty that our bold companion had found the death he had so rashly courted, when I was inexpressibly relieved by hearing the crackling of the bushes near, which was immediately followed by the appearance of the missing man himself.

He was in an excessively bad humor, and grumbled audibly about the " Blackfoot rascal getting off in that cowardly fashion," without at all heeding the congratulations which I was showering upon him for his almost miraculous escape. He was evidently not aware of having been peculiarly exposed, and was regretting, like the hunter who loses his game by a sudden shift of wind, that his human prey had escaped him.

The appearance of this Indian is a proof that others are lurking near; and if the party happens to be large, they may give us some trouble. We are now in a part of the country which is almost constantly infested by the Blackfeet; we have seen for several mornings past, the tracks of moccasins around our camp, and not unfrequently the prints of unshod horses, so that we know we are narrowly watched; and the slumbering of one of the guard, or the slightest appearance of carelessness in the conduct of the camp, may bring the savages whooping upon us like demons.

Our encampment this evening is on one of the head branches of the Blackfoot river, from which we can see the three remarkable conic summits known by the name of the *"Three Butes"* or *"Tetons."* Near these flows the Portneuf, or south branch of Snake or Lewis' river. Here is to be another place of rest, and we look forward to it with pleasure both on our own account and on that of our wearied horses.

12th.—In the afternoon we made a camp on Ross's creek, a small branch of Snake river. The pasture is better than we have had for two weeks, and the stream contains an abundance of excellent trout. Some of these are enormous, and very fine eating. They bite eagerly at a grasshopper or minnow, but the largest fish are shy, and the sportsman requires to be carefully concealed in order to take them. We have here none of the fine tackle, jointed rods, reels, and silkworm gut of the accomplished city sportsman; we have only a piece of common cord, and a hook seized on with half-hitches, with a willow rod cut on the banks of the stream; but with this rough equipment we take as many trout as we wish, and who could do more, even with all the curious contrivances of old Izaac Walton or Christopher North?

The band of Indians which kept company with us from the rendezvous, left us yesterday, and fell back to join Captain Bonneville's party, which is travelling on behind. We do not regret their absence; for although they added strength to our band, and would have been useful in case of an attack from Blackfeet, yet they added very materially to our cares, and gave us some trouble by their noise, confusion, and singing at night.

On the 14th, we travelled but about six miles, when a halt was called, and we pitched our tents upon the banks of the noble Shoshone or Snake river. It seems now, as though we were really nearing the western extremity of our vast continent. We are now on a stream which pours its waters directly into the Columbia, and we can form some idea of the great Oregon river by the beauty and magnitude of its tributary. Soon after we stopped, Captain W., Richardson, and two others left us to seek for a suitable spot for building a fort, and in the evening they returned with the information that an excellent and convenient place had been pitched upon, about five miles from our present encampment.[8] On their route, they killed a buffalo, which they left at the site of the fort, suitably protected from wolves, &c. This is very pleasing intelligence to us, as our stock of dried meat is almost exhausted, and for several days past we have been depending almost exclusively upon fish.

The next morning we moved early, and soon arrived at our destined camp. This is a fine large plain on the south side of the Portneuf, with an abundance of excellent grass and rich soil. The opposite side of the river is thickly covered with large timber of the cottonwood and willow, with a dense undergrowth of the same, intermixed with service-berry and currant bushes.

Most of the men were immediately put to work, felling trees, making horse-pens, and preparing the various requisite materials for the building, while others were ordered to get themselves in readiness for a start on the back track, in order to make a hunt, and procure meat for the camp. To this party I have attached myself, and all my leisure time to-day is employed in preparing for it.

Our number will be twelve, and each man will lead a mule with a pack-saddle, in order to bring in the meat that we may kill. Richardson is the principal of this party, and Mr. Ashworth has also consented to join us, so that I hope we shall have an agreeable trip. There will be but little hard work to perform; our men are mostly of the best, and no rum or cards are allowed.

Chapter VI

Departure of the hunting camp—A false alarm—
Blackfeet Indians—their ferocity—Requisites of a
mountain man—Good fare, and good appetites—An
experiment—Grizzly bears—Visit of a Nez Percé
Indian—Adventure with a grizzly bear—Hunters'
anecdotes—Homeward bound—Accident from
gunpowder—Arrival at "Fort Hall"—A salute—
Emaciation of some of the party from low diet—Mr.
McKay's company—Buffalo lodges—Progress of the
building—Effects of judicious training—Indian
worship—A "Camp Meeting"—Mr. Jason Lee, a
favorite—A fatal accident and a burial.

July 16th—Our little hunting party of twelve men, rode out of the encampment this morning, at a brisk trot, which gait was continued until we arrived at our late encampment on Ross' creek, having gone about thirty miles. Here we came to a halt, and made a hearty meal on a buffalo which we had just killed. While we were eating, a little Welshman, whom we had stationed outside our camp to watch the horses, came running to us out of breath, crying in a terrified falsetto, "*Indians, Indians!*" In a moment every man was on his feet, and his gun in his hand; the horses were instantly surrounded, by Richardson's direction, and driven into the bushes, and we were preparing ourselves for the coming struggle, when our hunter, peering out of the thick copse to mark the approach of the enemy, burst at once into a loud laugh, and muttering something about a Welsh coward, stepped boldly from his place of concealment, and told us to follow him. When we had done so, we perceived the band approaching steadily, and it seemed warily, along the path directly in our front. Richardson said something to them in an unknown tongue, which immediately brought several of the strangers towards us at full gallop. One of these was a Canadian, as his peculiar physiognomy, scarlet sash, and hat ribbons of gaudy colors, clearly proved, and the two who accompanied him, were Indians. These people greeted us with great cordiality, the more so, perhaps, as they had supposed, on seeing the smoke from our fire, that we were a band of Blackfeet, and that, therefore, there was no alternative for them but to fight. While we were conversing, the whole party, of about thirty, came up, and it needed but a glance at the motley group of tawdrily dressed hybrid boys, and blanketted Indians, to convince us that this was McKay's company travelling on to join him at Fort Hall.

They inquired anxiously about their leader, and seemed pleased on being informed that he was so near; the prospect of a few days' rest at the fort, and the *regale* by which their arrival was sure to be commemorated, acted upon the spirits of the mercurial young half-breeds, like the potent liquor which they expected soon to quaff in company with the kindred souls who were waiting to receive them.

They all seemed hungry, and none required a second invitation to join us at our half finished meal. The huge masses of savoury fleece meat, hump-ribs, and side-ribs disappeared, and were polished with wonderful dispatch; the Canadians ate like half famished wolves, and the sombre Indians, although slower and more sedate in their movements, were very little behind their companions in the agreeable process of mastication.

The next day we rode thirty-four miles, and encamped on a pretty little stream, fringed with willows, running through the midst of a large plain. Within a few miles, we saw a small herd of buffalo, and six of our company left the camp for a hunt. In an hour two of them returned, bringing the meat of one animal. We all commenced work immediately, cutting it in thin slices, and hanging it on the bushes to dry. By sundown, our work was finished, and soon after dark, the remaining hunters came in, bringing the best parts of three more. This will give us abundance of work for to-morrow, when the hunters will go out again.

Richardson and Sansbury mention having seen several Blackfeet Indians to-day, who, on observing them, ran rapidly away, and, as usual, concealed themselves in the bushes. We are now certain that our worst enemies are around us, and that they are only waiting for a favorable time and opportunity to make an attack. They are not here for nothing, and have probably been dogging us, and reconnoitering our outposts, so that the greatest caution and watchfulness will be required to prevent a surprise. We are but a small company, and there may be at this very moment hundreds within hearing of our voices.

The Blackfoot is a sworn and determined foe to all white men, and he has often been heard to declare that he would rather hang the scalp of a "pale face" to his girdle, than kill a buffalo to prevent his starving.

The hostility of this dreaded tribe is, and has for years been, proverbial. They are, perhaps, the only Indians who do not fear the power, and who refuse to acknowledge the superiority of the white man; and though so often beaten in conflicts with them, even by their own mode of warfare, and generally with numbers vastly inferior, their indomitable courage and perseverance still urges them on to renewed attempts; and if a single scalp is taken, it is considered equal to a great victory, and is hailed as a presage of future and more extensive triumphs.

It must be acknowledged, however, that this determined hostility does not originate solely in savage malignity, or an abstract thirst for the blood of white men; it is fomented and kept alive from year to year by incessant provocatives on the part of white hunters, trappers, and traders, who are at best but intruders on the rightful domains of the red man of the wilderness. Many a night have I sat at the camp-fire, and listened to the recital of bloody and ferocious scenes, in which the narrators were the actors, and the poor Indians the victims, and I have felt my blood tingle with shame, and boil with indignation, to hear the diabolical acts applauded by those for whose amusement they were related. Many a precious villain, and merciless marauder, was made by these midnight tales of rapine, murder, and robbery; many a stripling, in whose tender mind the seeds of virtue and honesty had never germinated, burned for an opportunity of loading his packhorse with the beaver skins of some solitary Blackfoot trapper, who was to be murdered and despoiled of the property he had acquired by weeks, and perhaps months, of toil and danger.

Acts of this kind are by no means unfrequent, and the subjects of this sort of atrocity are not always the poor and despised Indians: white men themselves often fall by the hands of their companions, when by good fortune and industry they have succeeded in loading their horses with fur. The fortunate trapper is treacherously murdered by one who has eaten from the same dish and drank from the same cup, and the homicide returns triumphantly to his camp with his ill gotten property. If his companion be inquired for, the answer is that some days ago they parted company, and he will probably soon join them.

The poor man never returns —no one goes to search for him —he is soon forgotten, or is only remembered by one more steadfast than the rest, who seizes with avidity the first opportunity which is afforded, of murdering an unoffending Indian in revenge for the death of his friend.

On the 20th, we moved our camp to a spot about twelve miles distant, where Richardson, with two other hunters, stopped yesterday and spent the night. They had killed several buffalo here, and were busily engaged in preparing the meat when we joined them. They gave us a meal of excellent cow's flesh, and I thought I never had eaten anything so delicious. Hitherto we have had only the bulls which are at this season poor and rather unsavory, but now we are feasting upon the *best food in the world.*

It is true we have nothing but meat and good cold water, but this is all we desire: we have excellent appetites, no dyspepsia, clear heads, sharp ears, and high spirits, and what more does a man require to make him happy?

We rise in the morning with the sun, stir up our fires, and *roast* our breakfast, eating usually from one to two pounds of meat at a morning meal. At ten o'clock we lunch, dine at two, sup at five, and lunch at eight, and during the night-watch commonly provide ourselves with two or three " hump-ribs" and a marrow bone, to furnish employment and keep the drowsy god at a distance.

Our present camp is a beautiful one. A rich and open plain of luxuriant grass, dotted with buffalo in all directions, a high picturesque hill in front, and a lovely stream of cold mountain water flowing at our feet. On the borders of this stream, as usual, is a dense belt of willows, and under the shade of these we sit and work by day, and sleep soundly at night. Our meat is now dried upon scaffolds constructed of old timber which we find in great abundance upon the neighboring hill. We keep a fire going constantly, and when the meat is sufficiently dried, it is piled on the ground, preparatory to being baled.

21st.—The buffalo appear even more numerous than when we came, and much less suspicious than common. The bulls frequently pass slowly along within a hundred yards of us, and toss their shaggy and frightful looking heads as though to warn us against attacking or approaching them.

Towards evening, to-day, I walked out with my gun, in the direction of one of these prowling monsters, and the ground in his vicinity being covered densely with bushes, I determined to approach as near him as possible, in order to try the efficacy of a ball planted directly in the centre of the forehead. I had heard of this experiment having been tried without success and I wished to ascertain the truth for myself.

"Taking the wind" of the animal, as it is called, (that is, keeping to leeward, so that my approach could not be perceived by communicating a taint to the air,) I crawled on my hands and knees with the utmost caution towards my victim. The unwieldy brute was quietly and unsuspiciously cropping the herbage, and I had arrived to within feet of him, when a sudden flashing of the eye, and an impatient motion, told me that I was observed. He raised his enormous head, and looked around him, and so truly terrible and grand did he appear, that I must confess, (in your ear,) I felt awed, almost frightened, at the task I had undertaken. But I had gone too far to retreat; so, raising my gun, I took deliberate aim at the bushy centre of the forehead, and fired. The monster shook his head, pawed up the earth with his hoofs, and making a sudden spring, accompanied by a terrific roar, turned to make his escape. At that instant, the ball from the second barrel penetrated his vitals, and he measured his huge length upon the ground. In a few seconds he was dead. Upon examining the head, and cutting away the enormous mass of matted hair and skin which enveloped the skull, my large bullet of twenty to the pound, was found completely flattened against the bone, having carried with it, through the interposing integument, a considerable portion of the coarse hair, but without producing the smallest fracture. I was satisfied; and taking the tongue, (the hunter's perquisite,) I returned to my companions.

This evening the roaring of the bulls in the gang near us is terrific, and these sounds are mingled with the howling of large packs of wolves, which regularly attend upon them, and the hoarse screaming of hundreds of ravens flying over head. The dreaded grizzly bear is also quite common in this neighborhood; two have just been seen in some bushes near, and they visit our camp almost every night, attracted by the piles of meat which are heaped all around us. The first intimation we have of his approach is a great *grunt* or *snort,* unlike any sound I ever heard, but much more querulous than fierce; then we hear the scraping and tramping of his huge feet, and the snuffing of his nostrils, as the savory scent of the meat is wafted to them. He approaches nearer and nearer, with a stealthy and fearful pace, but just as he is about to accomplish the object of his visit, he suddenly stops short; the snuffing is repeated at long and trembling intervals, and if the slightest motion is then made by one of the party, away goes "*Ephraim,*" like a cowardly burglar as he is, and we hear no more of him that night.

On the 23d a Nez Percé Indian, belonging to Mr. McKay's company visited us. He is one of several hundred who have been sent from the fort on the same errand as ourselves. This was a middle aged man, with a countenance in which shrewdness or cunning, and complaisance, appeared singularly blended. But his person was a perfect wonder, and would have served admirably for the study of a sculptor. The form was perfection itself. The lower limbs were entirely naked, and the upper part of the person was only covered by a short checked shirt. His blanket lay by his side as he sat with us, and was used only while moving. I could not but admire the ease with which the man squatted on his haunches immediately as he alighted, and the position both of body and limbs was one that, probably, no white man unaccustomed to it, could have endured for many minutes together. The attitude, and indeed the whole figure was graceful and easy in the extreme; and on criticising his person, one was forcibly reminded of the Apollo Belvidere of Canova. His only weapons were a short bow and half a dozen arrows, a scalping knife and tomahawk; with these, however, weak and inefficient as they seemed, he had done good service, every arrow being smeared with blood to the feathers. He told Richardson that he and his three or four companions had killed about sixty buffalo, and that now, having meat enough, they intended to return to their camp to-morrow.

This afternoon I observed a large flock of wild geese passing over; and upon watching them, perceived that they alighted about a mile and a half from us, where I knew there was a lake. Concluding that a little change of diet might be agreeable, I sallied forth with my gun across the plain in quest of the birds. I soon arrived at a thick copse of willow and currant bushes, which skirted the water, and was about entering, when I heard a sort of angry growl or grunt directly before me —and instantly after, saw a grizzly bear of the largest kind erect himself upon his hind feet within a dozen yards of me, his savage eyes glaring with horrible malignity, his mouth wide open, and his tremendous paws raised as though ready to descend upon me. For a moment, I thought my hour had come, and that I was fated to die an inglorious death away from my friends and my kindred; but after waiting a moment in agonizing suspense, and the bear showing no inclination to advance, my lagging courage returned, and cocking both barrels of my gun, and presenting it as steadily as my nerves would allow, full at the shaggy breast of the creature, I retreated slowly backwards. Bruin evidently had no notion of braving gunpowder, but I did not know whether, like a dog, if the enemy retreated he would not yet give me a chase; so when I had placed about a hundred yards between us, I wheeled about and flew, rather than ran, across the plain towards the camp. Several times during this run for life, (as I considered it,) did I fancy that I heard the bear at my heels; and not daring to look over my shoulder to ascertain the fact, I only increased my speed, until the camp was nearly gained, when, from sheer exhaustion I relaxed my efforts, fell flat upon the ground, and looked behind me. The whole space between me and the copse was untenanted, and I was forced to acknowledge, with a feeling strongly allied to shame, that my fears alone had represented the bear in chase of me.

When I arrived in camp, and told my break-neck adventure to the men, our young companion, Mr. Ashworth, expressed a wish to go and kill the bear, and requested the loan of my double-barrelled gun for this purpose. This I at first peremptorily refused, and the men, several of whom were experienced hunters, joined me in urging him not to attempt the rash adventure. At length, however, finding him determined on going, and that rather than remain, he would trust to his own single gun, I was finally induced to offer him mine, with a request, (which I had hoped would check his daring spirit,) that he would leave the weapon in a situation where I could readily find it; for after he had made one shot, he would never use a gun again.

He seemed to heed our caution and advice but little, and, with a dogged and determined air, took the way across the plain to the bushes, which we could see in the distance. I watched him for some time, until I saw him enter them, and then with a sigh that one so young and talented should be lost from amongst us, and a regret that we did not forcibly prevent his going I sat myself down distressed and melancholy. We all listened anxiously to hear the report of the gun; but no sound reaching our ears, we began to hope that he had failed in finding the animal, and in about fifteen minutes, to my inexpressible relief, we saw him emerge from the copse, and bend his steps slowly towards us. When he came in, he seemed disappointed, and somewhat angry. He said he had searched the bushes in every direction, and although he had found numerous footprints, no bear was to be seen. It is probable that when I commenced my retreat in one direction, bruin made off in the other, and that although he was willing to dispute the ground with me, and prevent my passing his lair, he was equally willing to back out of an engagement in which his fears suggested that he might come off the loser.

This evening, as we sat around the camp fire, cozily wrapped in our blankets, some of our old hunters became garrulous, and we had several good "*yarns,*" as a sailor would say. One told of his having been shot by a Blackfoot Indian, who was disguised in the skin of an elk, and exhibited, with some little pride, a great cicatrix which disfigured his neck. Another gave us an interesting account of an attack made by the Comanche Indians upon a party of Santa-Fee traders, to which he had been attached. The white men, as is usual in general engagements with Indians, gained a signal victory, not, however, without the loss of several of their best hunters; and the old man who told the story, — "uncle John," as he was usually called, —shed tears at the recollection of the death of his friends; and during that part of his narrative, was several times so much affected as to be unable to speak.*

The best story, however, was one told by Richardson, of a meeting he once had with three Blackfeet Indians. He had been out alone hunting buffalo, and towards the end of the day was returning to the camp with his meat, when he heard the clattering of hoofs in the rear, and, upon looking back, observed three Indians in hot pursuit of him.

He immediately *discharged his cargo* of meat to lighten his horse, and then urged the animal to his utmost speed, in an attempt to distance his pursuers. He soon discovered, however, that the enemy was rapidly gaining upon him, and that in a few minutes more, he would be completely at their mercy, when he hit upon an expedient, as singular as it was bold and courageous. Drawing his long scalping knife from the sheath at his side, he plunged the keen weapon through his horse's neck, and severed the spine. The animal dropped instantly dead, and the determined hunter, throwing himself behind the fallen carcass, waited calmly the approach of his sanguinary pursuers. In a few moments, one Indian was within range of the fatal rifle, and at its report, his horse galloped riderless over the plain. The remaining two then thought to take him at advantage by approaching simultaneously on both sides of his rampart; but one of them, happening to venture too near in order to be sure of his aim, was shot to the heart by the long pistol of the white man, at the very instant that the ball from the Indian's gun whistled harmlessly by. The third savage, being wearied

---

*I have repeatedly observed these exhibitions of feeling in some of our people upon particular occasions, and I have been pleased with them, as they seemed to furnish an evidence, that amid all the mental sterility, and absence of moral rectitude, which is so deplorably prevalent, there yet lingers some kindliness of heart, some sentiments which are not wholly depraved.

of the dangerous game, applied the whip vigorously to the flanks of his horse, and was soon out of sight, while Richardson set about collecting the trophies of his singular victory.

He caught the two Indians' horses; mounted one, and loaded the other with the meat which he had discarded, and returned to his camp with two spare rifles, and a good stock of ammunition.

On the morning of the 25th, we commenced baling up our meat in buffalo skins dried for the purpose. Each bale contains about a hundred pounds, of which a mule carries two; and when we had finished, our twelve long-eared friends were loaded. Our limited term of absence is now nearly expired, and we are anxious to return to the fort in order to prepare for the journey to the lower country.

At about 10 o'clock, we left our pleasant encampment, and bade adieu to the cold spring, the fat buffalo, and grizzly bears, and urging our mules into their fastest walk, we jolted along with our *provant* towards the fort.

In about an hour after, an unpleasant accident happened to one of our men, named McCarey. He had been running a buffalo, and was about reloading the gun, which he had just discharged, when the powder in his horn was ignited by a burning wad remaining in the barrel; the horn was burst to fragments, the poor man dashed from his horse, and his face, neck, and hands, burnt in a shocking manner. We applied, immediately, the simple remedies which our situation and the place afforded, and in the course of an hour he was somewhat relieved, and travelled on with us, though in considerable suffering. His eyes were entirely closed, the lids very much swollen, and his long, flowing hair, patriarchal beard and eye-brows, had all vanished in smoke. It will be long ere he gets another such crop.

The weather here is generally uncomfortably warm, so much so, that we discard, while travelling, all such encumbrances as coats, neckcloths, &c., but the nights are excessively cold, ice often forming in the camp kettles, of the thickness of half an inch, or more. My custom has generally been to roll myself in my blanket at night, and use my large coat as a pillow; but here the coat must be worn, and my saddle has to serve the purpose to which the coat is usually applied.

We travelled, this day, thirty miles, and the next afternoon, at 4 o'clock, arrived at the fort. On the route we met three hunters, whom Captain W. had sent to kill game for the camp. They informed us that all hands have been for several days on short allowance, and were very anxious for our return.

When we came in sight of the fort, we gave them a mountain salute, each man firing his gun in quick succession. They did not expect us until to-morrow, and the firing aroused them instantly. In a very few minutes, a score of men were armed and mounted, and dashing out to give battle to the advancing Indians, as they thought us. The general supposition was, that their little hunting party had been attacked by a band of roving Blackfeet, and they made themselves ready for the rescue in a space of time that did them great credit.

It was perhaps "*bad medicine,*" (to use the mountain phrase,) to fire a salute at all, inasmuch as it excited some unnecessary alarm, but it had the good effect to remind them that danger might be near when they least expected it, and afforded them an opportunity of showing the promptness and alacrity with which they could meet and brave it.

Our people were all delighted to see us arrive, and I could perceive many a longing and eager gaze cast upon the well filled bales, as our mules swung their little bodies through the camp. My companion, Mr. N., had become so exceedingly thin that I should scarcely have known him; and upon my expressing surprise at the great change in his appearance, he heaved a sigh of inanity, and remarked that I "would have been as thin as he if I had lived on old *Ephraim* for two weeks, and short allowance of that." I found, in truth, that the whole camp had been subsisting, during our absence, on little else than two or three grizzly bears which had been killed in the neighborhood; and with a complacent glance at my own rotund and *cow-fed* person, I wished my *poor* friend better luck for the future.

We found Mr. McKay's company encamped on the bank of the river within a few hundred yards of our tents. It consists of thirty men, thirteen of whom are Indians, Nez Percés, Chinooks and Kayouse, with a few squaws. The remainder are French-Canadians, and half-breeds. Their lodges,—of which there are several,—are of a conical form, composed of ten long poles, the lower ends of which are pointed and driven into the ground; the upper blunt, and drawn together at the top by thongs. Around these poles, several dressed buffalo skins, sewed together, are stretched, a hole being left on one side for entrance.

These are the kind of lodges universally used by the mountain Indians while travelling: they are very comfortable and commodious, and a squaw accustomed to it, will erect and prepare one for the reception of her husband, while he is removing the trapping, from his horse. I have seen an expert Indian woman stretch a lodge in half the time that was required by four white men to perform the same operation with another in the neighborhood.

At the fort, affairs look prosperous: the stockade is finished; two bastions have been erected, and the work is singularly good, considering the scarcity of proper building tools. The house will now soon be habitable, and the structure can then be completed at leisure by men who will be left here in charge, while the party travels on to its destination, the Columbia.

On the evening of the 26th, Captain W, Mr. Nuttall and myself supped with Mr. McKay in his lodge. I am much pleased with this gentleman: he unites the free, frank and open manners of the mountain man, with the grace and affability of the Frenchman. But above all, I admire the order, decorum, and strict subordination which exists among his men, so different from what I have been accustomed to see in parties composed of Americans. Mr. McKay assures me that he had considerable difficulty in bringing his men to the state in which they now are. The free and fearless Indian was particularly difficult to subdue; but steady, determined perseverance, and bold measures, aided by a rigid self-example, made them as clay in his hand, and has finally reduced them to their present admirable condition. If they misbehaved, a commensurate punishment is sure to follow: in extreme cases, flagellation is resorted to, but it is inflicted only by the hand of the Captain; were any other appointed to perform this office *on an Indian,* the indignity would be deemed so great, that nothing less than the blood of the individual could appease the wounded feelings of the savage.

After supper was concluded, we sat ourselves down on a buffalo robe at the entrance of the lodge, to see the Indians at their devotions. The whole thirteen were soon collected at the call of one whom they had chosen for their chief, and seated with sober, sedate countenances around a large fire. After remaining in perfect silence for perhaps fifteen minutes, the chief commenced an harangue in a solemn and impressive tone, reminding them of the object for which they were thus assembled, that of worshipping the "Great Spirit who made the light and the darkness, the fire and the water," and assured them that if they offered up their prayers to him with but "one tongue," they would certainly be accepted. He then rose from his squatting position to his knees, and his example was followed by all the others. In this situation he commenced a prayer, consisting of short sentences uttered rapidly but with great apparent fervor, his hands clasped upon his breast, and his eyes cast upwards with a beseeching look towards heaven. At the conclusion of each sentence, a choral response of a few words was made, accompanied frequently by low moaning. The prayer lasted about twenty minutes. After its conclusion, the chief, still maintaining the same position of his body and hands, but with his head bent to his breast, commenced a kind of psalm or sacred song in which the whole company presently joined. The song was a simple expression of a few sounds, no intelligible words being uttered. It resembled the words, *Ho-hă-ho-hă-ho-hă-hā-ā,* commencing in a low tone, and gradually swelling to a full, round, and beautifully modulated chorus. During the song, the clasped hands of the worshippers were moved rapidly across the breast, and their bodies swung with great energy to the time of the music. The chief ended the song that he had commenced, by a kind of swelling groan, which was echoed in chorus. It was then taken up by another, and the same routine was gone through. The whole ceremony occupied perhaps one and a half hours; a short silence then succeeded, after which each Indian rose from the ground, and disappeared in the darkness with a step noiseless as that of a spectre.

I think I never was more gratified by any exhibition in my life. The humble, subdued, and beseeching looks of the poor untutored beings who were calling upon their heavenly father to forgive their sins, and continue his mercies to them, and the evident and heart-felt sincerity which characterized the whole scene, was truly affecting, and very impressive.

The next day being the Sabbath, our good missionary, Mr. Jason Lee, was requested to hold a meeting, with which he obligingly complied. A convenient, shady spot was selected in the forest adjacent, and the greater part of our men, as well as the whole of Mr. McKay's company, including the Indians, attended. The usual forms of the Methodist service, (to which Mr. L. is attached,) were gone through, and were followed by a brief, but excellent and appropriate exhortation by that gentleman, The people were remarkably quiet and attentive, and the Indians sat upon the ground like statues. Although not one of them could understand a word that was said, they nevertheless maintained the most strict and decorous silence, kneeling when the preacher kneeled, and rising when he rose, evidently with a view of paying him and us a suitable respect, however much their own notions as to the proper and most acceptable forms of worship, might have been opposed to ours.

A meeting for worship in the Rocky mountains is almost as unusual as the appearance of a herd of buffalo in the settlements. A sermon was perhaps never preached here before; but for myself, I really enjoyed the whole scene; it possessed the charm of novelty, to say nothing of the salutary effect which I sincerely hope it may produce.

Mr. Lee is a great favorite with the men, deservedly so, and there are probably few persons to whose preaching they would have listened with so much complaisance. I have often been amused and pleased by Mr. L.'s manner of reproving them for the coarseness and profanity of expression which is so universal amongst them. The reproof, although decided, clear, and strong, is always characterized by the mildness and affectionate manner peculiar to the man; and although the good effect of the advice may not be discernible, yet it is always treated with respect, and its utility acknowledged.

In the evening, a fatal accident happened to a Canadian belonging to Mr. McKay's party. He was running his horse, in company with another, when the animals were met in full career by a third rider, and horses and men were thrown with great force to the ground. The Canadian was taken up completely senseless, and brought to Mr. McKay's lodge, where we were all taking supper. I perceived at once that there was little chance of his life being saved. He had received an injury of the head which had evidently caused concussion of the brain. He was bled copiously, and various local remedies were applied, but without success; the poor man died early next morning.

He was about forty years of age, healthy, active, and shrewd, and very much valued by Mr. McKay as a leader in his absence, and as an interpreter among the Indians of the Columbia.

At noon the body was interred. It was wrapped in a piece of coarse linen, over which was sewed a buffalo robe. The spot selected, was about a hundred yards south of the fort, and the funeral was attended by the greater part of the men of both camps. Mr. Lee officiated in performing the ordinary church ceremony, after which a hymn for the repose of the soul of the departed, was sung by the Canadians present. The grave is surrounded by a neat palisade of willows, with a black cross erected at the head, on which is carved the name "*Casseau.*"[1]

Chapter VII

Departure of Mr. McKay's party, Captain Stewart, and
the missionaries—Debauch at the fort—Departure of the
company—Poor provision—Blackfeet hunting ground—
A toilsome journey and sufferings from thirst—Goddin's
creek—Antoine Goddin, the trapper—Scarcity of
game—A buffalo—Rugged mountains—Comforting
reflections of the traveller—More game—Unusual
economy—Habits of the white wolf—"Thornburg's
pass"—Difficult travelling—The captain in jeopardy
among the snow—A countermarch—Deserted Banneck
camp—Toilsome and dangerous passage of the
mountain—Mallade river—Beaver dams, and beaver—
A party of Snake Indians—Scarcity of pasture—Another
Banneck camp—"Kamas prairie"—Indian mode of
preparing the kamas—Racine blanc, or biscuit root—
Travelling over the hills—Loss of horses by fatigue—
Boisée or Big-wood river—Salmon—Choke-cherries, &c.

O n the 30th of July, Mr. McKay and his party left us for Fort
Vancouver, Captain Stewart and our band of missionaries
accompanying them. The object of the latter in leaving us,
is, that they may have an opportunity of travelling more slowly than
we should do, on account, and for the benefit of the horned cattle
which they are driving to the lower country. We feel quite sad in the
prospect of parting from those with whom we have endured some toil
and danger, and who have been to some of us as brothers, throughout
our tedious journey; but, if no unforeseen accident occurs, we hope
to meet them all again at Walla-Walla, the upper fort on the Columbia.
As the party rode off, we fired three rounds, which were promptly
answered, and three times three cheers wished the travellers success.

August 5th.—At sunrise this morning, the "star-spangled banner" was
raised on the flag-staff at the fort, and a salute fired by the men, who,
according to orders, assembled around it. All in camp were then allowed
the free and uncontrolled use of liquor, and, as usual, the consequence

was a scene of rioting, noise, and fighting, during the whole day; some became so drunk that their senses fled them entirely, and they were therefore harmless; but by far the greater number were just sufficiently under the influence of the vile trash, to render them in their conduct disgusting and tiger-like. We had "gouging," biting, fisticuffing, and "stamping" in the most "scientific" perfection; some even fired guns and pistols at each other, but these weapons were mostly harmless in the unsteady hands which employed them. Such scenes I hope never to witness again; they are absolutely sickening, and cause us to look upon our species with abhorrence and loathing. Night at last came, and cast her mantle over our besotted camp; the revel was over, and the men retired to their pallets peaceably, but not a few of them will bear palpable evidence of the debauch of the 5th of August.

The next morning we commenced packing, and at 11 o'clock bade adieu to "Fort Hall." Our company now consists of but thirty men, several Indian women, and one hundred and sixteen horses. We crossed the main Snake or Shoshoné river, at a point about three miles from the fort. It is here as wide as the Missouri at Independence, but, beyond comparison, clearer and more beautiful.

Immediately on crossing the river, we entered upon a wide, sandy plain, thickly covered with wormwood, and early in the afternoon, encamped at the head of a delightful spring, about ten miles from our starting place.

On the route, our hunters killed a young grizzly bear, which, with a few grouse, made us an excellent dinner. Fresh meat is now very grateful to our palates, as we have been living for weeks past on nothing but poor, dried buffalo, the better, and far the larger part, having been deposited in the fort for the subsistence of the men who remain. We have no flour, nor vegetables of any kind, and our meat may be aptly compared to dry chips, breaking short off in our fingers; and when boiled to soften it a little, and render it fit for mastication, not a star appears in the pot. It seems astonishing that life can be sustained upon such miserable fare, and yet our men (except when under the influence of liquor) have never murmured, but have always eaten their crusty meal, and drunk their cold water with light and excellent spirits. We hope soon to fall in with the buffalo, and we shall then endeavor to prepare some good provision to serve until we reach the salmon region.

We shall now, for about ten days, be travelling through the most dangerous country west of the mountains, the regular hunting ground of the Blackfeet Indians, who are said to be often seen here in parties of hundreds, or even thousands, scouring the plains in pursuit of the buffalo. Traders, therefore, seldom travel this route without meeting them, and being compelled to prove their valor upon them; the white men are, however, generally the victors, although their numbers are always vastly inferior.

7th.—We were moving this morning with the dawn, and travelled steadily the whole day, over one of the most arid plains we have seen, covered thickly with jagged masses of lava, and twisted wormwood bushes. Both horses and men were jaded to the last degree; the former from the rough, and at times almost impassable nature of the track, and the latter from excessive heat and parching thirst. We saw not a drop of water during the day, and our only food was the dried meat before spoken of, which we carried and chewed like biscuits as we travelled. There are two reasons by which the extreme thirst which the way-farer suffers in these regions, may be accounted for; first, the intense heat of the sun upon the open and exposed plains; and secondly, the desiccation to which every thing here is subject. The air feels like the breath of a sirocco, the tongue becomes parched and horny, and the mouth, nose, and eyes are incessantly assailed by the fine pulverized lava, which rises from the ground with the least breath of air. Bullets, pebbles of chalcedony, and pieces of smooth obsidian, were in great requisition to-day; almost every man was mumbling some of these substances, in an endeavor to assuage his burning thirst. The camp trailed along in a lagging and desponding line over the plain for a mile or more, the poor horses' heads hanging low, their tongues protruding to their utmost extent, and their riders scarcely less drooping and spiritless. We were a sad and most forlorn looking company, certainly; not a man of us had any thing to say, and none cared to be interrupted in his blissful dream of cool rivers and streams. Occasionally we would pass a ravine or gorge in the hills, by which one side of the plain was bounded, and up this some of the men would steer, leaping over blocks of lava, and breaking a path through the dense bushes; but the poor searcher soon returned, disheartened and wo-begone, and those who had waited anxiously to hear his cheering call, announcing success, passed onward without a word. One of our men, a mulatto, after failing in a forage of this sort, cast himself resolutely from his horse to the ground, and declared that he would lie there till he died; "there was no water in the cursed country and he might as well die here as go farther." Some of us tried to infuse a little courage into him, but it proved of no avail, and each was too much occupied with his own particular grief to use his tongue much in persuasion; so we left him to his fate.

Soon after night-fall, some signs of water were seen in a small valley to our left, and, upon ascending it, the foremost of the party found a delightful little cold spring; but they soon exhausted it, and then commenced, with axes and knives, to dig it out and enlarge it. By the time that Mr. N., and myself arrived, they had excavated a large space which was filled to overflowing with muddy water. We did not wait for it to settle, however, but throwing ourselves flat upon the ground, drank until we were ready to burst. The tales which I had read of suffering travellers in the Arabian deserts, then recurred with some force to my recollection, and I thought I could,—though in a very small measure,—appreciate their sufferings by deprivation, and their unmingled delight and satisfaction in the opportunity of assuaging them.

Poor Jim, the mulatto man, was found by one of the people, who went back in search of him, lying where he had first fallen, and either in a real or pretended swoon, still obstinate about dying, and scarcely heeding the assurances of the other that water was within a mile of him. He was, however, at length dragged and carried into camp, and soused head foremost into the mud puddle, where he guzzled and guzzled until his eyes seemed ready to burst from his head, and he was lifted out and laid dripping and flaccid upon the ground.

The next morning we made an early start towards a range of willows which we could distinctly see, at the distance of fifteen or twenty miles, and which we knew indicated Goddin's creek, so called from a Canadian of that name who was killed in this vicinity by the Blackfeet. Goddin's son, a half-breed, is now with us as a trapper; he is a fine sturdy fellow, and of such strength of limb and wind, that he is said to be able to run down a buffalo on foot, and kill him with arrows.

Goddin's creek was at length gained, and after travelling a few miles along its bank we encamped in some excellent pasture. Our poor horses seemed inclined to make up for lost time here, as yesterday their only food was the straggling blades of a little dry and parched grass growing among the wormwood on the hills.

We have been considerably disappointed in not seeing any buffalo to-day, and their absence here has occasioned some fear that we may not meet with them on our route. Should this be the case, we shall have to depend upon such small game, hares, grouse, &c., as may happen to lie in our path. In a short time, however, even this resource will fail; and if we do not happen to see Indians on the upper waters of the Columbia, from whom we can purchase dried salmon, we shall be under the necessity of killing our horses for food.

We perhaps derive one advantage, however, from the absence of game here, —that of there being less probability of lurking Blackfeet in the vicinity; but this circumstance, convenient as it is, does not compensate for empty stomachs, and I believe the men would rather fight for the privilege of obtaining food, than live without it.

The next morning we left Goddin's creek, and travelled for ten miles over a plain, covered as usual with wormwood bushes and lava. Early in the day, the welcome cry of "a buffalo! a buffalo!" was heard from the head of the company, and was echoed joyfully along the whole line. At the moment, a fine large bull was seen to bound from the bushes in our front, and tear off with all his speed over the plain. Several hunters gave him chase immediately, and in a few minutes we heard the guns that proclaimed his death. The killing of this animal is a most fortunate circumstance for us: his meat will probably sustain us for three or four days, and by that time we are sanguine of procuring other provision. The appearance of this buffalo is not considered indicative of the vicinity of others: he is probably a straggler from a travelling band, and has been unable to proceed with it, in consequence of sickness or wounds.

On leaving the plain this morning, we struck into a defile between some of the highest mountains we have yet seen. In a short time we commenced ascending, and continued passing over them, until late in the afternoon, when we reached a plain about a mile in width, covered with excellent grass, and a delightful cool stream flowing through the middle of it. Here we encamped, having travelled twenty-seven miles.

Our journey, to-day, has been particularly laborious. We were engaged for several hours, constantly in ascending and descending enormous rocky hills, with scarcely the sign of a valley between them; and some of them so steep, that our horses were frequently in great danger of falling, by making a mis-step on the loose, rolling stones. I thought the Black Hills, on the Platte, rugged and difficult of passage, but they sink into insignificance when compared with these.

We observed, on these mountains, large masses of greenstone, and beautiful pebbles of chalcedony and fine agate; the summits of the highest are covered with snow. In the mountain passes, we found an abundance of large, yellow currants, rather acid, but exceedingly palatable to men who have been long living on animal food exclusively. We all ate heartily of them; indeed, some of our people became so much attached to the bushes, that we had considerable difficulty to induce them to travel again.

10th.—We commenced our march at seven this morning, proceeding up a narrow valley, bordering our encampment in a north-easterly direction. The ravine soon widened, until it became a broad, level plain, covered by the eternal "sage" bushes, but was much less stony than usual. About mid-day, we left the plain, and shaped our course over a spur of one of the large mountains; then taking a ravine, in about an hour we came to the level land, and struck Goddin's creek again, late in the afternoon.

Our provision was all exhausted at breakfast, this morning, (most of our bull meat having been given to a band of ten trappers, who left us yesterday,) we had seen no game on our route, and we were therefore preparing ourselves to retire supperless to our pallets, when Richardson and Sansbury were descried approaching the camp and, to our great comfort, we observed that they had meat on their saddles. When they arrived, however, we were somewhat disappointed to find that they had only killed a calf, but they had brought the entire little animal with them, the time for picking and choosing of choice pieces having passed with us; and after making a hearty meal, we wrapped ourselves in our blankets and slept soundly. Although but a scant breakfast was left for us in the morning, and we knew not if any dinner would fall in our way, yet "none of these things moved us;" we lived altogether upon the present, and heeded not the future. We had always been provided for; often, when we had despaired of procuring sustenance, and when the pangs of hunger had soured our temper, and made us quarrelsome, when we thought there was no prospect before us but to sacrifice our valuable horses, or die of starvation, have the means been provided for our relief. A buffalo, an elk, or an antelope, has appeared like the goat provided for the faithful Abraham, to save a more valuable life, and I hope that some of us have been willing, reverently to acknowledge from whom these benefits and blessings have been received.

On the day following, Richardson killed two buffalo, and brought his horse heavily laden with meat to the camp. Our good hunter walked himself, that the animal might be able to bear the greater burthen. After depositing the meat in the camp, he took a fresh horse, and accompanied by three men, returned to the spot where the game had been killed, (about four miles distant,) and in the evening, brought in every pound of it, leaving only the heavier bones. The wolves will be disappointed this evening; they are accustomed to dainty picking when they glean after the hunters, but we have now abandoned the "wasty ways" which so disgraced us when game was abundant; the despised leg bone, which was wont to be thrown aside with such contempt, is now polished of every tendon of its covering, and the savory hump is used as a kind of *dessert* after a meal of coarser meat.

Speaking of wolves, I have often been surprised at the perseverance and tenacity with which these animals will sometimes follow the hunter for a whole day, to feed upon the carcass he may leave behind him. When an animal is killed, they seem to mark the operation, and stand still at a most respectful distance, with drooping tail and ears, as though perfectly indifferent to the matter in progress. Thus will they stand until the game is butchered, the meat placed upon the saddle, and the hunter is mounted and on his way; then, if he glances behind him, he will see the wily forager stealthily crawling and prowling along towards the smoking remains, and pouncing upon it, and tearing it with tooth and nail, immediately as he gets out of reach.

During the day, the wolves are shy, and rarely permit an approach to within gun-shot; but at night, (where game is abundant,) they are so fearless as to come quite within the purlieus of the camp, and there sit, a dozen together, and howl hideously for hours. This kind of serenading, it may be supposed, is not the most agreeable; and many a time when on guard, have I observed the unquiet tossing of the bundles of blankets near me, and heard issue from them, the low, husky voice of some disturbed sleeper, denouncing heavy anathemas on the unseasonable music.

12th.—We shaped our course, this morning, towards what appeared to us a gap in a high and rugged mountain, about twenty miles ahead. After proceeding eight or ten miles, the character of the country underwent a remarkable and sudden change. Instead of the luxuriant sage bushes, by which the whole plains have hitherto been covered, and the compact and dense growth of willows which has uniformly fringed every stream and rivulet, the ground was completely denuded; not a single shrub was to be seen, nor the smallest appearance of vegetation, except in small patches near the water. The mountains, also, which had generally been rocky, and covered with low, tangled bushes, here abound in beautiful and shapely pine trees. Some of the higher peaks are, however, completely bare, and capped with enormous masses of snow.

After we had travelled about twelve miles, we entered a defile between the mountains, about five hundred yards wide, covered, like the surrounding country, with pines; and, as we proceeded, the timber grew so closely, added to a thick undergrowth of bushes, that it appeared almost impossible to proceed with our horses. The farther we advanced, the more our difficulties seemed to increase; obstacles of various kinds impeded our progress; —fallen trees, their branches tangled and matted together, large rocks and deep ravines, holes in the ground, into which our animals would be precipitated without the possibility of avoiding them, and an hundred other difficulties which beggar description.

We travelled for six miles through such a region as I have attempted to describe, and at 2 o'clock encamped in a clear spot of ground, where we found excellent grass, and a cold, rapid stream. Soon after we stopped, Captain W. and Richardson left us, to look for a pass through the mountains, or for a spot where it would be possible to cross them. Strange as it may appear, yet in this desolate and almost impassable region we have observed, to-day, the tracks of a buffalo which must have passed here last night, or this morning; at least so our hunters say, and they are rarely deceived in such matters.

Captain W. and Richardson returned early next morning, with the mortifying intelligence that no practicable pass through the mountain could be found. They ascended to the very summit of one of the highest peaks, above the snow and the reach of vegetation, and the only prospect which they had beyond, was a confused mass of huge angular rocks, over which even a wild goat could. scarcely have made his way. Although they utterly failed in the object of their exploration, yet they were so fortunate as to kill a buffalo, (*the* buffalo,) the meat of which they brought on their horses.

Wyeth told us of a narrow escape he had while travelling on foot near the summit of one of the peaks. He was walking on a ridge which sloped from the top at an angle of about forty degrees, and terminated, at its lower part, in a perpendicular precipice of a thousand or twelve hundred feet. He was moving along in the snow cautiously, near the lower edge, in order to attain a more level spot beyond, when his feet slipped and he fell. Before he could attempt to fix himself firmly, he slid down the declivity till within a few feet of the frightful precipice.

At the instant of his fall, he had the presence of mind to plant the rifle which he held in one hand, and his knife which he drew from the scabbard with the other, into the snow, and as he almost tottered on the verge, he succeeded in checking himself, and holding his body perfectly still. He then gradually moved, first the rifle and then the knife, backward up the slanting hill behind him, and fixing them firmly, drew up his body parallel to them. In this way he moved slowly and surely until he had gained his former station, when, without further difficulty, he succeeded in reaching the more level land.

After a good breakfast, we packed our horses, and struck back on our trail of yesterday, in order to try another valley which we observed bearing parallel with this, at about three miles distant, and which we conclude must of course furnish a path through the mountain. Although our difficulties in returning by the same wretched route were very considerable, yet they were somewhat diminished by the road having been partially broken, and we were enabled also to avoid many of the sloughs and pitfalls which had before so much incommoded us. We have named this rugged valley, "Thornburg's *pass,*" after one of our men of this name, (a tailor,) whom we have to thank for leading us into all these troubles. Thornburg crossed this mountain two years ago, and might therefore be expected to know something of the route, and as he was the only man in the company who had been here, Captain W. acted by his advice, in opposition to his own judgment, which had suggested the other valley as affording a more probable chance of success. As we are probably the only white men who have ever penetrated into this most vile and abominable region, we conclude that the name we have given it must stand, from priority.

In the bushes, along the stream in this valley, the blacktailed deer (*Cervus macrourus*) is abundant.[1] The beautiful creatures frequently bounded from their cover within a few yards of us, and trotted on before us like domestic animals; "they are so unacquainted with man" and his cruel arts, that they seem not to fear him.

We at length arrived on the open plain again, and in our route towards the other valley, we came to a large, recent Indian encampment, probably of Bannecks,* who are travelling down to the fisheries on Snake river. We here took their trail which led up the valley to which

---

*We afterwards learned, that only three days before our arrival, a hard contested, and most sanguinary battle, had been fought on this spot, between the Bannecks and Blackfeet, in which the former gained a signal and most

we had been steering. The entrance was very similar in appearance to that of Thornburg's pass, and it is therefore not very surprising that our guide should have been deceived. We travelled rapidly along the level land at the base of the mountain, for about three miles; we then began to ascend, and our progress was necessarily slow and tedious. The commencement of the Alpine path was, however, far better than we had expected, and we entertained the hope that the passage could be made without difficulty or much toil, but the farther we progressed, the more laborious the travelling became. Sometimes we mounted steep banks of intermingled flinty rock, and friable slate, where our horses could scarcely obtain a footing, frequently sliding down several feet on the loose, broken stones: —again we passed along the extreme verge of tremendous precipices at a giddy height, whereat almost every step the stones and earth would roll from under our horses' feet, and we could hear them strike with a dull, leaden sound on the craggy rocks below. The whole journey, to-day, from the time we arrived at the heights, until we had crossed the mountain, has been a most fearful one. For myself, I might have diminished the danger very considerably, by adopting the plan pursued by the rest of the company, that of walking, and leading my horse over the most dangerous places, but I have been suffering for several days with a lame foot, and am wholly incapable of such exertion. I soon discovered that an attempt to guide my horse over the most rugged and steepest ranges was worse than useless, so I dropped the rein upon the animal's neck, and allowed him to take his own course, closing my eyes, and keeping as quiet as possible in the saddle. But I could not forbear starting occasionally, when the feet of my horse would slip on a stone, and one side of him would slide rapidly towards the edge of the precipice, but I always recovered myself by a desperate effort, and it was fortunate for me that I did so.

---

complete victory, killing upwards of forty of their adversaries, and taking about three dozen scalps. The Blackfeet, although much the larger party, were on foot, but the Bannecks, being all well mounted, had a very decided advantage; and the contest occurring on an open plain, where there was no chance of cover, the Blackfeet were run down with horses, and, without being able to load their guns, were trampled to death, or killed with salmon spears and axes. This was not the first time that we narrowly escaped a contest with this savage and most dreaded tribe. If we had passed there but a few days earlier, there is every probability to suppose that we should have been attacked, as our party at that time consisted of but twenty-six men.

Late in the afternoon, we completed the passage across the mountain, and with thankful hearts, again trod the level land. We entered here a fine rich valley or plain, of about half a mile in width, between two ranges of the mountain. It was profusely covered with willow, and through the middle of it, ran a rapid and turbulent mountain torrent, called Mallade river. It contains a great abundance of beaver, their recent dams being seen in great numbers, and in the night, when all was quiet, we could hear the playful animals at their gambols, diving from the shore into the water, and striking the surface with their broad tails. The sound, altogether, was not unlike that of children at play, and the animated description of a somewhat similar scene, in the "Mohicans," recurred to my recollection, where the single-minded Gamut is contemplating with feelings of strong reprobation, the wayward freaks of what he supposes to be a bevy of young savages.

14th—We travelled down the Mallade river, and followed the Indian trail through the valley. The path frequently passed along near the base of the mountain, and then wound its way a considerable distance up it, to avoid rocky impediments and thick tangled bushes below, so that we had some climbing to do; but the difficulties and perils of the route of yesterday are still so fresh in our memory, that all minor things are disregarded, at least by *us.* Our poor horses, however, no doubt feel differently, as they are very tired and foot sore.

The next day we came to a close and almost impenetrable thicket of tangled willows, through which we had great difficulty in urging our horses. The breadth of the thicket was about one hundred yards, and a full hour was consumed in passing through it. We then entered immediately a rich and beautiful valley, covered profusely with a splendid blue Lupin. The mountains on either side are of much less height than those we have passed, and entirely bare, the pine trees which generally cover and ornament them, having disappeared. During the morning, we ascended and descended several high and stony hills, and early in the afternoon, emerged upon a large, level prairie, and struck a branch of Mallade river, where we encamped.

While we were unloading, we observed a number of Indians ahead, and not being aware of their character, stood with our horses saddled, while Captain W. and Richardson rode out to reconnoitre. In about half an hour they returned, and informed us that they were Snakes who were returning from the fisheries, and travelling towards the buffalo on the " big river," (Shoshoné.)[2] We therefore unsaddled our poor jaded horses and turned them out to feed upon the luxuriant pasture around the camp, while we, almost equally jaded, threw ourselves down in our blankets to seek a little repose and quiet after the toils and fatigues of a long day's march.

Soon after we encamped, the Snake chief and two of his young men visited us. We formed a circle around our lodge and smoked the pipe of peace with them, after which we made them each a present of a yard of scarlet cloth for leggings, some balls and powder, a knife, and a looking glass. Captain W. then asked them a number of questions, through an interpreter, relative to the route, the fishery, &c. &c.,— and finally bought of them a small quantity of dried salmon, and a little fermented kamas or *quamash* root.[3] The Indians remained with us until dark, and then left us quietly for their own camp. There are two lodges of them, in all about twenty persons, but none of them presumed to come near us, with the exception of the three men, two squaws, and a few children. The chief is a man about fifty years of age, tall, and dignified looking, with large, strong aqualine features. His manners were cordial and agreeable, perhaps remarkably so, and he exhibited very little of that stoical indifference to surrounding objects which is so characteristic of an Indian. His dress consisted of plain leggings of deer skin, fringed at the sides, unembroidered moccasins, and a *marro* or waist-covering of antelope skin dressed without removing the hair. The upper part of his person was simply covered with a small blanket, and his ears were profusely ornamented with brass rings and beads. The men and squaws who accompanied him, were entirely naked, except that the latter had marro's of deer skin covering the loins.

The next morning we steered west across the wide prairie, crossing within every mile or two, a branch of the tortuous Mallade, near each of which good pasture was seen; but on the main prairie scarcely a blade of grass could be found, it having lately been fired by the Indians to improve the crops of next year. We have seen to-day some lava and basalt again on the sides of the hills, and on the mounds in the plain, but the level land was entirely free from it.

At noon on the 17th, we passed a deserted Indian camp, probably of the same people whose trail we have been following. There were many evident signs of the Indians having but recently left it, among which was that of several white wolves lurking around in the hope of finding remnants of meat, but, as a Scotchman would say, "I doubt they were mistaken," for meat is scarce here, and the frugal Indians rarely leave enough behind them to excite even the famished stomach of the lank and hungry wolf. The encampment here has been but a temporary one occupying a little valley densely overgrown with willows, the tops of which have been bent over, and tied so as to form a sort of lodge; over these, they have probably stretched deer skins or blankets, to exclude the rays of the sun. Of these lodges there are about forty in the valley, so that the party must have been a large one.

In the afternoon we arrived at *"Kamas prairie,"* so called from a vast abundance of this esculent root which it produces, (the *Kamassa esculenta* of Nuttall.) The plain is a beautiful level one of about a mile over, hemmed in by low, rocky hills, and in spring, the pretty blue flowers of the Kamas are said to give it a peculiar, and very pleasing appearance. At this season, the flowers do not appear, the vegetable being indicated only by little dry stems which protrude all over the ground among the grass.

We encamped here, near a small branch of Mallade river; and soon after, all hands took their kettles and scattered over the prairie to dig a mess of kamas. We were, of course, eminently successful, and were furnished thereby with an excellent and wholesome meal. When boiled, this little root is palatable, and somewhat resembles the taste of the common potato; the Indian mode of preparing it, is, however, the best —that of fermenting it in pits under ground, into which hot stones have been placed. It is suffered to remain in these pits for several days; and when removed, is of a dark brown color, about the consistence of softened glue, and sweet, like molasses. It is then often made into large cakes, by being mashed, and pressed together, and slightly baked in the sun. There are several other kinds of bulbous and tuberous roots, growing in these plains, which are eaten by the Indians, after undergoing a certain process of fermentation or baking. Among these, that which is most esteemed, is the white or biscuit root, the *Racine blanc* of the Canadians,— (*Eulophus ambiguus,* of Nuttall.) This is dried, pulverized with stones, and after being moistened with water, is made into cakes and baked in the sun. The taste is not unlike that of a stale biscuit, and to a hungry man, or one who has long subsisted without vegetables of any kind, is rather palatable.[4]

On the morning of the 18th, we commenced ascending the hills again, and had a laborious and toilsome day's march. One of our poor wearied horses gave up, and stopped; kicking, and cuffing, and beating had no effect to make him move; the poor animal laid himself down with his load, and after this was detached and shifted to the back of another, we left him where he fell, to recruit, and fall into the hands of the Indians, or die among the arid hills. This is the first horse we have lost in this manner; but we have great fears that many others will soon fail, as their riders and drivers are compelled to use the whip constantly, to make them walk at the slowest gait. We comfort ourselves, however, by supposing that we have now nearly passed the most rugged country on the route, and hope, before many days, to reach the valley of the Shoshoné, where the country will be level, and the pasture good. We are anxious, also, to fall in with the Snake Indians, in order to get a supply of salmon, as we have been living for several days on a short allowance of wretched, dry meat, and this poor pittance is now almost exhausted.

19th.—This morning was cold, the thermometer stood at 28° and a thick skim of ice was in the camp kettles at sunrise. Another hard day's travel over the hills, during which we lost two of our largest and stoutest horses. Towards evening, we descended to a fine large plain, and struck *Boisée,* or Big Wood river, on the borders of which we encamped. This is a beautiful stream, about one hundred yards in width, clear as crystal, and, in some parts, probably twenty feet deep. It is literally *crowded* with salmon, which are springing from the water almost constantly. Our mouths are watering most abundantly for some of them, but we are not provided with suitable implements for taking any, and must therefore depend for a supply on the Indians, whom we hope soon to meet.

We found, in the mountain passes, to-day, a considerable quantity of a small fruit called the choke-cherry, a species of prunus, growing on low bushes. When ripe, they are tolerable eating, somewhat astringent, however, producing upon the mouth the same effect, though in a less degree, as the unripe persimmon. They are now generally green, or we should feast luxuriantly upon them, and render more tolerable our miserable provision. We have seen, also, large patches of service bushes, but no fruit. It seems to have failed this year, although ordinarily so abundant that it constitutes a large portion of the vegetable food of both Indians and white trappers who visit these regions.

Chapter VIII

A substitute for game, and a luxurious breakfast—
Expectations of a repast, and a disappointment—Visit of
a Snake chief—his abhorrence of horse meat—A band of
Snake Indians—their chief—Trade with Indians for
salmon—Mr. Ashworth's adventure—An Indian horse-
thief—Visit to the Snake camp—its filthiness—A
Banneck camp—Supercilious conduct of the Indians—
Arrival at Snake river—Equipment of a trapping
party—Indian mode of catching salmon—Loss of a
favorite horse—Powder river—Cut rocks—Recovery of
the lost trail—Grand Ronde—Captain Bonneville—his
fondness for a roving life—Kayouse and Nez Percé
Indians—their appearance—An Indian beauty—Blue
mountains—A feline visit.

August 20th.—At about daylight this morning, having charge of the last guard of the night, I observed a beautiful, sleek little *colt*, of about four months old, trot into the camp, winnying with great apparent pleasure, and dancing and curvetting gaily amongst our sober and sedate band. I had no doubt that he had strayed from Indians, who were probably in the neighborhood; but as here, every animal that comes near us is fair game, and as we were hungry, not having eaten any thing of consequence since yesterday morning, I thought the little stranger would make a good breakfast for us. Concluding, however, that it would be best to act advisedly in the matter, I put my head into Captain W.'s tent, and telling him the news, made the proposition which had occurred to me. The captain's reply was encouraging enough,—"Down with him, if you please, Mr. T., it is the Lord's doing; let us have him for breakfast." In five minutes afterwards, a bullet sealed the fate of the unfortunate visitor, and my men were set to work making fires, and rummaging out the long-neglected stew-pans, while I engaged myself in flaying the little animal, and cutting up his body in readiness for the pots.

When the camp was aroused, about an hour after, the savory steam of the cookery was rising and saluting the nostrils of our hungry people with its fragrance, who, rubbing their hands with delight, sat themselves down upon the ground, waiting with what patience they might, for the unexpected repast which was preparing for them.

It was to me almost equal to a good breakfast, to witness the pleasure and satisfaction which I had been the means of diffusing through the camp.

The repast was ready at length, and we did full justice to it; every man ate until he was filled, and all pronounced it one of the most delicious meals they had ever assisted in demolishing. When our breakfast was concluded, but little of the colt remained; that little was, however, carefully packed up, and deposited on one of the horses, to furnish, at least, a portion of another meal.

The route, this morning, lay along Boisée. For an hour, the travelling was toilsome and difficult, the Indian trail, leading along the high bank of the river, steep and rocky, making our progress very slow and laborious. We then came to a wide plain, interrupted only by occasional high banks of earth, some of them of considerable extent, across which ran the path. Towards mid-day, we lost sight of these banks, the whole country appearing level, with the exception of some distant hills in the south-west, which we suppose indicate the vicinity of some part of Snake river.

We have all been disappointed in the distance to this river, and the length of time required to reach it. Not a man in our camp has ever travelled this route before, and all we have known about it has been the general course.

In the afternoon, we observed a number of Indians on the opposite side of the river, engaged in fishing for salmon. Captain W. and two men immediately crossed over to them, carrying with them a few small articles to exchange for fish. We congratulated ourselves upon our good fortune in seeing these Indians, and were anticipating a plentiful meal, when Captain W. and his companions returned, bringing only *three* small salmon. The Indians had been unsuccessful in fishing, not having caught enough for themselves, and even the offer of exorbitant sums was not sufficient to induce them to part with more.

In the afternoon, a grouse and a beaver were killed, which, added to the remains of the colt, and our three little salmon, made us a tolerable supper. While we were eating, we were visited by a Snake chief, a large and powerful man, of a peculiarly dignified aspect and manner. He was naked, with the exception of a small blanket which covered his shoulders, and descended to the middle of the back, being fastened around the neck with a silver skewer. As it was pudding time with us, our visitor was of course invited to sit and eat; and he, nothing loath, deposited himself at once upon the ground, and made a remarkably vigorous assault upon the mixed contents of the dish. He had not eaten long, however, before we perceived a sudden and inexplicable change in his countenance, which was instantly followed by a violent ejectment of a huge mouthful of our luxurious fare. The man rose slowly, and with great dignity, to his feet, and pronouncing the single word "shekum," (horse,) in a tone of mingled anger and disgust, stalked rapidly out of the camp, not even wishing us a good evening. It struck me as a singular instance of accuracy and discrimination in the organs of taste. We had been eating of the multifarious compound without being able to recognize, by the taste, a single ingredient which it contained; a stranger came amongst us, who did not know, when he commenced eating, that the dish was formed of more than one item, and yet in less than five minutes he discovered one of the very least of its component parts.

It would seem from this circumstance that the Indians, or it may be the particular tribe to which this man belongs, are opposed to the eating of horse flesh, and yet, the natural supposition would be, that in the gameless country inhabited by them they would often be reduced to such shifts, and thus readily conquer any natural reluctance which they might feel to partake of such food. I did not think until after he left us, that if the chief knew how the horse meat he so much detested was procured, and where, he might probably have expressed even more indignation, for it is not at all unlikely that the colt had strayed from his own band.

21st—The timber along the river banks is plentiful, and often attains a large size. It is chiefly of the species called balsam poplar, (*Populus balsamifera.*)[1]

Towards noon to-day, we observed ahead several groups of Indians, perhaps twenty in each, and on the appearance of our cavalcade, they manifested their joy at seeing us, by the most extravagant and grotesque gestures, dancing and capering most ludicrously. Every individual of them was perfectly naked, with the exception of a small thong around the waist, to which was attached a square piece of flannel, skin, or canvass, depending half way to the knees. Their stature was rather below the middle height, but they were strongly built and very muscular. Each man carried his salmon spear, and these, with the knives stuck in their girdles, appeared to be their only weapons, not one of them having a gun. As we neared them, the first group ran towards us, crying "Shoshoné, Shoshoné," and caused some delay by their eagerness to grasp our hands and examine our garments. After one group had become satisfied with fingering us, we rode on and suffered the same process by the next, and so on until we had passed the whole, every Indian crying with a loud voice, "*Tabiboo sant, tabiboo sant!*" (white man is good, white man is good.)

In a short time the chief joined us, and our party stopped for an hour, and had a "talk" with him. He told us, in answer to our questions, that his people had fish, and would give them for our goods if we would sleep one night near their camp, and smoke with them. No trade, of consequence, can ever be effected with Indians, unless the pipe be first smoked, and the matter calmly and seriously deliberated upon. An Indian chief would think his dignity seriously compromised if he were expected to do *any thing* in a hurry, much less so serious a matter as a salmon or beaver trade; and if we had refused his offered terms, he would probably have allowed us to pass on, and denied himself the darling rings, bells, and paint, rather than infringe a custom so long religiously practised by his people. We were therefore inclined to humor our Snake friend, and accordingly came to a halt, on the bank of the river.

The chief and several of his favored young braves sat with us on the bank, and we smoked with them, the other Indians forming a large circle around.

The chief is a man rather above the ordinary height, with a fine, noble countenance, and remarkably large, prominent eyes. His person, instead of being naked, as is usual, is clothed in a robe made of the skin of the mountain sheep; a broad band made of large blue beads, is fastened to the top of his head, and hangs over on his cheeks, and around his neck is suspended the foot of a huge grizzly bear. The possession of this uncouth ornament is considered among them, a great honor, since none but those whose prowess has enabled them to kill the animal, are allowed to wear it, and with their weak and inefficient weapons, the destruction of so fierce and terrible a brute, is a feat that may well entitle them to some distinction.

We remained two hours at the spot where we halted, and then passed on about four miles, accompanied by the chief and his people, to their camp, where we pitched our tents for the night. In a short time the Indians came to us in great numbers, with bundles of dried salmon in their arms, and a few recent ones. We commenced our trading immediately, giving them in exchange, fish-hooks, beads, knives, paint, &c., and before evening, had procured sufficient provision for the consumption of our party until we arrive at the falls of Snake river, where we are told we shall meet the Bannecks, from whom we can doubtless trade a supply, which will serve us until we reach Walla-walla.

While we were pursuing our trade, Richardson and Mr. Ashworth rode into the camp, and I observed by the countenance of the latter, that something unusual had occurred. I felt very certain that no ordinary matter would be capable of ruffling this calm, intrepid, and almost fool-hardy young man; so it was with no little interest that I drew near, to listen to the tale which he told Captain W. with a face flushed with unusual anger, while his whole person seemed to swell with pride and disdain.

He said that while riding about five miles behind the party, (not being able to keep up with it on account of his having a worn out horse,) he was attacked by about fifty of the Indians whom we passed earlier in the day, dragged forcibly from his horse and thrown upon the ground. Here, some held their knives to his throat to prevent his rising, and others robbed him of his saddle bags, and all that they contained. While he was yet in this unpleasant situation, Richardson came suddenly upon them, and the cowardly Indians released their captive instantly, throwing the saddle bags and every thing else upon the ground and flying like frightened antelopes over the plain. The only real damage that Mr. Ashworth sustained, was the total loss of his saddle bags, which were cut to pieces by the knives of the Indians, in order to abstract the contents. These, however, we think he deserves to lose, inasmuch, as with all our persuasion, we have never been able to induce him to carry a gun since we left the country infested by the Blackfeet; and to-day, the very show of such a weapon would undoubtedly have prevented the attack of which he complains.

Richardson gives an amusing account of the deportment of our young English friend while he was lying under the knives of his captors. The heavy whip of buffalo hide, which was his only weapon, was applied with great energy to the naked backs and shoulders of the Indians, who winced and stamped under the infliction, but still feared to use their knives, except to prevent his rising. Richardson, says, that until he approached closely, the blows were descending in rapid succession, and our hunter was in some danger of losing his characteristic dignity in his efforts to repress a loud and hearty laugh at the extreme ludicrousness of the whole scene.

Captain W., when the circumstances of the assault were stated to him, gave an immediate order for the suspension of business, and calling the chief to him, told him seriously, that if an attempt were again made to interrupt any of his party on their march, the offenders should be tied to a tree and whipped severely. He enforced his language by gestures so expressive that none could misunderstand him, and he was answered by a low groan from the Indians present, and a submissive bowing of their heads. The chief appeared very much troubled, and harangued his people for considerable time on the subject, repeating what the captain had said, with some additional remarks of his own, implying that even a worse fate than whipping would be the lot of future delinquents.

22d.—Last night during the second guard, while on my walk around the camp, I observed one of my men squatted on the ground, intently surveying some object which appeared to be moving among the horses. At his request, I stooped also, and could distinctly perceive something near us which was certainly not a horse, and yet was as certainly a living object. I supposed it to be either a bear or a wolf, and at the earnest solicitation of the man, I gave the word "fire." The trigger was instantly pulled, the sparks flew from the flint, but the rifle was not exploded. At the sound, an Indian sprang from the grass where he had been crouching, and darted away towards the Snake camp. His object certainly was to appropriate one of our horses, and very fortunate for him was it that the gun missed fire, for the man was an unerring marksman. This little warning will probably check other similar attempts by these people.

Early in the morning I strolled into the Snake camp. It consists of about thirty lodges or wigwams, formed generally of branches of trees tied together in a conic summit, and covered with buffalo, deer, or elk skins. Men and little children were lolling about the ground all around the wigwams, together with a heterogeneous assemblance of dogs, cats, some tamed prairie wolves, and other "*varmints.*" The dogs growled and snapped when I approached, the wolves cowered and looked cross, and the cats ran away and hid themselves in dark corners. They had not been accustomed to the face of a white man, and all the quadrupeds seemed to regard me as some monstrous production, more to be feared than loved or courted. This dislike, however, did not appear to extend to the bipeds, for many of every age and sex gathered around me, and seemed to be examining me critically in all directions. The men looked complacently at me, the women, the dear creatures, smiled upon me, and the little naked, pot~bellied children crawled around my feet, examining the fashion of my hard shoes, and playing with the long fringes of my leathern inexpressibles. But I scarcely know how to commence a description of the *tout en semble* of the camp, or to frame a sentence which will give an adequate idea of the extreme filth, and most horrific nastiness of the whole vicinity. I shall therefore but transiently glance at it, omitting many of the most disgusting and abominable features.

Immediately as I entered the village, my olfactories were assailed by the most vile and mephitic odors, which I found to proceed chiefly from great piles of salmon entrails and garbage which were lying festering and rotting in the sun, around the very doors of the habitations. Fish, recent and half dried, were scattered all over the ground, under the feet of the dogs, wolves and Indian children; and others which had been split, were hanging on rude platforms erected within the precincts of the camp. Some of the women were making their breakfast of the great red salmon eggs as large as peas, and using a wooden spoon to convey them to their mouths. Occasionally, also, by way of varying the repast, they would take a huge pinch of a drying fish which was lying on the ground near them. Many of the children were similarly employed, and the little imps would also have hard contests with the dogs for a favorite morsel, the former roaring and blubbering, the latter yelping and snarling, and both rolling over and over together upon the savory soil. The whole economy of the lodges, and the inside and outside appearance, was of a piece with every thing else about them —filthy beyond description —the very skins which covered the wigwams were black and stiff with rancid salmon fat, and the dresses (if dresses they may be called) of the women, were of the same color and consistence, from the same cause. These *dresses* are little square pieces of deer skin, fastened with a thong around the loins, and reaching about half way to the knees; the rest of the person is entirely naked. Some of the women had little children clinging like bullfrogs to their backs, without being fastened, and in that situation extracting their lactiferous sustenance from the breast, which was thrown over the shoulders.

It is almost needless to say, that I did not remain long in the Snake camp; for although I had been a considerable time estranged from the abodes of luxury, and had become somewhat accustomed to, at least, a partial assimilation to a state of nature, yet I was not prepared for what I saw here. I never had fancied any thing so utterly abominable, and was glad to escape to a purer and more wholesome atmosphere.

When I returned to our camp, the trading was going on as briskly as yesterday. A large number of Indians were assembled around, all of whom had bundles of fish, which they were anxious to dispose of. The price of a dried salmon is a straight awl, and a small fish hook, value about one cent; ten fish are given for a common butcher knife that costs eight cents. Some, however, will prefer beads, paint, &c., and of these articles, about an equal amount in value is given. A beaver skin can be had for a variety of little matters, which cost about twelve and a half cents; value, in Boston, from eight to ten dollars!

Early in the afternoon, we repacked our bales of goods and rode out of the encampment, the Indians yelling an adieu to us as we passed them. We observed that one had wrapped a buffalo robe around him, taken a bow and arrows in his hand, and joined us as we went off. Although we travelled rapidly during the afternoon, the man kept with us without apparent over-exertion or fatigue, trotting along constantly for miles together. He is probably on a visit to a village of his people who are encamped on the "Big river."

23d.—Towards noon, to-day, we fell in with a village, consisting of thirty willow lodges of Bannecks. The Indians flocked out to us by hundreds, leaving their fishing, and every other employment, to visit the strangers. The chief soon made himself known to us, and gave us a pressing invitation to stop a short time with them, for the purpose of trade. Although we had a good supply of fish on hand, and did not expect soon to suffer from want, yet we knew not but we might be disappointed in procuring provision lower in the country, and concluded, therefore, to halt for half an hour, and make a small increase to our stock. We were in some haste, and anxious to travel on as quickly as possible, to Snake river. Captain W., therefore, urged the chief to have the fish brought immediately, as he intended soon to leave them. The only reply he could obtain to this request, was "*te sant,*" (it is good,) accompanied by signs, that he wished to smoke. A pipe was provided, and he, with about a dozen of his young men, formed a circle near, and continued smoking, with great tranquillity, for half an hour.

Our patience became almost exhausted, and they were told that if their fish were not soon produced, we should leave them empty as we came; to this, the only answer of the chief was a sign to us to remain still, while he deliberated yet farther upon the subject.

We sat a short time longer in silent expectation, and were then preparing to mount our horses and be off, when several squaws were despatched to one of the lodges. They returned in a few minutes, bringing about a dozen dried fish. These were laid in small piles on the ground, and when the usual price was offered for them, they refused it scornfully, making the most exorbitant demands. As our articles of trade were running low, and we were not in immediate want, we purchased only a sufficiency for one day, and prepared for our departure, leaving the ground strewn with the neglected salmon. The Indians were evidently very much irritated, as we could perceive by their angry countenances, and loud words of menace. Some loosed the bows from their shoulders, and shook them at us with violent gestures of rage, and a boy, of seventeen or eighteen years of age, who stood near me, struck my horse on the head with a stick, which he held in his hand. This provoked me not a little; and spurring the animal a few steps forward, I brought my heavy whip several times over his naked shoulders, and sent him screeching into the midst of his people. Several bows were drawn at me for this act, and glad would the savages have been to have had me for a short time at their mercy, but as it was, they feared to let slip their arrows, and soon dropped their points, contenting themselves with vaporing away in all the impotence of childish rage. As we rode off, they greeted us, not with the usual gay yell, but with a scornful, taunting laugh, that sounded like the rejoicings of an infernal jubilee. Had these people been provided with efficient arms, and the requisite amount of courage to use them, they might have given us some inconvenience.

Towards evening, we arrived on Snake river, crossed it at a ford, and encamped near a number of lodges along the shore. Shortly afterwards, Captain W., with three men, visited the Indians, carrying with them some small articles, to trade for fish. In about half an hour they returned, bringing only about ten salmon. They observed, among the Indians, the same disinclination to traffic that the others had manifested; or rather, like the first, they placed a higher value than usual upon the commodity, and wanted, in exchange, articles which we were not willing to spare them. They treated Captain W. with the same insolence and contempt which was so irritating from those of the other village.

This kind of conduct is said to be unusual among this tribe, but it is probably now occasioned by their having recently purchased a supply of small articles from Captain Bonneville, who, they inform us, has visited them within a few days.

Being desirous to escape from the immediate vicinity of the village, we moved our camp about four miles further, and stopped for the night.

24th.—The sudden and entire change from flesh exclusively, to fish, ditto, has affected us all more or less, with diarrhoea and pain in the abdomen; several of the men have been so extremely sick, as scarcely to be able to travel; we shall, however, no doubt, become accustomed to it in a few days.

We passed, this morning, over a flat country, very similar to that along the Platte, abounding in wormwood bushes, the pulpy-leaved thorn, and others, and deep with sand, and at noon stopped on a small stream called *Malheur's creek.*[2]

Here a party of nine men was equipped, and despatched up the river, and across the country, on a trapping expedition, with orders to join us early in the ensuing winter, at the fort on the Columbia. Richardson was the chief of this party, and when I grasped the hand of our worthy hunter, and bade him farewell, I felt as though I were taking leave of a friend. I had become particularly attached to him, from the great simplicity and kindness of his heart, and his universally correct and proper deportment. I had been accustomed to depend upon his knowledge and sagacity in every thing connected with the wild and roving life which I had led for some months past, and I felt that his absence would be a real loss, as well to myself, as to the whole camp, which had profited so much by his dexterity and skill.

Our party will now consist of only seventeen men, but the number is amply sufficient, as we have passed over the country where danger is to be apprehended from Indians. We followed the course of the creek during the afternoon, and in the evening encamped on Snake river, into which Malheur empties. The river is here nearly a mile wide, but deep and clear, and for a considerable distance, perfectly navigable for steamboats, or even larger craft, and it would seem not improbable, that at some distant day, these facilities, added to the excellence of the alluvial soil, should induce the stout and hardy adventurers of our country to make permanent settlements here.

I have not observed that the Indians often attempt fishing in the "big river," where it is wide and deep; they generally prefer the slues, creeks, &c. Across these, a net of closely woven willows is stretched, placed vertically, and extending from the bottom to several feet above the surface. A number of Indians enter the water about a hundred yards above the net, and, walking closely, drive the fish in a body against the wicker work. Here they frequently become entangled, and are always checked; the spear is then used dexterously, and they are thrown out, one by one, upon the shore. With industry, a vast number of salmon might be taken in this manner; but the Indians are generally so indolent and careless of the future, that it is rare to find an individual with provision enough to supply his lodge for a week.

25th.—Early in the day the country assumed a more hilly aspect. The rich plains were gone. Instead of a dense growth of willow and the balsam poplar, low bushes of wormwood, &c., predominated, intermixed with the tall, rank prairie grass.

Towards noon, we fell in with about ten lodges of Indians, (Snakes and Bannecks,) from whom we purchased eighty salmon. This has put us in excellent spirits. We feared that we had lost sight of the natives, and as we had not reserved half the requisite quantity of provisions for our support to the Columbia, (most of our stock having been given to Richardson's trapping party,) the prospect of several days abstinence seemed very clear before us.

In the afternoon, we deviated a little from our general course, to cut off a bend in the river, and crossed a short, high hill, a part of an extensive range which we have seen for two days ahead, and which we suppose to be in the vicinity of Powder river, and in the evening encamped in a narrow valley, on the borders of the Shoshoné.

26th.—Last night I had the misfortune to lose my favorite, and latterly my only riding horse, the other having been left at Fort Hall, in consequence of a sudden lameness, with which he became afflicted only the night before our departure.* The animal was turned out as

---

*I afterwards ascertained that this lameness of my "buffalo horse," was intentionally caused by one of the hopeful gentry left in charge of the fort, for the purpose of rendering the animal unable to travel, and as a consequence, confining him to the fort at the time of our departure. The good qualities of the horse as a buffalo racer, were universally known and appreciated, and I had repeatedly refused large sums for him, from those who desired him for this purpose.

usual, with the others, in the evening, and as I have never known him to stray in a single instance, I conclude that some lurking Indian has stolen him. It was the fattest and handsomest horse in the band, and was no doubt carefully selected, as there was probably but a single Indian, who was unable to take more, for fear of alarming the guard. This is the most serious loss I have met with. The animal was particularly valuable to me, and no consideration would have induced me to part with it here. It is, however, a kind of accident that we are always more or less liable to in this country, and as a search would certainly be fruitless, must be submitted to with as good a grace as possible. Captain W. has kindly offered me the use of horses until we arrive at Columbia.

We commenced our march early, travelling up a broad, rich valley, in which we encamped last night, and at the head of it, on a creek called Brulé, we found one family, consisting of five Snake Indians, one man, two women, and two children. They had evidently but very recently arrived, probably only last night, and as they must certainly have passed our camp, we feel little hesitation in believing that my lost horse is in their possession. It is, however, impossible to prove the theft upon them in any way, and time is not allowed us to search the premises. We cannot even question them concerning it, as our interpreter, McCarey, left us with the trapping party.

We bought, of this family, a considerable quantity of dried choke-cherries, these being the only article of commerce which they possessed. This fruit they prepare by pounding it with stones, and drying it in masses in the sun. It is then good tasted, and somewhat nutritive, and it loses, by the process, the whole of the astringency which is so disagreeable in the recent fruit.

Leaving the valley, we proceeded over some high and stony hills, keeping pretty nearly the course of the creek. The travelling was, as usual in such places, difficult and laborious, and our progress necessarily slow and tedious. Throughout the day, there was no change in the character of the country, and the consequence was, that three of our poor horses gave up and stopped.

27th.—This morning, two men were left at the camp, for the purpose of collecting and bringing on, moderately, the horses left yesterday, and others that may hereafter fail. We were obliged to leave with them a stock of provision greater in proportion than our own rather limited allowance, and have thus somewhat diminished our chance of performing the remainder of the journey with satisfied appetites, but there is some small game to be found on the route, grouse, ducks, &c., and occasionally a beaver may be taken, if our necessities are pressing. We made a noon camp on Brulé, and stopped at night in a narrow valley, between the hills.

28th.—Towards noon to-day, we lost the trail among the hills, and although considerable search was made, we were not able to find it again. We then directed our course due north, and at 2 o'clock struck Powder river, a narrow and shallow stream, plentifully fringed with willows. We passed down this river for about five miles and encamped. Captain W. immediately left us to look for the lost trail, and returned in about two hours, with the information that no trace of it could be found. He therefore concludes that it is up stream, and to-morrow we travel back to search for it in that direction. Our men killed, in the afternoon, an antelope and a deer fawn, which were particularly acceptable to us; we had been on an allowance of one dried salmon per day, and we had begun to fear that even this poor pittance would fail before we could obtain other provision. Game has been exceedingly scarce, with the exception of a few grouse, pigeons, &c. We have not seen a deer, antelope, or any other quadruped larger than a hare, since we left the confines of the buffalo country. Early this morning, one of our men, named Hubbard, left us to hunt, and as he has not joined us this evening, we fear he is lost, and feel some anxiety about him, as he has not been accustomed to finding his way through the pathless wilds. He is a good marksman, however, and will not suffer much for food; and as he knows the general course, he will probably join us at Walla-walla, if we should not see him earlier.

29th.—We commenced our march early this morning, following the river to a point about six miles above where we struck it yesterday. We then took to the hills, steering N. N. W.,—it being impossible, from the broken state of the country, to keep the river bank.

Soon after we commenced the ascent, we met with difficulties in the shape of high, steep, banks, and deep ravines, the ground being thickly strewed with sharp, angular masses of lava and basalt. As we proceeded, these difficulties increased to such a degree, as to occasion a fear that our horses could never proceed. The hills at length became like a consolidated mass of irregular rock, and the small strips of earthy matter that occasionally appeared, were burst into wide fissures by the desiccation to which the country at this season is subject. Sometimes, as we approached the verges of the cliffs, we could see the river winding its devious course many hundred fleet below, rushing and foaming in eddies and whirlpools, and fretting against the steep sides of the rocks, which hemmed it in. These are what are called the cut-rocks, the sides of which are in many places as smooth and regular as though they had been worked with the chisel, and the opening between them, through which the river flows, is frequently so narrow that a biscuit might be thrown across it.

We travelled over these rocks until 1 o'clock in the day, when we stopped to rest in a small ravine, where we found a little water, and pasture for our horses. At 3, we were again on the move, making across the hills towards the river, and after a long, circuitous march, we arrived on its banks, considerably wearied, and every horse in our band lamed and completely exhausted. We have not yet found any clue to the trail for which we have been searching so anxiously; indeed it would be impossible for a distinguishable trace to be left over these rugged, stony hills, and the difficulty of finding it, or determining its direction is not a little increased by a dense fog which constantly envelopes these regions, obscuring the sun, and rendering it impossible to see an object many hundred yards in advance.

The next day we were still travelling over the high and steep hills, which, fortunately for our poor horses, were far less stony than hitherto. At about noon we descended to the plain, and struck the river in the midst of a large level prairie.. We proceeded up stream for an hour, and to our great joy suddenly came in sight of a broad, open trail stretching away to the S. W. We felt, in some degree, the pleasure of a sailor who has found the port of which he has been long and anxiously in search. We made a noon camp here, at which we remained two hours, and then travelled on in fine spirits over a beautiful, level, and unobstructed country. Our horses seemed to participate in our feelings, and trotted on briskly, as though they too rejoiced in the opportunity of escaping the dreaded hills and rocks. Towards evening we crossed a single range of low hills and came to a small round prairie, with good water and excellent pasture. Here we found a family of *Kayouse* Indians, and encamped within sight of them. Two squaws from this family, visited us soon after, bringing some large kamas cakes and fermented roots, which we purchased of them.

31st—Our route this morning, was over a country generally level and free from rocks; we crossed, however, one short, and very steep mountain range, thickly covered with tall and heavy pine trees, and came to a large and beautiful prairie, called the *Grand ronde*. Here we found Captain Bonneville's company, which has been lying here several days, waiting the arrival of its trapping parties. We made a noon camp near it, and were visited by Captain Bonneville. This was the first time I had seen this gentleman. His manners were affable and pleasing, and he seemed possessed of a large share of bold, adventurous, and to a certain extent, romantic spirit, without which no man can expect to thrive as a mountain leader. He stated that he preferred the "free and easy" life of a mountain hunter and trapper, to the comfortable and luxurious indolence of a dweller in civilized lands, and would not exchange his homely, but wholesome mountain fare, and his buffalo lodge, for the most piquant dishes of the French *artiste*, and the finest palace in the land. This came well from him, and I was pleased with it, although I could not altogether agree with him in sentiment, for I confess I had become somewhat weary of rough travelling and rough fare, and looked forward with no little pleasure to a long rest under a Christian roof, and a general participation in Christian living.

With the captain, came a whole troop of Indians, Kayouse, Nez Percés, &c. They were very friendly towards us, each of the chiefs taking us by the hand with great cordiality, appearing pleased to see us, and anxious to point out to us the easiest and most expeditious route to the lower country. These Indians are, almost universally, fine looking, robust men, with strong aqualine features, and a much more cheerful cast of countenance than is usual amongst the race. Some of the women might almost be called beautiful, and none that I have seen are homely. Their dresses are generally of thin deer or antelope skin, with occasionally a bodice of some linen stuffs, purchased from the whites, and their whole appearance is neat and cleanly, forming a very striking contrast to the greasy, filthy, and disgusting Snake females. I observed one young and very pretty looking woman, dressed in a great superabundance of finery, glittering with rings and beads, and flaunting in broad bands of scarlet cloth. She was mounted astride,— Indian fashion,—upon a fine bay horse, whose head and tail were decorated with scarlet and blue ribbons, and the saddle, upon which the fair one sat, was ornamented all over with beads and little hawk's bells. This damsel did not do us the honor to dismount, but seemed to keep warily aloof, as though she feared that some of us might be inordinately fascinated by her fine person and splendid equipments, and her whole deportment proved to us, pretty satisfactorily, that she was no common beauty, but the favored companion of one high in office, who was jealous of her slightest movement.

After making a hasty meal, and bidding adieu to the captain, and our friendly Indian visitors', we mounted our horses, and rode off. About half an hour's brisk trotting brought us to the foot of a steep and high mountain, called the *Blue*. This is said to be the most extensive chain west of the dividing ridge, and, with one exception perhaps the most difficult of passage. The whole mountain is densely covered with tall pine trees, with an undergrowth of service bushes and other shrubs, and the path is strewed, to a very inconvenient degree, with volcanic rocks. In some of the ravines we find small springs of water; they are, however, rather rare, and the grass has been lately consumed, and many of the trees blasted by the ravaging fires of the Indians. These fires are yet smouldering, and the smoke from them effectually prevents our viewing the surrounding country, and completely obscures the beams of the sun. We travelled this evening until after dark, and encamped on a small stream in a gorge, where we found a plot of grass that had escaped the burning.

September 1st.—Last evening, as we were about retiring to our beds, we heard, distinctly, as we thought, a loud halloo, several times repeated, and in a tone like that of a man in great distress. Supposing it to be a person who had lost his way in the darkness, and was searching for us, we fired several guns at regular intervals, but as they elicited no reply, after waiting a considerable time, we built a large fire, as a guide, and lay down to sleep.

Early this morning, a large panther was seen prowling around our camp, and the hallooing of last night was explained. It was the dismal, distressing yell by which this animal entices its prey, until pity or curiosity induces it to approach to its destruction. The panther is said to inhabit these forests in considerable numbers, and has not unfrequently been known to kill the horses of a camp. He has seldom the temerity to attack a man, unless sorely pressed by hunger, or infuriated by wounds.

Chapter IX

*S*eptember 1st.—The path through the valley, in which we encamped last night, was level and smooth for about a mile; we then mounted a short, steep hill, and began immediately to descend. The road down the mountain wound constantly, and we travelled in short, zig-zag lines, in order to avoid the extremely abrupt declivities; but occasionally, we were compelled to descend in places that made us pause before making the attempt: they were, some of them, almost perpendicular, and our horses would frequently slide several yards, before they could recover. To this must be added enormous jagged masses of rock, obstructing the road in many places, and pine trees projecting their horizontal branches across the path.

The road continued, as I have described it, to the valley in the plain, and a full hour was consumed before we reached it. The country then became comparatively level again to the next range, where a mountain was to be ascended of the same height as the last. Here we dismounted and led our horses, it being impracticable, in their present state, to ride them. It was the most toilsome march I ever made, and we were all so much fatigued, when we arrived at the summit, that rest was as indispensable to us as to our poor jaded horses. Here we made a noon camp, with a handful of grass and no water. This last article appears very scarce, the ravines affording none, and our dried salmon and kamas bread were eaten unmoistened. The route, in the afternoon, was over the top of the mountain, the road tolerably level, but crowded with stones. Towards evening, we commenced descending again, and in every ravine and gulley we cast our anxious eyes in search of water; we even explored several of them, where there appeared to exist any probability of success, but not one drop did we find. Night at length came on, dark and pitchy, without a moon or a single star to give us a ray of light; but still we proceeded, depending solely upon the vision and sagacity of our horses to keep the track. We travelled steadily until 9 o'clock, when we saw ahead the dark outline of a high mountain, and soon after heard the men who rode in front, cry out, joyously, at the top of their voices, "*water! water!*" It was truly a cheering sound, and the words were echoed loudly by every man in the company. We had not tasted water since morning, and both horses and men have been suffering considerably for the want of it.

2d.—Captain W. and two men, left us early this morning for Walla-walla, where they expect to arrive this evening, and send us some provision, of which we shall be in need, to-morrow.

Our camp moved soon after, under the direction of Captain Thing, and in about four miles reached *Utalla river,* where it stopped, and remained until 12 o'clock.[1]

As we were approaching so near the abode of those in whose eyes we wished to appear like fellow Christians, we concluded that there would be a propriety in attempting to remove at least one of the heathenish badges which we had worn throughout the journey; so Mr. N.'s razor was fished out from its hiding place in the bottom of his trunk, and in a few minutes our encumbered chins lost their long-cherished ornaments; we performed our ablutions in the river, arrayed ourselves in clean linen, trimmed our long hair, and then arranged our toilet before a mirror, with great self-complacence and satisfaction. I admired my own appearance considerably, (and this is, probably, an acknowledgement that few would make,) but I could not refrain from laughing at the strange, party-colored appearance of my physiognomy, the lower portion being fair, like a woman's, and the upper, brown and swarthy as an Indian.

Having nothing prepared for dinner to-day, I strolled along the stream above the camp, and made a meal on rose buds, of which I collected an abundance; and on returning, I was surprised to find Mr. N. and Captain T. picking the last bones of a bird which they had cooked. Upon inquiry, I ascertained that the subject was an unfortunate owl which I had killed in the morning, and had intended to preserve, as a specimen. The temptation was too great to be resisted by the hungry Captain and naturalist, and the bird of wisdom lost the immortality which he might otherwise have acquired.

In the afternoon, soon after leaving the Utalla, we ascended a high and very steep hill, and came immediately in view of a beautiful, and regularly undulating country of great extent. We have now probably done with high, rugged mountains; the sun shines clear, the air is bracing and elastic, and we are all in fine spirits.

The next day, the road being generally level, and tolerably free from stones, we were enabled to keep our horses at the swiftest gait to which we dare urge them. We have been somewhat disappointed in not receiving the expected supplies from Walla-walla, but have not suffered for provision, as the grouse and hares are very abundant here, and we have shot as many as we wished.

At about noon we struck the Walla-walla river, a very pretty stream of fifty or sixty yards in width, fringed with tall willows, and containing a number of salmon, which we can see frequently leaping from the water. The pasture here, being good, we allowed our horses an hour's rest to feed, and then travelled on over the plain, until near dark, when, on rising a sandy hill, the noble Columbia burst at once upon our view. I could scarcely repress a loud exclamation of delight and pleasure, as I gazed upon the magnificent river, flowing silently and majestically on, and reflected that I had actually crossed the vast American continent, and now stood upon a stream that poured its waters directly into the Pacific. This, then, was the great Oregon, the first appearance of which gave Lewis and Clark so many emotions of joy and pleasure, and on this stream our indefatigable countrymen wintered, after the toils and privations of a long, and protracted journey through the wilderness. My reverie was suddenly interrupted by one of the men exclaiming from his position in advance, "there is the fort." We had, in truth approached very near, without being conscious of it.[2] There stood the fort on the bank of the river; horses and horned cattle were roaming about the vicinity, and on the borders of the little Walla-walla, we recognized the white tent of our long lost missionaries. These we soon joined, and were met and received by them like brethren. Mr. N. and myself were invited to sup with them upon a dish of stewed hares which they had just prepared, and it is almost needless to say that we did full justice to the good men's cookery. They told us that they had travelled comfortably from Fort Hall, without any unusual fatigue, and like ourselves, had no particularly stirring adventures. Their route, although somewhat longer, was a much less toilsome and difficult one, and they suffered but little for food, being well provided with dried buffalo meat, which had been prepared near Fort Hall.

Mr. Walker, (a young gentleman attached to the band,) related an anecdote of Mr. Lee, the principal, which I thought eminently characteristic. The missionaries were, on one occasion, at a considerable distance behind the main body, and had stopped for a few moments to regale themselves on a cup of milk from a cow which they were driving. Mr. L. had unstrapped the tin pan from his saddle, and was about applying himself to the task, when a band of a dozen Indians was descried at a distance, approaching the little party at full gallop. There was but little time for consideration. The rifles were looked to, the horses were mounted in eager haste, and all were ready for a long run, except Mr. Lee himself, who declared that nothing should deprive him of his cup of milk, and that he meant to "lighten the old cow before he moved." He accordingly proceeded coolly to fill his tin pan, and, after a hearty drink, grasped his rifle, and mounted his horse, at the very moment that the Indians had arrived to within speaking distance. To the great relief of most of the party, these proved to be of the friendly Nez Percé tribe, and after a cordial greeting, they travelled on together.

The missionaries informed us that they had engaged a large barge to convey themselves and baggage to Fort Vancouver, and that Captain Stewart and Mr. Ashworth were to be of the party. Mr. N. and myself were very anxious to take a seat with them, but to our disappointment, were told that the boat would scarcely accommodate those already engaged. We had therefore to relinquish it, and prepare for a journey on horseback to the *Dalles*, about eighty miles below, to which place Captain W. would precede us in the barge, and engage canoes to convey us to the lower fort.

This evening, we purchased a large bag of Indian meal, of which we made a kettle of mush, and mixed with it a considerable quantity of horse tallow and salt. This was, I think, one of the best meals I ever made. We all ate heartily of it, and pronounced it princely food. We had been long without bread stuff of any kind, and the coarsest farinaceous substance, with a proper allowance of grease, would have been highly prized.

The next morning, we visited Walla-walla Fort, and were introduced, by Captain W., to Lieutenant Pierre S. Pambrun, the superintendent.[3] Wyeth and Mr. Pambrun had met before, and were well acquainted; they had, therefore, many reminiscences of by-gone days to recount, and long conversations, relative to the variety of incidents which had occurred to each, since last they parted.

The fort is built of drift logs, and surrounded by a stoccade of the same, with two bastions, and a gallery around the inside. It stands about a hundred yards from the river, on the south bank, in a bleak and unprotected situation, surrounded on every side by a great, sandy plain, which supports little vegetation, except the wormwood and thorn-bushes. On the banks of the little river, however, there are narrow strips of rich soil, and here Mr. Pambrun raises the few garden vegetables necessary for the support of his family. Potatoes, turnips, carrots, &c., thrive well, and Indian corn produces eighty bushels to the acre.

At about 10 o'clock, the barge got under way, and soon after, our company with its baggage, crossed the river in canoes, and encamped on the opposite shore.

There is a considerable number of Indians resident here, Kayouse's and a collateral band of the same tribe, called Walla-wallas. They live along the bank of the river, in shantys or wigwams of drift wood, covered with buffalo or deer skins. They are a miserable, squalid looking people, are constantly lolling around and in the fort, and annoy visitors by the importunate manner in which they endeavor to force them into some petty trade for a pipe, a hare, or a grouse. All the industrious and enterprising men of this tribe are away trading salmon, kamas root, &c. to the mountain companies.

Notwithstanding the truly wretched plight in which these poor people live, and the privations which they must necessarily have to suffer, they are said to be remarkably honest and upright in their dealings, and generally correct in their moral deportment. Although they doubtless have the acquisitive qualities so characteristic of the race, they are rarely known to violate the principles of common honesty.

A man may leave his tent unguarded, and richly stored with every thing which ordinarily excites the cupidity of the Indian, yet, on returning after a long absence, he may find all safe. What a commentary is this on the habits and conduct of our *Christian* communities!

The river is here about three-fourths of a mile in width, a clear, deep, and rapid stream, the current being generally from three to four miles an hour. It is the noblest looking river I have seen since leaving our Delaware. The banks are in many places high and rocky, occasionally interrupted by broad, level sandy beaches. The only vegetation along the margin, is the wormwood, and other low, and plants, but some of the bottoms are covered with heavy, rank grass, affording excellent pasture for horses.

5th.—This morning we commenced our march down the Columbia. We have no provision with us except flour and horse tallow, but we have little doubt of meeting Indians daily, with whom we can trade for fish. Our road will now be a rather monotonous one along the bank of the river, tolerably level, but often rocky, so that very rapid travelling is inadmissible. The mallard duck, the widgeon, and the green-winged teal are tolerably abundant in the little estuaries of the river. Our men have killed several, but they are poor, and not good.

6th.—We have observed to-day several high, conical stacks of drift-wood near the river. These are the graves of the Indians. Some of these cemeteries are of considerable extent, and probably contain a great number of bodies. I had the curiosity to peep into several of them, and even to remove some of the coverings, but found nothing to compensate for the trouble.

We bought some salmon from Indians whom we met to-day, which, with our flour and tallow, enable us to live very comfortably.

7th.—We frequently fall in with large bands of Indian horses. There are among them some very beautiful animals, but they are generally almost as wild as deer, seldom permitting an approach to within a hundred yards or more. They generally have owners, as we observe upon many of them strange hieroglyphic looking characters, but there are no doubt some that have never known the bit, and will probably always roam the prairie uncontrolled. When the Indians wish to catch a horse from one of these bands, they adopt the same plan pursued by the South Americans for taking the wild animal.

8th.—Our road to-day has been less monotonous, and much more hilly than hitherto. Along the bank of the river, are high mountains, composed of basaltic rock and sand, and along their bases enormous drifts of the latter material. Large, rocky promontories connected with these mountains extend into the river to considerable distances, and numerous islands of the same dot its surface.

We are visited frequently as we travel along, by Indians of the Walla-walla and other tribes, whose wigwams we see on the opposite side of the river. As we approach these rude huts, the inhabitants are seen to come forth in a body; a canoe is immediately launched, the light bark skims the water like a bird, and in an incredibly short time its inmates are with us. Sometimes a few salmon are brought to barter for our tobacco, paint, &c., but more frequently they seem impelled to the visit by mere curiosity. To-day a considerable number have visited us, and among them some very handsome young girls. I could not but admire the gaiety and cheerfulness which seemed to animate them. They were in high spirits, and evidently very much pleased with the unusual privilege which they were enjoying.

At our camp in the evening, eight Walla-walla's came to see us. The chief was a remarkably fine looking man, but he, as well as several of his party, was suffering from a severe purulent ophthalmia which had almost deprived him of sight. He pointed to his eyes, and contorting his features to indicate the pain he suffered, asked me by signs to give him medicine to cure him. I was very sorry that my small stock of simples did not contain anything suited to his complaint, and I endeavored to tell him so. I have observed that this disease is rather prevalent among the Indians residing on the river, and I understood from the chief's signs that most of the Indians towards the lower country were similarly affected.

9th.—The character of the country has changed considerably since we left Walla-walla. The river has become gradually more narrow, until it is now but about two hundred yards in width, and completely hemmed in by enormous rocks on both sides. Many of these extend for considerable distances into the stream in perpendicular columns, and the water dashes and breaks against them until all around is foam. The current is here very swift, probably six or seven miles to the hour; and the Indian canoes in passing down, seem literally to *fly* along its surface. The road to-day has been rugged to the very last degree. We have passed over continuous masses of sharp rock for hours together, sometimes picking our way along the very edge of the river, several hundred feet above it; again, gaining the back land, by passing through any casual chasm or opening in the rocks, where we were compelled to dismount, and lead our horses.

This evening, we are surrounded by a large company of Chinook Indians, of both sexes, whose temporary wigwams are on the bank of the river. Many of the squaws have young children sewed up in the usual Indian fashion, wrapped in a skin, and tied firmly to a board, so that nothing but the head of the little individual is seen.

These Indians are very peaceable and friendly. They have no weapons except bows, and these are used more for amusement and exercise, than as a means of procuring them sustenance, their sole dependence being fish and beaver, with perhaps a few hares and grouse, which are taken in traps. We traded with these people for a few fish and beaver skins, and some roots, and before we retired for the night, arranged the men in a circle, and gave them a smoke in token of our friendship.

10th.—This afternoon we reached the *Dalles*. The entire water of the river here flows through channels of about fifteen feet in width, and between high, perpendicular rocks; there are several of these channels at distances of from half a mile to a mile apart, and the water foams and boils through them like an enormous cauldron.

On the opposite side of the river there is a large Indian village, belonging to a chief named Tilki, and containing probably five hundred wigwams. As we approached, the natives swarmed like bees to the shore, launched their canoes, and joined us in a few minutes. We were disappointed in not seeing Captain W. here, as this was the spot where we expected to meet him; the chief, however, told us that we should find him about twelve miles below, at the next village. We were accordingly soon on the move again, and urging our horses to their fastest gait, we arrived about sunset. The captain, the chief of the village, and several other Indians, came out to meet us and make us welcome. Captain W. has been here two days, and we were pleased to learn that he had completed all the necessary arrangements for transporting ourselves and baggage to Vancouver in canoes. The route by land is said to be a very tedious and difficult one, and, in some places, almost impassable, but even were it otherwise, I believe we should all much prefer the water conveyance, as we have become very tired of riding.

Since leaving the upper village this afternoon, we have been followed by scores of Indians on foot and on horseback; some of the animals carrying three at a time; and although we travelled rapidly, the pedestrians were seldom far behind us.

We have concluded to leave our horses here, in charge of the chief of the village, who has promised to attend to them during the winter, and deliver them to our order in the spring. Captain W. having been acquainted with this man before, is willing to trust him.

11th.—Early this morning, we launched our three canoes, and each being provided with an Indian, as helmsman, we applied ourselves to our paddles, and were soon moving briskly down the river. In about an hour after, the wind came out dead ahead, and although the current was in favor, our progress was sensibly checked. As we proceeded, the wind rose to a heavy gale, and the waves ran to a prodigious height. At one moment our frail bark danced upon the crest of a wave, and at the next, fell with a surge into the trough of the sea, and as we looked at the swell before us, it seemed that in an instant we must inevitably be engulphed. At such times, the canoe ahead of us was entirely hidden from view, but she was observed to rise again like a seagull, and hurry on into the same danger. The Indian in my canoe soon became completely frightened; he frequently hid his face with his hands, and sang, in a low melancholy voice, a prayer which we had often heard from his people, while at their evening devotions. As our dangers were every moment increasing, the man became at length absolutely childish, and with all our persuasion and threats, we could not induce him to lay his paddle into the water. We were all soon compelled to put in shore, which we did without sustaining any damage; the boats were hauled up high and dry, and we concluded to remain in our quarters until to-morrow, or until there was a cessation of wind. In about an hour it lulled a little, and Captain W. ordered the boats to be again launched, in the hope of being able to weather a point about five miles below, before the gale again commenced, where we could lie by until it should be safe to proceed. The calm proved, as some of us had suspected, a treacherous one; in a very few minutes after we got under way, we were contending with the same difficulties as before, and again our cowardly helmsman laid by his paddle and began mumbling his prayer. It was too irritating to be borne. Our canoe had swung round broad side to the surge, and was shipping gallons of water at every dash.

At this time it was absolutely necessary that every man on board should exert himself to the utmost to head up the canoe and make the shore as soon as possible. Our Indian, however, still sat with his eyes covered, the most abject and contemptible looking thing I ever saw. We took him by the shoulders and threatened to throw him overboard, if he did not immediately lend his assistance: we might as well have spoken to a stone. He was finally aroused, however, by our presenting a loaded gun at his breast; he dashed the muzzle away, seized his paddle again, and worked with a kind of desperate and wild energy, until he sank back in the canoe completely exhausted. In the mean time the boat had become half full of water, shipping a part of every surf that struck her, and as we gained the shallows every man sprang overboard, breast deep, and began hauling the canoe to shore. This was even a more difficult task than that of propelling her with the oars; the water still broke over her, and the bottom was a deep kind of quicksand, in which we sank almost to the knees at every step, the surf at the same time dashing against us with such violence as to throw us repeatedly upon our faces. We at length reached the shore, and hauled the canoe up out of reach of the breakers. She was then unloaded as soon as possible, and turned bottom upwards. The goods had suffered considerably by the wetting; they were all unbaled and dried by a large fire, which we built on the shore.

We were soon visited by several men from the other boats, which were ahead, and learned that their situation had been almost precisely similar to our own, except that their Indians had not evinced, to so great a degree, the same unmanly terror which had rendered ours so inefficient and useless. They were, however, considerably frightened, much more so than the white men. It would seem strange that Indians, who have been born, and have lived during their whole lives, upon the edge of the water, who have been accustomed, from infancy, to the management of a canoe, and in whose childish sports and manly pastimes these frail barks have always been employed, should exhibit, on occasions like this, such craven and womanly fears; but the probability is, as their business is seldom of a very urgent nature, that they refrain from making excursions of any considerable extent in situations known to be dangerous, except during calm weather; it is possible, also, that such gales may be rare, and they have not been accustomed to them. Immediately after we landed, our redoubtable helmsman broke away from us, and ran at full speed back towards the village. We have doubtless lost him entirely, but we do not much regret his departure, as he proved himself so entirely unequal to the task he had undertaken.

12th.—The gale continues with the same violence as yesterday, and we do not therefore think it expedient to leave our camp. Mr. N.'s large and beautiful collection of new and rare plants was considerably injured by the wetting it received; he has been constantly engaged since we landed yesterday, in opening and drying them. In this task he exhibits a degree of patience and perseverance which is truly astonishing; sitting on the ground, and steaming over the enormous fire, for hours together, drying the papers, and re-arranging the whole collection, specimen by specimen, while the great drops of perspiration roll unheeded from his brow. Throughout the whole of our long journey, I have had constantly to admire the ardor and perfect indefatigability with which he has devoted himself to the grand object of his tour. No difficulty, no danger, no fatigue has ever daunted him, and he finds his rich reward in the addition of nearly *a thousand* new species of American plants, which he has been enabled to make to the already teeming flora of our vast continent. My bale of birds, which was equally exposed to the action of the water, escaped without any material injury.

In the afternoon, the gale not having abated, Captain W. became impatient to proceed, as he feared his business at Vancouver would suffer by delay; he accordingly proposed taking one canoe, and braving the fury of the elements, saying that he wished five men, who were not afraid of water, to accompany him. A dozen of our fearless fellows volunteered in a moment, and the captain selecting such as he thought would best suit his purpose, lost no time in launching his canoe, and away she went over the foaming waters, dashing the spray from her bows, and laboring through the heavy swells until she was lost to our view. The more sedate amongst us did not much approve of this somewhat hasty measure of our principal; it appeared like a useless and daring exposure of human life, not warranted by the exigencies of the case. Mr. N. remarked that he would rather lose all his plants than venture his life in that canoe.

On the 13th the wind shifted to due north, and was blowing somewhat less furiously than on the previous day. At about noon we loaded our canoes, and embarked; our progress, however, during the afternoon, was slow; the current was not rapid, and the wind was setting up stream so strongly that we could not make much headway against it; we had, also, as before, to contend with turbulent waves, but we found we could weather them with much less difficulty, since the change of the wind.

14th.—Before sunrise, a light rain commenced, which increased towards mid-day to a heavy shower, and continued steadily during the afternoon and night. There was, in the morning, a dead calm, the water was perfectly smooth, and disturbed only by the light rain pattering upon its surface. We made an early start, and proceeded on very expeditiously until about noon, when we arrived at the "cascades," and came to a halt above them, near a small Indian village. These cascades, or cataracts are formed by a collection of large rocks, in the bed of the river, which extend, for perhaps half a mile. The current for a short distance above them, is exceedingly rapid, and there is said to be a gradual fall, or declivity of the river, of about twenty feet in the mile. Over these rocks, and across the whole river, the water dashes and foams most furiously, and with a roar which we heard distinctly at the distance of several miles.

It is wholly impossible for any craft to make its way through these difficulties, and our light canoes would not live an instant in them. It is, therefore, necessary to make a portage, either by carrying the canoes over land to the opposite side of the cataracts, or by wading in the water near the shore, where the surges are lightest, and dragging the unloaded boat through them by a cable. Our people chose the latter method, as the canoes felt very heavy and cumbersome, being saturated with the rain which was still falling rapidly. They were accordingly immediately unloaded, the baggage placed on the shore, and the men entered the water to their necks, headed by Captain Thing, and addressed themselves to the troublesome and laborious task. In the meantime, Mr. N., and myself were sent ahead to take the best care of ourselves that our situation and the surrounding circumstances permitted. We found a small Indian trail on the river bank, which we followed in all its devious windings, up and down hills, over enormous piles of rough flinty rocks, through brier bushes, and pools of water, &c. &c., for about a mile, and descending near the edge of the river, we observed a number of white men who had just succeeded in forcing a large barge through the torrent, and were then warping her into still water near the shore. Upon approaching them more closely, we recognised, to our astonishment, our old friend Captain Stewart, with the good missionaries, and all the rest who left us at Walla-walla on the 4th. Poor fellows! Every man of them had been over breast deep in water, and the rain, which was still falling in torrents, was more than sufficient to drench what the waves did not cover, so that they were most abundantly soaked and bedraggled. I felt sadly inclined to laugh heartily at them, but a single glance at the sorry appearance of myself and my companion was sufficient to check the feeling. We joined them, and aided in kindling a fire to warm and dry ourselves a little, as there was not a dry rag on us, and we were all in an ague with cold. After a very considerable time, we succeeded in igniting the wet timber, and had a tolerably large fire. We all seated ourselves on the ground around it, and related our adventures. They had, like ourselves, suffered somewhat from the head-wind and heavy swells, but unlike us they had a craft that would weather it easily; even they, however, shipped some water, and made very little progress for the last two days. They informed us that Captain W.'s canoe had been dashed to pieces on the rocks above, and that he and all his crew were thrown into the water, and forced to swim for their lives. They all escaped, and proceeded down the river, this morning, in a canoe, hired of the Indians here, one of whom accompanied them, as pilot.

After a hasty meal of fish, purchased on the spot, our friends reloaded their boat and got under way, hoping to reach Vancouver by next morning. Mr. N. and myself remained some time longer here, expecting intelligence from our people behind; we had begun to feel a little uneasy about them, and thought of returning to look into their situation, when Captain T. came in haste towards us, with the mortifying intelligence that one canoe had been stove upon the rocks, and the other so badly split, that he feared she would not float; the latter was, however, brought on by the men, and moored where we had stopped. A man was then despatched to an Indian village, about five miles below, to endeavor to procure one or two canoes and a pilot. In the mean time, we had all to walk back along the circuitous and almost impassable Indian trail, and carry our wet and heavy baggage from the spot where the boats had been unloaded. The distance, as I have stated, was a full mile, and the road so rough and encumbered as to be scarcely passable. In walking over many of the large and steep rocks, it was often necessary that the hands should be used to raise and support the body; this, with a load, was inconvenient. Again, in ascending and descending the steep and slippery hills, a single mis-step was certain to throw us in the mud, and bruise us upon the sharp rocks which were planted all around. This accident occurred several times with us all.

Over this most miserable of all roads, with the cold rain dashing and pelting upon us during the whole time, until we felt as though we were frozen to the very marrow, did we all have to travel and return four separate times, before our baggage was properly deposited. It was by far the most fatiguing, cheerless, and uncomfortable business in which I was ever engaged, and truly glad was I to lie down at night on the cold, wet ground, wrapped in my blankets, out of which I had just wrung the water, and I think I never slept more soundly or comfortably than that night.*

I arose the next morning rested and refreshed, though somewhat sore from sundry bruises received on the hills to which I have alluded.

15th.—The rain still continued falling, but lightly, the weather calm and cool. The water immediately below the cascades foams and boils in a thousand eddies, forming little whirlpools, which, however insignificant they may appear, are exceedingly dangerous for light canoes, whirling, their bows around to the current, and capsising them in an instant. Near the shore, at the foot of the cataract, there is a strong backward tow, through which it is necessary to drag the canoe, by a line, for the distance of a hundred yards; here it feels the force of the opposite current, and is carried on at the rate of seven or eight miles to the hour.

The man whom we sent yesterday to the village, returned this morning; he stated that one canoe only could be had, but that three Indians, accustomed to the navigation, would accompany us; that they would soon be with us, and endeavor to repair our damaged boat. In an hour they came, and after the necessary clamping and caulking of our leaky vessel, we loaded, and were soon moving rapidly down the river. The rain ceased about noon, but the sun did not appear during the day.

16th.—The day was a delightful one; the sky was robed in a large flaky cumulus, the glorious sun occasionally bursting through among the clouds, with dazzling splendor. We rose in the morning in fine spirits, our Indians assuring us that "King George," as they called the fort, was but a short distance from us. At about 11 o'clock, we arrived, and stepped on shore at the *end of our journey.*

---

*I could not but recollect at that time, the last injunction of my dear old grandmother, not to sleep in damp beds!!

It is now three days over six months since I left my beloved home. I, as well as the rest, have been in some situations of danger, of trial, and of difficulty, but I have passed through them all unharmed, with a constitution strengthened, and invigorated by healthful exercise, and a heart which I trust can feel deeply, sincerely thankful to that kind and overruling Providence who has watched over and protected me.

We have passed for months through a country swarming with Indians who thirsted for our blood, and whose greatest pride and glory consisted in securing the scalp of a white man. Enemies, sworn, determined enemies to all, both white and red, who intrude upon his hunting grounds, the Blackfoot roams the prairie like a wolf seeking his prey, and springing upon it when unprepared, and at the moment when it supposes itself most secure. To those who have always enjoyed the comforts and security of civilized life, it may seem strange that persons who know themselves to be constantly exposed to such dangers —who never lie down at night without the weapons of death firmly grasped in their hands, and who are in hourly expectation of hearing the terrific war whoop of the savage, should yet sleep soundly and refreshingly, and feel themselves at ease; such however is the fact. I never in my life enjoyed rest more than when travelling through the country of which I speak. I had become accustomed to it: I felt constant apprehension certainly, but not to such an extent as to deprive me of any of the few comforts which I could command in such an uncomfortable country. The guard might pass our tent, and cry " all's well," in his loudest key, without disturbing my slumbers: but if the slightest *unusual* noise occurred, I was awake in an instant, and listening painfully for a repetition of it.

On the beach in front of the fort, we were met by Mr. Lee, the missionary, and Dr. John McLoughlin, the chief factor, and Governor of the Hudson's Bay posts in this vicinity.[4] The Dr. is a large, dignified and very noble looking man, with a fine expressive countenance, and remarkably bland and pleasing manners. The missionary introduced Mr. N. and myself in due form, and we were greeted and received with a frank and unassuming politeness which was most peculiarly grateful to our feelings. He requested us to consider his house our home, provided a separate room for our use, a servant to wait upon us, and furnished us with every convenience which we could possibly wish for. I shall never cease to feel grateful to him for his disinterested kindness to the poor houseless and travel-worn strangers.

Chapter X

Fort Vancouver is situated on the north bank of the Columbia on a large level plain, about a quarter of a mile from the shore. The space comprised within the stoccade is an oblong square, of about one hundred, by two hundred and fifty feet. The houses built of logs and frame-work, to the number of ten or twelve, are ranged around in a quadrangular form, the one occupied by the doctor being in the middle. In front, and enclosed on three sides by the buildings, is a large open space, where all the in-door work of the establishment is done. Here the Indians assemble with their multifarious articles of trade, beaver, otter, venison, and various other game, and here, once a week, several scores of Canadians are employed, beating the furs which have been collected, in order to free them from dust and vermin.[1]

Mr. N. and myself walked over the farm with the doctor, to inspect the various improvements which he has made. He has already several hundred acres fenced in, and under cultivation, and like our own western prairie land, it produces abundant crops, particularly of grain, without requiring any manure. Wheat thrives astonishingly; I never saw better in any country, and the various culinary vegetables, potatoes, carrots, parsnips, &c., are in great profusion, and of the first quality. Indian corn does not flourish so well as at Walla-walla, the soil not being so well adapted to it; melons are well flavored, but small; the greatest curiosity, however, is the apples, which grow on small trees, the branches of which would be broken without the support of props. So profuse is the quantity of fruit that the limbs are covered with it, and it is actually *packed* together precisely in the same manner that onions are attached to ropes when they are exposed for sale in our markets.

On the farm is a grist mill, a threshing mill, and a saw mill, the two first, by horse, and the last, by water power; besides many minor improvements in agricultural and other matters, which cannot but astonish the stranger from a civilized land, and which reflect great credit upon the liberal and enlightened chief factor.

In the propagation of domestic cattle, the doctor has been particularly successful. Ten years ago a few head of neat cattle were brought to the fort by some fur traders from California; these have now increased to near seven hundred. They are a large framed, long horned breed, inferior in their milch qualities to those of the United States, but the beef is excellent, and in consequence of the mildness of the climate, it is never necessary to provide them with fodder during the winter, an abundant supply of excellent pasture being always found.

On the farm, in the vicinity of the fort, are thirty or forty log huts, which are occupied by the Canadians, and others attached to the establishment. These huts are placed in rows, with broad lanes or streets between them, and the whole looks like a very neat and beautiful village. The most fastidious cleanliness appears to be observed; the women may be seen sweeping the streets and scrubbing the door-sills as regularly as in our own proverbially cleanly city.*

---

*I have given this notice of the suburbs of the fort, as I find it in my journal written at the time; I had reason, subsequently, to change my opinion with regard to the scrupulous cleanliness of the Canadians' Indian wives, and particularly after inspecting the internal economy of the dwellings. What a first struck me as neat and clean, by an involuntary comparison of it with the

Sunday, September 25th.—Divine service was performed in the fort this morning by Mr. Jason Lee. This gentleman and his nephew had been absent some days in search of a suitable place to establish themselves, in order to fulfil the object of their mission. They returned yesterday, and intend leaving us to-morrow with their suite for the station selected, which is upon the Wallammet river, about sixty miles south of the fort.[2]

In the evening we were gratified by the arrival of Captain Wyeth from below, who informed us that the brig from Boston, which was sent out by the company to which Wyeth is attached, had entered the river, and was anchored about twenty miles below, at a spot called Warrior's point, near the western entrance of the Wallammet.[3]

Captain W. mentioned his intention to visit the Wallammet country, and seek out a convenient location for a fort which he wishes to establish without delay, and Mr. N. and myself accepted an invitation to accompany him in the morning. He has brought with him one of the brig's boats, and eight oarsmen, five of whom are Sandwich Islanders.

We have experienced for several days past, gloomy, lowering, and showery weather; indeed the sun has scarcely been seen for a week past. This is said to indicate the near approach of the rainy season, which usually sets in about the middle of October, or even earlier. After this time, until December, there is very little clear weather, showers or heavy clouds almost constantly prevailing.

On the 29th, Captain Wyeth, Mr. N., and myself, embarked in the ship's boat for our exploring excursion. We had a good crew of fine robust sailors, and the copper-colored islanders,—or *Kanakas,* as they are called,—did their duty with great alacrity and good will.[4]

At about five miles below the fort, we entered the upper mouth of the Wallammet. This river is here about half the width of the Columbia, a clear and beautiful stream, and navigable for large vessels to the distance of twenty-five miles. It is covered with numerous islands, the largest of which is that called *Wappatoo Island,* about twenty miles in length.[5] The vegetation on the main land is good, the timber generally pine and post oak, and the river is margined in many places with a beautiful species of willow with large ob-lanceolate leaves like those of the peach, and white on their under surface. The timber on the islands is chiefly oak, no pine growing there. At about 10 o'clock we overtook

---

extreme filthiness to which I had become accustomed amongst the Indians, soon revealed itself in its proper light, and I can freely confess that my first estimate was too high.

three men whom Captain W. had sent ahead in a canoe and we all landed soon after on the beach and dined on a mess of salmon and peas which we had provided. We were under way again in the afternoon, and encamped at about sunset. We have as yet seen no suitable place for an establishment, and to-morrow we proceed to the falls of the river, about fifteen miles further. Almost all the land in the vicinity is excellent and well calculated for cultivation, and several spots which we have visited, would be admirably adapted to the captain's views, but that there is not a sufficient extent unincumbered, or which could be fitted. for the purposes of tillage in a space of time short enough to be serviceable. others are at some seasons inundated, which is an insurmountable objection.

We embarked early the next morning, and at 11 o'clock arrived at the falls, after encountering some difficulties from rapids, through which we had to warp our boat. There are here three falls on a line of rocks extending across the river, which forms the bed of the upper channel. The water is precipitated through deep abrazed gorges, and falls perhaps forty feet at an angle of about twenty degrees. It was a beautiful sight when viewed from a distance, but it became grand and almost sublime as we approached it nearer. I mounted the rocks and stood over the highest fall, and although the roar of the cataract was almost deafening, and the rays of the bright sun reflected from the white and glittering foam threatened to deprive me of sight, yet I became so absorbed in the contemplation of the scene, and the reflections which were involuntarily excited, as to forget every thing else for the time, and was only aroused by Captain W. tapping me on the shoulder, and telling me that every thing was arranged for our return. While I visited the falls, the captain and his men had found what they sought for; and the object of our voyage being accomplished, we got on board immediately and shaped our course down the river with a fair wind, and the current in favor.

About two miles below the cataract is a small village of Klikatat Indians. Their situation does not appear different from what we have been accustomed to see in the neighborhood of the fort. They live in the same sort of miserable loose hovels, and are the same wretched, squalid looking people. Although enjoying far more advantages, and having in a much greater degree the means of rendering themselves comfortable, yet their mode of living, their garments, their wigwams, and every thing connected with them, is not much better than the Snakes and Bannecks, and very far inferior to that fine, noble-looking race, the Kayouse, whom we met on the *Grand ronde.*

A custom prevalent, and almost universal amongst these Indians, is that of flattening, or mashing in the whole front of the skull, from the superciliary ridge to the crown. The appearance produced by this unnatural operation is almost hideous, and one would suppose that the intellect would be materially affected by it. This, however, does not appear to be the case, as I have never seen, (with a single exception, the Kayouse,) a race of people who appeared more shrewd and intelligent. I had a conversation on this subject, a few days since, with a chief who speaks the English language. He said that he had exerted himself to abolish the practice in his own tribe, but although his people would listen patiently to his talk on most subjects, their ears were firmly closed when this was mentioned; "they would leave the council fire, one by one, until none but a few squaws and children were left to drink in the words of the chief." It is even considered among them a degradation to possess a round head, and one whose *caput* has happened to be neglected in his infancy, can never become even a subordinate chief in his tribe, and is treated with indifference and disdain, as one who is unworthy a place amongst them.

The flattening of the head is practiced by at least ten or twelve distinct tribes of the lower country, the Klikatats, Kalapooyahs, and Multnomahs, of the Wallammet, and its vicinity; the Chinooks, Klatsaps, Klatstonis, Kowalitsks, Katlammets, Killemooks, and Chekalis of the lower Columbia and its tributaries, and probably by others both north and south. The tribe called Flatheads, or *Salish*, who reside near the sources of the Oregon, have long since abolished this custom.

The mode by which the flattening is effected, varies considerably with the different tribes. The Wallammet Indians place the infant, soon after birth, upon a board, to the edges of which are attached little loops of hempen cord or leather, and other similar cords are passed across and back, in a zig-zag manner, through these loops, enclosing the child, and binding it firmly down. To the upper edge of this board, in which is a depression to receive the back part of the head, another smaller one is attached by hinges of leather, and made to lie obliquely upon the forehead, the force of the pressure being regulated by several strings attached to its edge, which are passed through holes in the board upon which the infant is lying, and secured there.

The mode of the Chinooks, and others near the sea, differs widely from that of the upper Indians, and appears somewhat less barbarous and cruel. A sort of cradle is formed by excavating a pine log to the depth of eight or ten inches. The child is placed in it on a bed of little grass mats, and bound down in the manner above described. A little boss of tightly plaited and woven grass is then applied to the forehead, and secured by a cord to the loops at the side. The infant is thus suffered to remain from four to eight months, or until the sutures of the skull have in some measure united, and the bone become solid and firm. It is seldom or never taken from the cradle, except in case of severe illness, until the flattening process is completed.

I saw, to-day, a young child from whose head the board had just been removed. It was, without exception, the most frightful and disgusting looking object that I ever beheld. The whole front of the head was completely flattened, and the mass of brain being forced back, caused an enormous projection there. The poor little creature's eyes protruded to the distance of half an inch, and looked inflamed and discolored, as did all the surrounding parts. Although I felt a kind of chill creep over me from the contemplation of such dire deformity, yet there was something so stark-staring, and absolutely queer in the physiognomy, that I could not repress a smile; and when the mother amused the little object and made it laugh, it looked so irresistibly, so *terribly* ludicrous, that I and those who were with me, burst into a simultaneous roar, which frightened it and made it cry, in which predicament it looked much less horrible than before.

On the 1st of November we arrived at the brig. She was moored, head and stern, to a large rock near the lower mouth of the Wallammet. Captain Lambert with his ship's company, and our own mountain men, were all actively engaged at various employments; carpenters, smiths, coopers, and other artisans were busy in their several vocations; domestic animals, pigs, sheep, goats, poultry, &c., were roaming about as if perfectly at home, and the whole scene looked so like the entrance to a country village, that it was difficult to fancy oneself in a howling wilderness inhabited only by the wild and improvident Indian, and his scarcely more free and fearless neighbors, the bear and the wolf. An excellent temporary storehouse of twigs, thatched with grass, has been erected, in which has been deposited the extensive assortment of goods necessary for the settlement, as well as a number of smaller ones, in which the men reside. It is intended as soon as practicable, to build a large and permanent dwelling of logs, which will also include the store and trading establishment, and form the groundwork for an *American fort* on the river Columbia.

5th.—Mr. N. and myself are now residing on board the brig, and pursuing with considerable success our scientific researches through the neighborhood. I have shot and prepared here several new species of birds, and two or three undescribed quadrupeds, besides procuring a considerable number, which, though known to naturalists, are rare, and therefore valuable.[6] My companion is of course in his element; the forest, the plain, the rocky bin, and the mossy bank yield him a rich and most abundant supply.

We are visited daily by considerable numbers of Chinook and Klikatat Indians, many of whom bring us provisions of various kinds, salmon, deer, ducks, &c., and receive in return, powder and shot, knives, paint, and *Indian rum,* i. e. rum and water in the proportion of one part of the former to two of the latter. Some of these Indians would be handsome were it not for the abominable practice, which, as I have said, is almost universal amongst them, of destroying the form of the head. The features of many are regular, though often devoid of expression, and the persons of the men generally are rather symmetrical; their stature is low, with light sinewy limbs, and remarkably small delicate hands. The women are usually more rotund, and, in some instances, even approach obesity. The principal clothing worn by them is a sort of short petticoat made of strands of pine bark or twisted hempen strings, tied around the loins like a marro. This article they call a *kalaquarté;* and is often their only dress; some, however, cover the shoulders with a blanket, or robe made of muskrat or hare skins sewed together.

A disease of a very fatal character is prevalent among these Indians; many of them have died of it; even some of those in the neighborhood of the fort, where medical assistance was always at hand. The symptoms are a general coldness, soreness and stillness of the limbs and body, with violent tertian ague. Its fatal termination is attributable to its tendency to attack the liver, which is generally affected in a few days after the first symptoms are developed. Several of the white people attached to the fort have been ill with it, but no deaths have occurred amongst them, the disease in their case having yielded to the simple tonic remedies usually employed at home. This I have no doubt would be equally the case with the Indians, were they willing to submit to proper restrictions during the time of administering medicine.[7]

Captain Lambert informs me that on his first landing here the Indians studiously avoided his vessel, and all kind of intercourse with his crew, from the supposition, (which they have since acknowledged) that the malady which they dread so much was thus conveyed. As in a short time it became desirable, on account of procuring supplies of provision, to remove this impression, some pains were taken to convince the Indians of their error, and they soon visited the ship without fear.

Mr. N. and myself have been anxious to escape the wet and disagreeable winter of this region, and visit some other portion of the country, where the inclemency of the season will not interfere with the prosecution of our respective pursuits. After some reflection and consultation, we concluded to take passage in the brig, which will sail in a few weeks for the Sandwich Islands. We shall remain there about three months, and return to the river in time to commence our peregrinations in the spring.

23d.—At Fort Vancouver. A letter was received yesterday by Dr. McLoughlin, from Captain Wyeth, dated Walla-walla, stating that the twelve Sandwich Islanders whom he took with him a week since for a journey to Fort Hall, had deserted, each taking a horse. They had no doubt heard from some of their countrymen, whom they met at the fort, of the difficulties of the route before them, which were probably very much exaggerated. Captain W. is on the alert to find them, and is sending men on their trail in every direction, but it is more than probable that they will not be overtaken, and the consequence will then be, that the expedition must be abandoned, and the captain return to the fort to spend the winter.[8]

December 3d.—Yesterday Mr. N. and myself went down the river to the brig, and this morning early the vessel left her moorings, and with her sails unloosed stood out into the channel way. The weather was overcast, and we had but little wind, so that our progress during the morning was necessarily slow. In the afternoon we ran aground in one and a half fathoms water, but as the tide was low, we were enabled to get her clear in the evening. The navigation of this river is particularly difficult in consequence of numerous shoals and sand bars, and good pilots are scarce, the Indians alone officiating in that capacity. Towards noon the next day, a Kowalitsk Indian with but one eye, who said his name was *George*, boarded us, and showed a letter which he carried, written by Captain McNeall, in the Hudson's Bay service, recommending said George as a capable and experienced pilot. We accepted his services gladly, and made a bargain with him to take us into Baker's bay near the cape, for four bottles of rum; with the understanding, however, that every time the brig ran aground, one bottle of the precious liquor was to be forfeited. George agreed to the terms, and taking his station at the bow, gave his orders to the man at the wheel like one having authority, pointing with his finger when he wished a deviation from the common course, and pronouncing in a loud voice the single word *ookook*, (here.)

On the afternoon of the 4th, we passed along a bold precipitous shore, near which we observed a large isolated rock, and on it a great number of canoes, deposited above the reach of the tides. This spot is called *Mount Coffin,* and the canoes contain the dead bodies of Indians. They are carefully wrapped in blankets, and all the personal property of the deceased, bows and arrows, guns, salmon spears, ornaments, &c., are placed within, and around his canoe. The vicinity of this, and all other cemeteries, is held so sacred by the Indians, that they never approach it, except to make similar deposites; they will often even travel a considerable distance out of their course, in order to avoid intruding upon the sanctuary of their dead.

We came to anchor near this rock in the evening, and Captain Lambert, Mr. N., and myself visited the tombs. We were especially careful not to touch or disarrange any of the fabrics, and it was well we were so, for as we turned to leave the place, we found that we had been narrowly watched by about twenty Indians, whom we had not seen when we landed from our boat. After we embarked, we observed an old withered crone with a long stick or wand in her hand, who approached, and walked over the ground which we had defiled with our sacrilegious tread, waving her enchanted rod over the mouldering bones, as if to purify the atmosphere around, and exorcise the evil spirits which we had called up.

I have been very anxious to procure the skulls of some of these Indians, and should have been willing, so far as I alone was concerned, to encounter some risk to effect my object, but I have refrained on account of the difficulty in which the ship and crew would be involved, if the sacrilege should be discovered; a prejudice might thus be excited against our little colony which would not soon be overcome, and might prove a serious injury.

6th.—The weather is almost constantly rainy and squally, making it unpleasant to be on deck; we are therefore confined closely to the cabin, and are anxious to get out to sea as soon as possible, if only to escape this.

In the afternoon, the captain and myself went ashore in the long-boat, and visited several Indian houses upon the beach. These are built of roughly hewn boards and logs, usually covered with pine bark, or matting of their own manufacture, and open at the top, to allow the smoke to escape. In one of these houses we found men, women, and children, to the number of fifty-two, seated as usual, upon the ground, around numerous fires, the smoke from which filled every cranny of the building, and to us was almost stifling, although the Indians did not appear to suffer any inconvenience from it. Although living in a state of the most abject poverty, deprived of most of the absolute necessaries of life, and frequently enduring the pangs of protracted starvation, yet these poor people appear happy and contented. They are scarcely qualified to enjoy the common comforts of life, even if their indolence did not prevent the attempt to procure them.

On the afternoon of the 8th, we anchored off *Fort George,* as it is called, although perhaps it scarcely deserves the name of a fort, being composed of but one principal house of hewn boards, and a number of small Indian huts surrounding it, presenting the appearance, from a distance, of an ordinary small farm house with its appropriate outbuildings. There is but one white man residing here, the superintendent of the fort; but there is probably no necessity for more, as the business done is not very considerable, most of the furs being taken by the Indians to Vancouver. The establishment is, however, of importance, independent of its utility as a trading post, as it is situated within view of the dangerous cape, and intelligence of the arrival of vessels can be communicated to the authorities at Vancouver in time for them to render adequate assistance to such vessels by supplying them with pilots, &c. This is the spot where once stood the fort established by the direction of our honored countryman, John Jacob Astor. One of the chimneys of old Fort Astoria is still standing, a melancholy monument of American enterprise and domestic misrule. The spot where once the fine parterre overlooked the river, and the bold stoccade enclosed the neat and substantial fort, is now overgrown with weeds and bushes, and can scarce be distinguished from the primeval forest which surrounds it on every side.[9]

Captain Lambert, Mr. N. and myself visited the Indian houses in the neighborhood. In one of them we saw a poor little boy about three years of age who had been blind from his birth. He was sitting on the ground near the fire, surrounded by a quantity of fish bones which he had been picking. Our sympathy was very much excited for the poor little unfortunate, particularly as he was made a subject for the taunting jibes and laughter of a number of men and women, squatting around, and his mother sat by with the most cruel apathy and unconcern, and only smiled at the commiseration which we expressed for her innocent and peculiarly unhappy offspring. It seems difficult to believe that those who possess the form and countenance of human creatures, should so debase the natural good feelings which God has implanted in them: but these ignorant and gross wretches seemed to take credit to themselves in rendering this afflicted being unhappy, and smiled and looked at each other when we endeavored to infuse a little pity into them. The child had evidently been very much neglected, and almost starved, and the little articles which we presented it, (in the hope, that the Indians on seeing us manifest an interest in it, would treat it more tenderly,) it put to its mouth eagerly, but finding them not eatable, threw them aside in disgust. Oh! how I wished at that moment for a morsel of bread to give this little famished and neglected creature. We soon left the place, and returned to the brig, but I could think of nothing during the remainder of the evening but the little blind child, and at night I dreamed I saw it, and it raised its dim and sightless orbs, and stretched out its little emaciated arms towards me, as if begging for a crumb to prevent its starving.

These people, as I have already said, do not appear to possess a particle of natural good feeling, and in their moral character, they are little better than brutes. In the case of the blind boy, they seemed to take pride in tormenting it, and rendering it miserable, and vied with each other in the skill and dexterity with which they applied to it the most degrading and insulting epithets. These circumstances, with others, in regard to their moral character, which I shall not even mention, have tended very considerably to lower the estimation in which I have always held the red man of the forest, and serve to strengthen the opinion which I had long since formed, that nothing but the introduction of civilization, with its good and wholesome laws, can ever render the Indian of service to himself, or raise him from the state of wretchedness which has so long characterized his expiring race.

The next morning, we ran down into Baker's bay, and anchored within gunshot of the cape, when Captain Lambert and myself went on shore in the boat, to examine the channel, and decide upon the prospect of getting out to sea. This passage is a very dangerous one, and is with reason dreaded by mariners. A wide bar of sand extends from Cape Disappointment to the opposite shore,—called Point

Adams,—and with the exception of a space, comprehending about half a mile, the sea at all times breaks furiously, the surges dashing to the height of the mast head of a ship, and with the most terrific roaring. Sometimes the water in the channel is agitated equally with that which covers the whole length of the bar, and it is then a matter of imminent risk to attempt a passage. Vessels have occasionally been compelled to lie in under the cape for several weeks, in momentary expectation of the subsidence of the dangerous breakers, and they have not unfrequently been required to stand off shore, from without, until the crews have suffered extremely for food and water. This circumstance must ever form a barrier to a permanent settlement here; the sands, which compose the bar, are constantly shifting, and changing the course and depth of the channel, so that none but the small coasting vessels in the service of the company can, with much safety, pass back and forth.

Mr. N. and myself visited the sea beach, outside the cape, in the hope of finding peculiar marine shells, but although we searched assiduously during the morning, we had but little success. We saw several deer in the thick forest on the side of the cape, and a great number of black shags, or cormorants, flying over the breakers, and resting upon the surf-washed rocks.

On the morning of the 11th, Mr. Hanson, the mate, returned from the shore, and reported that the channel was smooth; it was therefore deemed safe to attempt the passage immediately. While we were weighing our anchor, we descried a brig steering towards us, which soon crossed the bar, and ran up to within speaking distance. It was one of the Hudson's Bay Company's coasters, and, as we were getting under way, a boat put off from her, and we were boarded by Mr. Ogden, a chief factor from one of the Company's forts on the coast.[10] He informed us that the brig left Naas about the first of October, but had been delayed by contrary winds, and rough, boisterous weather. Thus the voyage which usually requires but about eight days for its performance, occupied upwards of *two months*. They had been on an allowance of a pint of water per day, and had suffered considerably for fresh provision. Mr. Ogden remained with us but a short time, and we stood out past the cape.

When we entered the channel, the water which had before been so smooth, became suddenly very much agitated, swelling, and roaring, and foaming around us, as if the surges were upheaved from the very bottom, and as our vessel would fall in the trough of the sea, pitching down like a huge leviathan seeking its native depths, I could not but feel positive, that the enormous wave, which hung like a judgment over our heads, would inevitably engulph us; but the good ship, like a creature instinct with life, as though she knew her danger, gallantly rose upon it, and but dipped her bows into its crest, as if in scorn of its mighty and irresistible power. This is my first sea voyage, and every thing upon the great deep is of course novel and interesting to me. During the scene which I have just described, although I was aware of our imminent peril, and the tales that I had frequently heard of vessels perishing in this very spot, and in precisely such a sea, recurred to my mind with some force, yet I could not but feel a kind of secret and wild joy at finding myself in a situation of such awful and magnificent grandeur. I thought of the lines of Shelley, and repeated them to myself in a kind of ecstasy.

> "And see'st thou, and hear'st thou,
> And fear'st thou, and fear'st thou,
> And ride we not free
> O'er the terrible sea,
> I and thou?"

In about twenty minutes we had escaped all the danger, and found ourselves riding easily in a beautiful placid sea. We set the sails, which had been shortened on the bar, and the gallant vessel feeling the impulse of the wind, rushed ahead as if exulting in the victory she had achieved.[11]

We saw, outside the bar, a great number of birds, of various kinds—ducks of several species, two or three kinds of guillemots, (*Uria*,)—shags, (*Phalacrocorax*,) among which was a splendid new species,* brown albatross, (*Diomedea fusca*,) the common dusky pelican, (*P. fuscus*,) and numerous *Procellariæ*,—also, the beautiful marine animal, called *Medusa*. It is a cartilaginous or gummy substance, flattish, and about the size of a man's hand, with a tube projecting from it, expanded or flared out like the end of a clarionet. Within the body, near the posterior part is a large ovate ball, of a bright orange color, resembling the yolk of an egg.

14th—There is to-day a heavy sea running, and we landsmen are affording some merriment to the seasoned crew, by our "lubberly" manner of "fetching away" in our attempts to walk the deck. I find, for myself, that I must for the present consent to relinquish an erect

---

*See appendix.

and dignified carriage, and adopt the less graceful, but safer method of clinging to the rails, & c., to assist locomotion. One thing, however, I cannot but feel thankful for, which is, that I have never felt in the least degree sea sick; and having so far escaped, I have no apprehension for the future.

Saw, in the afternoon, a large sperm. whale, lazily rolling about a quarter of a mile ahead of the vessel. It occasionally spouted up a stream of water to the height of six or seven feet, but was perfectly quiescent until we approached near it, when it suddenly sank away and was lost to sight.

20th—We observe constantly around us several species of dark albatross, puffins, petrels, &c. They follow closely in our wake, sailing over the surges with astonishing ease and grace, frequently skimming so near the surface that the eye loses them for an instant between the swells, but at such time they never touch the water, although we not infrequently see them resting upon it.

23d—The weather has become very mild; the thermometer ranging from 65° to 75°, indicating our approach to the tropics; and as a further proof of it, we saw, this morning, a beautiful tropic bird, (*Phæton.*) It sails around the vessel with an easy, graceful sweep, its long train being very conspicuous, and sufficiently distinguishing it from a tern, which, in other respects, it closely resembles. Its voice is very much like that of the great tern, (*Sterna hirundo,*) being a harsh, loud, and guttural croak, emitted while sailing high, and with its head curved downwards, examining the surface of the sea in search of its finny prey.[12]

30th—For the last four or five days we have been making but little headway, having been, occasionally, almost becalmed, and not going at any time more than two, or two and a half knots. The weather is so warm that our upper garments have become uncomfortable, the mean of the thermometer being about 77°, but we have, for several days past, been favored with cool, refreshing showers in the evening, which tend very much to our comfort.

Saw, this afternoon, in latitude 23°20' N., longitude 149°30' W., a "school" of eight or ten sperm. whales. Several passed within twenty yards of the vessel, and we had an excellent opportunity of observing them. They were so near that we could distinctly see the expansion of the nostrils as they spouted the brine before them, with a noise like the blowing of a mighty forge. There were among them several calves, which were sporting around their dames, sometimes dashing against them head foremost, and gliding half out of water upon the backs of the old ones.

We were followed to-day by several large dolphins. I had often heard of the surpassing beauty of this fish, but my imagination had never pictured any thing half so splendid as I then witnessed. We were going at about three knots, and the fish easily kept up with us, swimming in the wake without any apparent exertion, or even motion of their fins. At one moment they appeared to be of a clear, uniform grass-green, glistening and sparkling in the waves like emeralds, and in the next, they had changed their color wholly, appearing of an iridescent purple, with large oval spots of green and shining red; again, they were speckled and striped with all the colors of the rainbow, but without any one appearing predominant, and these changes were going on every minute while they remained near us, which was for the space of half an hour. When caught, and taken from the water, it is said that these changes occur precisely as when in their native element, with scarcely any diminution of brilliancy; and as vitality becomes less active, the variations are less frequent, until the colors finally settle into a dark greenish hue, and the animal is dead.

January 2d, 1835.—This evening at 5 o'clock, we made distinctly, the head land of three of the Sandwich group, Hawaii, Maui, and Morokai, being within about eighteen miles of the nearest. We have now light trade winds which bear us at the rate of five knots, and an unusually smooth and placid sea. This, combined with the free, unwavering breeze, is considered by our mariners as a fortunate circumstance for us, particularly, as we shall approach, and perhaps pass the dangerous rocky coast of Maui in the night. It is much more common for vessels to feel the land breeze, as they near it, setting them off shore, while the trades, operating in a contrary direction, they become unmanageable, and not unfrequently founder upon the rocks. This has been the fate of a number of vessels approaching as we are at present, and our skillful and careful captain, always on the alert and anxious in situations of apprehended danger, is at this moment pacing the quarter-deck, giving directions regarding the management of the vessel, in tones as firm, and with a decision as prompt as ever; but through it all, he cannot conceal the anxiety under which he is evidently laboring. We passengers consider ourselves perfectly safe under such good guardianship, but cannot help feeling for the captain, who to insure our safety is losing the repose which he absolutely requires.

On the afternoon of the 4th, we ran by several islands, and all within five miles. We could distinctly see the lofty and precipitous rocks of the coast, the deep ravines between them, and, by the assistance of our glasses, the green and rich looking vegetation of the interrupted plains.

At noon next day, we made the island of Oahu, our destination, distant about forty miles. In the evening we were enabled to run, the moon shining brightly, and the atmosphere being unusually free from haze. At 10 o'clock we were within a few miles of the island, so that we could distinctly see a number of lights form the huts on the beach; we let go our anchor off a point called Diamond hill; and soon after, the mountain ranges, and the quiet valleys echoed the report of our pilot gun.

As I leaned over the rail this evening, gazing at the shore on our quarter, with its lofty peaks, and lovely sleeping vales, clearly defined by the light of the full orbed moon, I thought I never had witnessed any thing so perfectly enchanting. The warm breeze which came in gentle puffs from the land, seemed to bear fragrance on its wings, and to discourse of the rich and sunny climes from which it came. The whole scene was to me like fairy land. I thought of Captain Cook, and fancied his having been here, and gazing with delighted eyes upon the very prospect before me, little dreaming, that after all he had endured, he should here be sacrificed by the very people to whom he hoped to prove a benefactor and friend. The noise and bustle on deck, sailors running to and fro making the ship "snug" for harbor, and all the preparation for an arrival, effectually banished my meditations, and I descended to my state room, to sleep away the tedious hours, 'till the morrow should reveal all the new and strange features of the land to which we had come.

Chapter XI

*Honoruru—Native canoes—Amphibious habits—
Captain Charlton, his Britanic Majesty's consul—Mr.
Jones, the American consul—reception by him—
Description of the town, and of the natives—Party-
colored hair of the women—The pagoda—A visit from
Rev. Hiram Bingham, the missionary—Opinions
regarding the missionary fraternity—First view of the
king, Kauikeaouli—his train—Seaman's chapel—A
visit to the native church—Kinau and Kekuanoa—
Orderly conduct of the natives during worship—
Introduction to the king—His fondness for the chase, and
athletic exercises—Native food—Manner of eating—The
rumi-rumi—its efficacy—A Lu au party—The valley of
Nuano—A visit to the Pari—The last battle of
Tamehemaha—A feast—Manner of cooking—A party of
native ladies—An adventure.*

Early on the morning of the 5th, Mr. Reynolds, the deputy pilot, boarded us in a whale boat manned by natives, and accompanied by two American gentlemen, residents of the town of Honoruru,—Captain William S. Hinckley and P.A. Brinsmade, Esq. Our anchor was soon weighed, and with a fine, free wind, we rounded Diamond hill, and passed along a beautiful indentation in the shore, called Waititi bay, within sight of a large coral reef, by which the whole island is surrounded. We very soon came in view of the lovely, sylvan looking village of Honoruru. The shore below the town the Waititi, to a considerable distance above, is fringed with graceful cocoanut trees, with here and there a pretty little grass cottage, reposing under their shade. As we approached the harbor, these cottages became more numerous, until at last they appeared thickly grouped together, with occasionally a pretty garden dividing them. The fort, too, which fronts the ocean, with its clean, white washed walls, and cannon frowning from the embrasures, adds very much to the effect of the scene; while behind, the noble hills and fertile valleys between, clothed with the richest verdure, soften down and mellow the whole, and render the prospect indescribably beautiful.

On nearing the shore, we observed some scores of curiously formed canoes, with large outriggers, which had just put off, and were bound out on a fishing excursion. A number of these passed close to our vessel, and usually paused when opposite, that the denuded mariners might have an opportunity of surveying the strangers, and of bidding them welcome to their shores, by a loud and gay *Aroha*. Near the land a number of natives, of both sexes, were swimming and playing in the surf, and diving to the bottom searching for *echinae*, and sea weeds, remaining under the water for a considerable time, while their heels were seen moving to and fro above the surface.

Our brig soon entered the narrow channel, opposite the harbor, and with a light, but steady breeze, stood in close to the town and let go her anchor within a hundred yards of the shore. As we were about leaving the vessel, Captain Charlton, H.B.M. consul, and Captain W. Darby of the H.B. Co.'s brig Eagle came on board, and gave Mr. N. and myself a passage to the shore in their boat. They walked with us to the house of Mr. Jones, the American consul, to whom I had a letter from my friend Doctor M. Burrough, of Philadelphia. We were received by this gentleman in a manner calculated to make us feel perfectly at home; a good and comfortable house was immediately provided for us, and every assistance was offered in forwarding our views. We dined at the sumptuous table of W. French, Esq., an American gentleman, and one of the most thriving merchants of the town, and were here introduced to several highly respectable foreign residents, Captain E. Grimes, Doctor Thomas, Dr. Rooke, Mr. Paty, and others.[1] In the afternoon we strolled out with two or three gentlemen to view the village and its environs.

The town of Honoruru contains about three hundred houses, the great majority of which are composed of grass exclusively, and those occupied by the natives consist of a single room. Others, in which many of the foreigners reside, are partitioned with boards, and form as comfortable and agreeable residences as could be desired in a climate always warm. There are some few houses of frame, and several of coral rock, built by the resident merchants and missionaries; but they are certainly not superior, except in being more durable, to those of grass, and probably not so comfortable in the intensely hot seasons. The houses are scattered about without any regard to regularity, the hard, clay passage-ways winding amongst them in every direction; but an air of neatness and simple elegance pervades the whole, which cannot fail to make a favorable impression on the stranger.

The natives are generally remarkably well formed, of a dark copper color, with pleasant and rather intellectual countenances, and many of the women are handsome.

The dress of the men, not in the employment of the whites, consists of a large piece of native cloth, called a *Tapa*, or a robe of calico thrown loosely round the body, somewhat like the Roman toga, and knotted on the left shoulder. The women wear a loose gown of calico, or native cloth, fastened tightly round the neck, but not bound at the waist, and often with the addition of several yards of cotton cloth tied round above the hips.

Their hair is generally of a beautiful glossy black, and of unusual fineness; it is folded around the back part of the head, very much in the manner common to our ladies at home, and splendid tortoise shell combs, of their own manufacture, are used to confine it. They display much taste in the arrangement of wild flowers amongst their hair, and a common ornament for the forehead is the *Re* of beautiful yellow feathers which is bound upon it. I have repeatedly seen women with hair of two, and, in some instances, of three distinct colors. Deep black and chestnut brown; not promiscuously mingled throughout, but lying in separate masses; and in the rare instances of which I have spoken, they were black, brown, and a kind of ash color, giving to the head a most singular appearance. I had supposed that this party-colored character of the hair was the effect of art, but was soon informed to the contrary, and perceived that by the natives themselves it was considered a deformity.

8th.—Mr. N. and myself are now fairly domiciliated. We occupy a large and commodious room, in a building called the Pagoda, which is in a central part of the town; from our front windows we have a fine view of the harbor and the shipping, and from a balcony in the rear, we can see almost the entire length of the lovely valley of Nuano, with its bold and rugged rocks, and the luxuriant verdure on their sides; while nearer, the little square taro patches, crowded together over the intermediate plain, look like pretty garden plots, as the broad green leaves of the plant are tinted by the sunbeams.

In the afternoon, a gentleman somewhat past middle age, in a plain, but neat garb, called upon me, and introduced himself as the Rev. Hiram Bingham, one of the missionaries resident upon the island.[2]

He gave me a very interesting account of the first landing and establishment of the missionaries at the Sandwich Islands, and discoursed very pleasantly upon ordinary topics for half an hour. As Mr. N. was absent on a conchological excursion, I had the good man all to myself, and I may truly say, I have rarely spent a half hour more agreeably. I was particularly interested in Mr. Bingham, from the circumstance of his being one of the oldest missionaries at these islands, and from the knowledge (which I had before acquired) of the very great influence he had exerted in the establishment of the missions, and of the excellent condition to which they had attained under his supervision and guardianship.

It is well known to all who visit the Sandwich Islands, as well as to many at home who have friends residing there, that the missionaries are exceedingly unpopular amongst the resident foreigners. Why it is, or should be so, I will not stop to inquire, but will merely remark, that so far as my own intercourse with these missionaries has extended, and according to the opportunities I have had of judging of the relative merits of the case, my opinion decidedly is, that there is no good and sufficient reason for this ill-feeling. Who are the missionaries? They are men who have left the homes of their childhood, the parents, the brothers, the sisters, the friends of their bosoms, and for what? To dwell in distant lands, among the uncivilized and the barbarous; to labor for these with all the energy of their minds and bodies; and for this they receive so trifling a compensation, that nothing except the reward of a good conscience, and of a life spent in the noblest service that can engage the bodily and mental powers of a Christian, could ever induce them to engage in it. Why, then, should they be opposed? Why should those calling themselves Christians, take every possible opportunity of thwarting and rendering null the labors of men such as these? Grant that there may be bad and designing persons among them, does this circumstance affect the cause itself? Surely not. Why then should not the foreigners, instead of opposing and laboring to subvert their measures, endeavor to aid these devoted people in their most laborious task, or if they do not aid, let them at least assume a neutrality, and neither place themselves in the ranks of opposition, nor endeavor to induce others to do so.

10th.—This morning I saw the king for the first time.[3] He is a very young man, only about twenty years of age, of ordinary size, and rather ordinary appearance. He was dressed in a little blue jacket, such as is worn by sailors when ashore, white pantaloons, and common black hat. He was walking in the street at a rapid, and not very dignified gate, and was followed closely by about twenty natives. Some of these were rather fantastically dressed, with old naval coats and rusty epaulets, which had seen long service, and huge sabres with iron scabbards, which jingled on the ground as the wearer stalked majestically along. Others were habited plainly, like their master, and some few were of the true tatterdemalion school. I had the curiosity to follow the royal escort for a little way to see what would become of them all; they soon turned a corner and halted near a little waggon which had just stopped. The king approached the vehicle and handed from it an old and venerable looking native, (who I afterwards learned was the chief *Kekeoeva*, the former guardian of the king,) and they walked off arm in arm in a very affectionate manner, followed, as before, by the motley group of retainers.

The natives have very generally become acquainted with the pursuits of my companion and myself, and at almost all hours of the day, our mansion is beseiged by men, women and children. Some bring shells, pearls, living birds, cocoanuts, bananas, &c., to sell, and others are attracted by curiosity to see us, which is no doubt much excited in regard to the use which we intend making of all the strange things they bring us.

Sunday, 11th.—Mr. Jones, the consul, called for us this morning, and we accompanied him to the Seamen's chapel in our neighborhood, the only church in the town in which English service is performed. The chapel is a handsome building of *adobes*, or sun-dried bricks, lately erected, and, as its name imports, is intended chiefly for the benefit of the mariners who visit the island. It is surmounted by a handsome dome and belfry of wood, from which the bell was pealing out its solemn notes as we approached it. The Rev. John Deill, the pastor, officiated, to whom we were introduced at the conclusion of the service.

In the afternoon, Mr. N. and myself walked with the consul to the native church, at the lower extremity of the town. This is an enormous building, one hundred and ninety-six feet in length by sixty in breadth, and capable of containing four thousand people. It is built in the native style, of grass tied in bundles on a rude frame work of sticks, and the ridge pole, which extends along the whole length of the apex of the roof within, is supported by numerous roughly hewn pillars driven into the ground. The natives, in great numbers, were flocking to the church; men in every variety of costume, from the plain and dignified dress of the European gentleman, to the simple and primitive tapa or native cloth; and women, from the gay hat and feathers, silk gowns and stays of polished life, to the light and much better adapted robe of the country, with its invariable accompaniment, the *pau* or waist-fillet of figured calico. While we were standing, surveying the moving throng, we observed a little two wheeled cart approach, drawn by four men in the native dress, in which sat one of the great rotund beauties of the island, attired in gay silk, with a large black hat, from which drooped a magnificent ostrich feather. This was *Kinau*, the ex-queen, and wife of *Kekuanoa*, the commandante of the fort, commonly called the colonel. At the door of the church she was assisted to dismount; and as she swept along by us and entered the aisle, she made us a low and graceful bow, tossing back her great head, and looking around upon the company assembled, with the air of one who expected profound admiration and unlimited homage. In the church, we were invited by Kekuanoa to take a seat on the bench beside him and his wife; and when Mr. Bingham commenced the service by reading a native hymn, Kinau did me the honor to present me with her book, pointing to the place with a dignified and patronising air, which I acknowledged with all suitable respect.

The sermon, in the narrative language, by Mr. Bingham, was delivered in an easy and fluent manner, and in the whole of the great concourse there was scarcely a movement during the service. All seemed deeply engaged in the business for which they had assembled; and as I looked around upon the quiet and attentive multitude, a comparison with the wild and idolatrous scenes which their assemblies exhibited in times past was irresistibly forced upon me.

A few days after this I was introduced by Captain Charlton, his Britanic majesty's consul, to the king KAUIKEAOULI, or TAMEHAMEHA III, as he is sometimes called. He was accompanied by John Young, one of his prime favorites, a fine, noble looking young man, who I thought looked much more like a king than his master. His majesty was very condescending and kind. He conversed easily and freely, though in broken English, and having understood that I had been somewhat of a traveller, was very curious to hear my adventures through the wild regions of the west. The stories of buffalo and grizzly bear hunting pleased him particularly, and his dark eye actually glittered as I recounted to him the stirring and thrilling incidents of the wild buffalo chace, and the no less moving perils of the encounter with the fierce bear of the prairies. He remarked that he should enjoy such hunting; that here there was nothing for his amusement but the chasing of wild cattle, and the common athletic exercise of quoits, bar-heaving, &c., but he should like to see these big buffalo and bears, and then asked me, with great simplicity, if I suppose he could kill them.

The king is said to be one of the strongest and most active men on the island. He is not yet encumbered with flesh, like most of the chiefs, and he has all the elasticity and vigor of youth, superadded to a naturally strong and robust frame. He has a great fancy for all kinds of break-neck adventures, and I have no doubt, that, were he transplanted to the plains of the west, he would soon be a hunter of the first water.

The food of the natives consists principally of an article called *poe*, which is made by beating the baked roots of the taro; (*Arum eaculanium*,) on a sort of wooden trencher, with a large oval stone. The mass so prepared is mixed with a small quantity of water, and set aside for several days to ferment, when it becomes about of the consistence of paper hanger's paste. This, with fish, either raw or baked, constitutes almost the sole food of the common people. Give a Sandwich Islander plenty of poe, with a raw fish or two, at each meal, and he asks for nothing more; deprive him of his dear loved sour paste, and he loses his spirits, and is miserable. I have seen this strikingly shown in the case of the Islanders at the Columbia. The poor Kanakas tried their utmost to manufacture a sort of poe—sweet potatoes, Irish potatoes, and even wappatoos, were operated upon, but all to no purpose; and when our brig left the river, their farewell's to us were mingled with desires loudly expressed, that on our return, we would bring them each a calabash of poe.

The manner in which an islander takes his food is primitive to the last degree. He seats himself cross-legged upon the ground with his calabash before him, and a fish and a little pile of salt on a wooden dish by his side. His two first fingers are immersed in the paste, and stirred round several times until enough adheres to coat them thickly, when they are carried by a quick motion to the mouth, which is open to receive them, and are sucked clean—a little pinch with the fingers is then taken of the fish which is perhaps floundering beside him, followed by a similar pinch of salt, to season the whole repast.

The principal beauty of the islanders, in their own estimation, consists in their being enormously fat, some of them weighing upwards of three hundreds pounds, and measures are consequently resorted to, that will successfully and expeditiously produce this much desired result. With this view, the chiefs take but little exercise and eat enormously of the nutritive paste before spoken of. After they have stuffed as much as their stomachs will contain, without the risk of positive suffocation, they roll over on their backs upon the ground, grunting like huge swine, when two attendance approach and place themselves on each side of the patient. One wields a *kahili*, or feather fly brush, to cool his master, and keep off the mosquetoes, while the other commences his operations by punching his fist violently into the stomach of the fallen man, who, with a great snort, acknowledges his consciousness, and the pleasure he derives from it. Soon the other fist of the serving man follows, and the regular *kneading* process is performed; at first, slowly and cautiously, but gradually increasing in quickness and severity until the attendant is forced to stop for breath, and the poor stupified lump of obesity forgets to grunt in unison with the rapidly descending blows. This is the operation called *rumi-rumi,* and is usually continued from ten to fifteen minutes, after which the patient rises, yawns, stretches his limbs, and calls loudly for another calabash of poe. This custom is followed almost exclusively by the chiefs, but is not confined to the male sex, the women enjoying the luxury equally with the men. The rumi-rumi is also practised in cases of abdominal pains, and in dyspeptic complaints. Even the foreigners sometimes resort to it, and find it beneficial.

17th—Mr. N. and myself were invited to participate in a *lu-au* dinner, to be given in the valley of Nuano this afternoon. At about 2 o'clock, Mr. Jones called for us, and furnished us with good horses, upon which we mounted, and galloped off to the valley. After a delightful ride of about five miles, over a good, though rather stony road, between the hills which enclose the valley, we arrived at a pretty little temporary cottage, formed entirely of the broad green leaves of the *ti* plant, and perched on a picturesque hill, overlooking the whole extent of our ride. Here we found a number of the foreign gentlemen; others soon joined us, and our company consisted of fifty or sixty persons, the king, John Young, and several other distinguished natives being of the party.

As the collation was not yet ready to be served up, Mr. Jones, Captain Hinckley, Mr. N. and myself remounted our horses for a visit to the great *pari*, or precipice, two miles above. We found the road somewhat rough, and very hilly, in some places extremely narrow, and the path wound constantly through bushes and tall ferns to the elevated land which, we were approaching. When within a few hundred yards of the precipice, we left our horses in charge of several native boys, who had followed us for the purpose, and ascended to the edge of the pari. The wind was blowing a gale, so that it was necessary to remove our hats and bind up our heads with handkerchiefs, and when we stood upon the cliff, some care was required to keep our footing, and to brace ourselves against the furious blast which was eddying around the summit.

The pari is an almost perpendicular precipice, of about six hundred feet, composed of basaltic rock, with occasional strata of hard white clay.[4]

On the north is seen the fertile and beautiful valley of Kolau, with its neat little cottages, taro-patches and fields of sugar cane, spread out before you like a picture; and beyond, is the indented shore, with its high and pointed cliffs, margining the ocean as far as the eye can discern. Down this precipice on the north side, is a sort of rude path, which the natives have constructed, and up this we saw a number of them toiling, clinging with their hands to the jutting crags above, to raise and support their bodies in the ascent. As they approached nearer to us, I was surprised to perceive that every man bore a burthen on his shoulder; some had large calabashes of poe, suspended one on each end of a long pole, and others carried living pigs, similarly suspended, by having their feet tied together, and the pole passed between them. The porkers, although hanging back downwards, in a position not the most comfortable, did not complain of the treatment, until they were deposited on the terra firma of the summit, when they tuned their pipes to a lusty squeal, and made amends for their former silence.

This spot is the scene of the last great battle of King Tamehameha, by which he acquired the sole and absolute sovereignty of the whole Sandwich group. The routed army of the petty island king was driven to take refuge among the wild crags of the pari, and hither it was followed by the conquering forces of the invader. No quarter was shown. The fugitives were hunted like savage beasts, and, almost to a man, were hurled from the giddy height and dashed to pieces on the frightful rocks below.

On returning to the cottage, we found that the dinner had been *dished* up, and that the guests were about taking their seats. Our table was the green grass, upon which had been arranged, with native taste, a circular *table cloth*, composed of ti leaves, placed one above another.

On this the viands were laid. They consisted of fat pigs, and fat dogs, turkies, chickens, boiled ham, and fish, with vegetables of various kinds, taro, sweet potatoes, &c.,—all cooked in the native manner, in pits made in the ground, in which heated stones had been placed. Each pig and dog had such a stone within him, and around it had been wrapped a quantity of ti leaves, which were eaten as greens, and were excellent. The whole of the cookery was, in fact, very superior, and would have delighted the most fastidious epicure of our own enlightened land. We had also various liquors: Champagne, cherry, Madeira, and mountain dew, and were waited upon by native men and boys, with chaplets of green bound around their heads, and their persons profusely ornamented with the "fern and heather of their native valleys." Among the attendants, Mr. Mills, or Deacon Mills, as he is sometimes called, stood preeminent; he acted as purveyor and major domo; was every where at the same moment, and showed, by his uniform conduct, that he was fully alive to the high responsibilities of his office.

When the meats were removed, wine usurped the board, toasts were drunk, and songs were sung, and all was hilarity and cheerfulness.

Towards evening the whole party mounted their horses and galloped down the valley into the town. As we entered the precincts we formed ourselves into a battalion, and reined in our horses to a dignified trot, in order to pass a troop of gay native ladies who were returning from a visit to Waititi. At the head of this equestrian cavalcade, I was surprised to observe the large person of Madam Kinau, sitting astride upon a noble steed which evidently made an effort to curvet and appear proud of its queenly burthen.

While we were proceeding at this slow gait, a man suddenly sprang up behind my saddle and fixed his arms firmly around my waist. I was not more astonished than my horse at this intrusion; and the spirited animal which I rode, not being accustomed to carrying double, and feeling unwilling to be so imposed upon, began kicking up his heels, and darting wildly about the road. I requested the intruder to dismount instantly, but the only attention which was paid to this was a reply, in the native language, which I did not understand. Supposing him to be one of the servants who had been heated by the refuse wine of the feast, and considering myself in real danger from the unruly conduct of my horse, I turned half round and dealt my merry companion a blow in the chest, which I intended should have unseated him. How was I astonished to hear the exclamation, "don't strike so hard, *hauri*," from him who occupied my crupper, and I was not long in discovering that the joker was the king, Kauikeaouli, himself. I apologized in the best manner I could, though out of breath with the exertion of restraining the fiery horse. His majesty did not seem in the least offended, but passing one arm each side of me, and taking the bridle in his hands, he guided the animal into one of the largest stores of the town, through which we went jumping and prancing, followed by all the king's train, and several white men of the party.

Chapter XII

February 10th.—Mr. Nuttall and myself were kindly invited by Captain Hinckley, to take a trip with him to the island of Kauai, in the brig Avon, owned by him. We embarked this morning, and with the pilot on board sailed out of the harbor. This being one of the leeward islands, towards which the trade-winds always blow, we made the passage quickly; and in the evening ran into the harbor of Koloa, and anchored within half a mile of the shore.

The next morning we landed in our boat, and took possession of a large untenanted native house, near the beach, belonging to Captain H. Our servant busied himself in making our new residence comfortable, arranging the bedding and mosquitoe curtains, procuring mats for partitions, and, finally, in setting before us a good breakfast, cooked on the spot. We had scarcely finished our meal, when two horsemen rode up, and dismounting at the door, entered the house. Our visitors proved to be the king and John Young, who had mounted their horses this morning for a cattle hunt on the hills, but hearing of the arrival of the foreigners, had hastened to pay their respects to us, and assure us of their protection. The king, and his train came a few days since to this island, and propose remaining two or three weeks longer; his majesty's object appears to be to inspect the condition of his people here, and to give them an opportunity of evincing their loyalty and affection. He was so kind as to express much interest for Mr. N. and myself, gave us one of his own body servants for our attendant, while we remain, and promised that in the afternoon he would send us some provisions.

Shortly after the king left us, we were visited by the Rev. P. J. Gulick, the missionary of this station, to whom I had a letter from my kind friend, Mr. Deill, and after sitting half an hour, we accompanied him to his house, about a mile distant.[1]

This part of the island of Kauai exhibits no particularly interesting features: from the beach to the mission station there is a good road made by the natives over a gentle ascent of about two miles, on each side of which taro patches, yam and maize fields abound. Back from the ocean and at right angles with it, are seen several ranges of long, high hills, with narrow valleys between; the hills are covered with low trees of *Tu-tui* and *Pandanus,* and the valleys with dense bushes, tall ferns, and broad leaved bananas.

The good missionary introduced us to his wife, a very intelligent and agreeable woman, and to his three pretty children, and we spent an hour with them very pleasantly. In the afternoon we returned to our cottage near the beach, where we found a native waiting for us with a hand cart filled with provisions of various kinds, which he said the king had sent to us as a present. There was a very large hog, three pigs, three or four turkies, and several pairs of chickens, all living; with vegetables in great abundance, taro, sweet-potatoes, melons, &c. I thought the man must certainly have made a mistake, but he assured me that it was right: "the king had sent them to the '*hauris*' (foreigners) who had just arrived, and wished him to say that in *tree* days he would send them as much more." His majesty had evidently measured our appetites by the standard of his own people, and we determined to see him immediately, and countermand the sumptuous order which he had given. It may be proper here to remark, that when the king, or chiefs, wish a supply of provisions, or any other articles in which the common people deal, or of which they are possessed, a messenger is sent to demand such things in the name of the master, and a levy is made upon the property of the poor native, without any kind of compensation being ever offered. We were aware that our provision had been obtained in this way, and were unwilling that the industrious poor should lose their labor to contribute to our wants, preferring to buy from them the necessary supplies.

The next day we paid another visit to Mr. Gulick, and accepted a pressing invitation to make our home with him, his house being much more convenient to the valleys, which we wished to explore in search of birds and other natural objects. Here we had another interview with the king, who insisted upon our occupying a fine large house in the neighborhood of Mr. Gulick's residence, as a depository for our collection. We accepted this offer with pleasure, and the missionary's accommodation being somewhat contracted, we used the king's house as our study and sleeping apartment, taking our meals with the family of our kind friend.

We made here several long excursions over the hills and through the deep valleys, without much success. The birds are the same as those we found and collected at Oahu, but are not so numerous.[2] They are principally creepers (*Certhia*) and honey-suckers (*Nectarinia;*) feed chiefly upon flowers, and the sweet juice of the banana, and some species are very abundant. The native boys here have adopted a singular mode of catching the honey sucking birds. They lay themselves flat upon their backs on the ground, and cover their whole bodies with bushes, and the campanulate flowers of which the birds are in search. One of these flowers is then held by the lower portion of the tube between the finger and thumb; the little bird inserts his long, curved bill to the base of the flower, when it is immediately seized by the fingers of the boy, and the little flutterer disappears beneath the mass of bushes. In this way, dozens of beautiful birds are taken, and they are brought to us living and uninjured.

20th.—We expected to have left the island several days ago, but the Avon has not returned, and she would not now be able to come, in consequence of a steady S. W. wind which has prevailed for the last week. Our ammunition, and materials for the preparation of birds, are entirely exhausted, and we cannot here obtain a supply, so we amuse ourselves in collecting shells on the beaches, plants, and fishes, &c. We are living very comfortably in the house furnished us by the king, and we have become completely domesticated in the agreeable family of Mr. Gulick. We sometimes spend whole days wandering along the rocky coast in search of shells, and in these journeys we are always accompanied by a troop of boys and girls, and sometimes men and women, often to the number of twenty or thirty.[3] They are indefatigable shell-hunters, and prove of great service to us, being compensated for each one that they bring us, with pins or needles. In their habits they are perfectly amphibious, diving into the sea, and through the dashing surf without the least hesitation, and exploring the bottom for an almost incredible time without rising to breathe.

In these sub-marine excursions they frequently find the echinus with spines four or five inches in length, and the black, lumpish substance called *beche la mer*. Both these animals are eaten by them as they are taken living from the water; the spines of the former are knocked off against the rocks, and the soft contents of the case sucked out; the latter, after having the tough outside skin removed, are eaten like biscuits to qualify the meal. There is also another sea animal which is considered by the natives a great delicacy, the sepia, or cuttle fish. This is a large, ill-looking creature, with an oval body, and eight or ten long arms or tentacula; within the cavity of the thorax is a sack, containing a fluid resembling ink, and as the teeth are sunk into this, the black juice squirts into the face of the masticator, while the long feelers are twisting about his head like serpents.

March 5th.—The king, and Kakeoeva, the governor of the island, called on us before breakfast this morning, and participated in our family worship. After the usual prayer in English, by Mr. Gulick, Kakeoeva supplicated in his own language, in a tone peculiarly solemn and impressive, which concluded the service. This chief is, I believe, a sincerely good and pious man, and his piety consists not in profession alone, but is exhibited in numerous acts of unassuming benevolence to his oppressed people and in uniform and well directed efforts for meliorating their condition. He enforces all the *tabus*, which have for their object the suppression of vice and immorality, and while his people fear to disobey his injunctions in the smallest particular, they love and venerate him as their father and friend.

The principal object of the king in calling upon us, was to request, (which he did with great apparent diffidence,) the *loan* of his house for a few days, as he wished to move his residence to a point nearer the sea, in order to catch the first glimpse of the white sails of the Avon, the arrival of which he is expecting with great anxiety. His impatience to return to Oahu is said, sometimes, to exceed all reasonable bounds; he works himself into a perfect fury; fancies that every thing is going wrong at home, and that his people are in mourning for his protracted absence; but although he is a king, the winds of heaven will not obey him, and, with the meanest follower in his train, he must wait the appointed time.

We, of course, relinquished the house cheerfully, and, with the assistance of our native servants, transferred all our commodities to the mansion of the good missionary.

In the afternoon, the natives from all parts of the island began to flock to the king's temporary residence. The petty chiefs, and head men of the villages, were mounted upon all sorts of horses, from the high-headed and high-mettled Californian steed, to the shaggy and diminutive poney raised on their native hills; men women and children were running on foot, laden with pigs, calabashes of poe, and every production of the soil; and though last, certainly not least, in the evening there came the troops of of the island, with fife and drum, and "tinkling cymbal," to form a body guard for his majesty, the king. Little houses were put up all around the vicinity, and thatched in an incredibly short space of time, and when Mr. N. and myself visited the royal mansion, after nightfall, we found the whole neighborhood metamorphosed; a beautiful little village had sprung up as by magic, and the retired studio of the naturalists had been transformed into a royal banquet hall. His majesty soon recognised us in the crowd, and taking us each by the hand, led us into the house, and introduced us to the queen, Kalama, who received us in a dignified and very pleasant manner, and made room for us near her at the supper, which the attendants were spreading upon the ground. This consisted of a variety of meats *lu aued*, fish, potatoes and taro, and before each guest was placed a little calabash of poe. As I have before stated, this last article is an indispensable requisite in the economy of every meal; and even the refined Kauikeaouli who has abolished in his own person so many of the rude customs of his forefathers, must sip a little poe to conclude his supper. I remarked, however, that on this occasion, he did not soil his fingers, as is usual, but fed himself with a spoon as delicately as possible. The queen, on the contrary, and all the chiefs assembled at the board, plunged their hands into the paste, and sucked their fingers after the approved fashion.

When the supper was concluded, the people were all assembled under a *ranai*, or shed, which had been constructed for the occasion, and prayer was made in a loud and solemn tone, by John Ii, the king's chaplain. At its conclusion, the people scattered themselves about as before; some were collected in little groups on the ground, smoking their short pipes, and regaling themselves with sea-urchins and succulent cuttle-fish, while the stentor voices of the royal guard pealed out an "all's well" from their station near the palace of the monarch.

This royal guard, which we had an opportunity of seeing next morning, would not do discredit to a militia gathering in yankee land. Like our own redoubtable troops, the men were of all sizes, in every variety of costume, and with all sorts of weapons; muskets without bayonets or locks, and no muskets at all, broomsticks, and tin pans, swords, pistols, and taro tops. They were arranged every morning in the line before the door of the palace, and laboriously drilled in the manual exercise, by James Young, a half-caste who has been in America. Poor fellows they had hard duty to perform, and were no doubt longing for the time when his majesty should depart, that they might exchange the arduous and uncongenial duties of the camp, for the toil of their simple husbandry.

About a week after, as I was strolling near the palace, which, being on a hill, commanded a fine view of the ocean, the cry of "sail, O!" was uttered in a joyful tone, by a bevy of urchins, who were on the look out, and was echoed all round the neighborhood. The king, who had of late become unusually dull and spiritless, seemed suddenly to have acquired new life. He was seen rushing out of the house, like one distraught, and jumping and capering all about in a perfect agony of joy. Seeing me near him, he grasped my hand in the most cordial manner, while his eyes filled with tears: "We shall go back to Oahu, hauri, my people want me again; the wind has changed, and this ship is sent to take me away."

I participated in the anxiety of the king to return; for, in addition to the ennui which is always the accompaniment of a forced detention, even in pleasant places, I feared that our brig would leave the islands for the Columbia without us, and we should thus lose the opportunity of hailing the opening of spring, in our western world, the season which, of all others, is the most interesting to us.

Next morning a messenger came to the king from Waimea, a port about fourteen miles distant, with information that the schooner which we had seen had put in there, and only waited the embarkation of this majesty to steer direct for Oahu. No time was lost in taking advantage of this opportunity; and at noon, the spot, which the day before had swarmed with hundreds of dingy natives, was silent and untenanted.

On the day following, learning that the schooner had not sailed, and fearing that the Avon would not arrive early enough, I wrote a letter to the king, requesting a passage for Mr. N. and myself, with him. To this,—which I sent by a runner,—the following laconic reply was received. It was directed, "To the missionary, Mr. Gulick," and is rendered literally from the native language: "Say thou to the foreigners, we have sailed. Let them look out when we arrive there. KING KAUIKEAOULI."

The arrival spoken of, alluded to the vessel passing the port of Koloa, where the schooner would back her topsails and lie to that we might board her in a canoe.

After some consideration, and consultation with Mr. Gulick, we concluded that we would decline the king's offer, as we knew the vessel would be crowded, and therefore uncomfortable; and as the wind now blew steadily in its accustomed quarter, we had little doubt of the early arrival of the Avon. In the afternoon we saw the schooner of the king come booming along past us, the deck, and even the rigging, alive with natives, but a messenger whom we had previously sent off, saved them the trouble of bringing to; and away went the little vessel on a wind, and soon became a dim and ill-defined speck upon the far horizon.

15th.—A sail was descried at daylight this morning, bearing towards our island; and while we were at breakfast, two fishermen called, to tell us that it was the Avon come at last. She was standing towards the harbor of Koloa, with a fair wind, and when Mr. N. and myself arrived at the beach, she was hauling in under the land. The captain and Mr. Smith, a resident of Honoruru, came on shore to meet us. They informed us that the king arrived at Oahu last evening, after an unusually boisterous and uncomfortable passage, and that his majesty was almost beside himself with joy to receive once more the warm and affectionate greetings of his people at home.

The brig was detained here a day, in order to take in a cargo of live stock, pigs, goats, &c.; and the next morning we bade adieu to the kind and affectionate family of the missionary, and went on board. In the afternoon our anchor was weighed, and we were soon ploughing the wide ocean, while the rugged, iron-bound coast of Kanai rapidly receded from our view. We had on board several distinguished natives, as passengers, the principal of whom was Kekeoeva, the governor, and at each meal which we took on board, the old gentleman asked an audible blessing on the viands, and regularly returned thanks at its conclusion.

After a pleasant passage of two days we arrived at Oahu, and were warmly greeted by our friends, who sympathized with us, and thought that our long tarriance must have been peculiarly irksome. They knew but little of the resources of the naturalist; they knew not that the wild forest, the deep glen, and the rugged mountain-top possess charms for him which he would not exchange for gilded palaces; and that to acquaint himself with nature, he gladly escapes from the restraints of civilization, and buries himself from the world which cannot appreciate his enjoyment.

22d.—I joined a party of ladies and gentlemen this morning, in an excursion to Pearl river, on the west side of the island. We embarked in several small schooners and barges, and had a delightful trip of two hours. The king, who was with us, with a number of his favorites, John Young, Kanaina, Halileo, &c., procured for our accommodation several native houses, in which we slung our cots and hammocks, and slept at night. We took our meals under a large shaded ranai, and the amusements of the party were riding, shooting, and a variety of sylvan games, which rendered our pic-nic of three days a constant scene of pleasant festivity.

The night before we left, the gentlemen of the party were invited by the king to witness the curious exhibition called the "calabash dance." We entered a large house, crowded with natives, with the exception of a wide space in the middle, which had been reserved for the performers. These were men and women to the number of ten or twelve, in a state of almost perfect nudity, having no covering, except the small maro of tapa bound around the loins. Each was furnished with a very large gourd, having the neck attached, and from the under surface the contents had been removed through a small aperture. The performers kneeled upon the ground, and each grasped his gourd by the neck and lifted it, when one of the number commenced a strange kind of howling song, lifting his calabash with one hand and beating it with the other so as to keep accurate time to his music. This song was soon taken up by the others, until the whole company joined, and every one thumped his calabash most musically. I was astonished at the exceeding nicety with which this was done. No band of civilized drummers could have kept time more perfectly, nor flourished their sticks with more grace, than did these unsophisticated people their inartificial instruments. During the whole time of the singing, the bodies of the performers were not idle; every muscle seemed to have something to do; and was incessantly brought into action by the strange motions, twistings and contortions of the frame, which were also as evanescent as the sound of their voices. This singular exhibition possessed interest for me, as being one of the idolatrous games, which in former years constituted a portion of their religious exercises. The calabash dance is now almost exploded, the natives generally not understanding the manipulations, and like other relics of heathenism it is of course discouraged by the missionaries, and will probably soon be unknown amongst them.

On the 26th of March we embarked on board the brig May Dacre, upon our return to the Columbia. As we sailed out of the harbor, and the lovely shore of the island became more and more indistinct, I felt sad and melancholy in the prospect of parting, perhaps for ever, from the excellent friends who had treated me with such uniform kindness and hospitality.

We have had an accession to our crew of thirty Sandwich Islanders, who are to be engaged in the salmon fishery on the Columbia, and six of these have been allowed the unusual privilege of taking their wives with them. Some six or eight natives, of both sexes, friends and relatives of the crew, came on board when we weighed anchor, and their parting words were prolonged until the brig cleared the reef, and her sails had filled with the fresh trade wind. They thought it then time to withdraw, and putting their noses together after their fashion, they bade their friends an affectionate farewell, and without hesitation dashed into the sea, and made directly for shore. I thought of blue sharks, tiger sharks, and shovel-noses, and would not have run such a risk for all the wealth of all the islands.

April 5th.—Yesterday we had an *inkling* of a storm. Some rain fell in the morning early; and at noon, while sitting in the cabin, I was startled by hearing a flapping, as if all the sails in the ship were being torn to pieces, and a roaring not unlike the escape of steam from the boiler of a boat. Upon ascending to the deck, I observed the whole ocean covered with glittering white foam, the surges boiling, and dashing, and breaking over our vessel as she labored heavily amongst them. The sails were flapping about most unmanageably. The studding-sails,—all of which had been set before the storm,—were immediately taken in, and hands were sent aloft to furl the remaining canvas, until in a very short time we were scudding under bare poles, and defying the utmost fury of the elements. In about half an hour, the storm abated, and, soon after, entirely ceased; the wind became steady and fresh; the white folds of our canvas were again let loose, and away we went before a "smashing breeze" at the rate of ten knots an hour.

12th.—The mate has several times spoken of having seen large flocks of a small species of land bird sailing around the vessel. As it is scarcely possible they could have emigrated from the distant continent, Captain L. supposes that they are residents of a small uninhabited island, somewhere in these latitudes, which has long been supposed to exist, but has never been found. He who may hereafter be so fortunate as to discover this land, will probably be rendered a rich man for the remainder of his days, for it doubtless abounds in seal, which never having been interrupted, will be easily taken. I have not seen the birds spoken of, but suppose them to be some of the small *grallæ*.[4]

On the 15th, the wind, which had for several days been light, began steadily to increase, until we were running ten knots by the log. In the afternoon, the atmosphere became thick and hazy, indicating our approach to the shores of the continent. In a short time, a number of the small Auks,—of which we saw a few immediately after leaving the Columbia,—were observed sporting in the waves, close under our bows; then several gulls of the species common on the river, and soon after large flocks of geese and canvass-back ducks.

The sea gradually lost its legitimate deep blue color, and assumed a dirty, green appearance, indicating soundings. Upon heaving the lead here, we got only eleven fathoms, and found that we had approached nearer than was prudent, having been misled by the haze. Wore ship immediately, and soon saw land, bearing east, which we ascertained to be south of Cape Disappointment. Stood off during the night, and the next morning at 4 o'clock, the wind favoring us, we bore up for the cape, and at 7 crossed the dangerous bar safely, and ran direct for the river.

Chapter XIII

Passage up the Columbia—Birds—A trip to the
Wallammet—Methodist missionaries—their prospects—
Fort William—Band-tail pigeons—Wretched condition
of the Indians at the falls—A Kallapooyah village—
Indian cemetery—Superstitions—Treatment of
diseases—Method of steaming—"Making medicine"—
Indian sorcerers—An interruption of festivities—Death
of Thornburg—An inquest—Verdict of the jury—
Inordinate appetite for ardent spirits—Misfortunes of
the American Company—Eight men drowned—Murder
of two trappers by the Banneck Indians—Arrival of
Captain Thing—His meeting and skirmish with the
Blackfeet Indians—Massacre—A narrow escape.

O n the 16th, we anchored abreast of Oak point.[1] Our decks
were almost immediately crowded with Indians to welcome
us, and among them we recognised many faces with which
we were familiar. *Chinamus*, the Chinook chief, was the principal of
these, who, with his wife, *Aillapust*, or *Sally*, as she is called at the fort,
paid us an early visit, and brought us red deer and sturgeon to regale
upon after our voyage.

On the afternoon of the next day, we ran up to Warrior's point, the
brig's old mooring ground. The people here had been anxious to see
us; extensive preparations had been made to prosecute the salmon
fishery, and the coopers have been engaged the whole winter in making
barrels to accommodate them. Mr. Walker, the missionaries' quondam
associate, was in charge of the post, and he informed us that Captain
Wyeth had returned only a few weeks since from the upper country,
where he had been spending the winter, engaged in the arduous
business of trapping, in the prosecution of which he had endured great
and various hardships.[2]

May 12th.—The rainy season is not yet over; we have had almost
constant showers since we arrived, but now the weather appears settled.

Birds are numerous, particularly the warblers, (*Sylvia.*) Many of these are migratory, remaining but a few weeks: others breed here, and reside during the greater part of the summer. I have already procured several new species.[3]

20th.—Mr. Wyeth, came down from Walla-walla yesterday, and this morning I embarked with him in a large canoe, manned by Kanakas, for a trip to the Wallammet falls in order to procure salmon. We visited fort William, (Wyeth's new settlement upon Wappatoo island,) which is about fifteen miles from the lower mouth of the Wallammet.[4] We found here the missionaries, Messrs. Lee and Edwards, who arrived to-day from their station, sixty miles above. They give flattering accounts of their prospects here; they are surrounded by a considerable number of Indians who are friendly to the introduction of civilization and religious light, and who treat them with the greatest hospitality and kindness. They have built several comfortable log houses, and the soil in their vicinity they represent as unusually rich and productive. They have, I think, a good prospect of being serviceable to this miserable and degraded people; and if they commence their operations judiciously, and pursue a steady, unwavering course, the Indians in this section of country may yet be redeemed from the thraldom of vice, superstition, and indolence, to which they have so long submitted, and above which their energies have not enabled them to rise.

The spot chosen by Captain W. for his fort is on a high piece of land, which will probably not be overflown by the periodical freshets, and the soil is the rich black loam so plentifully distributed through this section of country. The men now live in tents and temporary huts, but several log houses are constructing which, when finished, will vie in durability and comfort with Vancouver itself.

21st.—The large band-tail pigeon (*Colomba fasciata*) is very abundant near the river, found in flocks of from fifty to sixty, and perching upon the dead trees along the margin of the stream. They are feeding upon the buds of the balsam poplar; are very fat, and excellent eating. In the course of the morning, and without leaving the canoe, I killed enough to supply our people with provision for two days.

24th—We visited the falls to-day, and while Captain W. was inspecting the vicinity to decide upon the practicability of drawing his seine here, I strolled into the Indian lodges on the bank of the river. The poor creatures were all living miserably, and some appeared to be suffering absolute want. Those who were the best supplied, had nothing more than the fragments of a few sturgeons and lamprey eels, kamas bread, &c. To the roofs of the lodges were hung a number of crooked bladders, filled with rancid seal oil, used as a sort of condiment with the dry and unsavory sturgeon.

On the Klakamas river, about a mile below, we found a few lodges belonging to Indians of the Kalapooyah tribe.[5] We addressed them in Chinook, (the language spoken by all those inhabiting the Columbia below the cascades) but they evidently did not comprehend a word, answering in a peculiarly harsh and gutteral language, with which we were entirely unacquainted.[6] However, we easily made them understand by signs that we wanted salmon, and being assured in the same significant manner that they had none to sell, we decamped as soon as possible, to escape the fleas and other vermin with which the interior of their wretched habitations were plentifully supplied. We saw here a large Indian cemetery. The bodies had been buried under the ground, and each tomb had a board at its head, upon which was rudely painted some strange, uncouth figure. The pans, kettles, clothing, &c., of the deceased, were all suspended upon sticks, driven into the ground near the head board.

June 6th—The Indians frequently bring us salmon, and we observe that, invariably, before they part with them, they are careful to remove the hearts. This superstition, is religiously adhered to by all the Chinook tribe. Before the fish is split and prepared for eating, a small hole is made in the breast, the heart taken out, roasted, and eaten in silence, and with great gravity. This practice is continued only during the first month in which the salmon make their appearance, and is intended as a kind of propitiation to the particular deity or spirit who presides over the finny tribes. Superstition in all its absurd and most revolting aspects is rife among this people. They believe in "black spirits, and white, blue spirits, and grey," and to each grizzly monster some peculiar virtue or ghastly terror is attributed. When a chief goes on a hunting or fishing excursion, he puts himself under the care of one of these good spirits, and if his expedition is unsuccessful, he affirms that the antagonist evil principle has gained the victory; but this belief does not prevent his making another, and another attempt, in the hope, each time, that his guardian genius will have the ascendency.

In their treatment of diseases, they employ but few remedies, and these are generally simple and inefficacious. Wounds are treated with an application of green leaves, and bound with strips of pine bark, and in some febrile cases, a sweat is administered. This is effected by digging a hole two or three feet deep in the ground, and placing within it some hemlock or spruce boughs moistened with water; hot stones are then thrown in, and a frame work of twigs is erected over the opening, and covered closely with blankets to prevent the escape of the steam. Under this contrivance, the patient is placed; and after remaining fifteen or twenty minutes, he is removed, and plunged into cold water.

Their mode of *"making medicine,"* to use their own term, is, however, very different from this. The sick man is laid upon a bed of mats and blankets, elevated from the ground, and surrounded by a raised frame work of hewn boards. Upon this frame two "medicine men" (sorcerers) place themselves, and commence chaunting, in a low voice, a kind of long drawn, sighing song. Each holds a stout stick, of about four feet long, in his hand, with which he beats upon the frame work., and keeps accurate time with the music. After a few minutes, the song begins to increase in loudness and quickness, (a corresponding force and celerity being given to the stick,) until in a short time the noise becomes almost deafening, and may well serve, in many instances, to accelerate the exit of him whom it is their intention to benefit.

During the administration of the medicine, the relations and friends of the patient are often employed in their usual avocations in the same house with him, and by his bedside; the women making mats, moccasins, baskets, &c., and the men lolling around, smoking or conversing upon general subjects. No appearance of sorrow or concern is manifested for the brother, husband, or father, expiring beside them, and but for the presence and ear-astounding din of the medicine men, you would not know that anything unusual had occurred to disturb the tranquillity of the family circle.

These medicine men are, of course, all impostors, their object being simply the acquisition of property; and in case of the recovery of the patient, they make the most exorbitant demands of his relations; but when the sick man dies, they are often compelled to fly, in order to escape the vengeance of the survivors, who generally attribute the fatal termination to the evil influence of the practitioner.

July 4th.—This morning was ushered in by the firing of cannon on board our brig, and we had made preparations for spending the day in festivity, when, at about 9 o'clock, a letter was received from Mr. Walker, who has charge of the fort on Wappatoo island, stating that the tailor, Thornburg, had been killed this morning by Hubbard, the gunsmith, and requesting our presence immediately, to investigate the case, and direct him how to act.

Our boat was manned without loss of time, and Captain L. and myself repaired to the fort, where we found every thing in confusion.[7] Poor Thornburg, whom I had seen but two days previously, full of health and vigor, was now a lifeless corpse; and Hubbard, who was more to be pitied, was walking up and down the beach, with a countenance pale and haggard, from the feelings at war within.

We held an inquest over the body, and examined all the men of the fort severally, for the purpose of eliciting the facts of the case, and, if warranted by the evidence, to exculpate Hubbard from blame in the commission of the act. It appeared that, several weeks since, a dispute arose between Hubbard and Thornburg, and the latter menaced the life of the former, and had since been frequently heard to declare that he would carry the threat into effect on the first favorable opportunity. This morning, before daylight, he entered the apartment of Hubbard, armed with a loaded gun, and a large knife, and after making the most deliberate preparations for an instant departure from the room, as soon as the deed should be committed, cocked his gun, and prepared to shoot at his victim. Hubbard, who was awakened by the noise of Thornburg's entrance, and was therefore on the alert, waited quietly until this crisis, when cocking his pistol, without noise, he took deliberate aim at the assassin, and fired. Thornburg staggered back, his gun fell from his grasp, and the two combatants struggled hand to hand. The tailor, being wounded, was easily overcome, and was thrown violently out of the house, when he fell to the ground, and died in a few minutes. Upon examining the body, we found that the two balls from the pistol had entered the arm below the shoulder, and escaping the bone, had passed into the cavity of the chest. The verdict of the jury was "justifiable homicide," and a properly attested certificate, containing a full account of the proceedings, was given to Hubbard, as well for his satisfaction, as to prevent future difficulty, if the subject should ever be investigated by a judicial tribunal.

This Thornburg was an unusually bold and determined man, fruitful in inventing mischief, as he was reckless and daring in its prosecution.

His appetite for ardent spirits was of the most inordinate kind. During the journey across the country, I constantly carried a large two-gallon bottle of whiskey, in which I deposited various kinds of lizards and serpents and when we arrived at the Columbia the vessel was almost full of these crawling creatures. I left the bottle on board the brig when I paid my first visit to the Wallammet falls, and on my return found that Thornburg had decanted the liquor from the precious reptiles which I had destined for immortality, and he and one of his pot companions had been "happy" upon it for a whole day. This appeared to me almost as bad as the "tapping of the Admiral," practised with such success by the British seamen; but unlike their commander, I did not discover the theft until too late to save my specimens, which were in consequence all destroyed.[8]

11th.—Mr. Nuttall, who has just returned from the dalles, where he has been spending some weeks, brings distressing intelligence from above. It really seems that the "Columbia River Fishing and Trading Company" is devoted to destruction; disasters meet them at every turn, and as yet none of their schemes have prospered. This has not been for want of energy or exertion. Captain W. has pursued the plans which seemed to him best adapted for insuring success, with the most indefatigable perseverance and industry, and has endured hardships without murmuring, which would have prostrated many a more robust man; nevertheless, he has not succeeded in making the business of fishing and trapping productive, and as we cannot divine the cause, we must attribute it to the Providence that rules the destinies of men and controls all human enterprises.

Two evenings since, eight Sandwich Islanders, a white man and an Indian woman, left the cascades in a large canoe laden with salmon, for the brig. The river was as usual rough and tempestuous, the wind blew a heavy gale, the canoe was capsized, and eight out of the ten sank to rise no more. The two who escaped, islanders, have taken refuge among the Indians at the village below, and will probably join us in a few days.

Intelligence has also been received of the murder of one of Wyeth's principal trappers, named Abbot, and another white man who accompanied him, by the Banneck Indians. The two men were on their way to the Columbia with a large load of beaver, and had stopped at the lodge of the Banneck chief, by whom they had been hospitably entertained. After they left, the chief, with several of his young men, concealed themselves in a thicket, near which the unsuspicious trappers passed, and shot and scalped them both.

These Indians have been heretofore harmless, and have always appeared to wish to cultivate the friendship of the white people. The only reason that can be conceived for this change in their sentiments, is that some of their number may lately have received injury from the white traders, and, with true Indian animosity, they determined to wreak their vengeance upon the whole race. Thus it is always unsafe to travel among Indians, as no one knows at what moment a tribe which has always been friendly, may receive ill treatment from thoughtless, or evil-designing men, and the innocent suffer for the deeds of the guilty.

August 19th.—This morning, Captain Thing (Wyeth's partner) arrived from the interior. Poor man! he looks very much worn by fatigue and hardships, and seven years older than when I last saw him. He passed through the Snake country from Fort Hall, without knowing of the hostile disposition of the Bannecks, but, luckily for him, only met small parties of them, who feared to attack his camp. He remarked symptoms of distrust and coolness in their manner, for which he was, at the time, unable to account. As I have yet been only an hour in his company, and as a large portion of this time was consumed in his business affairs, I have not been able to obtain a very particular account of his meeting and skirmish with the Blackfeet last spring, a rumor of which we heard several weeks since. From what I have been enabled to gather, amid the hurry and bustle consequent upon his arrival, the circumstances appear to be briefly these. He had made a camp on Salmon river, and, as usual, piled up his goods in front of it, and put his horses in a pen erected temporarily for the purpose, when, at about daybreak, one of his sentries heard a gun discharged near. He went immediately to Captain T.'s tent to inform him of it, and at that instant a yell sounded from an adjacent thicket, and about five hundred Indians,—three hundred horse and two hundred foot,—rushed out into the open space in front. The mounted savages were dashing to and fro across the line of the camp, discharging their pieces with frightful rapidity, while those who had not horses, crawled around to take them in the rear.

Nothwithstanding the galling fire which the Indians were constantly pouring into them, Captain T. succeeded in driving his horses into the thicket behind, and securing them there, placing over them a guard of three men as a check to the savages who were approaching from that quarter. He then threw himself with the remainder of his little band, behind the bales of goods, and returned the fire of the enemy. He states that occasionally he was gratified by the sight of an Indian tumbling from his horse, and at such times a dismal, savage yell was uttered by the rest, who then always fell back a little, but returned immediately to the charge with more than their former fury.

At length the Indians, apparently wearied by their unsuccessful attempts to dislodge the white men, changed their mode of attack, and rode upon the slight fortification, rapidly and steadily. Although they lost a man or two by this (for them) unusually bold proceeding, yet they succeeded in driving the brave little band of whites to the cover of the bushes. They then took possession of the goods, &c., which had been used as a defence, and retired to a considerable distance, where they were soon joined by their comrades on foot, who had utterly failed in their attempt to obtain the horses. In a short time, a man was seen advancing from the main body of Indians towards the scene of combat, holding up his hand as a sign of amity, and an intimation of the suspension of hostilities, and requested a "talk" with the white people. Captain T., with difficulty repressing his inclination to shoot the savage herald down, was induced, in consideration of the safety of his party, to dispatch an interpreter towards him. The only information that the Blackfeet wished to communicate was, that having obtained all the goods of the white people, they were now willing that they should continue their journey in peace, and that they should not again be molested. The Indians then departed, and the white men struck back on their trail, towards Fort Hall. Captain Thing lost every thing he had with him, all his clothing, papers, journals, &c. But he should probably be thankful that he escaped with his life, for it is known to be very unusual for these hostile Indians to spare the lives of white men, when in their power, the acquisition of property being generally with them only a secondary consideration.

Captain T. had two men severely, but not mortally, wounded. The Indians had seven killed, and a considerable number wounded.

20th—Several days since a poor man came here in a most deplorable condition, having been gashed, stabbed, and bruised in a manner truly frightful. He had been travelling on foot constantly for fifteen days, exposed to the broiling sun, with nothing to eat during the whole of this time, except the very few roots which he had been able to find.

He was immediately put in the hospital here, and furnished with every thing necessary for his comfort, as well as surgical attendance. He states that he left Monterey, in California, in the spring, in company with seven, men, for the purpose of coming to the Wallammet to join Mr. Young, an American, who is now settled in that country. They met with no accident until they arrived at a village of *Potameos* Indians,* about ten days journey south of this. Not knowing the character of these Indians, they were not on their guard, allowing them to enter their camp, and finally to obtain possession of their weapons. The Indians then fell upon the defenceless little band with their tomahawks and knives, (having no fire arms themselves, and not knowing the use of those they had taken,) and, ere the white men had recovered from the panic which the sudden and unexpected attack occasioned, killed four of of them. The remaining four fought with their knives as long as they were able, but were finally overpowered, and this poor fellow left upon the ground, covered with wounds, and in a state of insensibility. How long he remained in this situation, he has no means of ascertaining; but upon recovering, the place was vacated by all the actors in the bloody scene, except his three dead companions, who were lying stark and stiff where they fell. By considerable exertion, he was enabled to drag himself into a thicket near, for the purpose of concealment, as he rightly conjectured that their captors would soon return to secure the trophies of their treacherous victory, and bury the corpses. This happened almost immediately after; the scalps were torn from the heads of the slain, and the mangled bodies removed for interment. After the most dreadful and excruciating sufferings, as we can well believe, the poor man arrived here, and is doing well under the excellent and skilful care of Doctor Gairdner.[9] I examined most of his wounds yesterday. He is literally covered with them, but one upon the lower part of his face is the most frightful. It was made by a single blow of a tomahawk, the point of which entered the upper lip, just below the nose, cutting entirely through both the upper and lower jaws and chin, and passing deep into the side of the neck, narrowly missing the large jugular vein. He says he perfectly recollects receiving this wound. It was inflicted by a powerful savage, who at the same time tripped him with his foot, accelerating his fall. He also remembers distinctly feeling the Indian's long knife pass five separate times into his body; of what occurred after this he knows nothing. This is certainly

---

*Called by the inhabitants of this country, the *"rascally Indians"* from their uniformly evil disposition, and hostility to white people.

by far the most horrible looking wound I ever saw, rendered so, however, by injudicious treatment and entire want of care in the proper apposition of the sundered parts; he simply bound it up as well as he could with his handkerchief, and his extreme anguish caused him to forget the necessity of accuracy in this respect. The consequence is, that the lower part of his face is dreadfully contorted, one side being considerably lower than the other. A union by the first intention has been formed, and the ill-arranged parts are uniting.

This case has produced considerable excitement in our little circle. The *Potameos* have more than once been guilty of acts of this kind, and some of the gentlemen of the fort have proposed fitting out an expedition to destroy the whole nation, but this scheme will probably not be carried into effect.

Chapter XIV

❦

*Indians of the Columbia—their melancholy condition—
Departure of Mr. Nuttall and Dr. Gairdner—A new
vocation—Arrival of the Rev. Samuel Parker—his
object—Departure of the American brig—Swans—
Indian mode of taking them—A large wolf—An Indian
mummy—A night adventure—A discovery, and
restoration of stolen property—Fraternal tenderness of
an Indian—Indian vengeance—Death of Waskéma, the
Indian girl—"Busy-body" the little chief—A village of
Kowalitsk Indians—Ceremony of "making medicine"—
Exposure of an impostor—Success of legitimate
medicines—Departure from Fort Vancouver for a visit
to the interior—Arrival of a stranger—"Cape Horn"—
Tilki, the Indian chief—Indian villages—Arrival at
Fort Walla-walla—Sharp-tailed grouse—
Commencement of a journey to the Blue mountains.*

The Indians of the Columbia were once a numerous and powerful people; the shore of the river, for scores of miles, was lined with their villages; the council fire was frequently lighted, the pipe passed round, and the destinies of the nation deliberated upon. War was declared against neighboring tribes; the deadly tomahawk was lifted, and not buried until it was red with the blood of the savage; the bounding deer was hunted, killed, and his antlers ornamented the wigwam of the red man; the scalps of his enemies hung drying in the smoke of his lodge, and the Indian was happy. Now, alas! where is he?—gone;—gathered to his fathers and to his happy hunting grounds; his place knows him no more. The spot where once stood the thickly peopled village, the smoke curling and wreathing above the closely packed lodges, the lively children playing in the front, and their indolent parents lounging on their mats, is now only indicated by a heap of undistinguishable ruins. The depopulation here has been truly fearful. A gentleman told me, that only four years ago, as he wandered near what had formerly been a thickly peopled village, he counted no less than sixteen dead, men and women, lying unburied and festering in the sun in front of their habitations. Within the houses all were sick; not one had escaped the contagion; upwards of a hundred individuals, men, women, and children, were writhing in agony on the floors of the houses, with no one to render them any assistance. Some were in the dying struggle, and clenching with the convulsive grasp of death their disease-worn companions, shrieked and howled in the last sharp agony.[1]

Probably there does not now exist one, where, five years ago, there were a hundred Indians; and in sailing up the river, from the cape to the cascades, the only evidence of the existence of the Indian, is an occasional miserable wigwam, with a few wretched, half-starved occupants. In some other places they are rather more numerous; but the thoughtful observer cannot avoid perceiving that in a very few years the race must, in the nature of things, become extinct; and the time is probably not far distant, when the little trinkets and toys of this people will be picked up by the curious, and valued as mementoes of a nation passed away for ever from the face of the earth. The aspect of things is very melancholy. It seems as if the fiat of the Creator had gone forth, that these poor denizens of the forest and the stream should go hence, and be seen of men no more.

In former years, when the Indians were numerous, long after the establishment of this fort, it was not safe for the white men attached to it to venture beyond the protection of its guns without being fully armed. Such was the jealousy of the natives towards them, that various deep laid schemes were practised to obtain possession of the post, and massacre all whom it had harbored; now, however, they are as submissive as children. Some have even entered into the services of the whites, and when once the natural and persevering indolence of the man is worn off, he will work well and make himself useful.

About two hundred miles southward, the Indians are said to be in a much more flourishing condition, and their hostility to the white people to be most deadly. They believe that we brought with us the fatal fever which has ravaged this portion of the country, and the consequence is, that they kill without mercy every white man who trusts himself amongst them.

October 1st.—Doctor Gairdner, the surgeon of Fort Vancouver, took passage a few days ago to the Sandwich Islands, in one of the Company's vessels. He has been suffering for several months, with a pulmonary affection, and is anxious to escape to a milder and more salubrious climate. In his absence, the charge of the hospital will devolve on me, and my time will thus be employed through the coming winter. There are at present but few cases of sickness, mostly ague and fever, so prevalent at this season. My companion, Mr. Nuttall, was also a passenger in the same vessel. From the islands, he will probably visit California, and either return to the Columbia by the next ship, and take the route across the mountains, or double Cape Horn to reach his home.[2]

16th.—Several days since, the Rev. Samuel Parker, of Ithaca, N. York, arrived at the fort.[3] He left his home last May, travelled to the rendezvous on the Colorado, with the fur company of Mr. Fontinelle, and performed the remainder of the journey with the Nez Percé or Cheaptin Indians. His object is to examine the country in respect to its agricultural and other facilities, with a view to the establishment of missions among the Indians. He will probably return to the States next spring, and report the result of his observations to the board of commissioners, by whose advice his pioneer journey has been undertaken.*

On the 17th, I embarked with this gentleman in a canoe, for a visit to the lower part of the river. We arrived at the American brig in the afternoon, on board of which we quartered for the night, and the next morning early, the vessel cast off from the shore. She has her cargo of furs and salmon on board, and is bound to Boston, via the Sandwich and Society Islands. Mr. Parker took passage in her to Fort George, and in the afternoon I returned in my canoe to Vancouver.

December 1st.—The weather is now unusually fine. Instead of the drenching rains which generally prevail during the winter months, it has been for some weeks clear and cool, the thermometer ranging from 35° to 45°. The ducks and geese, which have swarmed throughout the country during the latter part of the autumn, are leaving us, and the swans are arriving in great numbers. These are here, as in all other places, very shy; it is difficult to approach them without cover; but the Indians have adopted a mode of killing them which is very successful; that of drifting upon the flocks at night, in a canoe, in the bow of

---

*Mr. Parker has since published an account of this tour, to which the reader is referred, for much valuable information, relative to the condition of the Indians on our western frontier.

which a large fire of pitch pine has been kindled. The swans are dazzled, and apparently stupefied by the bright light, and fall easy victims to the craft of the sportsman.

20th—Yesterday one of the Canadians took an enormous wolf in a beaver-trap. It is probably a distinct species from the common one, (*lupus,*) much larger and stronger, and of a yellowish cinereous color. The man states that he found considerable difficulty in capturing him, even after the trap had been fastened on his foot. Unlike the lupus, (which is cowardly and cringing when made prisoner,) he showed fight, and seizing the pole in his teeth, with which the man attempted to despatch him, with one backward jerk, threw his assailant to the ground, and darted at him, until checked by the trap chain. He was finally shot, and I obtained his skin, which I have preserved.

I have just had a visit from an old and intelligent Indian chief, who lives near. It is now almost midnight, but for the last hour I have heard the old man wandering about like an unquiet spirit, in the neighborhood of my little mansion, and singing snatches of the wild, but sweetly musical songs of his tribe. It is a bitter night, and supposing the old man might be cold, I invited him to a seat by my comfortable fire.

He says, "eighty snows have chilled the earth since *Maniquon* was born." Maniquon has been a great warrior; he has himself taken twenty scalps between the rising and setting of the sun. Like most old people, he is garrulous, and, like all Indians, fond of boasting of his warlike deeds. I can sit for hours and hear old Maniquon relate the particulars of his numerous campaigns, his ambushes, and his "scrimmages" as old Hawk-eye would say. When he once gets into the spirit of it, he springs upon his feet, his old, sunken eyes sparkle like diamonds set in bronze, and he whirls his shrunken and naked arm around his head, as though it still held the deadly tomahawk. But in the midst of his excitement, seeming suddenly to recollect his fallen state, he sinks into his chair.

"Maniquon is not a warrior now—he will never raise his axe again—his young men have deserted his lodge—his sons will go down to their graves, and the squaws will not sing of their great deeds."

I have several times heard him speak the substance of these words in his own language, and in one instance he concluded thus:

"And who made my people what they are?" This question was put in a low voice, almost a whisper, and was accompanied by a look so savage and malignant, that I almost quailed before the imbecile old creature. I, however, answered quickly, without giving him time to reply to his own question.

"The Great Spirit, Maniquon," pointing with my finger impressively upwards.

"Yes, yes—it *was* the Great Spirit; it was not the *white man!*" I could have been almost angry with the old Indian for the look of deadly hostility with which he uttered these last words, but that I sympathized with his wounded pride, and pitied his sorrows too much to harbor any other feeling than commiseration for his manifold wrongs.

February 3d, 1836.—During a visit to Fort William, last week, I saw, as I wandered through the forest, about three miles from the house, a canoe, deposited, as is usual, in the branches of a tree, some fourteen feet from the ground. Knowing that it contained the body of an Indian, I ascended to it for the purpose of abstracting the skull; but upon examination, what was my surprise to find a perfect, embalmed body of a young female, in a state of preservation equal to any which I had seen from the catacombs of Thebes. I determined to obtain possession of it, but as this was not the proper time to carry it away, I returned to the fort, and said nothing of the discovery which I had made.

That night, at the witching hour of twelve, I furnished myself with a rope, and launched a small canoe, which I paddled up against the current to a point opposite the mummy tree. Here I ran my canoe ashore, and removing my shoes and stockings, proceeded to the tree, which was about a hundred yards from the river. I ascended, and making the rope fast around the body, lowered it gently to the ground ; then arranging the fabric which had been displaced, as neatly as the darkness allowed, I descended, and taking the body upon my shoulders, bore it to my canoe, and pushed off into the stream. On arriving at the fort, I deposited my prize in the store house, and sewed around it a large Indian mat, to give it the appearance of a bale of guns. Being on a visit to the fort, with Indians whom I had engaged to paddle my canoe, I thought it unsafe to take the mummy on board when I returned to Vancouver the next day, but left directions with Mr. Walker to stow it away under the hatches of a little schooner, which was running twice a week between the two forts.

On the arrival of this vessel, several days after, I received, instead of the body, a note from Mr. Walker, stating that an Indian had called at the fort, and demanded the corpse. He was the brother of the deceased, and had been in the habit of visiting the tomb of his sister every year. He had now come for that purpose, from his residence near the "*tum-water*," (cascades,) and his keen eye had detected the intrusion of a stranger on the spot hallowed to him by many successive pilgrimages. The canoe of his sister was tenantless, and he knew the spoiler to have been a white man, by the tracks upon the beach, which did not incline inward like those of an Indian.

The case was so clearly made out, that Mr. W. could not deny the fact of the body being in the house, and it was accordingly delivered to him, with a present of several blankets, to prevent the circumstance from operating upon his mind to the prejudice of the white people. The poor Indian took the body of his sister upon his shoulders, and as he walked away, grief got the better of his stoicism, and the sound of his weeping was heard long after he had entered the forest.

25th.—Several weeks ago the only son of Ke-ez-a-no, the principal chief of the Chinooks, died. The father was almost distracted with grief, and during the first paroxysm attempted to take the life of the boy's mother, supposing that she had exerted an evil influence over him which had caused his death. She was compelled to fly in consequence, and put herself under the protection of Dr. McLoughlin, who found means to send her to her people below. Disappointed in this scheme of vengeance, the chief determined to sacrifice all whom he thought had ever wronged his son, or treated him with indignity; and the first victim whom he selected was a very pretty and accomplished Chinook girl, named Waskéma, who was remarkable for the exceeding beauty of her long black hair. Waskéma had been solicited by the boy in marriage, but had refused him, and the matter had been long forgotten, until it was revived in the recollection of the father by the death of his son. Ke-ez-a-no despatched two of his slaves to Fort William, (where the girl was at that time engaged in making moccasins for Mr. W. and where I had seen her a short time previously,) who hid themselves in the neighborhood until the poor creature had embarked in her canoe alone to return to her people, when they suddenly rushed upon her from the forest which skirted the river, and shot two balls through her bosom. The body was then thrown into the water, and the canoe broken to pieces on the beach.

Tapeo the brother of Waskéma delivered to me a letter from Mr. W. detailing these circumstances, and amid an abundance of tears which he shed for the loss of his only and beloved sister, he denounced the heaviest vengeance upon her murderer. These threats, however, I did not regard, as I knew the man would never dare to raise his hand against his chief, but as expression relieves the overcharged heart, I did not check his bursts of grief and indignation.

A few days after this, Ke-ez-a-no himself stalked into my room. After sitting a short time in silence, he asked if I believed him guilty of the murder of Waskéma. I replied that I did, and that if the deed had been committed in my country, he would be hanged. He denied all agency in the matter, and placing one hand upon his bosom, and pointing upwards with the other, called God to witness that he was innocent. For the moment I almost believed his asseverations. but calling to mind the strong and undeniable evidence against him, with a feeling of horror and repugnance, I opened the door and bowed him out of the house.

March 1st.—There is an amusing little Indian living in this neighborhood, who calls himself "*tanas tie,*" (little chief,) and he is so probably in every sense of the term. In person, he stands about four feet six, in his moccasins; but no exquisite in the fashionable world, no tinselled dandy in high life, can strut and stamp, and fume with more dignity and self consequence. His name, he says, is Quâlaskin; but in the fort, he is known by the cognomen of *"busy body,"* from his restless anxiety to pry into every body's business, and his curiosity to know the English name of every article he sees; *ikata ookook?—ikata ookook?* (what is this?—what is this?) *kahtah pasiooks yahhalle?* (what is its English name?) are expressions which he is dinning in your ears, whenever he enters a room in the fort. If you answer him, he attempts the pronunciation after you, and it is often not a little ludicrous. He is evidently proud of the name the white people have given him, not understanding its import, but supposing it to be a title of great honor and dignity. If he is asked his Indian name, he answers very modestly, Quâlaskin, (muddy river,) but if his *pasiooks yahhalle* is required, he puffs up his little person to its utmost dimensions, and tells you with a simper of pride and self complacency, that it is "*mizzy moddy.*"

16th.—Doctor W. F. Tolmie, one of the surgeons of the Hudson's Bay Company, has just arrived from Fort Langley, on the coast, and has relieved me of the charge of the hospital, which will afford me the opportunity of peregrinating again in pursuit of specimens. [4] The spring is just opening, the birds are arriving, the plants are starting from the ground, and in a few weeks, the wide prairies of the Columbia will appear like the richest flower gardens.

May 13th.—Two days ago I left the fort, and am now encamped on a plain below Warrior's point. Near me are several large lodges of Kowalitsk Indians; in all probably one hundred persons. As usual, they give me some trouble by coming around and lolling about my tent, and importuning me for the various little articles that they see. My camp-keeper, however, (a Klikatat) is an excellent fellow, and has no great love for Kowalitsk Indians, so that the moment he sees them becoming troublesome, he clears the coast, *sans ceremonie*. There is in one of the lodges a very pretty little girl, sick with intermittent fever; and to-day the "medicine man" has been exercising his functions upon the poor little patient; pressing upon its stomach with his brawny hands until it shrieked with the pain, singing and muttering his incantations, whispering in its ears, and exhorting the evil spirit to pass out by the door, &c. These exhibitions would be laughable did they not involve such serious consequences, and for myself I always feel so much indignation against the unfeeling impostor who operates, and pity for the deluded creatures who submit to it, that any emotions but those of risibility are excited.

I had a serious conversation with the father of this child, in which I attempted to prove to him, and to some twenty or thirty Indians who were squatted about the ground near, that the "medicine man" was a vile impostor, that he was a fool and a liar, and that his manipulations were calculated to increase the sufferings of the patient instead of relieving them. They all listened in silence, and with great attention to my remarks, and the wily conjurer himself had the full benefit of them: he stood by during the whole time, assuming an expression of callous indifference which not even my warmest vituperations could affect. Finally I offered to exhibit the strongest proof of the truth of what I had been saying, by pledging myself to cure the child in three days, provided the "medicine man" was dismissed without delay. This, the father told me, required some consideration and consultation with his people, and I immediately left the lodge and took the way to my camp, to allow them an opportunity of discussing the matter alone.

Early next morning the Indian visited me, with the information that the "medicine man" had departed, and he was now anxious that I should make trial of my skill. I immediately administered to the child an active cathartic, followed by sulphate of quinine, which checked the disease, and in two days the patient was perfectly restored.[5]

In consequence of my success in this case, I had an application to administer medicine to two other children similarly affected. My stock of quinine being exhausted, I determined to substitute an extract of the bark of the dogwood, (*Cornus Nuttalli*) and taking one of the parents into the wood with his blanket, I soon chipped off a plentiful supply, returned, boiled it in his own kettle, and completed the preparation in his lodge, with most of the Indians standing by, and staring at me, to comprehend the process.

This was exactly what I wished; and as I proceeded, I took some pains to explain the whole matter to them, in order that they might at a future time be enabled to make use of a really valuable medicine, which grows abundantly every where throughout the country. I have often thought it strange that the sagacity of the Indians should not long ago have made them acquainted with this remedy; and I believe, if they had used it, they would not have had to mourn the loss of hundreds, or even thousands of their people who have been swept away by the demon of ague and fever.[6]

I administered to each of the children about a scruple of the extract per day. The second day they escaped the paroxysm, and on the third were entirely well.

June 26th.—I left Vancouver yesterday, with the summer brigade, for a visit to Walla-walla, and its vicinity. The gentlemen of the party are, Peter Ogden, Esq., chief factor, bound to New Caledonia, Archibald McDonald, Esq., for Colville, and Samuel Black, Esq., for Thompson's river, and the brigade consists of sixty men, with nine boats.

27th.—We arrived yesterday at the upper cascades, and made in the course of the day three portages. As is usual in this place, it rained almost constantly, and the poor men engaged in carrying the goods, were completely drenched. A considerable number of Indians are employed here in fishing, and they supply us with an abundance of salmon. Among them I recognise many of my old friends from below.

29th.—This morning the Indian wife of one of the men gave birth to a little girl. The tent in which she was lying was within a few feet of the one which I occupied, and we had no intimation of the matter being in progress until we heard the crying of the infant. It is truly astonishing with what ease the parturition of these women is performed; they generally require no assistance in delivery, being fully competent to manage the whole paraphernalia themselves. In about half an hour after this event we got under way, and the woman walked to the boat, carrying her new born infant on her back, embarked, laughed, and talked as usual, and appeared in every respect as well as if nothing had happened.

This woman is a most noble specimen of bone and muscle, and so masculine in appearance, that were she to cast the petticoat, and don the breeches, the cheat would never be discovered, and but few of the *lords of the creation* would be willing to face the Amazon. She is particularly useful to her husband. As he is becoming rather infirm, she can protect him most admirably. If he wishes to cross a stream in travelling without horses or boats, she plunges in without hesitation, takes him upon her back, and lands him safely and expeditiously upon the opposite bank. She can also kill and dress an elk, run down and shoot a buffalo, or spear a salmon for her husband's breakfast in the morning, as well as any man-servant he could employ. Added to all this, she has, in several instances, saved his life in skirmishes with Indians, at the imminent risk of her own, so that he has some reason to be proud of her.

In the afternoon, we passed the bold, basaltic point, known to the *voyageurs* by the name of "Cape Horn." The wind here blew a perfect hurricane, and but for the consummate skill of those who managed our boats, we must have had no little difficulty.

30th—We were engaged almost the whole of this day in making portages, and I had, in consequence, some opportunity of prosecuting my researches on the land. We have now passed the range of vegetation; there are no trees or even shrubs; nothing but huge, jagged rocks of basalt, and interminable sand heaps. I found here a large and beautiful species of marmot, (the *Arctomys Richardsonii)* several of which I shot.[7] Encamped in the evening at the village of the Indian chief, Tilki. I had often heard of this man, but I now saw him for the first time. His person is rather below the middle size, but his features are good, with a Roman cast, and his eye is deep black, and unusually fine. He appears to be remarkably intelligent, and half a century before the generality of his people in civilization.

July 3d.—This morning we came to the open prairies, covered with wormwood bushes. The appearance, and strong odor of these, forcibly remind me of my journey across the mountains, when we frequently saw no vegetation for weeks, except this dry and barren looking shrub.

The Indians here are numerous, and are now engaged in catching salmon, lamprey eels, &c. They take thousands of the latter, and they are seen hanging in great numbers in their lodges to dry in the smoke. As soon as the Indians see us approach, they leave their wigwams, and run out towards us, frequently wading to their breasts in the water, to get near the boats. Their constant cry is *pi-pi, pi-pi,* (tobacco, tobacco,) and they bring a great variety of matters to trade for this desirable article; fish, living birds of various kinds, young wolves, foxes, minks, &c.

On the evening of the 6th, we arrived at Walla-walla or Nez Percés fort, where I was kindly received by Mr. Pambrun, the superintendent.

The next day the brigade left us for the interior, and I shouldered my gun for an excursion through the neighborhood. On the west side of the little Walla-walla river, I saw, during a walk of two miles, at least thirty rattlesnakes, and killed five that would not get out of my way. They all seemed willing to dispute the ground with me, shaking their rattles, coiling and darting at me with great fury. I returned to the fort in the afternoon with twenty-two sharp-tailed grouse, *(Tetrao phasianellus,)* the product of my day's shooting.[8]

25th—I mounted my horse this morning for a journey to the Blue mountains. I am accompanied by a young half breed named Baptiste Dorion,*who acts as guide, groom, interpreter, &c., and I have a pack horse to carry my little *nick-nackeries.* We shaped our course about N. E. over the sandy prairie, and in the evening encamped on the Morro river, having made about thirty miles.

On our way, we met two Walla-walla Indians driving down a large band of horses. They inform us that the Snakes have crossed the mountain to commence their annual thieving of horses, and they are taking them away to have them secure. I shall need to keep a good look out to my own small caravan, or I shall be under the necessity of turning pedestrian.

---

*This is the son of old Pierre Dorion, who makes such a conspicuous figure in Irving's "Astoria."

Chapter XV

A village of Kayouse Indians—their occupation—
appearance and dresses of the women—family worship—
its good effects—Visit to the Blue mountains—Dusky
grouse—Return to Walla-walla—Arrival of Mr.
McLeod, and the missionaries—Letters from home—
Death of Antoine Goddin, the trapper—A renegado
white man—Assault by the Walla-walla Indians—
Missionary duties—Passage down the Columbia—
Rapids—A dog for supper—Prairies on fire—A
nocturnal visit—Fishing Indians—Their romantic
appearance—Salmon huts—The shoots—Dangerous
navigation—Death of Tilki—Seals—Indian stoicism
and contempt of pain—Skookoom, the strong chief—his
death—Maiming, an evidence of grief—Arrival at Fort
Vancouver—A visit to Fort George—Indian
cemeteries—Lewis and Clarke's house—A medal—Visit
to Chinook—Hospitality of the Indians—Chinamus'
house—The idol—Canine inmates.

July 26th.—At noon, to-day, we arrived at the Utalla, or Emmitilly river, where we found a large village of Kayouse Indians, engaged in preparing kamas. Large quantities of this root were strewed about on mats and buffalo robes; some in a crude state, and a vast quantity pounded, to be made into cakes for winter store. There are of the Indians, about twelve or fifteen lodges. A very large one, about sixty feet long by fifteen broad, is occupied by the chief, and his immediate family. This man I saw when I arrived at Walla-walla, and I have accepted an invitation to make my home in his lodge while I remain here. The house is really a very comfortable one; the rays of the sun are completely excluded, and the ground is covered with buffalo robes. There are in the chief's lodge about twenty women, all busy as usual; some pounding kamas, others making leathern dresses, moccasins, &c. Several of the younger of these are very good looking,— I might almost say handsome. Their heads are of the natural form,—

not flattened and contorted in the horrible manner of the Chinooks;
—their faces are inclining to oval, and their eyes have a peculiarly sleepy
and languishing appearance. They seem as if naturally inclined to
lasciviousness, but if this feeling exists, it is effectually checked by their
self-enacted laws, which are very severe in this respect, and in every
instance rigidly enforced. The dresses of the women, (unlike the
Chinooks, they all *have* dresses,) are of deer or antelope skin, more or
less ornamented with beads and *hyquâs.** It consists of one piece, but
the part covering the bust, projects over the lower portion of the
garment, and its edges are cut into strings, to which a quantity of blue
beads are generally attached.

In the evening all the Indians belonging to the village assembled in
our lodge, and, with the chief for minister, performed divine service,
or family worship. This, I learn, is their invariable practice twice every
twenty-four hours, at sunrise in the morning, and after supper in the
evening. When all the people had gathered, our large lodge was filled.
On entering, every person squatted on the ground, and the *clerk* (a
sort of sub-chief) gave notice that the Deity would now be addressed.
Immediately the whole audience rose to their knees, and the chief
supplicated for about ten minutes in a very solemn, but low tone of
voice, at the conclusion of which an amen was pronounced by the
whole company, in a loud, swelling sort of groan. Three hymns were
then sung, several of the individuals present leading in rotation, and at
the conclusion of each, another amen. The chief then pronounced a
short exhortation, Occupying about fifteen minutes, which was
repeated by the clerk at his elbow in a voice loud enough to be heard
by the whole assembly. At the conclusion of this, each person rose,
and walked to one of the doors of the lodge, where, making a low
inclination of his body, and pronouncing the words "*tots sekan,*"(good
night,) to the chief, he departed to his home.

I shall hear this ceremony every night and morning while I remain,
and so far from being irksome, it is agreeable to me. It is pleasant to
see these poor degraded creatures performing a religious service; for
to say nothing of the good influence which it will exert in improving
their present condition, it will probably soften and harmonize their
feelings, and render them fitter subjects for the properly qualified
religious instruction which it is desirable they may some day receive.

---

*A long white shell, of the genus *Dentalium*, found on the coast.

The next morning, my friend the chief furnished me with fresh horses, and I and my attendant, with two Indian guides, started for a trip to the mountain. We passed up one of the narrow valleys or gorges which here run at right angles from the alpine land, and as we ascended, the scenery became more and more wild, and the ground rough and difficult of passage, but I had under me one of the finest horses I ever rode; he seemed perfectly acquainted with the country; I had but to give him his head, and not attempt to direct him, and he carried me triumphantly through every difficulty. Immediately as we reached the upper land, and the pine trees, we saw large flocks of the dusky grouse, *(Tetrao obscurus,)* a number of which we killed.[1] Other birds were, however, very scarce. I am at least two months too late, and I cannot too much regret the circumstance. Here is a rich field for the ornithologist at the proper season. We returned to our lodge in the evening loaded with grouse, but with very few specimens to increase my collection.

29th.—Early this morning our Indians struck their lodges, and commenced making all their numerous movables into bales for packing on the horses. I admired the facility and despatch with which this was done; the women alone worked at it, the men lolling around, smoking and talking, and not even once directing their fair partners in their task. The whole camp travelled with me to Walla-walla, where we arrived the next day.

Sept. 1st.—Mr. John M'Leod, a chief trader of the Hudson's Bay Company, arrived this morning from the rendezvous, with a small trading party. I had been anxiously expecting this gentleman for several weeks, as I intended to return with him to Vancouver. He is accompanied by several Presbyterian missionaries, the Rev. Mr. Spalding and Doctor Whitman, with their wives, and Mr. Gray, teacher.[2] Doctor Whitman presented me with a large pacquet of letters from my beloved friends at home. I need not speak of the emotions excited by their reception, nor of the trembling anxiety with which I tore open the envelope and devoured the contents. This is the first intelligence which I have received from them since I left the state of Missouri, and was as unexpected as it was delightful.

Mr. M'Leod informed me of the murder of Antoine Goddin, the half-breed trapper, by the Blackfeet Indians, at Fort Hall.—A band of these Indians appeared on the shore of the Portneuf river, opposite the fort, headed by a white man named Bird.—This man requested Goddin, whom he saw on the opposite side of the river, to cross to him with a canoe, as he had beaver which he wished to trade. The poor man accordingly embarked alone, and landing near the Indians, joined the circle which they had made, and *smoked the pipe of peace with them*. While Goddin was smoking in his turn, Bird gave a sign to the Indians, and a volley was fired into his back. While he was yet living, Bird himself tore the scalp from the poor fellow's head, and deliberately cut Captain Wyeth's initials, N. J. W. in large letters upon his forehead. He then hallooed to the fort people, telling them to bury the carcass if they wished, and immediately went off with his party.

This Bird was formerly attached to the Hudson's Bay Company, and was made prisoner by the Blackfeet, in a skirmish several years ago. He has since remained with them, and has become a great chief, and leader of their war parties. He is said to be a man of good education, and to possess the most unbounded influence over the savage people among whom he dwells. He was known to be a personal enemy of Goddin, whom he had sworn to destroy on the first opportunity.

We also hear, that three of Captain Wyeth's men who lately visited us, had been assaulted on their way to Fort Hall, by a band of Walla-walla Indians, who, after beating them severely, took from them all their horses, traps, ammunition, and clothing. They were, however, finally induced to return them each a horse and gun, in order that they might proceed to the interior, to get fresh supplies. This was a matter of policy on the part of the Indians, for if the white men had been compelled to travel on foot, they would have come immediately here to procure fresh horses, &c., and thus exposed the plunderers. Mr. Pambrun is acquainted with the ringleader of this band of marauders, and intends to take the first opportunity of inflicting upon him due punishment, as well as to compel him to make ample restitution for the stolen property, and broken heads of the unoffending trappers.

I have had this evening, some interesting conversation with our guests, the missionaries. They appear admirably qualified for the arduous duty to which they have devoted themselves, their minds being fully alive to the mortifications and trials incident to a residence among wild Indians; but they do not shrink from the task, believing it to be their religious duty to engage in this work. The ladies have borne the journey astonishingly; they look robust and healthy.

3d.—Mr. M'Leod and myself embarked in a large batteau, with six men, and bidding farewell to Mr. Pambrun and the missionaries, were soon gliding down the river. We ran, to-day, several rapids, and in the evening encamped about fifteen miles below the mouth of the Utalla river.

This running of rapids appears rather a dangerous business to those unaccustomed to it, and it is in reality sufficiently hazardous, except when performed by old and skilful hands. Every thing depends upon the men who manage the bow and stern of the boat. The moment she enters the rapid, the two guides lay aside their oars taking in their stead paddles, such as are used in the management of a canoe. The middle-men ply their oars; the guides brace themselves against the gunwale of the boat, placing their paddles edgewise down her sides, and away she goes over the curling, foaming, and hissing waters, like a race horse.

We passed to-day several large lodges of Indians, from whom we wished to have purchased fish, but they had none, or were not willing to spare any, so that we were compelled to purchase a *dog* for supper. I have said *we,* but I beg leave to correct myself, as I was utterly averse to the proceeding; not, however, from any particular dislike to the quality of the food, (I have eaten it repeatedly, and relished it,) but I am always unwilling, unless when suffering absolute want, to take the life of so noble and faithful an animal. Our hungry oarsmen, however, appeared to have no such scruples. The Indian called his dog, and he came to him, *wagging his tail!* He sold his companion for ten balls and powder! One of our men approached the poor animal with an axe. I turned away my head to avoid the sight, but I heard the dull, *sodden* sound of the blow. The tried friend and faithful companion lay quivering in the agonies of death at its master's feet.

We are enjoying a most magnificent sight at our camp this evening. On the opposite side of the river, the Indians have fired the prairie, and the whole country for miles around is most brilliantly illuminated. Here am I sitting crosslegged on the ground, scribbling by the light of the vast conflagration with as much ease as if I had a ton of oil burning by my side; but my eyes are every moment involuntarily wandering from the paper before me, to contemplate and admire the grandeur of the distant scene. The very heavens themselves appear ignited, and the fragments of ashes and burning grass-blades, ascending and careering about through the glowing firmament, look like brilliant and glorious birds let loose to roam and revel amid this splendid scene.

It is past midnight: every one in the camp is asleep, and I am this moment visited by half a dozen Indian fishermen, who are peering over my shoulders, and soliciting a smoke, so that I shall have to stop, and fill my calamet.

5th.—The Indians are numerous along the river, and all engaged in fishing; as we pass along, we frequently see them posted upon the rocks overhanging the water, surveying the boiling and roaring flood below, for the passing salmon. In most instances, an Indian is seen entirely alone in these situations, often standing for half an hour perfectly still, his eyes rivetted upon the torrent, and his long fish spear poised above his head. The appearance of a solitary and naked savage thus perched like an eagle upon a cliff, is sometimes, —when taken in connexion with the wild and rugged river scenery, —very picturesque. The spear is a pole about twelve feet in length, at the end of which a long wooden fork is made fast, and between the tines is fixed a barbed iron point. They also, in some situations, use a hand scoopnet, and stand upon scaffolds ingeniously constructed over the rapid water. Their winter store of dried fish is stowed away in little huts of mats and branches, closely interlaced, and also in *caches* under ground. It is often amusing to see the hungry ravens tearing and tugging at the strong twigs of the houses, in a vain attempt to reach the savory food within.

In the afternoon, we passed John Day's river, and encamped about sunset at the "shoots." Here is a very large village of Indians, (the same that I noticed in my journal, on the passage down,) and we are this evening surrounded by some scores of them.

6th.—We made the portage of the shoots this morning by carrying our boat and baggage across the land, and in half an hour, arrived at one of the upper *dalles.* Here Mr. M'Leod and myself debarked, and the men ran the dall. We walked on ahead to the most dangerous part, and stood upon the rocks about a hundred feet above to observe them. It really seemed exceedingly dangerous to see the boat dashing ahead like lightning through the foaming and roaring waters, sometimes raised high above the enormous swells, and dashed down again as if she were seeking the bottom with her bows, and at others whirled around and nearly sucked under by the whirlpools constantly forming around her. But she stemmed every thing gallantly, under the direction of our experienced guides, and we soon embarked again, and proceeded to the lower dalles. Here it is utterly impossible, in the present state of the water, to pass, so that the boat and baggage had to be carried across the whole portage. This occupied the remainder of the day, and we encamped in the evening at a short distance from the lower villages. The Indians told us with sorrowful faces of the recent death of their principal chief, Tilki. Well, thought I, the white man has lost a friend, and long will it be before we see his like again! The poor fellow was unwell when I last saw him, with a complaint of his breast, which I suspected to be pulmonary. I gave him a few simple medicines, and told him I should soon see him again. Well do I remember the look of despondency with which he bade me farewell, and begged me to return soon and give him more medicine. About two weeks since he ruptured a blood vessel, and died in a short time.

We see great numbers of seals as we pass along. Immediately below the Dalles they are particularly abundant, being attracted thither by the vast shoals of salmon which seek the turbulent water of the river. We occasionally shoot one of them as he raises his dog-like head above the surface, but we make no use of them; they are only valuable for the large quantity of oil which they yield.

We observe on the breasts and bellies of many of the Indians here, a number of large red marks, mostly of an oval form, sometimes twenty or thirty grouped together. These are wounds made by their own hands, to display to their people the unwavering and stoical resolution with which they can endure pain. A large fold of the skin is taken up with the fingers, and sliced off with a knife; the surrounding fibre then retreats, and a large and ghastly looking wound remains. Many that I saw to-day are yet scarcely cicatrized. There is a chief here who obtained the dignity which he now enjoys, solely by his numerous and hardy feats of this kind. He was originally a common man, and possessed but one wife; he has now six, and any of the tribe would think themselves honored by his alliance. He is a most gigantic fellow, about six feet four inches in height, and remarkably stout and powerful. The whole front of his person is covered with the red marks of which I have spoken, and he displays with considerable pride the two scars of a bullet, which entered the left breast, and passed out below the shoulder blade. This wound he also made with his own hand, by placing the muzzle of his gun against his breast, and pressing the trigger with his toe; and by this last, and most daring act, he was raised to the chief command of all the Indians on the north side of the river. Now that Tilki is no more, he will probably be chosen chief of all the country from the cascades to Walla-walla. I asked him if he felt no fear of death from the wound in his chest, at the time it was inflicted. He said, no; that his heart was strong, and that a bullet could never kill him. He told me that he was entirely well in a week after this occurrence, but that for two days he vomited blood constantly. He is named by the Indians "*Skookoom,*" (the strong.)

About six weeks after, Mr. M'Leod, who again returned from a visit to Walla-walla, informed me that the strong chief was dead. A bullet, (or rather two of them,) killed him at last, in spite of his supposed invulnerability. He was shot by one of his people in a fit of jealousy. *Skookoom* had assisted Mr. M'Leod with his boats across the portage, and, being a chief, he of course received more for the service than a common man. This wretch, who was but a serf in the tribe, chose to be offended by it, and vented his rage by murdering his superior. He fired a ball from his own gun into his breast, which brought him to the ground, and then despatched him with a second, which he seized from another. So poor Skookoom has passed away, and such is the frail tenure upon which an Indian chief holds his authority and his life. The murderer will no doubt soon die by the hand of some friend or relative of the deceased; he in his turn will be killed by another, and as usual, the bloody business will go on indefinitely, and may even tend to produce an open war between the rival parties.

I saw an old man here, apparently eighty years of age, who had given himself three enormous longitudinal gashes in his leg, to evince his grief for the loss of Tilki. From the sluggishness of the circulation in the body of the poor old creature, combined with a morbid habit, these wounds show no disposition to heal. I dressed his limb, and gave him a strict charge to have it kept clean, but knowing the universal carelessness of Indians in this respect, I fear my directions will not be attended to, and the consequence will probably be, that the old man will die miserably. I spoke to him of the folly of such inflictions, and took this opportunity of delivering a short lecture upon the same subject to the others assembled in his lodge. At 11 o'clock next day we arrived at the cascades, where we made the long portage, and at nine in the evening encamped in an ash grove, six miles above *Prairie de Thé.*

On the 8th, reached Vancouver, where we found two vessels which had just arrived from England.

On the 24th, I embarked in a canoe with Indians for Fort George, and arrived in two days. Here I was kindly received by the superintendent, Sir. James Birnie, and promised every assistance in forwarding my views.[3]

30th.—I visited to-day some cemeteries in the neighborhood of the fort, and obtained the skulls of four Indians. Some of the bodies were simply deposited in canoes, raised five or six feet from the ground, either in the forks of trees, or supported on stakes driven into the earth. In these instances it was not difficult to procure the skulls without disarranging the fabric; but more frequently, —they were nailed in boxes, or covered by a small canoe, which was turned bottom upwards, and placed in a larger one, and the whole covered by strips of bark, carefully arranged over them. It was then necessary to use the utmost caution in removing the covering, and also to be careful to leave every thing in the same state in which it was found. I thought several times to-day, as I have often done in similar situations before:—Now suppose an Indian were to step in here, and see me groping among the bones of his fathers, and laying unhallowed hands upon the mouldering remains of his people, what should I say? —I know well what the Indian would *do*. He would instantly shoot me, unless I took the most effectual measures to prevent it; but could I have time allowed me to temporize a little, I could easily disarm his hostility and ensure his silence, by the offer of a shirt or a blanket; but the difficulty in most cases would be, that in a paroxysm of rage he would put a bullet through your head, and then good bye to temporizing. Luckily for my pursuits in this way, there are at present but few Indians here, and I do not therefore incur much risk; were it otherwise, there would be no little danger in these aggressions.

The corpses of the several different tribes which are buried here, are known by the difference in the structure of their canoes; and the *sarcophagi* of the chiefs from those of the common people, by the greater care which has been manifested in the arrangement of the tomb.

October 14th.—I walked to-day around the beach to the foot of Young's bay, a distance of about ten miles, to see the remains of the house in which Lewis and Clark's party resided during the winter which they spent here. The logs of which it is composed, are still perfect, but the roof of bark has disappeared, and the whole vicinity is overgrown with thorn and wild currant bushes.

One of Mr. Birnie's children found, a few days since, a large silver medal, which had been brought here by Lewis and Clark, and had probably been presented to some chief, who lost it. On one side was a head, with the name "Th. Jefferson, President of the United States,

1801." On the other, two hands interlocked, surmounted by a pipe and tomahawk; and above the words, "Peace and Friendship."

15th.—This afternoon I embarked in a canoe with *Chinamus,* and went with him to his residence at Chinook. The chief welcomed me to his house in a style which would do no discredit to a more civilized person. His two wives were ordered to make a bed for me, which they did by piling up about a dozen of their soft mats, and placing my blankets upon them, and a better bed I should never wish for. I was regaled, before I retired, with sturgeon, salmon, wappatoos, cranberries, and every thing else that the mansion afforded, and was requested to ask for any thing I wanted, and it should be furnished me. Whatever may be said derogatory to these people, I can testify that inhospitality is not among the number of their failings. I never went into the house of an Indian in my life, in any part of the country, without being most cordially received and welcomed.

The chief's house is built in the usual way, of logs and hewn boards, with a roof of cedar bark, and lined inside with mats. The floor is boarded and matted, and there is a depression in the ground about a foot in depth and four feet in width, extending the whole length of the building in the middle, where the fires are made.

In this, as in almost every house, there is a large figure, or idol, rudely carved and painted upon a board, and occupying a conspicuous place. To this figure many of the Indians ascribe supernatural powers. Chinamus says that if he is in any kind of danger, and particularly, if he is under the influence of an evil spell, he has only to place himself against the image, and the difficulty, of whatever kind, vanishes at once. This certainly savors of idolatry, although I believe they never address the uncouth figure as a deity. Like all other Indians, they acknowledge a great and invisible spirit, who governs and controls, and to whom all adoration is due.

Attached to this establishment, are three other houses, similarly constructed, inhabited by about thirty Indians, and at least that number of dogs. These, although very useful animals in their place, are here a great nuisance. They are of no possible service to the Indians, except to eat their provisions, and fill their houses with fleas, and a stranger approaching the lodges, is in constant danger of being throttled by a legion of fierce brutes, who are not half as hospitable as their masters.

I remained here several days, making excursions through the neighborhood, and each time when I returned to the lodge, the dogs growled and darted at me. I had no notion of being bitten, so I gave the Indians warning, that unless the snarling beasts were tied up when I came near, I would shoot every one of them. The threat had the effect desired, and after this, whenever I approached the lodges, there was a universal stir among the people, and the words, "*iskam kahmooks, iskam kahmooks, kalaklalah tie chahko,*" (take up your dogs, take up your dogs, the *bird chief is* coming,) echoed through the little village, and was followed by the yelping and snarling of dozens of wolf-dogs, and "curs of low degree," all of which were gathered in haste to the cover and protection of one of the houses.

Chapter XVI

Northern excursion—Large shoals of salmon—Indian
mode of catching them—House near the beach—
Flathead children—A storm on the bay—Loss of
provision—Pintail ducks—Simple mode of killing
salmon—Return to Chinook—Indian garrulity—
Return to Fort George—Preparations for a second trip to
the Sandwich Islands—Detention within the cape—
Anxiety to depart—The tropics, and tropic birds—Make
the Island of Maui—Arrival at Oahu—Accession to the
society—A visit with Mr. Cowie to the king—Illness of the
princess, Harieta Nahienaena—Abrupt exit of the
king—A ride to Waititi—Cocoanut grove—Native
mode of climbing—Death of the princess—grief of her
people—barbarous ceremonies—Residence in the valley of
Nuano—A visit to the palace—Kahiles—Coffin of the
princess, and inscription—appurtenances—ceremony of
carrying the body to the church—description of the
pageant—dress of the king—conclusion of the ceremony.

*O*ctober 17th.—I left Chinook this morning in a canoe with
Chinamus, his two wives, and a slave, to procure shell-fish,
which are said to be found in great abundance towards the
north. We passed through a number of narrow *slues* which connect
the numerous bays in this part of the country, and at noon debarked,
left our canoe, took our blankets on our shoulders, and struck through
the midst of a deep pine forest. After walking about two miles, we
came to another branch, where we found a canoe which had been left
there for us yesterday, and embarking in this, we arrived in the evening
at an Indian house, near the seaside, where we spent the night.

In our passage through some of the narrow channels today, we saw
vast shoals of salmon, which were leaping and curvetting about in
every direction, and not unfrequently dashing their noses against our
canoe, in their headlong course. We met here a number of Indians
engaged in fishing. Their mode of taking the salmon is a very simple
one. The whole of the tackle consists of a pole about twelve feet long,

with a large iron hook attached to the end. This machine they keep constantly trailing in the water, and when the fish approaches the surface, by a quick and dexterous jerk, they fasten the iron into his side, and shake him off into the canoe. They say they take so many fish that it is necessary for them to land about three times a day to deposit them.

The house in which we sleep to-night is not near so comfortable as the one we have left. It stinks intolerably of salmon, which are hanging by scores to the roof, to dry in the smoke, and our bed being on the dead level, we shall probably suffer somewhat from fleas, not to mention another unmentionable insect which is apt to inhabit these dormitories in considerable profusion. There are here several young children; beautiful, flat-headed, broad-faced, little individuals. One of the little dears has taken something of a fancy to me, and is now hanging over me, and staring at my book with its great goggle eyes. It is somewhat strange, perhaps, but I have become so accustomed to this universal deformity, that I now scarcely notice it. I have often been evilly disposed enough to wish, that if in the course of events one of these little beings should die, I could get possession of it. I should like to plump the small carcass into a keg of spirits, and send it home for the observation of the curious.

18th.—Last night the wind rose to a gale, and this morning it is blowing most furiously, making the usually calm water of these bays so turbulent as to be dangerous for our light craft. Notwithstanding this disadvantage, the Indians were in favor of starting for the sea, which we accordingly did at an early hour. Soon after we left, in crossing one of the bays, about three-quarters of a mile in width, the water suddenly became so agitated as at first nearly to upset our canoe. A perfect hurricane was blowing right ahead, cold as ice, and the water was dashing over us, and into our little bark, in a manner to frighten even the experienced chief who was acting as helmsman. In a few minutes we were sitting nearly up to our waistbands in water, although one of the women and myself were constantly bailing it out, employing for the purpose the only two hats belonging to the party, my own and that of the chief. We arrived at the shore at length in safety, although there was scarcely a dry thread on us, and built a tremendous fire with the drift-wood which we found on the beach. We then dried our clothes and blankets as well as we could, cooked some ducks that we killed yesterday, and made a hearty breakfast. My stock of bread, sugar, and tea, is completely spoiled by the salt water, so that until I return to

Fort George, I must live simply; but I think this no hardship: what has been done once can be done again.

In the afternoon the women collected for me a considerable number of shells, several species of *Cardium, Citherea, Ostrea, &c.,* all edible, and the last very good, though small.

The common pintail duck, *(Anas acuta,)* is found here in vast flocks. The chief and myself killed *twenty-six* to-day, by a simultaneous discharge of our guns. They are exceedingly fat and most excellent eating; indeed all the game of this lower country is far superior to that found in the neighborhood of Vancouver. The ducks feed upon a small submerged vegetable which grows in great abundance upon the reedy islands in this vicinity.

The next day we embarked early, to return to Chinook. The wind was still blowing a gale, but by running along close to the shore of the stormy bay, we were enabled, by adding greatly to our distance, to escape the difficulties against which we contended yesterday, and regained the slues with tolerably dry garments.

At about 10 o'clock, we arrived at the portage, and struck into the wood, shouldering our baggage as before. We soon came to a beautiful little stream of fresh water, where we halted, and prepared our breakfast. In this stream, (not exceeding nine feet at the widest part,) I was surprised to observe a great number of large salmon. Beautiful fellows, of from fifteen to twenty-five pounds weight, darting and playing about in the crystal water, and often exposing three-fourths of their bodies in making their way through the shallows. I had before no idea that these noble fish were ever found in such insignificant streams, but the Indians say that they always come into the rivulets at this season, and return to the sea on the approach of winter. Our slave killed seven of these beautiful fishy while we made our hasty breakfast, his only weapon being a light cedar paddle.

We reached Chinook in the evening, and as we sat around the fires in the lodge, I was amused by the vivid description given to the attentive inhabitants by Chinamus and his wives, of the perils of our passage across the stormy bay. They all spoke at once, and described most minutely every circumstance that occurred, the auditors continually evincing their attention to the relation by a pithy and sympathizing *hugh.* They often appealed to me for the truth of what they were saying, and, as in duty bound, I gave an assenting nod, although at times I fancied they were yielding to a propensity, not uncommon among those of Christian lands, and which is known by the phrase, "drawing a long bow."

21st.—The wind yesterday was so high, that I did not consider it safe to attempt the passage to Fort George. This morning it was more calm, and we put off in a large canoe at sunrise. When we had reached the middle of Young's bay, the wind again rose, and the water was dashing over us in fine style, so that we were compelled to make for the shore and wait until it subsided. We lay by about an hour, when, the water becoming more smooth, we again got under way, and arrived at Fort George about noon.

On the 5th of November, I returned to Vancouver, and immediately commenced packing my baggage, collection, &c., for a passage to the Sandwich Islands, in the barque Columbia, which is now preparing to sail for England. This is a fine vessel, of three hundred tons, commanded by Captain Royal; we shall have eight passengers in the cabin; Captain Darby, formerly of this vessel, R. Cowie, chief trader, and others.

On the 21st, we dropped down the river, and in two days anchored off the cape. We have but little prospect of being able to cross the bar; the sea breaks over the channel with a roar like thunder, and the surf dashes and frets against the rocky cape and drives its foam far up into the bay.

I long to see blue water again. I am fond of the sea; it suits both my disposition and constitution; and then the reflection, that now every foot I advance will carry me nearer to my beloved home, is in itself a most powerful inducement to urge me on. But much as I desire again to see home, much as I long to embrace those to whom I am attached by the strongest ties, I have nevertheless felt something very like regret at leaving Vancouver and its kind and agreeable residents. I took leave of Doctor McLoughlin with feelings akin to those with which I should bid adieu to an affectionate parent; and to his fervent, "God bless you, sir, and may you have a happy meeting with your friends," I could only reply by a look of the sincerest gratitude. Words are inadequate to express my deep sense of the obligations which I feel under to this truly generous and excellent man, and I fear I can only repay them by the sincerity with which I shall always cherish the recollection of his kindness, and the ardent prayers I shall breathe for his prosperity and happiness.

30th.—At daylight this morning, the wind being fair, and the bar more smooth, we weighed anchor and stood out. At about 9 o'clock we crossed the bar, and in a few minutes were hurrying along on the open sea before a six-knot breeze. We are now out, and so good bye to Cape Disappointment and the Columbia, and now for *home*, dear home again![1]

December 16th.—We are now in the delightful tropics, and more lovely weather I never saw—clear, warm and balmy, but not in the slightest degree debilitating—and a fine trade wind, before which we are going eight and a half knots. This morning we saw a number of beautiful tropic birds flying around the vessel. This is one of the loveliest birds in the world. With a plumage of the most unsullied white, a form which is grace itself, and with long red tail-feathers streaming in the wind, it looks like a beautiful sylph sporting over the desolate ocean.[2]

On the 22d, we made the island of Maui, distant about twenty-five miles. This evening is a most delightful one, as indeed are all the evenings in this latitude. The moon is shining most brilliantly, the atmosphere is deliciously warm, and we are sailing over a sea as smooth as a lake, with the island of Morokai about ten miles on our weather beam.

On the morning of the 23d, we made Oahu, and as we rounded Diamond Hill, Adams, the pilot, boarded us, and brought us close outside the harbor, where we anchored for want of wind. The captain, Mr. Cowie, and myself, went ashore in the pilot boat, and paid our respects to a number of old friends who were assembled on the wharf to meet and welcome us.

January 1st, 1837.—Since we arrived, we have been so constantly engaged in visiting, receiving visits, and performing the usual *penance* imposed upon strangers visiting the island, that I have not had an opportunity of continuing my notes. I am now so much in arrears that I scarcely know where to begin, and many little circumstances, in themselves, perhaps, trifling enough, but which, at the time of their occurrence interested me, must of necessity have escaped my recollection.

On my arrival, Mr. George Pelly, agent of the Honorable Hudson's Bay Company, kindly invited me to his house, where I remained three days, and at the end of that time, Mr. Jones procured for me a neat and very comfortable grass cottage, in which I live like a prince.

The society of the town has been considerably augmented and improved since my last visit, by the importation, from the United States, of some four or five young ladies, and they have routes and balls, and *lu au* parties in abundance.

3d.—This morning, Mr. Cowie and myself called at the palace to see the king. At the door, we were met by one of his numerous attendants, who informed us that his majesty was not within, and offered his services to conduct us to his *office*, where he usually spends his mornings. Here we found him, and made our greetings, which he received and returned in a handsome manner. He gave us a glass of excellent Madeira, and a cigar, and we smoked and chatted with him very pleasantly for half an hour. He does not look so well as when I last saw him; is even more careless in his person, and he never was remarkable for neatness or particularity in his attire. Some allowance should, however, be made for him now, as he is suffering great distress of mind on account of the extreme illness of his favorite and only sister, the princess *Harieta Nahienaena*.[3] This is the girl of whom mention is often made in Mr. Stewart's journals. She is said to be very amiable and kind, and is universally beloved and respected by her people. While we were yet conversing with the king, a messenger came to say that she was worse, and desired to see him. He excused himself to us in a rather flurried and impatient manner, but which was nevertheless not devoid of grace; and we saw his majesty dart out of the door and run across the street in the direction of his sister's house, without a coat or braces to his trousers, in a manner neither very dignified or kingly, but one which indicated most strongly the deep interest and attachment with which he regards the last scion of his noble house. Should Harieta die, the royal Hawaiian line will be broken for ever, the insignia of Sandwich Island rank will be buried in her tomb, and the children of her reigning brother will not inherit their father's rank. The princess is married to a chief named *Laleahoku*, commonly called "young Pitt." She has just given birth to a child, which died a few hours after, and she is now suffering from severe puerperal fever. Dr. Rooke, who attends her, feels very slight hopes of her recovery.

4th.—This afternoon Mr. Josiah Thompson, Mr. Cowie, and myself, rode down to Waititi, and to Diamond Hill. The day has been a most delightful one, our horses were excellent, and we enjoyed the ride highly. In the upper part of the Waititi district, we passed through an extensive and beautiful cocoanut grove, probably a mile in length, by half a mile in width.

In the midst of this grove, we came to a small group of native houses, the inhabitants of which came running around our horses, the younger branches, in a state of perfect nudity, and capering about like so many little imps of darkness. I told them I should like to have a couple of nuts from one of the trees. I had hardly spoken before two of them ran to the nearest, and commenced mounting, one each side, and then, best fellow reached the top soonest. They climbed just like monkeys, placing their arms half way round the tree, and their feet flat against it, and then actually *jumping* up the perpendicular trunk. The exhibition was so exceedingly ludicrous, that I was indulging myself in a hearty laughing fit, when my cachination was suddenly interrupted by two nuts falling so near me that I felt in some danger of having my brains knocked out. I suspended my mirth, to shake my fist threateningly at the young urchins, who immediately slid to the ground, and with the greatest good humor, held out their hands to receive a *rial* for their trouble.

The milk of the young cocoanut, when fresh from the tree, is peculiarly delicious and refreshing; no idea can be formed of its excellence by those who have only tasted the stale fruit at home.

6th.—Yesterday the princess Harieta died. Scarcely was the circumstance known in the town, when it was announced to all by the most terrific and distressing crying and wailing amongst all ranks and classes of people. The natives, particularly the women, walked the streets, weeping bitterly and loudly, and real briny tears were falling from their eyes in plenteous showers. This most lugubrious exhibition is common on the occasion of the death of any of the high chiefs; but in the present instance there is evidently evinced much real feeling. In the afternoon, Mr. Deppe, (a Prussian gentleman,) and myself, walked to the king's palace to see the mourners who were collected there.[4] We found the large enclosed space surrounding the house, filled with natives of both sexes, to the number of perhaps a thousand, all of whom were weeping in their loudest key. Young, active men and women, and the old and decrepid, who had just strength enough to crawl to the scene of action, chiefs and common people, public functionaries and beggars; all were mingled in one common herd, bewailing in chorus their common loss.

I observed several women of the higher class standing in a group somewhat apart from the great concourse, who appeared affected in a peculiar manner. Tossing their arms over their heads, and behind their necks, beating their breasts violently and frantically, and raging with their voices during the whole time, as though they were suffering the most acute agony. In a few minutes, this violent paroxysm would subside, and then the poor creatures would fall to the ground exhausted and breathless. After about a minute spent in total inactivity, and apparent stupor, the voice and physical powers were suddenly recovered, and the consequence was, a long succession of the most horrid shrieks, the mourners rolling over and over upon the ground, biting the earth, and sobbing loud enough to be heard above the dreadful din of the multitude. Soon after this, commenced the most disgusting and barbarous part of the whole exhibition. A number of men and women, and even some little boys and girls, laid themselves upon their backs on the ground, and a man approached them with a small ivory, or hard wood wedge, and a large oval stone in his hand. He commenced his operations upon the first of the victims, who was a fine looking young man, by placing a wedge between two of his front teeth, and striking it a hard and quick blow with the stone. This loosened it effectually; then by inserting the wedge upon the opposite side, and giving another similar blow, out flew the tooth in an instant. In this manner, every person who was lying there, lost, some two, others three of his front teeth, and during the whole time the crying was not suspended for a moment.

The question naturally arises?—Why have not the missionaries, who have such unbounded influence over this people, taken measures to abolish this most barbarous and shocking custom? They have, as I well know, used great exertions to do it away, and so far as the higher ranks of society are concerned, they have probably succeeded; but there are yet, and will for some time be, hundreds among the common people upon whom they can exert little or no influence. Reason and argument are thrown away upon such, as nothing will convince them of the inutility and absurdity of so old and long established a custom.

How often, how very often, do I thank Providence in my heart, that I was born in a Christian and enlightened country, free from the shackles of barbarism, and under the influence of benign and wholesome laws. It is a blessing which those only, who have witnessed a different state of things in other lands can properly appreciate.

15th.—Several days ago Mr. Deppe and myself visited Nuano valley, where we hired a native house, in which we are now living. Our object has been to procure birds, plants &c. and we have so far been very successful. I have already prepared about eighty birds which I procured here.[5] We have a very good and comfortable cottage, and a more delightful country residence I certainly never saw. The valley here is narrow, only about a quarter of a mile across, and the mountains on either side, at least two thousand feet in height, are clothed with the most beautiful verdure. Within gunshot of our dwelling, there is a cascade of delightfully cold mountain water, which falls perhaps thirty feet; the basin below gives us an excellent bath, and we can take a shower when we wish it, by standing under one of the jets. As our cottage is situated upon elevated ground, we have a fine view of the town of Honoruru, five miles from us, as well as the lovely harbor and the shipping. I am so pleased with this residence, on every account, that I shall be loath to leave it; I have escaped from the bustle, and confusion, and dissipation of the town, from the, at times, almost insufferable heat which prevails there, and am living exactly as I wish, in a retired and quiet manner. We never suffer from heat here, and although this is the rainy season, we have had, so far, fine, clear weather.

27th.—I went, this morning, again to the palace of the king, accompanied by Captain Charlton, the British Consul, to view the remains of the princess. We saw there the widowed husband, Governor Boki, Kanaina, and several other chiefs. Their grief appears to have almost entirely evaporated. The hand of time has had the effect, not only to soften down the pangs of recent sorrow, but even to render those who were but a few days ago under its severest influence, alive to all the joyousness and sprightly emotions attendant upon a reaction.

The leaden coffin is now enclosed in one of wood, covered with rich crimson velvet, and elaborately studded, and ornamented with brass. On the top is a brass plate, with this inscription:

"Harieta
Nahienaena,
22 Makahiki, i make
i detemaba, he 30
la, i ka makahiki,
o ko haku,
1836."*

---

*Harieta
Nahienaena,
aged 22 years, died
on the 30th of December,
in the year
of our Lord,
1836.

The coffin rests upon a tressel in the centre of the large house, and underneath it is a native mat of the finest and most delicate workmanship. This mat is considered a great curiosity. It was made in the time of Tamehameha, and was presented to his queen. The grass of which it is composed is about the thickness of a horse hair, and the fabric is soft and pliant as a silken cloth. The coffin is covered with a large cloak, made of the splendid yellow feathers of one of the native birds, and is surrounded by about a dozen of the magnificent insignia of royalty, called *kahiles*. These kahiles are made of the feathers of different birds, and some of the tail plumes of the common dung-hill cock, fastened together with light pieces of bamboo, and arranged cylindrically on a long pole. Many of the kahiles are as large in circumference as a hogshead, and some few not thicker than a man's leg. Including the handle, they are, most of them, from eighteen to twenty-five feet in length. The handle is composed of alternate rings of tortoise shell and fine ivory, so accurately fitted, and beautifully polished, as to appear at a short distance like one piece. I observed that one of these handles was tipped with the bone of a human leg, and upon inquiry learned that it had belonged to one of the ancient kings. This was also finely polished, and looked like ivory, but the joint by which it was terminated had a rather grim and ghastly appearance. One of these kahiles is of so ancient a date, that the natives have no tradition respecting its fabrication. It is indeed a most antiquated looking affair, composed of a wiry sort of white feather from a bird which is now either entirely extinct, or which had been brought from a distance.

All these splendid and costly ornaments will be buried in the tomb of Harieta, where they will always remain.

February 3d.—This was the day appointed for the ceremony of carrying the body of the princess to the church. After the rite was finished, it was brought back to the palace, where it will remain for a considerable time, previous to its removal to Maui. Yesterday the king sent invitations, through the consuls, to all the foreign residents and visiters,

---

This appears like a contradiction. It is stated on the coffin plate, that the princess died on the 30th of December, when it did not actually occur until the 5th of January. This is accounted for, by the peculiar, and in some measure, reasonable doctrine of the Sandwich Islanders, that a person experiences two deaths; one of the mind, and another of the body. Now the *mind* of the princess died, i.e., became deranged, on the 30th of December, although her body did not die until the 5th of January.

and at one o'clock to-day all were assembled at the palace. The coffin still remained in the situation in which I last saw it, surrounded by the kahiles. The house was well filled by foreigners and natives of rank, and the large enclosure without was crowded. The common men were variously attired, but the great concourse of women were clothed in black from head to foot. After we had waited about an hour, the king, and Leleahoku, (the husband of the deceased,) entered. The foreigners all uncovered their heads, and his majesty acknowledged the civility by removing his own hat, and making a low and very graceful bow. He was most magnificently attired in a fine blue regimental coat, richly embroidered with gold and silver lace, and two splendid gold epaulets on the shoulders. His pantaloons were of very delicate white cassimere, embroidered down the seams with gold lace, and from a crimson sash depended a beautiful, and highly ornamented dress sword, the scabbard of which was of fine gold. His *chapeau bras* was in keeping with the rest of his attire, being of black beaver, ornamented with broad bands of gold filigree.*

The *tout ensemble* was in the highest degree magnificent and kingly, and he wore the dress with most becoming dignity. His age is about two and twenty, his stature five feet ten, and the proportions of his person are most decidedly and strictly symmetrical. Like most of the chiefs, he appears to be inclining to obesity, and will probably in a few years lose much of the beauty of his form. He is now, however, one of the most graceful and dignified men in his appearance that I ever beheld. Young Pitt has a good, and rather handsome face, but the graces of his person bear no comparison with those of his brother-in-law. His attire was also rich, with uniform coat, epaulets, *chapeau bras* and sword, and all the high chiefs were nearly similarly habited.

The procession was headed by a band of very good music, most of the performers being negroes. Next followed the missionaries in double file; then the hearse, which was a small plain cart, drawn by about twenty natives. Next came the king, who walked immediately behind the coffin; he was followed closely by young Pitt, also alone, and then came the high chiefs, men and women, to the number of about thirty,

---

*This most splendid and appropriate uniform was presented some years ago to the king, by the subscription of the foreign residents at Oahu. It was made in Lima, and cost eight hundred dollars! The presentation is said to have been rather imposing. It took place at the palace, and most of the high chiefs were present. Mr. Jones made a speech on the occasion, which was promptly replied to by his majesty.

in double file. On either side of the hearse, the magnificent kahiles were borne aloft by a number of the sub-chiefs, and favorites of the royal household, and so enormously heavy were some of these, particularly when the wind struck them, that each of them required the utmost exertion of four or five strong men to keep it in a vertical position. After the chiefs, followed all the respectable foreigners, two and two, headed by the consuls, to the number of perhaps a hundred; then a long line of females, all habited in deep black, and the rear was brought up by a motley throng of all denominations, and in every variety of costume. From the head of the procession, nearly to the foot on each side, walked the king's guards in Indian file. They were dressed in a complete suit of white, with red and blue cuffs to their jackets, and every man carried his musket reversed. When the line was formed, the band played a solemn dead march, and the procession moved toward the native church at the lower end of the town. During the whole distance, about a mile, the ground had been strown with fresh grass, forming a pleasant carpet, and preventing, in a great measure, the rising of clouds of dust, which would otherwise have been uncomfortable.

The whole pageant was "got up" with the greatest splendor and was conducted with singular order and regularity, nothing occurring which in the slightest degree tended to produce confusion.

When the procession arrived at the church, the music ceased; a large bell which hands in the area, was tolled every ten seconds, and the whole company entered the house and sought their seats. The bier was placed on the ground opposite the pulpit, the king and the other chiefs sitting by the side of it, and the bearers kneeling beneath the cart. The service was opened by an address in the native language by the Rev. Mr. Bingham; this was followed by hymns, short addresses, and prayers alternately, by several other missionaries who were present. At the conclusion of the service, which occupied about one and a half hours, the procession again formed, and returned in the same order to the palace, when, after a short prayer, in the native language, from Mr. Bingham, the cavalcade dispersed.

Chapter XVII

9th.—Mr. French kindly offered me a passage in his brig Diana, Captain Hinckley, to make a short tour of the islands. The object of the trip is to carry lumber to several of the ports, to trade with the natives, and to bring to Oahu a cargo of live stock, cattle, &c. The time allowed will be so short that I shall probably not be able to do much in my vocation, but I shall at least be furnished with an opportunity of visiting several islands, and as we have pleasant companions as passengers, besides our agreeable and accomplished captain, we anticipate a delightful trip.

We stood out of the harbor in the afternoon, and the next evening made Maui, but as we came under the land it fell calm, with a heavy ground swell, and we were tossing about most uncomfortably the whole night.

14th.—Yesterday we made Maui again, after having been cruising around the islands at the mercy of contrary winds, since Friday. Several of our passengers have been constantly seasick, and our anticipated pleasure has been thus very much lessened.

When I rose this morning, we were off the pretty village of Lahaina, and in about two hours after, we dropped our anchor within half a mile.

While the ship's people were engaged in discharging cargo, Mr. Paty, (one of our passengers,) and myself went ashore to see the town. The village is one of the prettiest I have seen: many of the houses are built of stone, handsomely whitewashed, and, as at Honoruru, a very picturesque looking fort frowns upon you as you approach the anchorage. These forts, although they add greatly to the appearance of the harbors in which they are situated, yet appear to me to be better calculated for show than service, as in case of an attack from the sea, they could not act efficiently, not being provided with bastions; and in addition to this, they are built in such a loose and unsubstantial manner, that the very means of defence would be more fatal than even the fire of an enemy. A cannonading from the fort, if long persisted in, would almost certainly level the walls with the ground.

The houses, composing the village of Lahaina, are, many of them, so obscured by cocoanut and kou trees, (*Cordia sebestena*,) that you cannot see the whole of the town from any single point of view, even from the offing. On a high hill, two miles back of the town, stands another village, called *Lahainaluna*, (or upper Lahaina,) composed entirely of white stone houses. It is here that the missionaries chiefly reside. The high school here is a large building of stone, thatched with grass, and stands on an elevated piece of ground, so as to be distinctly seen some miles out at sea. I called, with Mr. Paty, upon Mr. Andrews, to whom I had a letter of introduction from the Rev. Mr. Dieill, and here I met several other missionaries, Mr. Baldwin, Mr. Rogers, and Mr. Dibble. These gentlemen are all more or less concerned in the management of the high school, but Mr. Andrews is the principal.[1] It was commenced by him in the year 1831. For some time it was held under a simple *ranai*, or shed, made of grass, and since then it has gone on increasing and improving with a rapidity almost unprecedented. It now consists of about seventy-five scholars, chiefly boys, and the improvement of many of them is surprising. From all that I can learn, (for the school is at present closed, and I have not had an opportunity of seeing the pupils,) the advancement manifested by them is fully equal, in every respect, to those of similar seminaries in our own country. Attached to this branch of the mission is a printing office, in which the operatives are natives, under the superintendence of Mr. Rogers. Mr. Andrews showed us impressions of maps of different parts of the world, which have been engraved on copper by the pupils. These efforts are exceedingly creditable, not only to the boys themselves, but to their tutors, showing the untiring perseverance with which they must have labored, especially as none of them had ever before seen the operation performed. Mr. Andrews is a very indefatigable and most superior man, as his works abundantly testify. Contending, as he constantly is, against indisposition, he attends most diligently and faithfully to the peculiarly arduous duties of the school, and during the very few hours of relaxation which each day affords, he is busily engaged in writing for the benefit of the mission, and its objects. He is the author of "A Vocabulary of the Hawaiian Language," published at these islands some years since, and he is now employed on a new and much enlarged edition of the same work.[2]

On the morning of the 17th, we made the island of Hawaii, and, approaching with a free wind, soon let go our anchor in the bay of *Karakakua*. The land here is composed almost entirely of rough and irregular masses of lava, but towards the summit of the hills, as in Oahu, vegetation is abundant. The shore, for miles, in both directions, is sprinkled with the little sylvan looking hamlets of this country, and they are sometimes so thickly grouped together, as to form the most picturesque and beautiful villages. On the hill fronting the bay is one of these, at which the missionary, Mr. Forbes, resides, and about eighteen miles from this, there is a considerable town called *Kairua*, the residence of the chief, John Adams, governor of Hawaii.[3] In the afternoon Mr. Paty and myself went on shore, chiefly for the purpose of seeing the spot on which Captain Cook was killed, in the year 1779.

When we made this inquiry after we landed, a number of natives ran to the beach, and pointed out to us the exact spot where the gallant mariner received his death blow. I need not attempt to describe, for my sisters can in a measure understand the emotion with which I viewed the rock on which this brave and excellent man offered up his life in the service of his country. I had read the voyages of Cook, with great interest, when I was a child; I had pondered over his dangers, his magnificent discoveries, the intense excitement of his life, and his premature and violent death, but if at that time any one had told me that I should ever visit the scene of his discoveries, and stand upon the identical rock which was pressed by his bleeding bosom, I should have smiled at it as too chimerical for belief; here I am, however, although at times I can scarcely realize the possibility of it.

The rock is somewhat isolated, and at high tide the water breaks over its summit. It is said to be at present not one fourth its original size, as almost every visiter, for a number of years, has been in the habit of carrying away a fragment of it as a relic. A French man-of-war, which was lately here, is said to have taken off about a ton of it; and some Spaniards, who visited the island several years since, not only took specimens of the rock, but the whole ship's company knelt upon it, and offered up a prayer for the repose of their hero's soul.

There is perhaps no one unfortunate circumstance connected with foreigners, that has ever occurred here, which the natives of these islands so deeply regret, as the death of Cook. They all speak of it as a lamentable event, and some of the elder of them are said to even shed tears when the subject is mentioned. They have canonized him, and he is universally known by the title of "*Olono*," a particular deity.

18th.—This morning I met Mr. Forbes, the missionary of this station, at the lower village, and after delivering to him a letter from Mr. Dieill, accompanied him to his house on the hill, a distance of three miles. At about one mile from the shore on the hill is a monument, erected in 1825 by Lord Byron, Captain of his Britannic majesty's frigate "Blond," to the memory of Captain Cook. It consists of a simple wall of lava about five feet high, embracing a square of twenty feet, in the centre of which is a cedar post, twelve feet in height, and near the top a copper plate, with this inscription:

"In memory
of
Captain James Cook, R.N.,
Who discovered these islands,
in the year of our Lord,
1778.
This humble monument is erected
by his fellow countrymen,
in the year of our Lord,
1825."

This post is completely covered with the initials of persons who have from time to time visited the spot, chiefly the masters, officers, and crews of vessels, and among them I noticed the well known name of "*Coffin, Nantucket.*"

20th.—Mr. Paty and myself spent the day in traversing the extensive forests of this island, in search of birds, but with very little success. The walking was extremely difficult, and sometimes dangerous, in consequence of a thick undergrowth of bushes, intermixed with large masses of rough, porous lava. There is here a small species of crow, said to be numerous at times, but we did not see any, as, in consequence of a long drought, they, as well as most other birds, have retired back into the mountains to procure water.[4] We returned to Mr. Forbes' house late in the afternoon, and found him preparing his baggage, &c., for a passage to Oahu in our brig. He takes his wife and two children with him.

22d.—We sailed out of Karakakua last evening with the periodical land breeze, and this morning, at 9 o'clock, anchored off *Kawaihae*. This is a barren and most unattractive looking place, a rambling sort of village, containing about fifty houses, but no vegetation except a few scattered cocoanuts, and an occasional kou, and tutui tree. The soil is composed entirely of volcanic earth, or the pulverization of lava and basalt. I observed none of the handsome taro patches here that form such a relief to the eye when scanning this rugged country in other places. From our anchorage we have a view of several of the colossal mountains and peaks of this island, among which the majestic point of *Mauna kea* stands pre-eminent. I have not yet seen *Mauna roa*, except from a considerable distance at sea, and I suppose that now the gratification of a nearer view will not be afforded me. I cannot too much regret that I have had no opportunity of visiting this celebrated and stupendous volcano.

23d.—Yesterday morning I went on shore with Captain Hinckley and others, and called upon Mrs. Young, widow of the late John Young, the oldest foreign resident of the Sandwich Islands. He came hither in the year 1789, remaining until his death, which took place about a year ago, in his 90th year. Mrs. Young is a sister of old king Tamehameha, and is now probably sixty years of age, a very pleasant and lady-like old woman.

In the afternoon we visited a large *heiau*, or temple, in the neighborhood. This temple, (which of course has not been used as such since the abolition of idolatry) was built in the early part of the reign of Tamehameha; in it were deposited the gods of wood and stone, which the natives worshipped, and at regular periods, a human victim was offered as a sacrifice to their imaginary deity. The victims consisted chiefly of convicts, or those who had been guilty of some misdemeanor, but whenever the stock commonly kept on hand, failed, (which not unfrequently happened,) the authorities rarely scrupled to supply the deficiency, either by forcing the common people to commit crimes worthy of the punishment, or by entrapping them into a confession of some petty transgression.

It was also a common practice to sacrifice a victim on the death of any of the higher chiefs, to propitiate the favor of the idol toward the departed. At such times they were even less scrupulous than ordinary; a victim must be procured for the repose of the troubled spirit, and it was therefore frequently made an excuse for the most open and cruel injustice.

The heiau is built of stones laid together, enclosing a square of about two hundred feet. The walls are thirty feet high, and about sixteen feet thick at the base, from which they gradually taper to the top, where they are about four feet across. In the centre, is a platform of smooth stones, carefully laid together, but without any previous preparation, raised to within ten feet of the top of the wall. It was on this platform that the victims were sacrificed, the gods standing around outside in niches made for their accommodation.

There is, near the heiau, another very similar, though smaller edifice of stone, called a *morai*. This was used for nearly similar purposes, and, in addition, it was the place to which the bodies of the dead chiefs were carried, previous to interment. After lying here in state for a longer or shorter time, according to the grade of rank held by the deceased, the flesh was stripped from the bones, and buried in the sea; the bones were then taken and deposited in caves, or subterranean vaults, which concluded the ceremony. On Oahu, near Diamond hill, in the district of Waititi, are several of these morais, but they have gone to decay, and are not so perfect as the above mentioned one.

24th.—The ship's people have been engaged the whole day in taking cattle on board, and we are now deep in the water, having upwards of one hundred and twenty head stowed under the hatches. These cattle are procured wild, on the island, by Spaniards, who live here for the purpose. They take them by means of lassos, and display great dexterity in the business. This operation has been so often described, that I need not repeat it here, suffice it to say, that all the bullocks on board have been taken expressly for us, by three Spaniards, since our arrival here on Wednesday.

25th.—We were under way at daylight this morning, bound for Oahu. We passed, in the course of the day, the islands of *Maui, Kaawalawi, Ranai, Morokai,* and *Morokini.* The weather was rough, and the sea high, and as usual, most of our passengers have been suffering from sea sickness, and at times the scene on the quarter deck is quite distressing.

Our vessel is now literally stowed full, so much so as to be somewhat unpleasant for passengers. All forward of the main mast, both above and below, is crowded with cattle; the 'tweendecks are stowed with hides, and the quarter deck with passengers of all colors, from the fair skinned European, to the deep copper-colored native, not omitting the intermediate grade of half-castes. Men, women, and children, of various families, are all huddled together in a mass, lolling about, talking and smoking during the day, and sleeping and grunting like swine at night. The effluvia arising from the mass of native bodies, during a still, warm evening, is not comparable to otto of roses, and I have often been compelled to forego the pleasure of a nocturnal lounge on deck, and dive to the cabin for purer air. This effluvia is owing to a common habit among these people, and particularly of the women, of anointing the hair and body with cocoanut oil. The oil, in a recent state, possesses an aromatic, and rather agreeable odor, but when allowed to become rancid, it is most insufferably rank and disgusting. When in this rancid state, its cosmetic properties are supposed to be improved, and it is then applied in large quantities to the whole person. Were it not for this disagreeable and unsavory practice, the women here would be well calculated to please the taste of a stranger, as many of them are truly handsome, and remarkably graceful in their deportment. I believe that most of those who are married to the foreigners have given up this disgusting practice.

On the 27th we anchored in the harbor of Oahu, and from this time, until the 16th of March, I was busily engaged in packing my multifarious collections, making calls upon my friends, &c., preparatory to embarking for Valparaiso, via Tahiti, in the ship Europa, Captain Shaw, of this port.

I have now been here nearly three months; much longer than I expected to have been detained. My time has been employed chiefly in pursuing my scientific avocations, collecting specimens, &c., in which I have been as successful as I anticipated. In this pursuit I have received much and very steady assistance from many of the resident foreigners, and, as a parting word, I wish them to accept my most unfeigned thanks; both for this and for the uniform hospitality and kindness with which they have treated me. To J.C. Jones, Esq.,—the American consul,—my acknowledgments are particularly due. I shall always remember, with gratitude, the many favors he has conferred upon me.

18th.—We cleared Oahu yesterday, and this evening, are sailing along delightfully before an eight knot breeze. I think that of all enjoyments I have ever experienced since I became a dweller in distant lands, there is none that has ever excited in me such a thrill of delight and pleasure, as an evening sail upon a moon-lit sea. I can hang for hours over the gunwale, as the ship ploughs the deep blue waters; I gaze upon the lovely moon, and turn my face towards my father-land, and then, oh then, do I fancy I can see my quiet, peaceful home, and commune with the loved objects there! All, all rise before me with a distinctness at times almost startling. I see my excellent and affectionate father, my beloved and tender mother, my dear sisters, brothers, all whom I love, and I think I can see them beckoning to the wanderer, and entreating him to turn his footsteps homeward. These images have risen before me, this evening, with uncommon vividness. It is now eight bells in the middle watch; the officer is pacing the quarter deck, muffled in his large pea jacket, the helmsman stands by the wheel, the drowsy watch are lolling on the forecastle, and all else are asleep. But I cannot sleep, nor would I if I could, on such a glorious night as this.

April 1st.—Nothing important has occurred to vary the monotony of a sea voyage. We have generally been favored with good breezes, though the sea has been mostly rough. On Thursday last, we crossed the line, and our latitude is now 3° 52' south.

8th.—Yesterday morning at 10 o'clock, "*land, ho!*" was sung out by a man at the mast head, and we ascertained it to be Dean's island, distant about fifteen miles. We had a fine seven knot breeze, and we rapidly approached, and soon passed it within five miles. This is a very long, low island, profusely covered with vegetation, very undulating, and with a fine sand beach surrounding it, upon which the surf breaks furiously. It is said to be sparsely inhabited by people of a very wild and unsocial nature. Ships rarely, if ever, touch here, as the island produces nothing to tempt the cupidity of our mariners. In the evening we had a heavy squall, with rain, and incessant and very vivid lightning. We shortened sail immediately, and lay to, under a double reefed maintopsail and reefed foresail, for about an hour, when the gale subsided, and a dead calm of about the same duration succeeded. During the storm, we observed a little speck of brilliant light, like a star, resting upon the main truck or top of the mainmast. In a few minutes after, a similar light appeared upon the summits of both the other masts, and continued visible for about an hour. This is what sailors call a "*complaisant*," and is of course occasioned by an excess of electricity in the atmosphere.

In the afternoon we made Tahiti, (or Otaheite,) and the next morning approached to within two miles of it, brought our vessel to, in a fine breeze, and hoisted our signal for a pilot. After waiting about two hours, a native, who spoke English well, boarded us in a whale boat, and announced himself as authorized pilot of the port. The charge of the vessel was of course given into his hands, and in another hour we were riding at anchor in a beautiful, and very safe harbor. Tahiti, like most islands in these seas, is nearly surrounded by a coral reef, a narrow passage only being found for entrance, but the native pilot appears to be skillful, and I am told that no accident has ever happened here.

The outline of this island is exceedingly uneven and rugged, being formed of high hills and valleys alternately, but the whole of the land is profusely covered with vegetation. The bay in which we are anchored, (Papeeté,) is one of the most beautiful I have seen; the water in the harbor is at all times so smooth and placid that no motion whatever can be felt on board a vessel riding at anchor, and the shore, fringed with cocoanut, bread-fruit, and banana trees, with the neat white-washed cottages sprinkled amongst them, forms a view at once striking and lovely. There are about eight whale ships now in the port, and several of the masters of these, as well as some resident gentlemen from the shore, visited us shortly after we came to anchor. Among the latter were the missionary of this station, the Rev. Mr. Pritchard, Doctor Vaughan, Mr. William Henry and others. Soon after, Mr. Skinner, the supercargo, and myself, went on shore, and called upon Mr. Moerenhaut, the U.S. consul, to whom I had a letter of introduction from Mr. Jones of Oahu.[5] He received us kindly, and we spent an hour with him very pleasantly. We partook of a good dinner at the house of Mr. Henry, after which Mr. Skinner and several other gentlemen with myself, took a stroll back of the village. If I was pleased with the appearance of the harbor from the anchorage, how much more was I delighted with the opportunity of rambling in the interior. Soon after we left the house, we entered upon an excellent turnpike road made by natives, chiefly convicts, and extending nearly the whole circuit of the island. This, as is almost every part of this lovely isle, is a complete orchard of the most delicious of the tropical fruits; vast groves of oranges, lemons, guavas, &c. &c., growing wild, and in the most prodigal profusion, patches of pine apples, interminable forests of bananas, cocoanuts, and *Vi's,** and all without an owner. Well may it be said, this is a highly favored, and most fruitful land. The natives do not require to cultivate the earth; it teems with every luxury that their unsophisticated palates crave. For a meal, they have but to enter the forest, and gather a mess of bread-fruit, bananas, and guavas, and kill a pig from the large droves which are constantly roaming the country, in a half wild state, and fattening to obesity on the ripe and luscious fruit which every where strews the ground.

10th.—I strolled, during the whole of this day, through the woods, and procured a number of very pretty birds, all new to me.[6] In this expedition I was accompanied by a stout boy, a Sandwich Islander, whom I have engaged as my servant while I remain. This is a convenience, inasmuch as I am not acquainted with the language of Tahitians, but am sufficiently familiar with that of the Sandwich Islanders, to ask for whatever I want, and understand ordinary conversation. In my ramble through the forest to-day, I was surprised to hear a stave of the old familiar song, *Jim Crow,* sung by a little puling voice, but with singular fidelity of tone and time, and after a short search, I perceived a little naked native girl, of not more than four years of age, washing her only calico garment in a creek which flowed by, and amusing herself at her work, by singing "wheel about, and turn about, and do just so." The child attempted to escape when she found she was observed, but I caught her, and by dint of persuasion, and the offer of a *rial,* induced her to sing several verses to me.

12th.—I went, with the consul, to the palace of the queen, *Pomaré Wahine,* (or the woman Pomaré.) The house did not differ, except in being somewhat larger, from the ordinary native habitations, and her majesty could not have been distinguished, by her appearance, from the poorest woman in her dominions. Her complexion is somewhat fairer than that of the generality, and the expression of her countenance

---

*This is the *Spondias dulcis* of botanists; a large and wide spreading of forest tree, bearing a most delicious fruit, somewhat like a pear, and about the same size.

is pleasing. She was dressed, like the maids of honor who surrounded her, in a loose wrapper of calico, but without any kind of ornament about her person, and her feet were bare. I was informed that she disliked all show and ostentation, and that she never donned her queenly garments except upon occasions of state or high ceremonial. Her husband is a young man of prepossessing appearance, who has been selected from the common ranks for his good looks. He is not burthened with the cares of sovereignty, and if his wife were to die, would return immediately to the humble walk from which he has been elevated. He is universally known by the title of the "queen's husband."

15th.—This day, although with us, in our ship account, Saturday the 15th, is Sunday the 16th, at Tahiti. This is accounted for by the fact of the early missionaries having made the passage around the Cape of Good Hope instead of Cape Horn, and making no allowance for easting, consequently gained nearly a day in their reckoning. The mistake has never since been corrected, and at the present time it would perhaps not be advisable to do so.

I attended, with most of the gentlemen of the place, the native church, at 9 o'clock in the morning. Mr. Pritchard performed the service, and I was pleased, not only with the order and regularity of the exercises, but with the strict and decorous deportment of the audience. The hymns were sung with much taste and skill, and many of the voices, particularly of the females, were sweet, and well trained.

The chapel is a very neat and pretty piece of workmanship, somewhat in the style of those at the Sandwich Islands, but more tasteful and lighter. The roof, instead of a thatch of grass, is neatly covered with the large leaves of a species of *Pandanus*, handsomely and ingeniously worked on light reeds, and the beams are wrapped, for about one-fourth of their length, with alternative strips of fine sinnit and mats of different colors, and adds very much to the general appearance of the building.

20th.—I observed to-day near the beach, in front of the village, an old, delapidated cottage, the trellised sides of which had fallen to pieces from decay, and I was surprised to hear issue from it a few notes of a low and plaintive song. Upon entering, I saw a poor old man lying on a board elevated upon posts about four feet from the ground, with no bedding except a small mat, and his long white hair drooping over a square wooden block, which was his only pillow. Attached to the rude ceiling, were several baskets of fruit, oranges, bananas, &c., suspended by cords over the old creature's head, and within reach of his hand. I dispersed the swine which were wallowing beneath him on the floor, and spoke to the old man. But he heeded me not. His dull eyes seemed fixed upon the fruit baskets over his head, and soon the low and melancholy song was renewed, in a voice palsied and broken from extreme age.

It is an immemorial custom of the Tahitians, so to dispose of their old and infirm people. When a man becomes too feeble, from age, to walk, and provide for his own necessities, he is laid out in this way, and furnished daily with a fresh supply of fruit, and a calabash of water, to sustain his flickering life, until the hand of death relieves his relatives from further care.

May 2d.—We are now quite ready for sea, and are only waiting a breeze to go out. I am as anxious as the rest to re-embark, for I have completed my ornithological collections, having prepared about a hundred and ten birds, most of them, I think, peculiar to this island.

The common dunghill fowl is found wild in the forests here. Some of the residents think that it is a jungle fowl, peculiar to the country, but, upon examination, I have not been able to perceive any material difference between it and the domesticated bird, and therefore incline to the belief that it is the common species returned to its original habits. In my excursions, I have killed about a dozen of them. Their plumage is generally more rich and brilliant than that of the domesticated bird, and there is not so much variety in the color of different individuals. Their flesh is exquisite. They are very shy, running away with singular rapidity, and concealing themselves on the approach of the sportsman. When flushed, they fly with great vigor and swiftness, and where the trees and bushes are not too dense, afford a very good mark.

4th.—This morning, the wind being fair, we took the pilot on board, and at 8 o'clock, stood out. While in the middle of the passage, the breeze fell very light, and our vessel began to swing towards the high and dangerous reef which was just beside us. For myself, I gave our good ship up for lost, and was waiting to see her dashed upon the rocks, which I thought was inevitable. This was evidently the opinion of our captain also. As he stood upon the rail, looking out ahead, and casting his eyes anxiously upon the sunken rocks under our quarter, I perceived his countenance change; but still he was calm, and gave his orders, in obedience to the signals of the pilot, with coolness and precision. At the instant when I fancied, (and I believe correctly,) that we were in the most imminent peril, a light breeze struck our sails, which were soon filled, and the ship made some headway; then followed a strong puff, and in about five minutes more, we were past all danger. The captain sprang down from the rail, ejaculating, "thank God, thank God!" and he had reason. A fine ship, a valuable cargo, and many lives still more valuable, in all probability, depended upon that single puff of wind.

After congratulating ourselves upon our escape, we all turned anxiously to look at the situation of a whale ship, which attempted the passage a few minutes after us, under the direction of a deputy appointed by the authorized pilot. While in difficulty ourselves, we had enough to do to look after our own ship, but now that it was past, all our sympathy was excited for our fellow probationer. He appeared to have more wind than ourselves, and was coming out beautifully, when suddenly, from a cause to us unknown, he sheered towards the reef, and the next moment, to our consternation and horror, the fine ship struck, hung by her keel, and leaned over 'till her yards were in the water. She soon righted again, only to go over upon the other side. Her sails were still set, and drew well with the wind which came freshly off the land, but she would not move ahead, and kept rolling and grinding upon the rough coral, showing her clean copper bottom at every moment. The intense and painful interest which we took in the situation of our poor neighbor, would not suffer us to run away and leave him in his extremity, and accordingly, Captain Shaw, Mr. Skinner, and myself went off to him in our boat. When we arrived, we found that the whale boats belonging to all the ships in the port, had come out with their commanders and crews to render all the assistance they could to their unfortunate brother. Most of the boats were made fast to the bowsprit of the ship, and it was attempted to tow her off; hawsers were carried out, and kedge anchors, and every other means resorted to to get her clear, but all to no purpose. The devoted vessel continued forging higher and higher upon the reef, and in a few minutes more it was found necessary to cut away the masts, in order to lighten and right her. I scarcely ever in my life felt more distressed than when I heard this order given; it was, however, necessary that it should be done for the sake of the cargo. The poor ship seemed like a human creature in its agony, tossing and groaning as on a bed of pain. A dozen men with axes in their hands mounted on the weather rail, and in a minute the shrouds and back-stays were cut away. The heavy masts reeled and swayed from side to side, for an instant, and then fell with a crash into the sea. Then indeed

"A wreck complete she roll'd."

One little hour before, she had been a noble and stately ship in all the majesty of her beauty, and contained within many a manly heart burning with the spirit of enterprise, or dwelling with delight upon the happy home and family which it was then about to seek. How changed the prospect now! The beautiful fabric is in ruins, and those who risked their all within her, are disheartened and undone. The sight is a melancholy one indeed, and I cannot but think, too, how nearly this deplorable situation had been ours.

When the masts went over the side, the ship righted, as if she felt relieved from a burthen, but in a very short time, the cry "she has bilged," arose from her decks, and the people were put to work getting out all the most valuable private articles, and passing them out of the cabin windows. Here they were received in boats and taken on shore, Soon after this, we observed, as the hull rose and fell, the water pouring in and out of her counter, and very soon she settled upon her side, and lay with one of her gunwales under water, fast anchored upon the coral reef. Nothing more could be done for her safety, and all the efforts of the crew were directed to getting out the cargo of oil. Meanwhile, we who could render no service, concluded to go ashore, and as we were about pushing off from the wreck, the captain of the ship requested a passage with us. As we pulled into the harbor, I wished to say something by way of consolation to the poor fellow, but I had no language in which to express my feelings. He is a young man, only twenty seven-years of age, highly spoken of for his activity, perseverance and honesty. He has raised himself from the lowest station to a command, entirely by his good conduct; this is his first voyage as master, and so far it had been remarkably successful. After we left the ship, he seemed more calm, but as we drew near the shore, he trusted himself with one look towards his former *home*, and it was too much for his philosophy,—he threw himself back in the boat and wept like a child! I could almost have wept with him, for I appreciated and respected his feelings. A ship is a sailor's home, his castle; he loves her next to his wife and family, and where is the man with a heart in his bosom, who can look upon his *home in ruins*, and not feel it bleed within him at the sight!

Chapter XVIII

Island of Eimeo—Juan Fernandez—Make the coast of
Chili—The shore—Town of Valparaiso—suburbs—
Indisposition—Kindness of the foreign residents, & c.—
Preparation by the Chilian government for an
expedition against Peru—Foreign adventurers—
Disaffection of Vidaurre and other officers in the
Chilian army—Murder of Signor Portales by the
rebels—Preparation for invading the town of
Valparaiso—consternation of the inhabitants—A
battle—defeat of the insurgents—Capture and
imprisonment of Vidaurre and seven officers—Florine,
the murderer—Sentence of the court martial—A
military execution—Appearance of the bodies after
death—Sail for the United States—Cape Horn—
Pernambuco—Cape Henlopen—A gale—Arrival at
Philadelphia.

May 5th.—This afternoon we got under way, and sailed along the north side of Eimeo, a beautiful island, only twenty miles from Tahiti, and the next morning, (having had a good wind during the night,) the loom only of the land was seen astern.

June 10th.—When I rose this morning, the island of Juan Fernandez was in sight, distant about thirty miles. The outline is very uneven and rugged, being composed of alternate rough peaks and vallies. We soon approached so near that I distinctly saw, with the glass, a herd of goats bounding over the rocky heights. I felt anxious to set my foot on the shore, hallowed by the romantic narrative of De Foe, but this was impracticable under the circumstances, and I was compelled to abandon it. This is the Botany Bay of Chili; the number of convicts at present is about two hundred.

12th.—We have had fine breezes since Saturday, and this morning, at 8 o'clock, we made the coast of Chili, distant about fifty miles. The day has been a lovely, clear one, so that we had a fine view of the land until evening closed. We were then within about eight miles of Valparaiso point, and as it was deemed unsafe to attempt to run in during the dusk, we were compelled to lie to all night. The coast here appears exceedingly bold, with a very small portion of level beach. In the back ground, hills rise upon hills to the far distance, where their summits are crowned by the snow-capt Andes. As the sun sank this evening, and gilded with his departing rays the frozen peaks of these lofty mountains, the effect was truly magnificent.

The hills in the vicinity of the shore appear to be totally devoid of vegetation, nor can the eye discern a single shrub in the whole of the vast space comprehended within the range of vision. From our present station, we can see two flag-staffs erected in different situations, upon the tops of two of the highest hills, intended, doubtless, as a guide for mariners; and in one of the little valleys, we observe a small, but neat looking village of white houses. The harbor of Valparaiso is deeply embayed within the hills, so that we have not yet had a sight of it.

13th.—Early this morning we passed the point, and came immediately in view of the town of Valparaiso. The houses appeared thickly grouped together, but without any attention to order or regularity, and between these groups, there often intervened large uninhabited spaces, producing the appearance, from the harbor, of several towns. Immediately in front of the bay; and for the space of a quarter of a mile east and west of it, is the principal part of the city, the place of commercial business and fashion. Back and westward of this, are three large groups of houses, occupying the summits and sides of three hills, commonly known to foreigners by the nautical names, *fore-top, main-top, and mizen-top.* Occasionally, also, a white cottage is seen to peep out from some little convenience nook among the loftiest hill behind.

About half a mile eastward of this on the low land, is the *Almendral,* (almond grove,) so called from a great number of these trees, which formerly grew there. The houses here are the same in appearance as the rest, and the city extends in this direction for perhaps a mile. Immediately after we dropped our anchor, the captain of the port came on board for the purpose of examining the ship's papers. Then followed the customhouse officers, who also made the requisite investigations, and in about an hour we were allowed to go on shore.

We landed accordingly on a large mole in front of the custom house, and Mr. Skinner and myself called upon Mr. Chauncey, of the house of Alsop & Co., to whom we had letters from Oahu, and by whom we were politely received. After sitting about an hour, we strolled out to look at the town. Every thing here is quite new to me; the style of building, the manner in which the streets are laid out, the customs, and even the language of the inhabitants. It is now more than three years since I saw a town which had any pretensions to civilization, and though so far inferior in every respect to our cities at home, yet from my first landing, I have enjoyed the opportunity of seeing an approximation to polite society, generally diffused. I do not mean that I have seen no polite society since I left home; far from it, but the little which I have seen has been so surrounded by baser material, that here, where civilization predominates, I am more deeply impressed with the contrast.

August 12th.—Here a considerable *hiatus* occurs in my journal, occasioned by a severe fit of illness which confined me for several weeks to my bed, and from which I did not wholly recover during my residence of two months in Chili. I was so fortunate as to meet here a gentleman from Philadelphia, Doctor Thomas S. Page, by whom I was assiduously attended, and to whose skillful and judicious treatment I consider myself indebted for my recovery. I also received much kindness from Captain E.L. Scott and his estimable lady, as well as from a number of the foreign residents and British naval officers in the port.

The political affairs of the country, and the events to which certain important and recently adopted measures have given rise, are worthy a slight notice.

An expedition is about being fitted out by this country against her sister, Peru. All the men of war belonging to her navy are to be brought into service, and before many weeks there will be bloody work on the shores of South America.

The Chilians have a large and efficient navy, commanded chiefly by foreign adventurers, English and Americans. Peru has also some officers of the same stamp, and thus brother will war against brother; and for what? For "filthy lucre," and bloody laurels, worthy to decorate the brow of the first murderer.

> "See from his native hills afar,
> The rude Helvetian flies to war:—

Careless for *what*—for *whom* he fights:—
For *slaves* or *despots*—*wrongs* or *rights*:—
A conqueror oft—*a hero never!*
Yet lavish of his life-blood still,
As if 'twere like his mountain rill,
And gushed for ever!"

The reason assigned by the Chilians for the necessity of the contemplated invasion, are manifold. They complain of aggressions and spoliations upon their subjects and commerce, ill treatment of their envoys, &c.; and some time since, a private citizen of Callao, upon his own responsibility, and with his own resources, without the advice of his government, visited the island of Chiloe in an armed vessel, and laid it under a heavy contribution. The Chilénos considered this a national outrage, and the fire of jealousy and furious animosity, which had been hitherto smothered, burst at once into a flame. A formal declaration of war has been the result, and it appears to be the opinion of the most calculating and discerning foreigners here, that the Chilian forces will be worsted in the conflict.

As might have been expected, many of the subjects of Chili, and some influential ones too, highly disapproved of the projected enterprise. Among these, were a colonel of the army, and his brother, the commandante of the Rezguardo, named *Vidaurre*, person of the first respectability in the government, and of considerable influence. These men openly expressed their disapprobation of the public proceedings, and in a short time induced many other officers in the service, as well as a considerable number of the regular troops, to join in a revolt, for the purpose of putting an immediate and summary end to an attempt which they argued could not fail to produce the most calamitous and fatal consequences. As a commencement of this bold and somewhat Quixotic measure, they sent an invitation to a man high in office in Valparaiso, named Don Diego Portales, a person of unbounded influence, and indeed the proposer and prime mover of the contemplated expedition, requesting him to meet the chief of the insurgents at Quillota, about five leagues from the town, on business of importance. Portales, without the slightest suspicion of foul play being intended, or the faintest idea of the meditated resistance to the laws, accepted the invitation unhesitatingly, and repaired to the place appointed, accompanied only by his private secretary. Here he was met by Colonel Vidaurre alone, who received him in a friendly manner, and immediately commenced a conversation relative to the invasion of Peru. The colonel expressed his sentiments freely on the subject, which of course gave great offence to Portales, by whom he was charged with traitorous and treasonable designs, and who threatened to order his arrest immediately on his return to Valparaiso. This threat had been anticipated, and was the preconcerted signal for the appearance of the troops of Vidaurre, who suddenly rose, like Clan Alpine's warriors, from the bushes where they had been concealed, surrounded and made prisoner the unfortunate commander-in-chief, stript him in a twinkling of his arms and equipments, loaded his hands and legs with heavy irons, and left him in sad and melancholy musing as to his probable fate. In a short time, a small detachment of the insurgents returned, headed by a young officer named Florine, a man who had made himself remarkable by several acts of wanton and bloody atrocity. Portales felt that his hour was come. He knew that he need expect no mercy from the man into whose hands he had fallen. He disdained therefore to plead for himself, but only requested that his secretary, (a young man belonging to one of the first families in Chili,) who was of course perfectly innocent, might be suffered to depart without molestation. This request the ruffian said he could not grant, but told them both to prepare instantly for death, for that they had not five minutes to live.

After both the victims had performed their devotions, which they did in the most calm and devout manner, a signal was given, and the whole detachment fired their pieces within a few yards of the unhappy prisoners. The young secretary was instantly killed, but Portales himself still stood, being but slightly wounded in the side; and it is said that, in this most trying moment, his admirable courage and self command, did not desert him.

He stood and looked with a proud, cold eye upon his executioners. Not a man among them dared to meet that glance, but every one cast down his eyes in admiration and profound awe. They stood in the presence of a superior mind, and they cowered like abject worms before its influence. Young Florine, however, was not to be so daunted. Enraged that he whom he chose to consider his enemy, still survived, he gnashed his teeth and rushed upon his bound and defenceless general with his sword. Three several times, did he pass his murderous blade clean through the body of Portales. That calm unwavering eye still kept its basilisk glance upon the convulsed features of the assassin, until with the third thrust its lustre was quenched in death; the poor body which encased the dauntless soul, quivered in the last agony, and fell a lump of senseless clay upon its parent earth.

These details were related by an eye witness, one who, although engaged in the revolt, opposed with manly energy the dastardly and most atrocious act by which it was commenced.

After the perpetration of this lawless and high-handed deed, (which it is generally believed even Vidaurre himself did not sanction, or approve of,) a pacific negotiation with the reigning powers was of course impossible. All engaged in the insurrection would be denounced as felons, and any one of them who should fall into the hands of the authorities would inevitably die the felon's death; so there was nothing for it but to strengthen their army as much and as rapidly as possible, and forthwith attack the stronghold of the enemies of misrule.

Accordingly the whole army retired to a short distance from the scene of the murder, leaving the dead bodies on the spot, and set on foot the most active measures to increase the number of their forces. In the mean time, the protracted absence of Portales, caused much anxiety among his friends, several of whom knew of his having gone to Quillota, and on the day following they repaired thither in all haste, where they found the corpses as they had been left, and conveyed them immediately to Valparaiso. The cause and manner of Portales' death was at once suspected, and naturally induced a supposition that this flagitious act of private animosity was but the prelude to public hostility, and therefore the Chilian commander lost no time in getting his regulars and militia under arms, and in readiness to repel the suspected invasion. On the day following, intelligence of the movements, and meditated attack of the rebel army was received in Valparaiso. All was consternation through the town. Every horse that could be found was seized upon for the use of the troops, not excepting private property even; the merchants sealed up all their specie in boxes, and sent it on board the men of war for sake keeping, and stood ready to embark themselves, with their most valuable effects, in case of the success of the invaders.

The Chilian general selected an eligible spot of ground within about four miles of the town, concealing his army as well as he could, in the *quebrados* or valleys by which it was bounded, and waited, with what patience he might, the approach of the enemy.

On the 3d of June, at three o'clock in the morning, Vidaurre came on, leading his men quietly and stealthily over the uneven ground, and no doubt thought to take the town by complete surprise, and secure an easy, and, perhaps, bloodless victory over the amazed regulars. But he was most sadly mistaken. As his army was silently and warily moving down one of the abrupt hills, in a perfectly unprepared state, a tremendous and most destructive fire was suddenly opened upon them from the bushes upon both sides of the declivity. A large body of men from one valley rushed to the top of the hill, and completely cut off their retreat in the direction from which they came; a detachment from the opposite valley filled off in front, and received them from the town side, and at the same instant, a number of gunboats, which were stationed in the bay, greeted them with a tremendous volley of grape shot and musket balls, which completed the panic of the insurgent army. Once, and once only, did they attempt to rally, and in answer to the deadly shower of bullets which was mowing down their ranks, did they discharge a few of their muskets at irregular and trembling intervals, but they were completely routed; resistance was utterly vain, and the whole mass fled in the utmost dismay and consternation. Some few effected their escape, but the greater number were taken prisoners, among whom were the colonel himself, the bloody Florine, and six other officers of distinction, besides about twenty subalterns. The number of killed and wounded I have not exactly ascertained, but I believe it exceeded a hundred.

The news of this victory was of course most agreeable to the inhabitants of the town, (a great number of whom witnessed the combat from the heights,) and quiet and security were immediately restored. When I arrived, (which was only ten days after,) matters were in the most tranquil state. One day more had elapsed than is, by common consent, allotted to the recollection of affairs of an unusual character, and the people were beginning to talk of it as an event which had left but little impression upon the memory.

But the poor officers of the ill-fated army had not forgotten it. They were languishing on board the Chilian ships of war in the harbor, laden with heavy irons, such as they had caused to be placed upon the limbs of the unfortunate Portales; they were stowed away in the darkest and most uncomfortable places, and fed upon a miserable allowance of hard bread and water. Add to this, that in consequences of the constant, and sometimes severe motion of the ships in this harbor, they were for weeks dreadfully sea-sick, without medical advice being allowed them, and of course utterly deprived of the power of moving about, and thereby diminishing its pangs, and we can readily believe that they were wretched enough. I felt a sincere commiseration for several of the officers whose history I inquired into, and particularly for a poor Swede, an almost innocent man, certainly innocent of any participation in the death of Portales; the same who related the interesting particulars of the murder.

For Florine, I never felt much pity. He was a miscreant of the deepest dye; and when I saw him, a few days after my arrival, brought with others on shore, I observed that the people seemed to contemplate, with savage pleasure, the haggard and disease-worn lineaments, which physical suffering, and the gnawing worm at his heart, had rendered hideous and forbidding.

A court martial was called immediately upon the capture of the prisoners, and after a tedious and protracted examination of some weeks, all the eight officers were sentenced to be publicly shot. The long, and most unnecessary delay which preceded the condemnation, was a refinement in cruelty, worthy of the most barbarous horde that ever existed, and sufficiently proved the savage origin of the examining judges. But they had to deal with firm and bold spirits;—men who had not attempted revolt without calculating the chances of defeat and capture, and their minds were therefore strung to meet the ignominious and painful death which they knew awaited them.

On the 4th of July, the day appointed for the execution, all the stores of the town were closed; the streets were thronged with people of both sexes, and a stranger, suddenly entering the city, would have supposed that some great national jubilee was about to take place. At 11 o'clock in the morning, the prisoners were brought on shore in boats, accompanied by several officers of the squadron, and a guard of soldiers. In consequence of the severe illness which most of them had so long suffered, added to the cumbrous shackles on their limbs, not one of them had strength to climb the short flight of steps from the water to the top of the mole. It was necessary for them to be lifted over this impediment, and almost carried to the carts which waited for them in front of the custom-house. I saw, by the countenances of the condemned men, that bodily fear or apprehension had not produced the illness under which they were laboring; it could be accounted for only by their rigid confinement, unwholesome living, and constant sea-sickness. They conversed with the cowled and shaven priests who occupied the carts with them in a calm, and even cheerful tone.

Poor fellows! they probably enjoyed the pure air and glorious canopy of heaven, for which, even though they heralded their way to an ignominious and violent death, they were glad to exchange the gloomy horrors of their prison-house on the sea.

After many delays, which always occur at such times, the carts moved off, preceded and followed by a file of soldiers. The streets were crowded with the populace of all ages, sexes, and conditions, and I, of course, was borne on in the throng towards the place of execution.

I never felt so oppressed with conflicting emotions in my life. Pity and commiseration for the wretched beings who were about to launch out upon the untried ocean of eternity, admiration for the calm and manly resolution which they had shown in this most trying hour, anticipation of the sufferings they were to endure in undergoing the dreadful sentence, and a doubt, a strong and irrepressible doubt of the right of poor fallible mortals to assume a power over the lives of their fellows, which should belong only to the good and righteous Judge of all. Under the influence of the last conclusion, (for such it had become,) I was several times on the point of returning to my lodgings, so as not to sanction by my presence, an act which I could not approve, but I had left with the intention of seeing the end of the tragedy, and as my presence or absence would not affect the event, I followed the rest.

In the course of an hour, the carts arrived at the place of execution, which was a large square, fronting on the sea, at the lower extremity of the city proper, and upper portion of the Almendral. Here the prisoners were lifted to the ground, their coats and hats removed, and thrown in a heap together, and each man placed by a sort of arm chair which had been previously provided, the legs of which had been driven firmly into the ground. A large body of troops, to the number of perhaps six hundred, was then brought forward, and stationed around the square; the city guards, on horseback, were arranged within these, and outside the whole open space was crowded with people, as well as the heights overlooking the spot.

After a long and painful pause, the culprits were seated in the chairs, their arms and legs firmly bound to the upright pieces, and a handkerchief tied around the eyes of each.

From this moment every thing was conducted with the greatest despatch. A file of twelve men was drawn up within about five yards of the victims; the commanding officer waved his sword over his head— every man clapt his musket to his shoulder and fired a rattling volley in the very faces of the poor criminals. It was most wretchedly, most cruelly managed. I had posted myself on the top of a high fence near, and could see clearly every thing that occurred. The volley was fired before even the executioners were prepared; they had evidently expected more exact and definite orders, and the saturnine priests were taken wholly by surprise, as, when the report of the muskets broke the awful silence, they were whispering ghostly comfort, and administering extreme unction to the unhappy sufferers. As the smoke cleared away, the terrified padres were seen scampering from the area, and mixing in the crowd without. As I anticipated, not one of the poor wretches was killed. Some were grievously wounded, and struggling convulsively in their bonds, but several seemed to have escaped altogether. Among these were the colonel and young Florine. The former raised his hand, and tapped his breast several times as though directing them where to fire; and Florine—the diabolical Florine, smiled in scorn and derision! A reserve of twelve men was then brought forward, and each of them walked up to some one of the victims, and placing his musket against the head or breast, fired at his leisure. The first file had by this time reloaded, and they also marched up, each one of them discharging his piece with the most perfect coolness and unconcern at those of the dying men who still struggled, until at last the horrid butchery ceased with the death of all the culprits. The heads lay flaccid and motionless upon the bosoms, and the thongs being cut asunder, the bodies fell heavily to the ground. The soldiers were then all marched in single file by the spot that they might look upon the remains of those who had been traitors to their country, and receive a fearful lesson from the sight, after which the bodies were thrown into one of the carts, and conveyed through the streets towards the place of sepulture. The concourse of people still followed, and I several times observed, when the cart was forced to stop for a few minutes by reason of the crowd, that when it moved on again, a pool of dark, frothy blood was always seen on the spot over which it had been delayed. It was very horrible, and I saw more than one man shudder as he looked upon it.

When the cart arrived at one of the small streets in the lower part of the city, on which the burial ground is situated, the bodies were lifted out by the arms and feet, and thrown upon the ground with about as much care and tenderness as the carcasses of so many dogs! I felt my blood boil at this, but the Chilian gentlemen who were present gave no evidence of such feeling. They had been *traitors*, and therefore indignity should be added to indignity, until the earth covered the mutilated remains.

While the bodies were thus lying, previous to interment, I requested of the guard permission to examine them, which being granted, I stept out from the surrounding crowd, which was kept back by the soldiery, and contemplated with great interest the countenances of the dead. On several of these, the traces of intense and protracted agony were frightfully apparent. The face of the colonel betrayed no evidence of suffering, and that of young Florine still wore its Caliban grin of defiance and derision. I turned away from it to look at the others. The next upon whom my eye fell was the poor Swede, in whom I had taken so much interest. He had received several balls through the breast, his hair was gory, and his lustreless and dead eyes wide open, but the muscles of the face were not contracted, and I hoped he had passed away without much suffering; but upon moving to the other side, my blood curdled, when I perceived that the whole back of the head had been blown away, exhibiting the empty, brainless skull. But enough, and too much of all this. I would not be thought a lover of the horrible.

The bodies were buried on the same day. The head of the colonel was severed from the trunk, and hung in chains near where the battle was fought. The head and right arm of Florine were similarly suspended on the spot where the murder of Portales was committed, and in a few days people ceased to talk, or even think of the tragical fate of the insurgents.

But there are some who will think of them, who will weep and lament for them through long years of sorrow. Mothers are mourning for their children, and "will not be comforted." Wives, sons, and daughters are drinking the waters of affliction, embittered an hundred fold by the violent death of those who were dear to them! Vidaurre had a mother, wife, and children; the Swede had a wife and mother in his own country; many more of them were similarly circumstanced, and even the ruffian Florine will be wept for by the partial eyes of maternal tenderness.

There was another actor in this revolt whom we have lost sight of for some time. Colonel Vidaurre's younger brother, the commandante of the Rezguardo. Although he was fully engaged in the insurrection, and was on the ground at the time of the murder of Portales, yet he was not in the battle which followed; and on his examination, found means to prove, that during the time when these scenes were transpiring, he was lying *dead drunk* at a house in the vicinity. This proof on an *alibi* cleared him, and his sentence will probably be committed to imprisonment or transportation.[1]

The squadron for Peru will sail in a few weeks, and it is expected that in a short time an embargo will be placed on all vessels in the port, which will continue in force for a month or more.

On the 22d of August, I embarked on board the brig B. Mezick, Captain Martin, bound for Philadelphia, and in the evening, sailed out of the harbor of Valparaiso.

September 7th.—During the past week we have had some Cape Horn weather—rain, snow, and hail, but happily, no ice. The sea has been tremendously high, and still continues so, with the weather excessively cold. We may, however, consider ourselves peculiarly favored, as not a day has passed, in which we did not see the sun and ascertain our longitude. Probably the greatest difficulty and danger of this vicinity is the constant darkness and gloom which is its usual characteristic. You are in consequence, unable to ascertain your true position by observation, and dead reckoning furnishes but an insecure guide when powerful currents are impelling you to leeward, and drifting your vessel towards the most frightful of all dangers, a rocky lee-coast. We have now doubled the cape, and are steering N.E., the island of Diego Ramirez bearing W. 130 miles. We have therefore left the Pacific, and are now in the South Atlantic ocean.

October 8th.—We are within about two degrees of the tropical line, and, with good breezes, only about twenty-five days sail from the capes of Delaware. Oh, who can describe the anxious longings of him who is approaching his beloved home, after having been long separated from it, or depict his feelings, his ardent, soul-absorbing feelings, in the prospect of soon holding to his bosom the dear beings who are twined around every fibre of his heart!

Yesterday we passed the latitude of Pernambuco, and are now steering N.W. along the northern coast of Brazil.[2]

On the 13th of November, we made Cape Henlopen, and took a pilot on board, at the distance of four miles from land. The next day ran in, and anchored within view of the light-house, during a heavy N.E. gale. In the night we were so unfortunate as to lose successively both our bower anchors, and were compelled to run out to sea again. The day following, however, was clear; we procured another anchor at the breakwater, and had a fine run of forty-eight hours to the city. I again trod the shore of my native land, after an absence of three years and eight months. I met again the dear relatives and friends, from whom I had been so long separated, and who had been spared in mercy to welcome the wanderer to a participation in the inestimable blessings of Home.

Appendix[1]

❦

Catalogue of Quadrupeds
Found in the Territory of the Oregon

The new species are designated by an * preceding the vulgar name.

American Bison, or Buffalo, *Bos americanus.*

Moose, *Cervus alces.*

Wapiti, or Red Deer, (Elk of the hunters,) *Cervus canadensis.*

Black-tailed Deer, *Cervus macrourus.*

White-tailed Deer, *Cervus leucurus.*

Prong-horned Antelope, *Antelope furcifer.*

Grizzly Bear, *Ursus ferox.*

Black Bear, *Ursus americanus.*

White Bear.

Brown Bear.

American Badger, *Meles labradoria.*

Racoon, *Procyon lotor.*

Common Wolf, *Canus lupus.*

Dusky Wolf, *Canus nubilus.**

Cinereous Wolf, *Canus.*

Prairie Wolf, *Canus latrans.*

Red Fox, *Canus vulpes.*

Grey Fox, *Canus cinereo-argentatus.*

Cross Fox, *Canus cinereo-argentatus.*

Black, or Silver Fox, *Canus cinereo-argentatus.*

Wolverene, or Glutton, *Gulo luscus.*

Beaver, *Castor fiber.*

Musk-rat, or Musquash, *Fiber zibethicus.*

Sea Otter, *Lutra marina.*

Land, or River Otter, *Lutra canadensis.*

Pine Marten, *Mustela martes.*

Ermine Weasel, *Mustela erminea.*

Fisher, *Mustela Pennanti.*

Mink, *Mustela vison.*

Mountain Sheep, *Ovis montana.*

Mountain Goat, *Capra americana.*

---

*This is probably a new species. It is much larger than *nubilus*, as described, and differs much in its habits.

Cougar, or Panther, *Felis concolor.**
Hudson's Bay Lynx, *Felis hudsonicus.*
*Townsend's Hare, *Lepus Townsendii,* (BACHMAN.)
*Wormwood Hare, *Lepus artemesia,* (BACHMAN.)
Marsh Hare, *Lepus palustris,* (BACHMAN.)
*Nuttall's little Hare, *Lepus Nuttallii,* (BACHMAN.)
Little Chief Hare, *Lagomys princeps,* (RICHARDSON.)
Prairie Dog, or Marmot, *Arctomys ludovicianus.*
Franklin's Marmot, *Arctomys Franklinii.*
Douglass' Marmot, *Arctomys Douglassii.*
Richardson's Marmot, *Arctomys Richardsonii.*
*Townsend's Marmot, *Spermophilus Townsendii,* (BACHMAN.)
Hood's Marmot, *Spermophilus tridecemlineatus.*
*Small-pouched Marmot, (the opening of the pouches within the
    mouth,) not in my collection.
Gopher, or Kamas Rat, *Geomys borealis.*
Townsend's Gopher, *Geomys Townsendii,* (*Richardson's M.S.S.*)
Jumping Mouse, *Meriones labradorius,* (RICHARDSON.)
White-footed Mouse, *Mus leucopus.*
Common Mouse, *Mus musculus.*
Rocky Mountain Rat, *Neotoma Drummondii.*
*Townsend's Meadow Mouse, *Arvicola Townsendii,* (BACHMAN.)
*Small Meadow Mouse, *Arvicola oregonii,* (BACHMAN.)
Douglass' Tree Squirrel, *Sciurus Douglassi,* (BENNETT.)
*Downy Squirrel, *Sciurus lanuginosus,* (BACHMAN.)
*Richardson's Squirrel, *Sciurus Richardsonii,* (BACHMAN.)
*Little Ground Squirrel, *Tamias minimus,* (BACHMAN.)
Four-lined Squirrel, *Tamias quadrivitatus,* (SAY.)
*Townsend's Ground Squirrel, *Tamias Townsendii,* (BACHMAN.)
Hudson's Bay Flying Squirrel, *Pteromys sabrinus.*
*Oregon's Flying Squirrel, *Pteromys oregonensis,* (BACHMAN.)
*Townsend's Shrew Mole, *Scalops Townsendii,* (BACHMAN.)
*Columbia Shrew, *Sorex,* (*undescribed.*)
Thick-tail Star-nose Mole, *Condylura macroura.*
Long-tail Star-nose, *Condylura longicaudata.*
Hair Seal, *Phoca vitulina.*
American Porcupine, *Hystrix dorsata.*
*Great-eared Bat, *Plecotus Townsendii,* (COOPER.)
Say's Bat, *Vespertilio subulatus,* (SAY.)
*?Little Bat, *Vespertilio,* (*undescribed.*)

---

*There is a second species of Panther, of which, unfortunately, I possess only
the skull and one foot. I believe it to be undescribed.

NUTTALL'S LITTLE HARE

Lepus *Nuttallii, (BACH.) in Journal Acad. Nat. Sciences, Vol. 7, part II. page 345, plate 22, No. 1.[2]

"*Characters.*—Very small: tail of moderate length; general color above, a mixture of light buff and dark brown; beneath, light yellowish-gray; ears broad and rounded; lower surface of the tail white."* * *

"The fur on the back is for three-fourths of its length from the roots of a plumbeous color, then light ash, mixed with buff; and the long interspersed hairs are all tipped with black. The ears are pretty well clothed internally and externally with hairs of an ash color, bordered with a line of black anteriorly, and edged with white. From behind the ears to the back there is a very broad patch of buff, and the same color, mixed with rufous, prevails on the outer surface of the legs, extending to the thighs and shoulders. The soles of the feet are yellowish-brown. The claws, which are slightly arched, are light brown for three-fourths of their length, and tipped with white. The under surface of the tail is white.

Length, from point of nose to insertion of tail,	$6^3/4$ inches
Length of heel,	2 inches
Length of fur on the back,	$^3/4$ inches
Length of head,	$2^1/8$ inches
Height of ear,	$1^1/2$ inches
Tail (vertebrae,)	$^3/4$ inches
Tail including fur,	$1^1/4$ inches

This description is from a single specimen brought by Mr. Nuttall from beyond the Rocky Mountains. It was captured on the banks of a small stream which flowed into the Snake or Shoshoné river, where it was not uncommon. We never heard of it on the Columbia, and presume, therefore, that it does not inhabit a very extended range.— TOWNS.

TOWNSEND'S SHREW MOLE

Scalops *Townsendii, (BACHMAN.) Journal Acad. Natural Sciences, vol. 8, part I. *Scalops canadensis,* (RICHARDSON,) Fauna boreali Americana, p. 9.

"This species first described by Dr. Richardson, was incorrectly referred to the common shrew mole of the United States. Its size and dentition are sufficient evidences of its being a new and distinct species, which, on account of the number and arrangement of its teeth, will either require the characters of the genus to be enlarged, or that it be placed under a new subgenus. A specimen of this quadruped was kindly presented to me, by Mr. Nuttall, who requested, that in case it should prove a distinct species, it might be given under the above name. I subsequently received from Mr. Townsend another specimen, a little larger, which I presume to be a mere variety, although very singularly marked.

Description of Mr. Nuttall's specimen.

Length of the head and body,	7 in. 6 lines.
Length of tail,	1 in. 6 lines.
Breadth of the fore palm,	7 lines

Dental formula. Incis. $^3/_4$. False molars $^{12}/_{12}$. True molars $^3/_6$. 44.

The body is thick and cylindrical, shaped like the shrew mole of the United States. The whole upper and under surface is of a dark color, in most lights appearing black. The hair, when blown aside, exhibits a grayish-black color from the roots to near the tips. The tail is slightly clothed with short strong bristles.

The specimen brought by Mr. Townsend, is thicker, and about an inch longer. It has a white stripe about two lines wide, commencing under the chin, and running in a somewhat irregular line along the under surface of the body, to within an inch and a half of the insertion of the tail; there is also a white streak commencing on the forehead and extending along the snout."   *   *   *

Inhabits the Columbia river.—TOWNS.

TOWNSEND'S MEADOW MOUSE.

*Avicola *Townsendii,* (BACH.) Journal Acad. Nat. Sciences, vol. 8, part I. *Hash-sho,* of the Chinook Indians.

"Body cylindrical, head rather small, whiskers nearly all white, intermingled with a few black hairs; eyes small; teeth large, yellow; ears large, broad, extending a little beyond the fur; feet of moderate size, toes like the rest of this genus; thumb protected by a rather short, acute nail; fur on the back, about three lines long, much shorter beneath. Tail scaly, sparingly covered with soft brown hair, a few white hairs at its extremity; feet clothed to the nails with short, brown, adpressed hairs; claws brown; fur above lead color from the roots to near the tips, which are dark brown; beneath cinerous.

Length of head and body,	6 inches, 0 lines
Length of tail,	2 inches, 0 lines
Fore feet to point of nails,	9 lines

From heel to point of nail,	1 inches, 0 lines
Breadth of ear,	5 lines"

Inhabits the Columbia river.—TOWNS.

OREGON MEADOW MOUSE.

Arvicola Oregoni, (BACH.) Journal Acad. Nat. Sciences, Vol. 8, part I.

"This dimunitive species is another of the discoveries of Mr. Townsend.

Head of moderate size, body slender, eyes very small for this genus; ears nearly naked, concealed by the fur; feet small; whiskers the length of the head, white and black, the latter predominating; color above, a shade lighter than that of the former species, inclining a little to hoary brown; ash-colored beneath; a very minute blunt thumb nail on the fore foot.

Length of the head and body,	3 inches
Length of tail	1 inch, 2 lines"

Inhabits the Columbia river.—TOWNS.

TOWNSEND'S MARMOT.

Spermophilus *Townsendii, (BACH.) Journal Acad. Nat. Sciences, Vol. 8, part I. *Tet no,* of the Walla-walla, and Nez Percés Indians.

"The body is long and rather slender. Head of moderate size; nose slightly obtuse. Ears short, scarcely a line in height; nails slender, compressed, and slightly arched; the thumb protected by an acute and prominent nail; the second claw in the fore foot, as in all the species of this genus, is longest, and not the third, as in the squirrels. Cheek-pouches not large. Tail thickly clothed with fur, and in the dried specimen appears much flattened; the fur is soft, smooth, and lustrous.

There is a line of white above and below the eye-brows. The fur on the whole of the upper surface is for one-fourth of its length from the roots of a nearly black color, then a broad line of silver gray, then a narrow line of dark brown, edged with yellowish-white, with a few black hairs interspersed, giving it a brownish-gray appearance. On the under surface, where the hair is a little longer than on the back, it is black at the roots, and cinereous at the points; on the forehead and nose, it is slightly tinged with brown. The line of separation between the colors of the upper and under surface, exists high up along the sides, and is very distinctly drawn. The tail on the upper surface is the color of the back, slightly tinged with brown beneath; the teeth are white.

Length of the head and body,	8 inches, 9 lines,
Length of the head,	1 inch, 10 lines
Length of the tail, (vertebræ,)	1 inch
Length of the tail including fur,	1 inch, 6 lines
Length from heel to middle hind claw,	1 inch, 4 lines"

I procured a single specimen of this animal on the Columbia river, about three hundred miles above its mouth, in July. It was said to be common there at that season, but as I was traveling in boats to the interior, had but little time to search for it. I know but little of its habits. It becomes excessively fat, and is eaten by the Indians. Disappears in August, and emerges in the spring in a very attentuated state.—TOWNS. in lit.

DOUGLASS' SQUIRREL.

Sciurus Douglassi, (BENNETT.) *Sciurus Townsendii*, (BACHMAN.) Journal Acad. Nat. Sciences, Vol. 8, part I. *Ap-poe-poe*, of the Chinook Indians.

"This species, in the form of its body, is not very unlike the *Sciurus hudsonicus*; its ears and tail, however, are proportionably much shorter; it is about a fourth larger, and in its markings differs widely from all other known species.

Head considerably broader than that of the *Sciurus hudsonicus*; nose less elongatged and blunter, body long and slender; ears rather small, nearly rounded, slightly tufted posteriorly. As usual in this genus, the third inner toe is the longest, and not the second, as in the Spermophile.

Color.—The whiskers, which are the length of the head, are black. The fur, which is soft and lustrous, is, on the back from the roots to near the points, plumbeous, tipped with brownish-gray, with a few lighter colored hairs interspersed, giving it a dark brown appearance; when closely examined, it has the appearance of being thickly sprinkled with minute points of rust color on a black ground. The tail, which is distichous, but not broad, is, for three-fourths of an inch, of the color of the back; in the middle, the fur is plumbeous at the roots, then irregular markings of brown and black, tipped with soiled white, giving it a hoary appearance; on the extremity of the tail, the hairs are black from the roots, tipped with light brown. The inner sides of the extremities, and the outer surface of the feet, together with the throat and mouth, and a line above and under the eye, are bright buff. The colors on the upper and under parts are separated by a line of black, commencing at the shoulders, and running along the flanks to the thighs. It is widest in the middle, about three lines, and tapers off to a point. The hairs which project beyond the outer margins of the ears, and forming a slight tuft, are dark brown, and, in some specimens, black.

> Length from point of nose to insertion of tail, 8 inches 4 lines.
> Length of tail, (vertebræ,)   4 inches, 6 lines
> Length of tail, including fur,   6 inches, 4 lines
> Height of ear posteriorly,   6 lines
> Sole and middle hind claw,   1 inch 11 lines"

This squirrel is common on the Columbia in pine forests. Feeds chiefly upon the seeds of the pine, and lays up a large quantity of them for winter store, in the hollows of decayed limbs.

It is very unsuspicious and tame; more so than *Sciurus hudsonicus.* Voice remarkably loud and harsh; may be heard several hundred yards. It is in the habit of nipping off small branches from the summits of the trees, and throwing them down, apparently in sport. I have seen at one time at least a dozen of them engaged in this way, within a short distance. The twigs were falling in every direction, and the loud call was not suspended for a moment. The nest is made of sticks and hair, usually in the hollow of a decayed branch, rarely in the bifurcation of limbs. Has four young at a birth, which remain longer in the nest than the common gray squirrel.

I have frequently seen this species tamed, and in the possession of the Indian boys. They were very lively and playful.—Towns. in lit.

COLUMBIA PINE SQUIRREL.

*Sciurus *Richardsonii,* (BACHMAN,) Journal Acad. Nat. Sciences, Vol. 8, part I. *Small brown squirrel, Lewis and Clarke,* Vol. 3, p. 37. *Sciurus hudsonicus, var. (Columbia Pine Squirrel, Richardson.)*

"This small species was first noticed by Lewis and Clarke, who deposited a specimen in the Philadelphia Museum, where it still exists. I have compared it with a specimen brought by Mr. Townsend, and find them identical. Richardson, who appears not to have seen it, supposes it to be a mere variety of the *Sciurus hudsonicus.* On the contrary, Mr. Townsend says in in his notes, 'It is evidently a distinct species; its habits are very different from those of the *Sciurus hudsonicus.* It frequents the pine trees in the high range of the Rocky Mountains, west of the great chain, feeding upon the seeds contained in the cones. These seeds are large and white, and contain a good deal of nutriment. The Indians eat a great quantity of them, and esteem them good. The note of this squirrel is a loud jarring chatter, very different from the voice of the *Sciurus hudsonicus.* It is not at all shy, frequently coming down to the foot of the tree to reconnoitre the passenger, and scolding at him vociferously. It is, I think, a scarce species.'

The difference between these two species can be detected at a glance by comparing the specimens. The present, in addition to its being about a fourth smaller, the size of the *Tamias lysteri*, has less of the reddish-brown on the upper surface, and may be always distinguished from the other by the blackness of its tail at the extremity.

The body of this most diminutive of all the known species of genuine squirrel in North America, is short, and does not present that appearance of lightness and agility which distinguishes the *Sciurus hudsonicus*. Head large, less elongated, and nose a little blunter than *Sciurus hudsonicus*, ears short; feet of moderate size, the third toe on the fore foot but slightly longer than the second. The claws are compressed, hooked and acute; tail shorter than the body; the thumb nail is broad, flat and blunt.

The fur on the back is dark plumbeous from the roots, tipped with rusty brown and black, giving it a rusty gray appearance. It is less rufous than the *Sciurus hudsonicus*, and lighter colored than the *S. Douglassi*. The feet, on their upper surface, are rufous; on the shoulders, forehead, ears, and along the thighs, there is a slight tinge of the same color. The whiskers, which are a little longer than the head, are black, the teeth yellowish-white. The whole of the under surface, as well as a line around the eyes, and a small patch above the nostrils, smoke gray. The tail for about one-half its length, presents on the upper surface a dark rufous appearance; many of the hairs being nearly black, pointed with light rufous. At the extremity of the tail, for about one inch in length, the hairs are black, a few of them slightly tipped with rufous. The hind feet, from the heels to the palms, are thickly clothed with short adpressed light colored hairs; the palms are naked. The sides are marked by a line of black commencing at the shoulder, and terminating abruptly on the flanks; it is about two inches in length, and four lines wide.

Length of head and body,	6 inches, 2 lines.
Length of tail (vertebræ,)	3 inches, 6 lines
Length of including fur,	5 inches
Length of ears posteriorly,	3 inches
Length of including fur,	5 inches
Length of sole and middle hind claw,	9 lines"

DOWNY SQUIRREL.

Sciurus lanuginosus, (BACH.) Journal Acad. Nat. Sciences, vol. 8, part I.

"A singular and beautiful little quadruped, to which I have conceived the above name appropriate, was sent to me with the collection of Mr. Townsend.

The head is broader than the *S. hudsonicus,* and the forehead much arched; the ears short and oval; whiskers longer than the head; feet and toes short, thumb armed with a broad, flat nail; nails slender, compressed, and acute; the third on the fore feet is the longest, as in the squirrels. The tail, which bears some resemblance to that of the flying squirrel, is composed of hairs a little coarser than those of the back, and much shorter than the body. On the fore feet the palms are nearly naked; the under surface of the toes being only partially covered with hair, but on the hind feet, the under surface, from the heel even to the extremity of the nails is thickly clothed with short soft hairs.

The fur is softer and more downy than that of any other of our species, and the whole covering of the animal indicates it to be a native of a cold region.

The teeth are dark orange; whiskers brown; the fur on the back, from the roots near the extremitites, light plumbeous, tipped with light chestnut-brown; on the sides with silver gray; there is a broad band of white around the eyes; a spot of white on the hind part of the head, a little in advance of the anterior portion of the ears. The nose is white, which color extends along the forehead till above the eyes, where it is gradually blended with the colors on the back. The whole of the under surface, including the feet and the inner surface of the legs, pure white. In the tail, the colors are irregularly blended with markings of black, light brown, and white, scarcely two hairs being uniform in color. In general, it may be said that the tail, when examined without reference to individual hairs, is light ash at the roots of the hair, then a broad, but not well defined, line of light rufous, then dark brown, and tipped with rufous and smoke gray.

Length of head and body,	7 inches 11 lines.
Length of tail, (vertebræ,)	4 inches 8 lines
Length of tail, including fur,	6 inches
Length of palm and middle fore claw,	1 inch
Length of sole and middle hind claw,	1 inch 9 lines
Length of fur on the back,	7 lines
Length of fur at the tip of the tail,	1 inch 10 lines
Height of ear, measured posteriorly,	5 lines
Distance between the orbits,	6 lines"

Of the habits, &c., of this animal, I know nothing. It was presented to me by William Fraser Tolmie, Esq., surgeon of the Honorable Hudson's Bay Company, by whom it was captured near Fort McLoughlin, on the N.W. coast of America.—Towns.

TOWNSEND'S GROUND SQUIRREL.

Tamias *Townsendii, (BACHMAN.) Journal Acad. Nat. Sciences, Vol. 8, part I. *Quiss-Quiss* of the Chinook Indians.

"This species bears some resemblance to our common ground squirrel of the middle and northern states, (*S. lysteri,*) it differs from it, however, in its larger size, longer tail, and several other striking particulars.

The body is stouter than that of the former species, the head broader, the nose more obtuse, and the tail nearly double the length. In the arrangement of the teeth and toes, this species does not differ widely from the Sciurus (*Tamias*) lysteri, except that they are much more robust. The teeth are dark orange; whiskers, which are a little shorter than the head, black; a line of fawn color, commencing at the nostrils, runs over the eyebrows, and terminates a little beyond them in a point of lighter color; a patch of similar commences under the eyelids, and running along the cheeks, terminates at the ear. There is a line of dark brown, commencing at the termination of the nose, where it forms a point, and bordering the fawn color above, is gradually blended with the lighter colors of the head. The ears, which are of moderate size, and ovate, are on the upper margins of the inner surface partially clothed with a few short, brown hairs; the outer surface is thickly clothed with fur, brown on the anterior parts, with a patch of white covering about one-fourth of the ear on the posterior portion. Behind the ear there is a slight marking of cinereous, of about six lines in length, terminating near the shoulder. A line of black commences on the hind part of the head, runs over the centre of the back, where it spreads out to the width of four lines, and terminates in a point at the insertion of the tail; a line of similar color commences at the shoulders, and running parallel, terminates a little beyond the hips; another, but narrower and shorter line of the same color, runs parallel with this, low down on the sides, giving it five black stripes. The head and back are light yellowish-brown, presenting on the upper surface a dusky ochre color. It has not the whitish stripes on the sides, nor the rufous color on the hips, which are so conspicuous in the Sciurus (*Tamias*) lysteri. On the throat, belly, and inner parts of the legs and thighs, the color is light cinereous; there is no line of separation between the colors of the back and belly. The tail, which is not bushy, is on the upper surface grayish-black, having a hoary appearance. Underneath it is reddish brown, for two-thirds of its breadth, then a narrow line of black, tipped with light ash. The nails are brown.

Length of the head and body,	6 inches 9 lines
Length of the tail (vertebrae)	4 inches
Length of tail, including fur	5 inches
Length of head	2 inches
Height of ear	6 lines
Length of heel to middle claw of hind foot,	1 inch 6 lines"

This pretty little animal, so much resembling our common *striatus*, is quite common on the Columbia river. It lives in holes in the ground, and is so tame, that it not unfrequently runs over your feet as you traverse the forests. It frequently perches itself upon a log or stump, and keeps up a continual *clucking*, which is usually answered by another at some distance, for a considerable time. Their note so much resembles that of the dusky grouse, (*Tetrao obscurus*,) that I have more than once been deceived by it.—Towns. in lit.

LEAST GROUND SQUIRREL.

*Tamias *minimus*, (BACHMAN.) Journal Acad. Nat. Sciences, Vol. 8, part I.

"This diminutive and beautiful species of Tamias, not half the size of the common ground squirrel, is another of the discoveries of Mr. Townsend.

Length of head and body,	3 inches, 9 lines.
Length of tail, (vertebræ,)	3 inches 2 lines
Length of tail to the end of fur,	4 inches
Height of ear, posteriorly,	$2^1/2$ lines
Length of head,	1 inch 3 lines
Length of heel to end of middle claw,	1 inch

The head is rather small; the nose very sharp pointed; claws moderately curved, compressed, acute, and dark brown. There is, as in all the species of this genus, a minute blunt nail on the thumb. The feet and legs rather long in proportion to the size of the animal.

The fur is soft to the touch, fine and silky. The teeth, which are not robust, are yellow; a white streak runs from above and behind the eye to the nostrils, giving the nose a sharp and pointed appearance. This white line is marked on the upper surface with an edge of brown; a minute line of rufous runs from the nose through the eye, terminating at the ear, another commencing under the eye, and running parallel with the last, terminates on the neck; a line of black commencing on the forehead, extends over the back and terminates at the tail; this is succeeded on each side by a broad line of whitish-ash, then by a narrower line of brown, commencing back of the neck and running parallel with the rest, till it is narrowed to a point on the hips; this is succeeded by a line of pure white on each side, similar to the last, and finally, by a broader and shorter stripe of brown, giving it on the back one stripe of black, two of light ash, and four of light brown. The head is cinereous; the ears have a white spot on their posterior surface, similar to the last species, and also to another described by Say, as the *Sciurus quadrivitatus*, with which I have compared it. The neck and whole of the under surface, including the legs and thighs, are white. The tail, which is quite narrow, is dark brown above, edged with light rufous. Beneath, it is rufous near the roots, then a line of black edged with light rufous; from the end of the vertebræ to the extremity, the hairs are black, a few of them are tipped with light rufous."

This species is found very plentiful along the banks of the Rio Colorado, but I think does not inhabit a very extensive range, as I never saw it after leaving this river. It keeps almost constantly among heaps of stones, on the tops of which it often perches, extending its long tail over its back, and curving it down in front of its head. At such times it emits a lively, garrulous note like the squeaking of a young puppy; but if approached, darts off with astonishing swiftness, carrying the tail level with the ground, and almost eluding the eye by the activity of its motions, and conceals itself under some jutting rock or in the interstices of a stone heap until the intruder has passed.—Towns. in lit.

TOWNSEND'S GREAT-EARED BAT.

*Plecotus *Townsendii*, (Cooper,) Annals of the Lyceum of Nat. History of N. York, Vol. 4, p. 73, [Plate 3, fig. 6, the head.] *So-capual* of the Chinook Indians.

"Fur on the back dusky at base, brown at the tips, with a ferruginous cast, the two tints appearing nearly uniform. The ears are fringed with fur. Beneath, the fur is of a reddish cinereous or ochreous hue, lighter towards the tail, but not in the least whitish. The nose is similar to the *P. Lecontii*, but the fleshy crests between the eyes and nostrils appear to be still larger, and in the preserved specimens are much more conspicuous. The ears are similar, though every way more ample in the present, and presenting a different outline immediately after rising from the forehead; the auricle broader and larger. The wing and tail membranes are entirely naked, dusky, of a thicker texture, and much more strongly reticulated than in the first species.

Incisors $^4/_6$, canines $^{1\text{-}1}/_{1\text{-}1}$, molars $^{5\text{-}5}/_{0\text{-}6}$ = 36.

Total length,	3.8 inches
Ears,	1.1 inches
Tail,	1.7 inches
Fore arm,	1.8 inches
Tibia,	0.8 inches
Spread,	11.0 inches

Three specimens of this very distinct new species were brought fromthe Columbia river by Mr. John K. Townsend, where he procured them on his late journey. It is very like the *P. Lecontii,* but they may be readily known by the color of the under part of the body, besides which they differ in almost all their details of color and proportions, the present being a larger and more robust animal. Together, they seem to form a small group in the genus, characterized by the double fleshy crest of the nose, which is not mentioned as occurring in any other species.

Verpertilio megalotis, (Raf.) *Plecotis Rafinesquii,* (Lesson,) which is described as having the auricle as long as the ears, cannot be either of our species. I am not acquainted with any other species within the United States."

Inhabits the Columbia river district, rather common. Frequents the store houses attached to the forts, seldom emerging from them even at night. This, and a species of *Verpertilio,* (*V. subulatus,*) which is even more numerous, are protected by the gentelmen of the Hudson's Bay Company, for their services in destroying the dermestes which abound in their fur establishments.—Towns.

TOWNSEND'S HARE.

*Lepus * Townsendii,* (BACHMAN.) Journal Acad. Nat. Sciences. Vol. 8, part I., figure. *Poolalik* of the Walla-walla and Nez Percés Indians.

"This species, which is another of the discoveries of Mr. Townsend, and of which no specimen exists in any museum that I have had an opportunity of examining, is one of the most singular hares that has fallen under my notice.

Characters.—Size of the northern hare, *(L. americanus.)* Ears, tail, legs, and tarsi, very long. Color above, light gray; beneath white. Crown of the head, cheeks, neck, and whole upper parts—the front of the ears and legs, externally—gray, with a faint cream-colored wash. Hairs whitish, or silver-gray at base, then brownish-white, then black,

witha faint cream tinge, and ultimately tipped with black; interspersed
with long, silky hairs, some of which are wholly black. Chin, throat,
whole under surface, interior of legs, the whole of the tail, (with the
exception of a narrow, dark line on the top,) pure white to the roots.
Irides light hazel; around the eyes white. The tips of the back parts of
the ears black; the external two-thirds of the hinder part of the ears
white, running down the back part of the neck, and there mingling
with the color of the upper surface; the interior third of the outer
portion of the ear, the same gray color as the back, fringed on the edge
with long hairs, which are reddish-fawn at the roots, and white at the
tips. The interior of the ear is very thinly scattered with beautiful, fine
white hairs, being more thickly clothed towards the edge, where it is
grizzled black and yellowish, but the edge itself is fringed with pure
white, becoming yellowish towards the tip, and at the tip is black.
Whiskers nearly as long as the head, for the most part white, black at
the roots; a few hairs are pure white, others wholly black.

Dimensions.

From nose to insertion of tail,	21 inches 0 lines.
From tail to end of hair,	5 inches 6 lines
From tail (vertebræ,) about	3 inches 3 lines
Ears measured posteriorly,	4 inches 9 lines
Length of head measured over the forehead,	4 inches 6 lines
Length from eye to nose,	2 inches 0 lines
Length from heel to longest nail,	5 inches 6 lines

The specimen from which the above description and drawing were
taken, was a female, procured by Mr. Townsend on the Walla-walla, one
of the sources of the Columbia river."

This species is common on the Rocky Mountains. I made particular
inquiries, both of the Indians and British traders, regarding the changes
it undergoes at different seasons, and they all assured me that it never
was lighter colored. We first saw it on the plains of Blackfoot river, west
of the mountains, and observed it in all similar situations during our
route to the Columbia. When first seen, which was in July, it was lean
and unsavory, having, like our common species, the larva of an insect
imbedded in its neck, but when we arrived at Walla-walla, in
September, we found the Indians, and the persons attached to the fort,
using them as a common article of food. Immediately after we arrived
we were regaled with a dish of hares, and I thought I had never eaten
anything more delicious. They are found here in great numbers on the
plains covered with wormwood, (*Artemesia*,) under the close branches
of which they often squat when pursued. I will not be qualified that this

animal "can leap *twenty-one feet* at a bound," but it is so exceedingly fleet, that no ordinary dog can catch it. I have frequently surprised it in its form, and shot it as it leapt away, but I found it necessary to be very expeditious, and to pull trigger at a particular instant, or the game was off amongst the wormwood, and I never saw it again.

The Indians kill them with arrows, by approaching them stealthily as they lie concealed under the bushes, and in winter take them with nets. To do this, some one or two hundred Indians, men, women, and children, collect and enclose a large space with a slight net, about five feet wide, made of hemp; the net is kept in a vertical position by pointed sticks attached to it, and driven into the ground. These sticks are placed about five or six feet apart, and at each one an Indian is stationed with a short club in his hand. After these arrangements are completed, a large number of Indians enter the circle, and beat the bushes in every direction. The frightened hares dart off toward the nets, and, in attempting to pass, are knocked on the head and secured.

Mr. Pambrun, the superintendent of Fort Walla-walla, from whom I obtained this account, says that he has often participated in this sport with the Indians, and has known several hundred to be thus taken in a day. When captured alive, it does not scream like the common gray rabbit, (*Lepus sylvaticus.*)

This species inhabits the plains exclusively, and seems particularly fond of the vicinity of the aromatic wormwood. Immediately as you leave these bushes, in journeying towards the sea, you lose sight of the hare.—Towns. in lit. to Dr. Bachman.

WORMWOOD HARE.

*Lepus *artemesia*, (BACHMAN.) Journal Acad. Nat. Sciences, vol. 8, part I. *I-iks*, of the Walla-walla, and Nez Percés Indians.

"*Characters.*—Small; of a gray color, with pale rusty on the back of the neck and legs. Tail above, the color of the body; beneath white. Under parts of the neck, and lower surface of the body white, all the fur being gray at the base. Ears as long as the head; tarsus well clothed.

Description.—The head is much arched—upper incisors deeply grooved. The color of this species is grizzled black, and brownish-white above. The fur is soft, pale gray at the base, shaded into brownish externally, annulated with brownish-white near the apex, and black at the tips. Under parts, and inner sides of limbs, white, the hairs pale gray at the base. Neck, with the hairs on the sides and under parts, gray, tipped with brownish-white, having a faint yellow hue. Chin and throat grayish-white, the hairs being gray at the base, and white at their tips.

The whole back of the neck, and limbs exteriorly, of a pale, rusty fawn color; those on the neck uniform to the base. Feet beneath, a very pale, soiled yellow-brown. Tail, colored above as the back, with an admixture of grayish-black hairs; beneath white. Ears externally on the anterior part, colored as the crown of the head, posteriorly ashy-white;—at the apex margined with black; internally nearly naked, excepting on the posterior part, where they are grizzled with grayish-black and white; in the apical portion, they are chiefly white.

Dimensions.

Length from nose to root of tail,	12 inches 0 lines,
From heel to point of longest tail,	3 inches 2 lines
Height of ear externally,	2 inches 8 lines
From ear to point of nose,	2 inches 7 lines
Tail, (vertebræ,) about,	1 inch 1 line
Do. to end of fur,	1 inch 9 lines"

This small hare, inhabits the wormwood plains near the banks of the streams in the neighborhood of Fort Walla-walla. I cannot define its range with any degree of certainty, but I have reason to believe that it is very contracted, never having met with it many miles from this locality. It is here abundant, but very shy and retired, keeping constantly in the densest wormwood bushes, and leaping, with singular speed, from one to another, when pursued. I have never seen it dart away, and run to a great distance like other hares. I found it very difficult to shoot this animal for the reasons stated. I had been residing at Fort Walla-walla for several weeks, and had procured only two, when, at the suggestion of Mr. Pambrun, I collected a party of a dozen Indians armed with bows and arrows, and sallied forth. We hunted through the wormwood, within about a mile of the fort, and in a few hours returned, bringing eleven hares. The keen eyes of the Indians discovered the little creatures squatting under the bushes, when, to a white man, they would have been totally invisible. This hare when wounded and taken, screams like our common species.—Towns. in lit. to Dr. Bachman.

OREGON FLYING SQUIRREL.

*Pteromys *Oregonensis*, (Bachman,) Journal Acad. Nat. Sciences, Vol. 8 part, I.

"*Characters.*—Intermediate in size, between *P. volucella*, and the northern *P. sabrinus*; ears longer than the latter species; fur more compact; the lobe of the flying membrane joining the fore foot, much longer in proportion, making that membrane broader; foot larger; general color above brown; beneath yellowish-white.

Description.—All the fur of this species is deep gray at the base; that of the back tipped with yellowish-brown; tail, pale brown above, dusky towards the extremity; beneath, brownish-white. Whiskers numerous, and very long, chiefly of a black color, and grayish at the tips. Hairs covering the flying membrane chiefly black, most of them slightly tipped with pale brown; feet dusky; around the eyes blackish; ears with minute, adpressed brown hairs externally, and brownish-white internally.

This species differs much from *P. sabrinus* in several very striking particulars. Although a smaller animal, the bone of the wrist, which supports the flying membrane, is eleven and a half lines in length, whilst that of the former is only nine; thus the smallest animal has the largest flying membrane. The fur of *P. sabrinus* is much the longest. The fur on the belly of the latter is white, whilst that of *oregonensis* has an ochreous tinge. The hairs on the tail of *P. sabrinus* are only slightly tinged with lead color at the roots, whilst in *oregonensis* it extends to half the length of the hairs. The greater length and less breadth, however, of the ear of the latter, is a sufficient mark of distinction.

From our little *Pteromys volucella*, the difference is so great, that it is unnecessary to institute a particular comparison. Besides being much larger than our little species, and not possessing the beautiful downy-white on the belly, the two species may be instantly detected, in the volucella having its hairs white to the roots, which is not the case in the other species.

Dimensions.

Length from point of nose to root of tail,	6 inches, 8 lines.
Length from tail to point of fur,	6 inches 0 lines
Height of ear posteriorly,	7 lines
Breadth between the outer edges of the flying membrane,	8 inches 0 lines
Longest hind toe, including nail,	$5^1/4$ lines
Longest fore toe, including nail,	$5^1/2$ lines
From heel to point of nail,	1 inch $6^1/2$ lines
From nose to ear,	1 inch 6 lines"

This species inhabits the pine woods of the Columbia, near the sea; very rare. Habits of the *P. volucella*.—TOWNS. in lit.

Townsend's Gopher.

Geomys *Townsendii, (*Richardson's manuscripts*,) Journal Acad. Nat. Sciences, Vol. 8, Part I.

General color very pale gray above, with a faint yellowish wash; muzzle dusky-gray; under parts grayish-white; chin pure white. Tail and feet white; the former grayish above. Hairs of the back very pale gray at the base, pale yellow at the apex, the extreme tip cinereous. Teeth yellowish-white. Upper incisors with a faint groove near the internal margin. Claws and fore feet moderate, white.

Dimensions.

From nose to tail,	7 inches, 6 lines.
Tail,	2 inches 9 lines
Tarsus,	1 inch $3^1/2$ lines
Central claw of fore foot,	5 lines
From nose to ear,	1 inch 5 lines

The specimen was procured by Mr. Townsend on the Columbia river.

I am obliged to confess that I should not have ventured to publish this species as distinct from *G. borealis,* on my own responsibility. The discriminating eye of Dr. Richardson, however, who has studied this genus more carefully than I have had an opportunity of doing, may have detected marks of difference which I have not been able to discover.—BACH.

Catalogue of Birds,
Found in the Territory of the Oregon.

The new species are designated by an * preceding the vulgar name.

Californian Vulture, *Cathartes californianus.*
Turkey Buzzard, or Vulture, *Cathartes aura.*
Golden Eagle, *Falco chrysætos.*
White-headed, or Bald Eagle, *Falco leucocephalus.*
Fish Hawk, *Falco haliætus.*
Sparrow Hawk, *Falco sparverius.*
Pigeon Hawk, *Falco columbarius.*
Merlin, *Falco æsalon.*
Great-footed, or Duck Hawk, *Falco peregrinus.*
Sharp-shinned Hawk, *Falco velox.*
Hen Harrier, or Marsh Hawk, *Falco cyaneus.*
Cooper's Hawk, *Falco Cooperii.*
Red-tailed Hawk, *Falco borealis.*
Black Hawk, *Falco sancti-johannes.*
Rough-legged Hawk, or Falcon, *Falco lagopus.*
Common Hawk, or Buzzard, *Falco (buteo) vulgaris.*
Winter Hawk, or Falcon, *Falco hyemalis.*
Great Cinereous Owl, *Strix cinerea.*
Great-horned Owl, *Strix virginiana.*
Red Owl, *Strix asio.*
Mottled Owl, *Strix nœvia.*
Long-eared Owl, *Strix otus.*
Short-eared Owl, *Strix brachyotus.*
Little Owl, *Strix acadica.*
Tengmalm's Owl, *Strix Tengmalmi.*
Burrowing Owl, *Strix cunicularia.*
Passerine Owl, *Strix passerinoides.*
Meadow Lark, or Starling, *Sturnus ludovicianus.*
Red-winged Starling, or Oriole, *Icterus phœniceus.*
Bullock's Oriole, *Icterus Bullocki.*
Rusty Blackbird, or Grakle, *Quiscalus ferrugineus.*
Raven, *Corvus corax.*
Common Crow, *Corvus corone.*
Fish Crow, *Corvus ossifragus.*
Magpie, *Corvus pica.*
Clark's Crow, *Corvus columbianus.*
Steller's Jay, *Garrulus Stelleri.*
Ultramarine Jay, *Garrulus ultramarinus.*

Canada Jay, *Garrulus canadensis.*
Black-capt Titmouse, *Parus atricapillus.*
*Chestnut-backed Titmouse, *Parus rufescens,* (TOWNSEND.)
*Brown-headed Titmouse, *Parus minimus,* (TOWNSEND.)
Cedar Bird, or Cherry Bird, *Bombycilla carolinensis.*
Great American Shrike, *Lanius septentrionalis.*
Loggerhead Shrike, *Lanius ludovicianus.*
Tyrant Flycatcher, or King Bird, *Muscicapa tyrannus.*
Cooper's Flycatcher, *Muscicapa Cooperi.*
Pewit Flycatcher, *Muscicapa fusca.*
Wood Pewee Flycatcher, *Muscicapa virens.*
Small Green-crested Flycatcher, *Muscicapa acadica.*
Traill's Flycatcher, *Muscicapa Trailli.*
Little Flycatcher, *Muscicapa pusilla,* (SWAINSON.)
Arkansas Flycatcher, *Muscicapa verticalis.*
Say's Flycatcher, *Muscicapa Saya.*
Yellow-breasted Chat, *Icteria viridis.*
Solitary Flycatcher, or Vireo, *Vireo solitarius.*
Warbling Flycatcher, or Vireo, *Vireo gilvus.*
White-eyed Flycatcher, or Vireo, *Vireo noveboracensis.*
*Mountain Mocking Bird, *Orpheus montanus,* (TOWNSEND.)
American Robin, *Turdus migratorius.*
Varying Thrush, *Turdus nœvia.*
Hermit Thrush, *Turdus minor.*
Wilson's Tawny Thrush, *Turdus Wilsonii.*
Golden-crowned Thrush, *Turdus aurocapillus.*
*White tailed Thrush, (*not in the collection.*)
*Townsend's Thrush, *Ptiliogonys Townsendi,* (AUDUBON.)
*Morton's Water Ouzel, *Cinclus Mortoni,* (TOWNSEND.)
*Columbian Water Ouzel, *Cinclus Townsendi,* (AUDUBON.)
Blue-eyed Yellow Warbler, *Sylvia œstiva.*
Maryland Yellow-throat, *Sylvia trichas.*
*Tolmie's Warbler, *Sylvia Tolmei.* (TOWNSEND.)
Cærulean Warbler, *Sylvia azurea.*
Wilson's Green-black Capt Warbler, *Sylvia Wilsoni.*
Orange-crowned Warbler, *Sylvia celata.*
*Hermit Warbler, *Sylvia occidentalis,* (TOWNSEND.)
*Black-throated Gray Warbler, *Sylvia nigrescens,* (TOWNSEND.)
*Audubon's Warbler, *Sylvia Auduboni,* (TOWNSEND.)
*Townsend's Warbler, *Sylvia Townsendi,* (NUTTALL.)
*Ash-headed Warbler, *Sylvia* (*not described.*)
Ruby-crowned Wren, *Regulus calendula.*

Golden-crested Wren, *Regulus cristatus*.
Common Wren, *Troglodytes ædon*.
Winter Wren, *Troglodytes hyemalis*.
Bewick's Wren, *Troglodytes Bewicki*.
Rocky-mountain Wren, *Troglodytes obsoleta*.
Arctic Blue Bird, *Sialia arctica*.
*Western Blue Bird, *Sialia occidentalis*, (TOWNSEND.)
Brown Lark, *Anthus spinoletta*.
Shore Lark, *Alanda cornuta*, (WILSON.)
Snow Bunting, *Emberiza nivalis*.
Louisiana Tanager, *Tanagra ludoviciana*.
*Brown Longspur, *Plectrophanes Townsendi*, (AUDUBON.)
Luzuli Finch, *Fringilla amœna*.
White-crowned Bunting, or Finch, *Fringilla leucophrys*.
Bay-winged Bunting, or Grass Finch, *Fringilla graminea*.
Chipping Sparrow, *Fringilla socialis*.
American Goldfinch, *Fringilla tristis*.
Pine Finch, *Fringilla pinus*.
Purple Finch, *Fringilla purpurea*.
Crimson-fronted Bullfinch, *Fringilla frontalis*.
Arctic Ground Finch, *Fringilla arctica*.
Savannah Finch, *Fringilla savanna*.
*Oregon Snow Finch, *Fringilla Oregona*, (TOWNSEND.)
Ash-colored Finch, *Fringilla cinerea*, (GM.)
Evening Grosbeak, *Fringilla vespertina*.
Mottled, or Spotted Grosbeak, *Fringilla maculata*.
*Green-tailed Finch, *Fringilla* (*not described.*)
Black-headed Finch, *Fringilla artricapilla*, (GM.)
Lark Finch, *Fringilla grammaca*.
Tree Sparrow, *Fringilla canadensis*.
Field Sparrow, *Fringilla pusilla*.
American Crossbill, *Loxia curvirostra*.
Yellow-billed Cuckoo, *Coccyzus americanus*.
Red-shafted Woodpecker, *Picus mexicanus*.
Pileated Woodpecker, *Picus pileatus*.
Lewis Woodpecker, *Picus torquatus*.
Red-breasted Woodpecker, *Picus ruber*.
*Black, White-Banded Woodpecker, (*not in the collection.*)
*Black, Red-Backed Woodpecker, (*not in the collection.*)
*Harris' Woodpecker, *Picus Harrisi*, (AUDUBON.)
Downy Woodpecker, *Picus pubescens*.
White-breasted Nuthatch, *Sitta carolinensis*.

Red-bellied Nuthatch, *Sitta canadensis.*
Common Creeper, *Certhia familiaris.*
Nootka Humming Bird, *Trochilus rufus.*
American Kingfisher, *Alcedo alcyon.*
Barn Swallow, *Hirundo rufa.*
Marten, *Hirundo purpurea.*
Cliff, or Republican Swallow, *Hirundo fulva.*
White-bellied Swallow, *Hirundo bicolor.*
Bank Swallow, *Hirundo riparia.*
Violet-green Swallow, *Hirundo thalassina.*
*Vaux's Chimney Swallow, *Cypselus Vauxi*, (TOWNSEND.)
Night Hawk, *Caprimulgus virginianus.*
Band-tail Pigeon, *Columba fasciata.*
Passenger Pigeon, *Columba migratoria.*
Turtle Dove, *Columba carolinensis.*
Plumed Partridge, *Perdix plumifera*, (GOULD.)
*Long-tailed Black Pheasant, (*not in the collection.*)
Ruffled Grouse or Pheasant, *Tetrao umbellus,*
Dusky Grouse, *Tetrao obscurus.*
Cock of the plains, *Tetrao urophasianus.*
Spotted Grouse, *Tetrao canadensis.*
Sharp-tailed Grouse, *Tetrao phasianellus.*
White-tailed Grouse, *Tetrao leucurus.*

Water Birds

*White-legged Oyster-catcher, *Hœmatopus Bachmani*, (AUD.)
Killdeer Plover, *Charadrius vociferus.*
*Rocky Mountain Plover, *Charadrius montanus,* (TOWNSEND.)
Hooping Crane, or Stork, *Grus americana.*
Brown, or Sandhill Crane, *Grus canadensis.*
Great Blue Heron, *Ardea herodias.*
Night Heron, *Ardea nycticorax.*
American Avocet, *Recurvirostra americana.*
Long-billed Curlew, *Numenius longirostris.*
Esquimaux Curlew, *Numenius borealis.*
Red-backed Sandpiper, *Tringa alpina.*
Little Sandpiper, *Tringa Wilsonii.*
Semipalmated Sandpiper, *Tringa semipalmata.*
*Townsend's Sandpiper, *Frinca Townsendi,* (AUDUBON.)
Spotted Sandpiper, *Totanus macularis.*
Yellow-shanks Snipe, *Totanus flavipes.*

Semipalmated Snipe, or Willet, *Totanus semipalmatus.*
Great Marbled Godwit, *Limosa fedoa.*
Common American Snipe, *Scolopax Wilsonii.*
Red-breasted Snipe, *Scolopax grisea.*
Soree, or Rail, *Rallus carolinus.*
Common Coot, *Fulica americana.*
Hyperborean Phalarope, *Phaluropus hyperboreus.*
Wilson's Phalarope, *Phalaropus Wilsonii.*
Red Phalarope, *Phalaropus fulicarius.*
Little Grebe, *Podiceps minor.*
Red-necked Grebe, *Podiceps rubricollis.*
Black Tern, *Sterna nigra.*
Glaucous Gull, *Larus glaucous.*
Common Gull, *Larus canus.*
Ring-billed Gull, *Larus zonorrhynchus.*
Wilson's Stormy Petrel, *Thalassidroma Wilsonii.*
Brown Albatross, *Diomedea fusca.*
White, or Snow Goose, *Anser hyperboreus.*
White-fronted Goose, *Anser albifrons.*
Black-headed Goose, *Anser canadensis.*
Hutchin's Brant Goose, *Anser Hutchinsii.*
Bewick's Swan, *Cygnus Bewickii.*
Trumpeter Swan, *Cygnus buccinator,* (RICHARDSON.)
Mallard Duck, *Anas boschas.*
American Widgeon, *Anas Americana.*
Summer, or Wood Duck, *Anas sponsa.*
Green-winged Teal, *Anas crecca.*
Shoveller Duck, *Anas clypeata.*
Dusky Duck, *Anas obscura.*
Pintail Duck, *Anas acuta.*
Black, or Surf Duck, *Fuligula perspicillata.*
Blue-bill, or Scaup Duck, *Fuligula marila.*
Canvass-back Duck, *Fuligula valisneria.*
Tufted, or Ring-necked Duck, *Fuligula rufitorques.*
Harlequin Duck, *Fuligula histrionica.*
Golden-eye Duck, *Fuligula clangula.*
Long-tailed Duck, *Fuligula glacialis.*
Goosander, *Mergus merganser.*
Hooded, or Crested Merganser, *Mergus cucullatus.*
White Pelican, *Pelecanus onocrotalus.*
Brown Pelican, *Pelecanus fuscus.*
Black Cormorant, *Phalacrocorax carbo.*

*Violet-green Cormorant, *Phalacrocorax splendens,* (Townsend.)
*Townsend's Cormorant, *Phalacrocorax Townsendi,* (Audubon.)
Loon, or Great Northern Diver, *Colymbus glacialis.*
Black Guillemot, *Uria grylle.*
*Slender-billed Guillemot, *Uria Townsendi.* (Audubon.)

CHESTNUT-BACKED TITMOUSE.

*Parus *rufescens,* (Townsend,) Journal Acad. Nat. Sciences, Vol. 7, part II., p. 190. Audubon's Birds of America, Vol. 4, pl. 353. Male and female. *T'nlooqualla* of the Chinook Indians.[3]

Bill black; head and throat sooty-brown, or dark umber; a white line from the bill under the eye, extending to the hind-head, where it increases considerably in breadth; whole back and rump chestnut; wings and emarginate tail dusky; the exterior edges of the feathers of the former, as well as the coverts, whitish; breast, belly and vent, grayish-white, the base of the plumage blackish; flanks chestnut; legs and feet blue. Length scarcely $4^1/2$ inches; extent of wings $6^1/2$ inches. The sexes are very nearly alike.

Inhabits the Columbia river; common, gregarious. Voice somewhat similar to *P. atricapillus,* but sharper and more squeaking.

BROWN-HEADED TITMOUSE.

*Parus *minimus,* (Townsend,) Journal Acad. Nat. Sciences, Vol. 7, part II., p. 190. Audubon's Birds of America, Vol. IV. pl. 353. Male, female and nest. *A-ka-ke-lok* of the Chinook Indians.

Bill short, stout, and entirely black; top of the head light-brown or rust color, paler on the cheeks; whole back and rump cinereous-gray; the wings and tail cinereous-brown, the feathers of the former edged exteriorly and interiorly with light gray; third and fourth primaries longest; tail remarkably long, of twelve rather narrow feathers; whole lower parts gray, the belly and flanks inclining to rust. Legs and feet blackish. Irides *yellow.* Whole length 4 inches; length of tail 2 inches; extent of wings 5 inches. The male and female are very similar in size and markings.

I first observed this little species on the Columbia river in May, 1835, and procured a pair. They hopped through the bushes, and hung from the twigs in the manner of other titmice, twittering all the time, with a rapid enunciation resembling the words, *tsisk-tsish-tsee-tsee.* Upon my return, I found that Mr. Nuttall had observed the same birds a few hours previously in another place. He said that they frequently flew to the ground from the bushes, where they appeared to institute a rapid search for insects, and quickly returned to the perch, emitting their weak, querulous note the whole time without intermission. The stomachs of these birds contained fragments of minute coleopterous insects, and in the ovary of the female was an egg nearly ready for expulsion.

The nest, which Mr. N. found a few days afterwards, is a very curious and beautiful fabric, somewhat like that of the bottle tit of Europe, being from eight to nine inches in length, formed of fine bent, lined with hair, and covered externally with mosses, the hole for entrance near the top. It was suspended from a low bush, and contained seven eggs, very small and beautifully shaped, and pure white.

Mountain Mocking-bird.

*Orpheus *montanus,* (Townsend,) Journal Acad. Nat. Sciences, Vol. 7, part II., p. 192. Audubon's Birds of America, Vol. IV., pl. 369. Male.

Mandibles black, the lower flesh-color at base; whole upper parts dull grayish-cinereous, slightly barred transversely with white; flexure of the wing and axillaries whitish; third primary longest, first and fifth nearly equal; tail long, rounded, of a dark cinereous color, the three lateral feathers with a large white spot on the tip of the inner vanes; lower parts white, with longitudinal, oblanceolate spots of black, largest and most numerous on the breast; a line formed of small black spots extends from the base of the lower mandible on either side, down upon the breast; flanks, vent, and inferior tail-coverts whitish, strongly tinged with bay. Legs and feet yellowish flesh-color. Irides bright yellow. Length 8 inches.

Female unknown.

Inhabits the banks of the Platte river, west of the Rocky Mountains.

Townsend's Thrush.

*Ptiligonys *Townsendi,* (Audubon.) Birds of America, Vol. IV., pl. 419. Female.

Bill black; whole upper parts of a dark, smoke-gray color, inclining to yellowish; tail somewhat emarginate, long, the feathers black, except the two middle ones, which are of the same color as the back, the outer one almost wholly white, and the two next largely tipped with white; wings blackish, the feathers broadly margined with light grayish-cinereous; a triangular spot of yellowish-rufous below the lesser coverts, which is scarcely visible when the wing is closed; lower parts nearly the same color as the back, but lighter; vent, and inferior tail-coverts yellowish-rusty. Legs and feet blackish-brown. Irides dark hazel. Length $7^1/2$ inches.

Of this singular bird I know nothing, but that it was shot by my friend Captain W. Brotchie, of the Honorable Hudson's Bay Company, in a pine forest near Fort George, (Astoria.) It was the only specimen seen.

MORTON'S WATER OUZEL.

*Cinclus *Mortoni,* (TOWNSEND.) Audubon's Birds of America, Vol. IV., pl. 435. Male.

Upper mandible black; lower brownish-yellow, the point black; head, and neck above, dark cinereous; back, rump and tail plumbeous; wings dusky, plumbeous on the edges, the two greater coverts tipped with soiled white; tail remarkably short; eyelids white; a semi-lunated spot of white over the eye; throat, breast, and upper portion of the belly, grayish-fuscous, inclining to brown, and slightly banded transversely with blackish; abdomen and vent, dull grayish-plumbeous; inferior tail-coverts, which are nearly the length of the tail, barred transversely with gray and blackish. Irides dark hazel. Legs and feet brownish-yellow. Length about 5 inches.

I have honored this species with the name of my excellent friend, Doctor Samuel George Morton, of Philadelphia. It was shot by Captain W. Brotchie, near Fort McLoughlin, on the N.W. coast of America, in latitude about 49° N. He stated that it was common there, and inhabited, like the rest of its tribe, the rapid fresh water streams. He procured but one specimen.

COLUMBIAN WATER OUZEL.

*Cinclus *Townsendi,*(AUDUBON.) Birds of America, Vol. IV., pl. 435. Female.

Upper mandible black, the inferior edge bright yellow; lower, yellow, black at the point; whole lower parts dark grayish-plumbeous, rather lighter on the head; a large lunate spot of white over the eye, which inclines toward the front; wings dark plumbeous, the shoulders lighter; the exterior vanes of the primaries, secondaries, and of some of the coverts, grayish-white; throat, breast, and medial portion of the belly dusky-cinereous; sides under the wings and flanks, dusky; the whole inferior surface of the body is banded transversely with blackish; the bands upon the throat are broken, and not well defined, but as they approach the tail they become more distinct; lower tail-coverts with strongly marked alternate transverse lines of blackish and white. The tail is much longer in proportion than that of the preceding species. Irides dark hazel. Legs and feet bright yellow. Length about 7 inches.

This fine bird inhabits the swiftly running streams of fresh water in the vicinity of Fort Vancouver. It is a very scarce species, as in all my peregrinations I have met with but two individuals, only one of which I was enabled to procure.

This I observed swimming about among the rapids of the stream, occasionally flying for short distances over the surface, and then diving into it, and reappearing after a long interval. Occasionally it would alight on the stones, and at such times jerked the tail in the manner of some of the sandpipers. I did not hear it utter any note.

Hermit Warbler.

*Sylvia *occidentalis,* (TOWNSEND.) Journal Acad. Nat. Sciences, Vol. 7, part II., p. 190. Audubon's Birds of America, Vol. IV., pl. 395. Male and female.

The bill is wholly black; the frontlet, crown, and sides of the head yellow, the former rather sparingly dotted with blackish near the nape, where the yellow color almost disappears, by the increase in the size of the spots; upper parts grayish, thickly spotted with black and most of the feathers tinged with olive; the rump is somewhat lighter, having few or no spots, and more strongly tinged with light olive; wings cinereous, with two bands of white; tail darker, the three lateral feathers with white on their inner vanes; throat deep black; whole lower parts white. Legs and feet blackish, the soles yellow. Length 5 inches. Extent 7 inches.

The female differs from the male in having the yellow of the crown and cheeks less bright, the dark spots upon the head are larger and more numerous; the back is of a lighter tint; the black centres of the feathers smaller, and the throat wants the jetty black which is so conspicuous in the male.

I shot a single pair of these birds in a pine forest on the Columbia river, on the 28th of May, 1836. They were flitting about among the pine trees, very actively engaged in searching for insects, and frequently hanging from the boughs like titmice.

BLACK-THROATED GRAY WARBLER.

*Sylvia *nigrescens,* (Townsend.) Journal Acad. Nat. Sciences, Vol. 7, part II, p. 191. Audubon's Birds of America, Vol. IV, pl. 395, male.

The bill is black, and stout; crown and hind head black, the feathers edged with grayish-plumbeous; a line from the lower mandible on each side of the head, extending to the neck, white; a similar broad white line above the cheeks, running parallel with the first, and approaching it on the neck; a small bright yellow spot on the lores; upper parts grayish-plumbeous, the back and upper tail-coverts with a few oblanceolate spots of black; wings and tail dusky, the former with two white bands; and the three exterior feathers of the latter with white on their inner vanes; throat and pectoral collar black; flanks with numerous spots of black; axillaries grayish-white; belly and vent white, with a tinge of yellowish. Legs and feet dusky-brown.

Length nearly 5 inches. Extent of wings 7 inches.

This species is not uncommon in the forests of oak on the Columbia river. It is, however, singularly retired and sedentary. Its note is a rather feeble, but agreeable warble. Sings chiefly in the morning early; silent at mid-day. I have reason to believe, that at least a few pairs breed on the Columbia, but I have never been so fortunate as to find the nest.

TOWNSEND'S WARBLER.

*Sylvia *Townsendi,* (Nuttall,) Jour. Acad. Nat. Sci. Vol. 7, pt. II., page 191. Audubon's Birds of America, Vol. IV. pl. 393. Male.

The crown, lores, a broad patch through the eye to the hind-head, and throat, deep black, the first thickly touched towards the back part, with greenish; back and rump greenish-yellow, spotted all over with black, the spots somewhat concealed by the recumbent plumage; wings dusky-cinereous, edged with grayish lead-color, and crossed by two rather broad bands of white; tail emarginate, of twelve dusky feathers, the three lateral ones, with white on their inner vanes; over the eye, from the bill to the hind-head, is a broad line of rich yellow; a similar yellow line from the lower mandible, round to the back of the neck, joining the first, and enclosing the black patch; a spot below the eye, also yellow; breast yellow; flanks marked with yellow, black and white, the black predominating; axillaries, belly and vent, pure white; bill and feet black, the soles of the latter, yellow. Length 5 inches. Extent of wings 7 inches.

I procured but one specimen of this beautiful bird, on the Columbia river, in the spring of 1835. Early in the autumn of the same year, I shot another male, in a somewhat plainer livery.

It does not breed there, and I know nothing of its habits.

AUDUBON'S WARBLER.

*Sylvia *Auduboni,* (TOWNSEND.) Journal Acad. Natural Sciences, Vol. 7, part II., p. 191. Audubon's Birds of America, Vol. IV., pl. 395. Male and female.

Bill slender, black; upper parts light plumbeous; crown, throat, rump, and sides under the wings, gamboge yellow; lores, and a broad space behind and below the eye, including the auriculars, black; a white spot above and below the eye; feathers of the back with large, pointed spots of black, occupying the shafts, and a portion of each vane; wings dusky, all the feathers edged exteriorly with grayish; wing-coverts tipped with white, forming a large spot below the shoulder; upper tail-coverts light plumbeous, largely tipped with black; tail long, nearly even, blackish, edged with dark gray, and every feather, except the two middle ones, with a large spot of white on the inner vane, near the tip; breast and sides of the belly, black; medial portion of the latter, vent and inferior tail-coverts, white; legs and feet brownish-black. Irides dark hazel. Length 5 inches.

The female has the upper parts brownish, spotted and streaked with black; the yellow on the crown, rump, and flanks is more restricted and fainter than in the male, and it wants the large bed of white upon the wing; throat white; breast and belly varied with black and white.

Very common on the Columbia river in the spring, where it breeds. It sings quite prettily, but, like some others of its family, is rather monotonous. The note very much resembles that of *S. coronata,* to which the species is closely allied, but unlike the bird just named, it keeps in the thickest and most impervious clumps of bushes while singing, and is always silent when engaged in seeking its food.

TOLMIE'S WARBLER.

*Sylvia *Tolmiei,* (TOWNSEND,) Journal Acad. Nat. Sciences, Vol. 8, part I. Audubon's Birds of America, Vol. IV., pl. 399. Male and female. (*S. philadelphia* in the plate.)[4]

The bill is brownish above, pale flesh-color beneath, darker at the point; lores and narrow frontlet black; whole head, neck, and upper part of the breast, dark sooty-ash, the feathers of the latter fringed with white; upper parts greenish yellow-olive; the tail brighter, and of a uniform color, without spots; wings lightish cinereous, the exterior vanes of all the feathers, including the coverts, yellow. Legs and feet flesh-color. Length 5 inches. Extent of wings $6^1/2$ inches.

The female differs from the male, chiefly by having the head and throat light ash-color, without any black, and in being destitute of the black frontlet and lores.

This pretty species, so much resembling the curious *S. philadelphia* of Wilson, is common in spring on the Columbia. It is mostly solitary, and extremely wary, keeping chiefly in the densest and most impenetrable thickets, and gliding through them in a very cautious and suspicious manner. It may, however, sometimes be seen towards mid-day, perched upon a dead twig over its favorite place of concealment, and at such times it warbles a very sprightly and pleasant little song, raising its head until the bill is almost vertial, and swelling its throat in the manner of many of its relatives.

I dedicate the species to my friend W.F. Tolmie, Esq., of Fort Vancouver.

WESTERN BLUE BIRD.

*Sialia *occidentalis,* (TOWNSEND,) Journal Acad. Nat. Sciences, Vol. 7, part II., p. 188. Audubon's Birds of America, Vol. IV., pl. 393. Male and female.

Bill dark horn color, or nearly black; head, upper portion of the back, and throat, of a fine deep mazarine blue, the last somewhat paler; a broad transverse band on the interscapular region, and the whole of the lower breast and belly, dark rufous bay; wings, back, upper tail-coverts and tail, of the same deep blue as the head; the inner vanes of all the wing feathers dark fuscous; vent and lower tail-coverts white; legs and feet blackish horn-color. Irides dark hazel. Length $6^1/2$ inches.

The female has the upper parts dark cinereous, slightly waved with blue; the shoulders, primary quills, upper tail-coverts and tail, are rich blue, as in the male; the greater coverts and interior edges of the scapulars and secondaries, whitish; whole lower parts light bay, the vent and lower tail-coverts white. About half and inch shorter than the male.

Common on the Columbia river in the spring. It arrives from the south early in April, and about the first week in May commences building. The nest is placed in the hollow of a decayed tree, and is very loose and unsubstantial. The eggs, four to five, are light blue, somewhat larger than those of the common blue bird, (*S. Wilsonii.*)

A flock of eight or ten of these birds visited the British fort on the Columbia, on a fine day in the winter of 1835. They confined themselves chiefly to the fences, occasionally flying to the ground and scratching among the snow for minute insects, the fragments of which were found in the stomachs of several which I killed. After procuring an insect, the male usually returned to the fence again, and warbled for a minute most delightfully. This note, although somewhat like that of our common *Wilsonii*, is still so different as to be easily recognised. It is equally sweet and clear, but of so little compass, (at this season,) as to be heard only a short distance. In the spring it is louder, but it is at all times much less strong than that of the common species.

CHESTNUT-COLORED FINCH.

*Plectrophanes *ornata*, (TOWNSEND,) Journal Acad. Nat. Sciences, Vol. 7, part II., p. 189. Audubon's Birds of America, Vol. IV., pl. 394. Male.

Mandibles pale flesh-color, the upper, black along the ridge, and both black at tip; upper portion of the head black; a line of white commences at the nostrils, and passes over the eye, where it is expanded so as to form a large semi-lunated spot, and is continued irregularly back to the nape; below this and towards the throat are several irregular alternate spots of white and black; auriculars, and gular region faint rufous; a broad transverse band of deep bay on the hind part of the neck, comprehending a portion of the back; upper part of the body light cinereous, with numerous spots of dusky; these spots run into each other so as to be scarcely distinguishable; wings dusky; first and second primaries nearly equal, and longest; upper coverts of the wing slightly edged with cream; a large transverse band of white upon the lower portion of the throat, margining the faint rufous of the gular region, and joining the bay on the hind part of the neck; breast and abdomen deep black, irregularly waved with cinereous and white; vent and inferior tail-coverts white; tail emarginate, the outer feathers nearly all white; all the others with a large portion of white, chiefly on their inner vanes, the tips dusky. Legs and feet yellowish-dusky. Irides dark hazel. Length $5^1/2$ inches.

Female unknown.

Inhabits the plains of the Platte river, near the first range of the Rocky Mountains. It appears to live exclusively upon the ground, and is a very rare and shy species. I procured but one specimen.

Townsend's Ground Finch, or Longspur.

*Plectrophanes *Townsendi,* (Audubon.) Birds of America, Vol. IV., pl. 424. Female.

Upper mandible cinnamon; lower, light yellow; whole upper parts, and tail, dark rufous; wing feathers blackish, edged with yellowish-rufous; throat, breast, and belly white, with numerous irregular spots and blotches of dark brown; a line of brown and black spots extends from the base of the lower mandible on each side, down upon the throat; inferior portion of the flanks, vent, and upper tail-coverts, yellowish-brown, with a few spots of black occupying the centre of the feathers. Legs and feet yellowish, claws black. Irides dark hazel. Length $6^1/2$ inches.

This species is common in the neighborhood of Fort Vancouver on the Columbia. It inhabits the dense bushes chiefly in the vicinity of low, marshy places, and feeds upon coleopterons insects and worms, for which it searches in the ground by scratching up the earth with its feet. It is observed only in the autumn and winter.

Oregon Snow Finch.

*Fringilla *oregona,* (Townsend.) Journal Acad. Natural Sciences, Vol. 7, part II., page 188. Audubon's Birds of America, Vol. IV., pl. 398. Male and female.

The bill is a pale fresh color, the upper mandible brownish at the point; head, neck, and upper part of the breast, black; the feathers slightly tipped with white; on the hind-head and back of the neck, are some touches of brown or bay, mixed with the white sprinkling; back rufous-brown or bay; rump grayish-plumbeous, slightly touched with bay; upper tail-coverts and tail cinereous, the former slightly tipped with pale brown, the outer vanes of the feathers of the latter edged with the same color; first lateral tail-feather pure white; second white, with the exception of a small edging of cinereous on the outer vane, near the tip; third, with a broad stripe of white on the inner vane, extending from the point nearly to the base; wings dark cinereous, the outer vanes edged with whitish, the greater coverts and tertials margined with bay; third and fourth primaries nearly equal, and longest; lower part of the breast and belly white; flanks light yellowish-bay, the lower tail-coverts with a lighter tint of the same color; tibial feathers cinereous, spotted with gray. Legs and feet flesh-color; claws light horn color. Length $5^1/2$ inches. Extent of wing $8^1/2$ inches.

The female is very similar to the male, except that the general colors are somewhat fainter.

Common on the Columbia river in winter. Gregarious. Voice, and general habits similar to *F. hyemalis.*

PRAIRIE FINCH.

*Fringilla *bicolor,* (TOWNSEND,) Journal Acad. Nat. Sciences, Vol. 7, part. II., p. 189. Audubon's Birds of America, Vol. IV., pl. 390. Male and female.

The head and back are black, shaded with ash; rump ash; superior tail-coverts and tail, blackish-brown, the former slightly edged with white; all the feathers of the latter tipped with white; a broad patch of white upon the wing; secondaries and tertials tipped and edged with white; throat, cheeks, and whole lower parts, deep black, the feathers on the belly, and the inferior tail-coverts, tipped with white. The upper mandible is of a lightish brown color, the lower, pale bluish-white. Legs and feet olive-brown. Length $7^1/2$ inches. Extent about 11 inches.

The female has the head, and whole upper parts, of a light ash, or cinereous color, varied with blackish; large patches of yellowish-white upon the wing-coverts; throat and breast varied with black and white; belly white; all the lateral tail-feathers tipped with white on their inner webs.

This very pretty and distinct species inhabits a portion of the Platte country, east of the first range of the Rocky Mountains. It appears to be strictly gregarious. Feeds upon the ground, along which it runs swiftly, like the grass finch (*F. graminea,*) to which it is somewhat allied. As the large flocks, (consisting often of from sixty to a hundred,) were started from the ground by our caravan in passing, the piebald appearance of the males and females promiscuously intermingled, presented a curious, but by no means unpleasing effect. While the flock is engaged in feeding, the males are frequently observed to rise suddenly to a considerable height, and poising themselves over their companions, with their wings in constant and rapid motion, they become nearly stationary. In this situation, they pour forth a number of very lively and sweetly modulated notes, and at the expiration of about a minute, descend to the ground, and course about as before. I never observed this bird west of the Black Hills.

HARRIS'S WOODPECKER.

*Picus *Harrisi,* (AUDUBON,) Birds of America, Vol. IV., pl. 417. Male and female.

Bill bluish-black; feather covering the nostrils cinereous-brown; upper part of the head, and an oblong spot below the eye, back; a stripe of white commences in front of the eye above, and extends back to the nape, where it is joined by a similar stripe, which begins at the lower mandible; the semicircle formed by this white line, encloses the black spot on the auriculars; another black line commences at the base of the lower mandible bounding the white, and is continued down upon the shoulder, where it is somewhat expanded anteriorly; a broad occipital band, red; upper parts black, the wings strongly glossed with blue; the primaries, secondaries, and a few of the tertails, with numerous spots of white; a stripe down the middle of the back, white; tail long, cuneiform, black, the three exterior feathers brownish-white; the whole of the lower plumage is of a deep sooty-brown, whitish on the flanks; legs and feet bluish-black. Irides dark hazel. Length 8 inches.

The female differs from the male, chiefly in the absence of the red occipital band.

This species, so much resembling the common *P. villosus,* is abundant in the forests on the Columbia river. Its habits are very similar to those of its near relative. Builds a loose and unsubstantial nest, in the hollow of a decayed tree, and lays four white eggs.

VAUX'S CHIMNEY SWALLOW.

*Cypcelus *Vauxi,* (TOWNSEND,) Journal Acad. Nat. Sciences, Vol. 8, part I. Female.[5]

Bill slender, black; upper parts of a dull smoke-brown, inclining to blackish upon the interscapular region; shoulders and primary quills blackish; the rump and tail are of a much lighter color than the back, being dull cinereous-brown; shafts of the tail-feathers, and their points, black; wings of ordinary length, extending about two inches beyond the tail; throat, and upper portion of the breast, grayish-white; belly, and all below, cinereous-gray. Legs and feet brownish-black. Irides dark hazel. Length $3^1/2$ inches. Extent of wings 10 inches. It differs from the *C. pelasgius,* with which it has been confounded, in several very striking particulars. It is one inch shorter, and two inches less in extent; the body is proportionally smaller in every aspect, and the color much lighter.

This species, (which I dedicate to my friend, Wm. S. Vaux, Esq., of Philadelphia,) is common on the Columbia river; breeds in hollow trees, forming its nest in the same manner as the *pelasgius*, and lays four white eggs.

WHITE-LEGGED OYSTERCATCHER.

*Hæmatopus *Bachmani*, (AUDUBON.) Birds of America, Vol. IV., pl. 427. Male.

Bill yellow, red at base, and on the superior portion of the upper mandible; whole head, neck, and throat black; back, wings, and rump, brownish-fuscous, varied with a darker tint; tail somewhat rounded, blackish, the feathers edged with lighter; flanks deep black; belly, vent, and upper tail-coverts, brownish-fuscous. Legs and feet white; claws yellowish-horn color; eyelids bright red; irides yellow. Length about 17 inches.

This fine species was shot near Puget's sound, by my friend William Fraser Tolmie, Esq., surgeon of the Honorable Hudson's Bay Company, by whom it was presented to me. I was anxious to give to it the name of its discoverer, but I have been overruled by Mr. Audubon, who has probably had good reasons for rejecting my proposed specific appellation, *Tolmiei*.

ROCKY MOUNTAIN PLOVER.

*Charadrius *montanus*, (TOWNSEND.) Journal Acad. Nat. Sciences, Vol. 7, part II., p. 192. Audubon's Birds of America, Vol. IV., pl. 350. Male.

Bill and lores black; front white, this color being continued in a narrow line over the eye to the nape; head-brownish-cinereous; back of the neck, and cheeks behind the eye, yellowish-tawney; whole upper parts yellowish-cinereous, varied with a darker tint; wings lighter, the shoulders and flexura whitish; nearly all the secondaries, and some of the primaries, edged with white; upper tail-coverts, and even tail, brownish-cinereous, the latter tipped with white; legs and feet yellowish-dusky; claws black. Irides dark hazel. Length $8^1/2$ inches.

Inhabits the table land of the Rocky Mountains. I saw but one specimen of this beautiful bird, and, as our party was on the move, I was compelled to kill it without delay.

TOWNSEND'S SANDPIPER.

*Frinca *Townsendi,* (AUDUBON.) Birds of America, Vol. IV., pl. 428.
Female.

Bill yellowish-brown, black at the point; a white line below the eye;
whole upper parts dark ashy-cinereous, the secondaries centred with
blackish; rump blackish; upper tail-coverts pure white; tail blackish-
brown, of ten feathers, the four lateral ones white from their insertion
half way to the points, and each tipped with white; greater wing-
coverts, and bases of all the primaries, white, forming a spot upon the
wing when closed; throat white; breast grayish-cinereous; under surface
of the wings white; belly, vent, and lower tail-coverts white; a few
oblong black spots, chiefly on the sides, and lower-coverts; legs and feet
greenish; claws black. Irides dark hazel. Length $10^1/2$ inches.

I shot one specimen of this curious bird on the base of the rocky cape
at the entrance of the Columbia river, in November 1836. It was sitting
on the edge of the steep rocks, and the heavy surf frequently dashed its
spray over it, as it foraged among the retreating waves. When it started,
it flew with a quick, jerking motion of its wing, and alighted again at a
short distance. Although I resided for many weeks in the vicinity of the
cape, I never saw a second specimen. The stomach, which was
remarkably strong and muscular, contained fragments of a small black
shell fish, of the genus *Modiola,* which adheres in clusters to the rocks.

VIOLET-GREEN CORMORANT.

*Phalacrocorax *splendens.* (TOWNS. *in lit. to Audubon.*) *P. resplendens*
(AUDUBON.) Birds of America Vol. IV., pl. 412. Female in winter.

Bill greenish-dusky, blackish above; front, light sea-green, which
color passes behind the eye, and around the gular region, occupying
the chief portion of the neck below; neck above, deep prussian blue,
with strong reflections of purple; lateral part of the neck lighter, with
numerous minute specks of white, formed by very small, hair-like
feathers; whole upper parts deep green, reflecting shades of purple and
violet; wings greenish, varied with dusky; bare space on the gullet
contracted, of a yellowish-red color; it includes the eye, but does not
extend in front of the lores; tail long, rounded, dusky; below, the colors
are nearly the same as the back; a few white spots on the inferior
portion of the flanks. Legs and feet black; the middle claw strongly
pectinated. Irides light sea-green. Length about 2 feet.

This most splendid of all the species of cormorants yet discovered,
inhabits in considerable number the Rocky Cape at the entrance of the

Columbia river, upon the sides of which it often rest, and no doubt rears its young within the natural cavities which front the tempestuous ocean, and in situations wholly inaccessible to man. Sometimes many weeks elapse in which not a singe cormorant is seen, when suddenly a flock of fifty or sixty, is observed to enter the bay, every individual of which immediately commences an assiduous search for the small fish and mollusca which constitute its food. It never ascends the river, but keeping almost constantly around the cape, under shelter of the enormous breakers which are incessantly dashing against it, successfully defies all attempts to shoot it. The procuring of the only specimen which I was ever enabled to kill, almost cost the lives of myself and eight men. Our boat was carried with frightful velocity into the furious breakers, and a full hour was consumed in unremitting efforts to escape the danger towards which the swift current was hurrying us.

The Indians of the N.W. coast make cloaks of the skins of this bird sewed together. It is probably even more numerous to the north of Cape Disappointment, and must necessarily frequent less inaccessible places.

TOWNSEND'S CORMORANT.

*Phalacrocorax *Townsendi*, (AUDUBON.) Birds of America, Vol. IV., pl. 412. Male.

Bill light-yellow, black above; crown, and upper part of the neck to the interscapulars, yellowish-fuscous; lateral part of the hind-head and neck, pointed with white like the preceding species; middle of the back, rump and upper tail-coverts, dark greenish, reflecting purple; tail long, dusky; lateral portion of the upper surface of the body, including the scapulars and wings, yellowish-fuscous, each feather edged with blackish; bare space on the gullet, which includes the eye, and extends upon the lores, light red, streaked with a deeper tint; sides of the head, and throat whitish-cinereous; breast and belly yellowish-rufous, slightly varied with dusky; vent and lower tail-coverts dark brownish-fuscous; a few longitudinal points of white on the tibial feathers; legs and feet black. Irides dark hazel. Length about 28 inches.

This species inhabits the Columbia river, and is not uncommon. It is seldom seen near the sea, but is mostly observed high up upon the river. It is, like most species of its genus, partially gregarious, and is fond of resting in company. The old trees which are fastened in the bottom of the river, and protrude above the surface, and the isolated rocks in the stream, are its favorite places of resort. Here it sits, sometimes for hours together, indolently gazing into the water, and only leaving its perch to seize an unsuspecting fish, which may happen to pass near it. It is very shy and cautious, and is seldom killed even by the Indians, who are fond of its flesh.

SLENDER-BILLED GUILLEMOT.

*Uria *Townsendi,* (AUDUBON.) Birds of America, Vol. IV., pl. 430. Male and female.

Bill very slender, black; nostrils small, rounded, open; an interrupted circle of white around the eye; head and neck above, dark umber brown, slightly waved with blackish; back, rump, and upper tail-coverts, light yellowish-fuscous, with broad transverse bands of black; wings blackish, edged with grayish-plumbeous, the greater coverts tipped with white; tail short, rounded, extending about an inch beyond the closed wings; throat cinereous-gray waved transversely with a darker tint; lower parts black, spotted with white; flanks white; legs and feet sulphur yellow; claws black. Irides dark hazel. Length 8 inches.

The female has the whole upper parts of a dull cinereous color; scapulars, and a narrow occipital band, white; whole lower parts white; a few black, longitudinal streaks on the flanks. Length about the same as the male.

Inhabits the bays of the N.W. Coast of America, in latitude 38° to 40°. The specimens were shot and presented to me by Captain W. Brotchie, to whom I am under very great obligations for the addition to my collection of several fine species.

Notes

Introduction

1. For a discussion of the second great age of discovery, see William H. Goetzmann, *New Lands, New Men: America and the Second Great Age of Discovery* (New York: Viking Penguin, 1986), 8-15. This work, along with Goetzmann, *Exploration and Empire: The Explorer and the Scientist in the Winning of the American West* (New York: Alfred Knopf, 1966), has been particularly helpful in my conceptualization of Townsend's place in American scientific exploration.

2. Although Witmer Stone, "John Kirk Townsend," *Cassinia* 7 (1903): 2, gives October 10 as the date of Townsend's birth, he elsewhere, *Dictionary of American Biography*, 18 (1936): 617, gives August 10. Theodore S. Palmer, "Notes on Persons Whose Names Appear in the Nomenclature of California Birds: A Contribution to the History of West Coast Ornithology," *Condor* 30 (1928): 299, uses October 10, but notes that Townsend's grave marker in the Congressional Cemetery, Washington, D.C., gives the birth date as August 10.

3. Goetzmann, *Exploration and Empire*, 183-84; Goetzmann, *New Lands, New Men*, 94-95; Richard S. Miller, "The Federal City, 1783-1800," in *Philadelphia: A 300-Year History*, ed. Russell F. Weigley (New York: W. W. Norton, 1982), 191; Edgar P. Richardson, "The Athens of America, 1800-1825," in *Philadelphia: A 300-Year History*, 242-43; Hans Huth, *Nature and the American: Three Centuries of Changing Attitudes* (Berkeley, CA: University of California Press, 1957; reprint, Lincoln, NE: University of Nebraska Press, Bison Books, 1972), 17; Dirk J. Struik, *Yankee Science in the Making*, new rev. ed. (New York: Collier Books, 1962), 43; and Larry T. Spencer, "Filling in the Gaps: A Survey of Nineteenth Century Institutions Associated with the Exploration and Natural History of the American West," *American Zoologist* 26 (1986): 372-74.

4. For the affinity of Quakers of this time with science and medicine, see Margaret H. Brown, *The Quiet Rebels: The Story of the Quakers in America* (New York: Basic Books, 1969), 159-61.

5. Marcia Bonta, "Graceanna Lewis: Portrait of a Quaker Naturalist, " *Quaker History* 74 (spring, 1985): 29, 30; Phebe [sic] A. Hanaford, *Daughters of America; or, Women of the Century* (Augusta, ME: True and Company, [1882]), 260-61; Deborah Jean Warner, *Graceanna Lewis, Scientist and Humanitarian* (Washington, D.C.: National Museum of History and Technology, 1979), 24-27, 46; Burton Lee Thorpe, *Biographies of Pioneer American Dentists and Their Successors*, vol. 3, of Charles R. E. Koch, ed., *History of Dental Surgery* (Fort Wayne, IN: National Art Publishing Company, 1910), 96.

6. *Dictionary of American Biography*, 18 (1936): 617; Stone, "John Kirk Townsend," 2; Frank L. Burns, *The Ornithology of Chester County, Pennsylvania* (Boston: Richard G. Badger, The Gorham Press, 1919), 13-

15; Ruthven Deane, "Some Original Manuscript Relating to the History of Townsend's Bunting," *Auk* 26 (1909): 270. Warner, *Graceanna Lewis*, 51, identifies Michener as a cousin.

7. Dean, "Some Original Manuscript," 270-72; John James Audubon, *Ornithological Biography*, 5 vols. (Edinburgh: Adam and Charles Black, 1832-39) 2:183; American Ornithologists' Union Committee, *Check-list of North American Birds*, 6th ed. (Lawrence, KS: American Ornithologists' Union, 1983), 791; Elliot Coues, *Key to North American Birds...*, 2nd ed. (Boston: Estes and Lauriate, 1884), 388. Audubon mentions this specimen again in *Ornithological Biography*, 5:90, and figured the species in plate 400 of his *Birds of America* (New York: The Macmillan Company, 1953). A line drawing, by Bob Hines, of how that remarkable specimen might have looked in life is in Peter Matthiessen, *Wildlife in America* (New York: The Viking Press, 1959), 123. American Ornithologists' Union Committee, *Check-list of North American Birds*, 5th ed. (Baltimore: American Onithologists' Union, 1957), 650, regards the genus as *Spiza*, but the sixth edition resurrects *Emberiza*, Audubon's and Townsend's original generic designation. Kenneth C. Parkes, "Audubon's Mystery Birds," *Natural History* 94 (1985): 92, disagrees that the specimen belongs in *Emberiza*, and regards it as an aberrant Dickcissel (*Spiza americana*), lacking the normal yellow pigments in its plumage. The Townsend's Bunting has been relegated to the hypothetical list of species since the first American Ornithologists' Union checklist; see American Ornithologists' Union Committee, *The Code of Nomenclature and Check-list of North American Birds...* (New York: American Ornithologists' Union, 1886), 354. Deane, "Some Original Manuscript," 270, notes that in his descriptive manuscript, Townsend gave the date of collection as June 12, 1833, but Deane accepts Michener's date of May 11, 1833, which is from a diary entry. All subsequent sources have followed Deane.

8. Bernard DeVoto, *Across the Wide Missouri* (Cambridge: Houghton Mifflin, 1947), 61-68; Jeanette E. Graustein, *Thomas Nuttall: Explorations in America, 1808-1841* (Cambridge: Harvard University Press, 1967), 278-80; F. G. Young, ed., "The Correspondence and Journals of Captain Nathaniel J. Wyeth, 1831-6," *Sources of the History of Oregon* 1 (1899): 180-81.

9. Nathaniel J. Wyeth to Thomas Nuttall, July 4, 1833, in Young, "Correspondence and Journals," 67.

10. M. L. Fernald, "Some Early Botanists of the American Philosophical Society," in *The Early History of Science and Learning in America, with Especial Reference to the Work of the American Philosophical Society During the Eighteenth and Nineteenth Centuries* (Philadelphia: American Philosophical Society, 1942), 66; Graustein, *Thomas Nuttall*, 292. Goetzmann, *Exploration and Empire*, 165, suggests that Wyeth "secured the services" of Townsend "to be the official ornithologist on the expedition." However, Wyeth to Nuttall, February 4, 1834, in Young, "Correspondence and Journals," 106, makes clear that it was Nuttall who either invited or recruited Townsend.

11. Wyeth to Nuttall, February 4, 1834, in Young, "Corresponce and Journals," 106.

12. There has been confusion over Townsend's age at the beginning of the second Wyeth expedition. Both DeVoto, *Across the Wide Missouri*, 184, and

Witmer Stone, "Philadelphia to the Coast in Early Days, and the Development of Western Ornithology Prior to 1850, *Condor* 18 (1916): 7, and Stone, "John Kirk Townsend," 2, give his age as twenty-five. However, since he was born in fall 1809 he would be twenty-four in March 1834, when he and Nuttall left Philadelphia. Graustein, *Thomas Nuttall*, 292, as well as popular accounts such as Joseph Kastner, *A Species of Eternity* (New York: Alfred A. Knopf, 1977), 277, and John I. Merritt III, "Naturalists Across the Rockies," *American West* 24 (1977): 4, give the correct age.

13. Donald Jackson, introduction to *Across the Rockies to the Columbia* by John Kirk Townsend (Lincoln, NE: University of Nebraska Press, Bison Books, 1978), v. Graustein, *Thomas Nuttall*, 292, and Spencer, "Filling in the Gaps," 372, 374, say Townsend received one hundred dollars from each institution.

14. For Morton's interest in craniographic research and his importance in early ethnographic work, see *Dictionary of American Biography*, 13 (1934):265-66, and Ales Hrdlicka, "Physical Anthropology in America: An Historical Sketch," *American Anthropologist*, n.s., 16 (1914): 512-23.

15. In a journal entry dated May 27, 1836, presumably from Fort Vancouver, and quoted in Audubon, *Ornithological Biography*, 4:515, Townsend mentioned consulting "the only two authors to whom I have access, Mr Nuttall and Prince Bonaparte [sic]...." The two volumes by Nuttall that Townsend might have used were *A Manual of the Ornithology of the United States and Canada: The Land Birds* (Cambridge: Hilliard and Brown, 1832), and *A Manual of the United States and of Canada. The Water Birds* (Boston: Hilliard, Gray, and Company, 1834). There are several possibilities for the work by Charles L. Bonaparte which Townsend consulted. Bonaparte continued Alexander Wilson's *American Ornithology*, four volumes which appeared in 1825-1833. In 1827 Bonaparte produced a "Catalogue of the Birds of the United States." His "Genera of North American Birds, and a Synopsis of the Species Found Within the Territory of the United States" (1828), and its supplement (though actually published earlier), "Supplement to the Generea of North American Birds" (1827), contain only scant reference to the West, Nuttall's volume on land birds (1832) only a trifle more, and the same author's volume on water birds (1834) virtually no reference to Oregon; see George A. Jobanek, *An Annotated Bibliography of Oregon Bird Literature Published Before 1935* (Corvallis, OR: Oregon State University Press, 1997), entries 330, 331, 1333, 1334. For more on Bonaparte's works, see Elliott Coues, *Birds of the Colorado Valley; A Repository of Scientific and Popular Information Concerning North American Ornithology* (Washington, D.C.: Government Printing office, 1878), 608-14; and Coues, *Key to North American Birds*, XX. Charles L. Bonaparte, "the father of systematic ornithology in America," was a nephew of Napolean Bonaparte and came to the United States after Waterloo to reside in Philadelphia and devote his attentions to ornithology; see Palmer, "Notes on Persons Whose Names Appear," 269; Edward S. Gruson, *Words for Birds: A Lexicon of North American Birds with Biographical Notes* (New York: Quadrangle Books, 1972), 122; and Barbara Mearns and Richard Mearns, *Audubon to Xántus: The Lives of Those Comemorated in North American Bird Names* (London: Academic Press, 1992), 95-100.

It is most likely that Townsend brought these volumes with him from Philadelphia since he was a literate and experienced naturalist. However, John McLoughlin was a well-read man who had compiled a sizeable library at Fort Vancouver. William Tolmie, the doctor who returned to Fort Vancouver from Fort Nisqually in March 1836, and relieved Townsend of the duties of fort surgeon, owned many scientific books, including Alexander Wilson's *American Ornithology*. Whether this was the continuation by Bonaparte is not known; see James W. Manning, "Books in Early Oregon, 1821-1883" (M.S. Thesis, University of Oregon, June, 1940), 7-10.

16. See Goetzmann, *New Lands, New Men*, 8-15; John K. Townsend to "My dear Sister," March 17, 1834, in John Kirk Townsend Papers, 1834-39, Collection 404, Academy of Natural Sciences of Philadelphia [hereinafter cited as Townsend Papers].

17. This is not to denigrate the efforts of Lewis and Clark and David Douglas in the scientific exploration of the Pacific Northwest, but their talents were other than ornithological. For Lewis and Clark's talents as naturalists, see Paul Russel Cutright, *Lewis and Clark: Pioneering Naturalists* (Urbana, IL: University of Illinois Press, 1969), passim; and C. Edward Quinn, "A Zoologist's View of the Lewis and Clark Expedition," *American Zoologist* 26 (1986); 299-306. David Douglas was primarily a botanist but did publish two important papers on the region's birdlife; see David Douglas, "Observations on Some Species of the Genera *Tetrao* and *Ortyx*, Natives of North America; With Descriptions of Four New Species of the Former, and Two of the Latter Genus," *Transactions of the Linnaean Society of London* 16 (1829): 133-49, and Douglas, Observations of the Vultur Californianus of Shaw," *Zoological Journal* 4 (1829): 328-30, as well as Douglas, *Journal Kept by David Douglas During His Travels in North America 1823-1827 ...* (London: W. Wesley, 1914; reprint, New York: Antiquarian Press, 1959), especially 152-55. I have discussed these elsewhere in Jobanek, *An Annotated Bibliography*, entries 541-43.

18. Townsend to "My dear Sister," March 17, 1834, Townsend Papers.

19. Townsend to "Dear Sister," n.d., but postmarked March 23, [1834], Townsend Papers.

20. Townsend to Charles Townsend, March 27, 1834, Townsend Papers; Townsend, *Narrative of a Journey Across the Rocky Mountains, to the Columbia River, and a Visit to the Sandwich Islands, Chili, &c., with a Scientific Appendix* (Philadelphia: Henry Perkins, 1839), 9-10 (this edition, p. 1).

21. Townsend, *Narrative*, 10 (this edition, p. 2).

22. Townsend to Charles Townsend, April 1, 1834, Townsend Papers. His discussion of the disagreeableness of St. Louis is much restrained in the *Narrative*, 12 (this edition, p. 3).

23. Townsend to Charles Townsend, April 1, 1834, Townsend Papers; Townsend, *Narrative*, 12-13.

24. Townsend to Charles Townsend, April 9, 1834, Townsend Papers; Townsend, *Narrative*, 20-21 (this edition, p.10). Burns, *Ornithology of Chester County, Pennsylvania*, does not list the Carolina Parakeet, *Conuropis carolinensis*, so it is probable that Townsend had not seen this bird before; the species was only a straggler to Pennsylvania; see American

Notes

Ornithologists' Union Committee, *The Code of Nomenclature*, 206.
Townsend's encounter here was already in the period of the parakeet's
population decline, which ultimately led to its extinction; see Errol Fuller,
Extinct Birds (New York: Facts on File Publications, 1988), 150, 152; James
C. Greenway, Jr., *Extinct and Vanishing Birds of the World*, 2nd rev. ed.
(New York: Dover Publications, 1967), 323-24.

25. Townsend to Charles Townsend, April 21, 1834, Townsend Papers.
26. Townsend to Charles Townsend, May 3, 1834, Townsend Papers;
Townsend, *Narrative*, 27-28 (this edition, pp. 14-15).
27. Townsend, *Narrative*, 42, 59-60 (this edition, pp. 26, 40); Graustein,
Thomas Nuttall, 298.
28. Townsend, *Narrative*, 60, 63 (this edition, pp. 40, 42-43). For two
examples of the difficulty Townsend and Nuttall faced in collecting while the
expedition marched westward, see Audubon, *Ornithological Biography*,
5:313-14, and Audubon and John Bachman, *The Quadrapeds of North
America*, 3 vols. (New York: V. G. Audubon, 1854; reprint, New York:
Arno Press, 1974), 2:298-99, regarding Townsend and Nuttall overlooking
the Black-footed Ferret, *Mustela nigripes*.
29. Townsend, *Narrative*, 64 (this edition, p. 43).
30. Regarding Nuttall's concentration on plants and Townsend's on birds, see
Nathaniel J. Wyeth to E. W. Metcalf, June 21, 1834, in Young,
"Correspondence and Journals," 137; Witmer Stone, "Some Philadelphia
Ornithological Collections and Collectors, 1784-1850," *Auk* 16 (1899):
171; and Stone, "A Study of the Type Specimens of Birds in the Collection
of the Academy of Natural Sciences of Philadelphia, With a Brief History of
the Collection," *Proceedings of the Academy of Natural Sciences of
Philadelphia* 1898 (1899): 13.
31. Townsend, *Narrative*, 338, 344-47 (this edition, pp. 249-68); Townsend,
"Description of Twelve New Species of Birds, Chiefly from the Vicinity of
the Columbia River," *Journal of the Academy of Natural Sciences of
Philadelphia* 8 (1839): 189, 192-93; Townsend, "List of the Birds
Inhabiting the Region of the Rocky Mountains, the Territory of the
Oregon, and the North West Coast of America," *Journal of the Academy of
Natural Sciences of Philadelphia* 8 (1839): 151-58; American Ornithologists'
Union Committee, *Check-list of North American Birds*, 6th ed., 172, 570,
683, 701, 719.
In his appendix to the *Narrative*, 331-36 (this edition, pp. 249-68),
Townsend included a "Catalogue of Birds, Found in the Territory of the
Oregon." His application of this geographical term was broad and the list
included plains species he encountered early on in the expedition, confusing
later ornithologists; see George A. Jobanek, "Dubious Reciords in the Early
Oregon Bird Literature," *Oregon Birds* 20 (1994): 3. For a striking example
of a later ornithologist crediting a species to Oregon on the basis of
Townsend's record when it was in fact seen elsewhere, see John Cassin,
*Illustrations of the Birds of California, Texas, Oregon, British and Russian
America* (Philadelphia: J. B. Lippincott, 1856; reprint, Austin: Texas State
Historical Association, 1991), 288.
32. Townsend to Charles Townsend, May 3, 1834, Townsend Papers;
Townsend, *Narrative*, 29-30, 34 (this edition, pp. 16, 19-20). Sublette later
died of the injury.

33. Townsend, *Narrative*, 52-53, 75-76, 99-100 (this edition, pp. 33-35, 52-53, 70-71).
34. Townsend, *Narrative*, 55-56 (this edition, pp. 36-37); Jason Lee, "Diary of Rev. Jason Lee," *Oregon Historical Quarterly* 17 (1916): 125-26.
35. Townsend, *Narrative*, 147 (this edition, p. 106).
36. Townsend to Charles Townsend, October 6, 1834, Townsend Papers; Townsend, *Narrative*, 168-69 (this edition, p. 122). John McLoughlin gives the date of Townsend's arrival at Fort Vancouver as September 6, 1834; see John McLoughlin to the "Governor Deputy Governor & Committee of the Honble. Hudsons Bay Coy.," November 18, 1834, in E. E. Rich, ed., *The Letters of John McLoughlin from Fort Vancouver to the Governor and Committee: First Series, 1825-38* (Toronto: The Champlain Society, 1941), 125-26.
37. Townsend, *Narrative*, 219, 311-52 (this edition, pp. 161, 231-68); Townsend, "Description of a New Species of *Cypcelus*, from the Columbia River," *Journal of the Academy of Natural Sciences of Philadelphia* 8 (1839): 148; Townsend, "Description of a New Species of *Sylvia*, from the Columbia River," *Journal of the Academy of Natural Sciences of Philadelphia* 8 (1839): 149-50; Townsend, "Notes on *Sylvia* Tolmoei [sic]," *Journal of the Academy of Natural Sciences of Philadelphia* 8 (1839): 159; John James Audubon to John Audubon, July 1, 1839, in Frances H. Herrick, *Audubon the Naturalist: A History of His Life and Time*, 2 vols., (New York: D. Appleton and Company, 1917), 2:179. These western subspecies are described in Robert Ridgway, *The Birds of North and Middle America: A Descriptive Catalogue...*, 8 vols. [under Ridgway's authorship] (Washington, D.C.: Government Printing Office, 1901-1919), 1:392-93 for the Fox Sparrow, and 1:420-21 for the Spotted Towhee.
An interesting issue is the type localities of Townsend's specimens. Townsend's locality records are ambiguous: "Forests near the Columbia river," on the Columbia river," see Townsend, "Description of Twelve New Species," 189-92; Townsend, "Description of a New Species of *Cypcelus*," 148. Since Townsend divided his time between Sauvie Island and its immediate vicinity and Fort Vancouver, as well as collecting on excursions to other areas, for several species no precise type locality can be established (the claim by Omar C. Spencer, *The Story of Sauvies Island* [Portland: Binfords & Mort, 1950], 122, that Townsend resided during his two years on the west coast solely at Wyeth's Fort William is not accurate). Recognizing the ambiguity, William Leon Dawson and J. Hooper Bowles, *The Birds of Washington*, 2 vols. (Seattle: The Occidental Publishing Company, 1909), 1:222, note a, questioned the value of Townsend's appended bird list in the *Narrative* in determining status relative to Washington. However, The American Ornithologists' Union Committee, *Check-list of North American Birds*, 3rd. ed., rev. (New York: American Ornithologists' Union, 1910), passim, identified Townsend's ambiguous locality records with Fort Vancouver, an identification that continues to the present (1983) *Check-list*, 6th ed. Stanley G. Jewett et al., *Birds of Washington State* (Seattle: University of Washington Press, 1953), 27, while acknowledging the ambiguity of Townsend's appended list, regarded all the northwest species in Townsend, "Description of Twelve New Species," as from Washington.
Frank L. Burns, "Type Localities of Townsend's 'Columbia River' Birds,"

Auk 51 (1934): 403-4, pointed out that as Townsend spent considerable time on or near Sauvie Island, where he did most of his initial collecting in the northwest, this area was the more likely type locality of several species. Spencer, *The Story of Sauvies Island*, 50, concurred. I have suggested the same in Jobanek, "John Kirk Townsend in the Northwest," *Oregon Birds* 12 (1986): 261-64. See also J. W. Slipp, "Swainson's Hawk in Western Washington with a Note on the Type Locality," *Auk* 64 (1947), 390-91, 393-97.

38. Samuel Parker, *Journal of an Exploring Tour Beyond the Rocky Mountains...* (Ithaca, NY: By the author, 1838; microfilm, New Haven, CT: Research Publications, Inc., 1975), 338-40. The abridged report from the 1844 edition of Parker's book is reprinted, only slightly edited, in Ira N. Gabrielson and Stanley G. Jewett, *Birds of Oregon* (Corvallis: Oregon State College, 1940), 51-52. We include the report Townsend submitted to Parker, in full, in Jobanek and David B. Marshall, "John K. Townsend's 1836 Report of the Birds of the Lower Columbia River Region, Oregon and Washington," *Northwestern Naturalist* 73 (1992): 1-14.

39. Townsend to Charles Townsend, October 6, 1834, Townsend Papers; Townsend, *Narrative*, 236-37, 241, 255, 258 (this edition, pp. 174-75, 177-78, 189, 191); Audubon and Bachman, *The Quadrapeds of North America*, 2:273; Whitfield J. Bell, Jr., and Murphy D. Smith, *Guide to the Archives and Manuscript Collections of the American Philosophical Society* (Philadelphia: American Philosophical Society, 1966), 141; Jobanek and Marshall, "John K. Townsend's 1836 Report of the Birds," 6-7. Pliny Earle Goddard, "The Present Condition of Our Knowledge of North American Languages," *American Anthropologist*, n.s., 16 (1914): 555-61, in an historical review of the field, does not mention Townsend. For more on Northwest Indian uses of dogwood and other plants, see Erna Gunther, *Ethnobotany of Western Washington: The Knowledge and Use of Indigenous Plants by Native Americans* (rev. ed.) (Seattle: University of Washington Press, 1973), 42-43, passim.

40. Townsend to Charles Townsend, October 6, 1834, Townsend Papers; Townsend, *Narrative*, 179 (this edition, p. 130); Daniel Lee and J. H. Frost, *Ten Years in Oregon* (New York: Published for the authors by J. Collard, Printer, 1844; microfilm, New Haven, CT: Research Publications, Inc., 1975), 132; Richard Henry Dana, *Two Years Before the Mast: A Personal Narrative of Life at Sea* (New York: Harper & Brothers, 1840; microfilm, New Haven, CT: Research Publications, Inc., 1875), 359. Regarding Nuttall's shyness and distaste for company, see Fernald, "Some Early Botanists," 66; and Spencer, *The Story of Sauvies Island*, 51. Charles V. Piper, *Flora of the State of Washington* (Washington, D.C.: Government Printing Office, 1906), 14, suggested that Nuttall resided primarily on Sauvie Island. John McLoughlin to the "Governor, Deputy Governor and Committee. Honble. H. Bay Compy," October 31, 1837, In Rich, *The Letters of John McLoughlin*, 203, mentions Townsend and Wyeth but not Nuttall as having been received at Fort Vancouver.

41. Townsend, *Narrative*, 233, 239 (this edition, pp. 171-72, 176); Townsend, "Description of a New Species of *Sylvia*," 150; Townsend, "Notes on *Sylvia* Tolmoei," 159; Rich, *The Letters of John McLoughlin*, 344; Lee and Frost, *Ten Years in Oregon*, 83; Murray L. Johnson, "Early Medical

Men in the Northwest Who Were Naturalists," *Western Journal of Surgery, Obstetrics and Gynecology* 51 (1943): 217; O. Larsell, "An Outline of the History of Medicine in the Pacific Northwest," *Northwest Medicine* 31 (1932): 484.

42. Townsend, *Narrative*, 223-24 (this edition, pp. 164-65); J. D. Cleaver, *Island Origins: Trappers, Traders & Settlers*, Sauvie Island Heritage Series, vol. 1 ([Portland]: Oregon Historical Society, 1986), 10-11. The appeal of alcohol used as a scientific preservative to men desiring alcohol appears to be a not unusual phenomenon. For an amusing, similar story, involving the Oregon ornithologist Charles E. Bendire, see Erskine Wood, *Life of Charles Erskine Scott Wood* (no place: Privately printed, 1978; reprint, Vancouver, WA: Rose Wind Press, 1991), 33-34, and George A. Jobanek, "Charles E. Bendire," *Oregon Birds* 20 (1994): 79.

43. Townsend, *Narrative*, 263-64 (this edition, p. 195). Venia T. Phillips and Maurice E. Phillips, *Guide to the Manuscript Collections in the Academy of Natural Sciences of Philadelphia* (Philadelphia: Academy of Natural Sciences of Philadelphia, 1963), 198, report incorrectly that Townsend returned to Philadelphia by an overland route.

44. Townsend, Journal, entries for December 22, 1836, January 1, 1837, January 3, 1837, Townsend Papers; Townsend, *Narrative*, 269 (this edition, pp. 199-200); American Ornithologists' Union Committee, *Check-list of North American Birds*, 6th ed., 587; George C. Munro, Birds of Hawaii, rev. ed. (Rutland, VT: Charles E. Tuttle Company, 1960), 88 Townsend collected types of at least the Hawaiian Hawk, *Buteo solitarius*, Hawaiian Crow, *Corvus hawaiiensis*, and the Kaui Oo, *Moho braccatus*, see Stone, "A Study of the Type Specimens of Birds," 43,45,46. The crow and the oo are now endangered; see H. Douglas Pratt, Phillip L. Bruner, and Delwyn G. Berrett, *A Field Guide to the Birds of Hawaii and the Tropical Pacific* (Princeton, NJ: Princeton University Press, 1987), 231-32, 280. Greenway, *Extinct and Vanishing Birds of the World*, 424, mentioned that Townsend collected with Deppe for three months, but this is unlikely, and mentioned that Townsend collected at least one Oahu Oo. Henry W. Henshaw, *Birds of the Hawaiian Islands, Being a Complete List of the Birds of the Hawaiian Possessions With Notes on Their Habits* (Honolulu: Thomas G. Thrum, 1902), 25-26; E. H. Bryan, Jr., and J. C. Greenway, Jr., "Contribution to the Ornithology of the Hawaiian Islands," *Bulletin of the Museum of Comparative Zoölogy* 94 (1944): 81-82; and Andrew J. Berger, *Hawaiian Birdlife* (Honolulu: The University Press of Hawaii, 1972), x, all raise criticisms that because Townsend's, Nuttall's, and Deppe's observations were not published, and their specimens bear ambiguous locality information, their contribution to an understanding of the ornithology and distribution of Hawaiian birds have been slight. Regarding Kamehameha III and Nahienaena's historical significance and their relationship, see Ralph S. Kuykendall, *The Hawaiian Kingdom, 1778-1854: Foundation and Transformation* (Honolulu: The University of Hawaii, 1938), passim; and Ruth Tabrah, *Hawaii: A Bicentennial History* (New York: W. W. Norton, 1980), 49-51.

45. Townsend, *Narrative*, 296 (this edition, p. 220). Townsend's seabird specimens proved controversial, with considerable debate in the 1930s between Witmer Stone and Frank Burns, over whether those specimens were

collected in Oregon waters, as labelled, or in waters off South America, which is most likely. The species in question are the Gray-headed Albatross, *Thalassarche chrystoma*, Light-mantled Albatross, *Phoebetria palpebrata*, Antarctic Giant-Petrel, *Macronectes giganteus*, and the Southern Fulmar, *Fulmarus glacialoides*. The American Ornithologists' Union Committee, *Check-list of North American Birds*, 6th ed., 771-77, now regards their North American occurrence as hypothetical, although one writer, Harvey I. Fisher, "Bird Records from Midway Atoll, Pacific Ocean," *Condor* 67 (1965): 356, regarded Townsend's Oregon record of the Antarctic Giant-Petrel as possible. The debate between Burns and Stone can be followed in Stone, "[Review of] Bent's Life Histories of North American Petrels and Pelican and Their Allies," *Auk* 40 (1923): 149-50; Stone, "Townsend's Oregon Tubinares," *Auk* 47 (1930): 414-15; Burns, "In Re 'Townsend's Oregon Tubinares'," *Auk* 48 (1931): 106-8; Stone, "[A Reply to Frank L. Burns's, "In Re 'Townsend's Oregon Tubinares'"]," *Auk* 48 (1931): 108-9; Burns, "Townsend's Sooty Albatross," *Auk* 51 (1934): 225; Stone, "[A Reply to Frank L. Burns's, 'Townsend's Sooty Albatross']," *Auk* 51 (1934): 225-26. I have summarized the debate in Jobanek, "Townsend's Tubenoses," *Oregon Birds* 12 (1986): 269-71.

46. Townsend, "Description of Twelve New Species," 187-88; Audubon to John Bachman, September 10, 1836, in Howard Corning, ed., *Letters of John James Audubon, 1826-1840*, 2 vol. (in one) (Boston: The Club of Odd Volumes, 1930; reprint, New York: Krauss Reprint Company, 1969), 2:130-31; Audubon to Edward Harris, September 12, 1836, in Herrick, *Audubon the Naturalist*, 2:147; Audubon, *Ornithological Biography*, 4:xi-xii; Witmer Stone, "On the Types of J. K. Townsend's Birds," *Auk* 53 (1936); 242; Graustein, *Thomas Nuttall*, 322-23.

47. Audubon to John Bachman, October 23, 1836, in Corning, *Letters of John James Audubon*, 2:135-36. This letter is also in Clive E. Driver, *Passing Through: Letters And Documents Written in Philadelphia by Famous Visitors* (Philadelphia: The Rosebach Museum & Library, 1982), 60.

48. Audubon to John Bachman, August 14, 1837, 2:179; Audubon to Bachman, December 20, 1837, 2:193; Audubon to Edward Harris, February 6, 1838, 2:196; Audubon to [Harris], n.d. [1838], 2:202; all in Corning, *Letters of John James Audubon*; Audubon, *Ornithological Biography*, 4:xiv; Stone, "A Study of the Type Specimens of Birds," 13; Stone, "On the Types of J. K. Townsend's Birds," 242; Alice Ford, *John James Audubon: A Biography* (New York: Abbeville Press, 1988), 319. For inadequacies of Audubon's plates of western species, arising from his painting them without personal experience of the species in life or with knowledge of Pacific Northwest flora and landscapes, see Waldemar H. Fries, *The Double Elephant Folio: The Story of Audubon's "Birds of America"* (Chicago: American Library Association, 1973), 99.

49. Audubon to Bachman, October 27, 1838, 2:207-8; Audubon to Bachman, February 15, 1840. 2:232; both in Corning, *Letters of John James Audubon*. Ford, *John James Audubon*, 359, records additional criticism that William MacGillivray, Audubon's collaborator on the *Ornithological Biography*, felt that the observations Nuttall and Townsend conveyed to Audubon were "sparse."

50. Witmer Stone, "A Bibliography and Nomenclator of the Ornithological Works of John James Audubon," *Auk* 23 (1906): 306, 312; Stone, "Philadelphia to the Coast," 10; Phillips and Phillips, *Guide to the Manuscript Collections*, 199.

51. Audubon to Edward Harris, February 6, 1838, in Corning, *Letters of John James Audubon*, 2:197; Coues, *Key to North American Birds*, xxiii; Coues, *Birds of the Colorado Valley*, 626, 636; Stone, "John Kirk Townsend," 4. Audubon's competing work is *The Birds of America, From Drawings Made in the United States and Their Territories*, 7 vols. (New York: J. J. Audubon, 1840-1844). Townsend's work presumably also appeared in the *Literary Record* of the Linnaean Association of Pennsylvania College, Gettysburg, Pennsylvania, vol. 4, no. 11 (September), 1848, pp. 249-55, 265-72, titled "Popular Monograph of the Acciptrine Birds of North America [sic]; no. 1: The Condor of the Andes Cathartes gryphus);" see Max Meisel, *A Bibliography of American Natural History: The Pioneer Century, 1769-1865*, 3 vols. (New York: The Premier Publishing Company, 1924-1929), 2:734. I see no justification for the remarks of Ford, *John James Audubon*, 355, that "Townsend was planning nothing more than a cheap, small book as his contribution to American ornithology. Even that little was painfully beyond his means."

52. William Baird to Spencer F. Baird, February 1, 1842, in William Healey Dall, *Spencer Fullerton Baird: A Biography, Including Selections from His Correspondence with Audubon, Agassiz, Dana, and Others* (Philadelphia: J. B. Lipincott Company, 1915), 75-76; Spencer F. Baird to William Baird, August 4, 1846, in Dall, *Spencer Fullerton Baird*; Dall, *Spencer Fullerton Baird*, 41; Meisel, *Bibliography of American Natural History*, 2:702, 703, 734; Stone, "John Kirk Townsend," 4-5; Stone, "Philadelphia to the Coast," 11.

53. William Baird to Spencer F. Baird, February 1, 1842, in Dall, *Spencer Fullerton Baird*, 76; Stone, "John Kirk Townsend," 4-5; Stone, "Philadelphia to the Coast," 11.

54. For example, see Kastner, *A Species of Eternity*, 281-82.

55. Palmer, "Notes on Some Persons Whose Names Appear," 299; Stone, "John Kirk Townsend," 1; Stone, "Philadelphia to the Coast," 10-11; Stone, "Some Philadelphia Ornithological Collections and Collectors," 171, 173; Richard C. Banks, Mary H. Clench, and Jon C. Barlow, "Bird Collections in the United States and Canada," *Auk* 90 (1973): 139.

56. See Thomas Nuttall, *A Manual of the Ornithology of the United States and of Canada. Second Edition, With Additions. The Land Birds* (Boston: Hilliard, Gray, and Company, 1840); Thomas M. Brewer, "North American Oölogy. Part I,—Raptores and Fissirostres," *Smithsonian Contributions to Knowledge* 11 (1859): 1-132; Spencer F. Baird, John Cassin, and George N. Lawrence, *Birds*, vol. 9, part 2, in *Reports of Explorations and Surveys to Ascertain the Most Practicable and Economical Route For a Railroad From the Mississippi River to the Pacific Ocean* (Washington, D.C.: Government Printing Office, 1858); Goetzmann, *Exploration and Empire*, 184, 185; Gordon Dodds, "Man and Nature in the Oregon Country: A Historical Survey," in Thomas Vaughn, ed., *The Western Shore: Oregon Country Essays Honoring the American Revolution* (Portland: Oregon Historical Society, [1976]), 354.

57. For the history of early medicine in the Pacific Northwest, see Larsell, "An Outline of the History of Medicine," passim.
58. Louis B. Wright, *Culture on the Moving Frontier* (New York:Harper & Row, 1955), 124-25.

Chapter I

1. For biographical information on Thomas Nuttall and Nathaniel Wyeth, see the introduction, as well as Jeanette E. Graustein, *Thomas Nuttall: Explorations in America, 1808-1841* (Cambridge: Harvard University Press, 1967), and Barbara Mearns and Richard Mearns, *Audubon to Xántus: The Lives of Those Commemorated in North American Bird Names* (San Diego, CA: Academic Press, 1992), 335-46; and Joseph Schafer, "Wyeth, Nathaniel Jarvis," *Dictionary of American Biography* 20 (1936): 576-77; and William R. Sampson, "Nathaniel Jarvis Wyeth," in LeRoy R. Hafen, ed., *The Mountain Men and the Fur Trade of the Far West*, X vols. (Glendale, CA: Arthur H. Clark Co., 1966), 5: 381-401.
2. For Black Hawk, see *Dictionary of American Biography* 2 (1929): 313-14.
3. St. Louis was at this time a principal center of the western fur trade industry. A year after Townsend and Nuttall's outfitting excursion, its population was over 8000, but in ten years had increased over fourfold. See James Neal Primm, *Lion of the Valley: St. Louis, Missouri* (Boulder, CO: Pruett Publishing Co., 1981), pp. 126ff.
4. This was the Carolina Parakeet, *Conuropsis carolinensis*, now extinct. Townsend's description of the ease of killing them, and the unease he felt at doing so, is quoted in Mikko Saikku, "The Extinction of the Carolina Parakeet," *Environmental History Review* 14 (no. 3, 1990): 9. Although Townsend here considered the parakeet present in vast numbers, it was thought even before this to be in decline (Audubon, *Ornithological Biography*, 1(1831): 138). The parakeet's extinction was precipitated by habitat destruction due to agricultural practises and settlement, as well as persecution by humans and the introduction to America of the European honeybee, which possibly competed with the parakeet for nest sites (Daniel McKinley, "The Carolina Parakeet in Pioneer Missouri," *Wilson Bulletin* 72(1960): 282-83; Saikku, "Extinction of the Carolina Parakeet," 10-15). The last Carolina Parakeet died in the Cincinnati Zoo in February 1918, just four years after the last Passenger Pigeon, *Ectopistes migratorius*, died at the same zoo (Mark V. Barrow, Jr., *A Passion for Birds: American Ornithology After Audubon* (Princeton, NJ: Princeton University Press, 1998): 106, 108; George Laycock, "The Last Parakeet," *Audubon Magazine* 71 (1969): 25.). Interestingly, an introduced parrot, the Monk Parakeet, *Myiopsitta monachus* (also known by aviculturists as the Quaker Parrot) is at present increasing in numbers in many of the areas once inhabited by the Carolina Parakeet.
5. For Jason and Daniel Lee, and their missionary efforts in Oregon, see especially Cornelius J. Brosnan, *Jason Lee: Prophet of the New Oregon* (New York: The Macmillan Company, 1932), and Robert J. Loewenberg, *Equality on the Oregon Frontier: Jason Lee and the Methodist Mission, 1834-43* (Seattle: Univ. of WA Press, 1976). Jason Lee's diary of the journey to Oregon on

the Wyeth expedition is in Jason Lee, "Diary of Rev. Jason Lee," *Oregon Historical Quarterly* 17 (1916): 116-46, 240-66, 397-430. Daniel Lee wrote an account of the mission in Lee and Frost, *Ten Years in Oregon.*

6. For more on the history of the Mormons in Missouri, and their persecutions, see Leonard J. Arrington and Davis Bitton, *The Mormon Experience: A History of the Latter-Day Saints* (New York: Alfred A. Knopf, 1979), 21, 44-64; Richard L. Bushman, "Mormon Persecutions in Missouri, 1833," *Brigham Young University Studies* 3 (1960): 11-20; and Warren Jennings, "The City in the Garden: Social Conflict in Jackson County, Missouri," in F. Mark McKiernan, Alma R. Blair, and Paul M. Edwards, eds., *The Restoration Movement: Essays in Mormon History* (Lawrence, KS: Coronado Press, 1973), 99-119.

Chapter II

1. Joseph Thing, Wyeth's second in command, was a Boston sea captain, born in Kentucky. Wyeth engaged him partly for his skill in making longitudinal and latitudinal observations. See Wyeth to Nuttall, February 4, 1834, in Young, "Correspondence and Journals," 106; Aubrey L. Haines, ed., *Osborne Russell's Journal of a Trapper* (Portland: Oregon Historical Society, 1955; reprint, Lincoln: University of Nebraska Press, Bison Books, 1965), 155, note 2; and Richard G. Beidleman, "Nathaniel Wyeth's Fort Hall," *Oregon Historical Quarterly* 58 (1957): 199.

2. Yellow-headed Blackbirds, *Xanthocephalus xanthocephalus*, a widespread western species. This species was here near the eastern edge of its range; see American Ornithologists' Union, *Check-list of North American Birds*, 6th ed. (Lawrence, KS: American Ornithologists' Union, 1983), 726. The other "black birds" were likely Red-winged Blackbirds, *Agelaius phoeniceus*. It was about this location that Townsend and Nuttall first encountered the Harris' Sparrow, *Zonotrichia querula*. Although the type specimen was collected by Edward Harris in Kansas and the species was named for him by his friend Audubon in 1844 (John J. Audubon, *Birds of America, From Drawings Made in the United States and Their Territories,* 7 vols (New York: J. J. Audubon, 1840-1844), 7: 331-32; and Herbert G. Deignan, "Type Specimens of Birds in the United States National Museum," *United States National Museum Bulletin* 221: 656-57), Nuttall was the first to describe the species; see Thomas Nuttall, *A Manual of the Ornithology of the United States and of Canada. Second Edition, with Additions* (Boston: Hilliard, Gray, and Company, 1840), 555; and AOU, *Check-list of North American Birds*, 6 ed., 1983: 715. Harry Harris, "Historical Notes on Harris's Sparrow (*Zonotrichia querula*), *Auk* 34 (1919); 180-90, provides a good discussion of the chronology of discovery and rediscovery of this large sparrow. Harris comments, p. 184, that Townsend did not mention the discovery of this species in the *Narrative* "of course due to courtesy to the discoverer [Nuttall] who had not yet given his species to science."

3. Reuben Gold Thwaites, ed., *Early Western Travels*, vol. 8 (Cleveland: Arthur H. Clark Company, 1905), 35, identifies "apishemeaus" as rush mats, "used for building wigwams, carpets, beds, and coverings of all sorts." E. S. Lohse, "Trade Goods," in Wilcomb E. Washburn, ed., *Handbook of North American Indians: History of Indian-White Relations* (Washington, D. C.:

Smithsonian Institution, 1988), 396-403, discusses the role trade goods played in Indian culture; and William R. Swagerty, "Indian Trade in the Trans-Mississippi West to 1870," in Washburn, *Handbook of North American Indians: History of Indian-White Relations*, 365-71, details trade in the period of Townsend's journey west.

4. For a biography of Milton Sublette, see Doyce B. Nunis, Jr., "Milton Sublette," in Hafen, *The Mountain Men and the Fur Trade of the Far West*, 4:331-49. Sublette died on April 5, 1837. Nunis remarks that Hiram M. Chittenden, *The American Fur Trade of the Far West*, 2 vols. (Stanford, CA: Academic Reprints, 1954), 1:254, incorrectly gives the date of Sublette's death as December 19, 1836 (given as 1838 in the 1935 edition), an error that has often been repeated.

5. For a biography of William Sublette, brother of Milton Sublette, see John E. Sunder, "William Lewis Sublette," in Hafen, *The Mountain Men and the Fur Trade of the Far West*, 5:347-59.

6. This is the Pronghorn, *Antilocapra americana*.

7. This is presumably Townsend's friend, Ezra Michener. For a biography of Michener, see *Dictionary of American Biography* 12 (1933): 596-97.

Chapter III

1. Franz Joseph Gall, born in Germany in 1758, originated the theory of phrenology, the belief that development of regions of the brain influenced the physiognomy of the cranium, and that an individual's character could be accurately analyzed by studying the shape of the skull. Gall's student and collaborator was Johann Gaspar Spurzheim, born in 1776, who coined the term phrenology. Through Gall's and Spurzheim's published works, and those of George Combe, who assiduosly attended Spurzheim's lectures in Edinburgh, phrenology enjoyed great popularity in England in the 1830s. Spurzheim himself brought popularity to the new science in America by a tour he began in 1832. He died in Boston on Novermber 10 of that year. For a review of phrenology's history, see John D. Davies, *Phrenology, Fad and Science: A 19th-Century American Crusade* (New Haven, CT: Yale Uiversity Press, 1955).

2. For Jason Lee's description of this incident, see Lee, "Diary," 125-26.

Chapter IV

1. Black-tailed Prairie Dog, *Cynomys ludovicianus*.

2. Plains Pocket Gopher, *Geomys bursarius*.

3. For the establishment of Fort Laramie, see LeRoy R. Hafen and Francis M. Young, *Fort Laramie and the Pageant of the West, 1834-1890* (Glendale, CA: Arthur H. Clark Co., 1988), 27-31; and Robert W. Frazer, *Forts of the West: Military Forts and Presidios and Posts Commonly Called Forts West of the Mississippi River to 1898* (Norman: University of Oklahoma Press, 1965), 181-82.

4. Probably the Prairie Rattlesnake, *Crotalus viridis*.

5. This was the Sage Thrasher, *Oreoscoptes montanus.*, named by Townsend in 1837 (Townsend, "Description of Twelve New Species of Birds," 192).

Chapter V

1. This was the tenth rendezvous of the fur trade. For a history of the rendezvous and the role it played in the fur trade, see Carl P. Russell, "Wilderness Rendezvous Period of the American Fur Trade," *Oregon Historical Quarterly* 42 (1941): 1-47; Russell discusses the rendezvous of 1834 on pp. 27-30.
2. Sage Grouse, *Centrocercus urophasianus.*
3. Sir William Drummond Stewart of Scotland adventured in the western United States in the 1830s and 1840s, returning home to assume a position among the Scottish nobility. For his biography, see Mae Reed Porter and Odessa Davenport, *Scotsman in Buckskin: Sir William Drummond Stewart and the Rocky Mountain Fur Trade* (New York: Hastings House, Publishers, 1963); Stewart's association with Townsend and the Wyeth expedition are detailed on pp. 85-100.
4. Of Ashworth's life, little is known. John McLoughlin wrote disparagingly of him, noting that "all that Captain [William] Stewart and the rest of [Wyeth's] party know of him is from his own story and that they found him in the Rocky Mountains among the American trappers without being employed by any one and going for his food from one party to another which to say the least of is discreditable" (McLoughlin to The Governor Deputy Governor & Committee of the Honble. Hudsons Bay Coy., November 18, 1834, in Rich, *The Letters of John McLoughlin*, 126-27). Ashworth is also mentioned in unflattering terms in Porter and Davenport, *Scotsman in Buckskins*, 81, 86, 89, 93-94.
5. Yellow Warbler, *Dendroica petechia.*
6. These are the Lewis' Woodpecker, *Melanerpes lewis,* and the Clark's Nutcracker, *Nucifraga columbiana,* discovered by Meriwether Lewis and William Clark on their expedition to the Pacific in 1803-1805, and named in their honor by Alexander Wilson (American Ornithologists' Union Committee, *Check-list of North American Birds,* 6th ed., 382, 507; Cutright, *Lewis and Clark: Pioneering Naturalists,* 384-87).
7. For a biography of Thomas McKay, see Annie Laurie Bird, "Thomas McKay," *Oregon Historical Quarterly* 40 (1939): 1-14.
8. For a history of the construction and operation of Fort Hall, see Beidleman, "Nathaniel Wyeth's Fort Hall," 196-250, and Carl P. Russell, *Firearms, Traps, & Tools of the Mountain Men* (New York: Alfred A. Knopf, 1967), 338-39.

Chapter VI

1. Jason Lee describes the accident and his service in Lee, "Diary," 241; and Nathaniel Wyeth describes the same in Young, "Correspondence and Journals," 227.

Chapter VII

1. Mule deer, *Odocoileus hemionus.*
2. The term Snake referred to several groups of Indians living in the northern Great Basin region. At this geographical location, the Indians present were

most likely Northern Shoshone or Bannock, although Northern Paiute and Western Shoshone are also possible; see Robert F. Murphy and Yolanda Murphy, "Northern Shoshone and Bannock," in Warren L. D'Azevedo, ed., *Handbook of North American Indians: Great Basin* (Washington, D. C.: Smithsonian Institution, 1986), 286, 305. For the synonymy of Snake with the at present preferred Shoshone, see Ives Goddard, "Synonymy," in Demitri B. Shimkin, "Eastern Shoshone," in D'Azevedo, *Handbook of North American Indians: Great Basin*, 334.

3. Common Camas, *Camassia quamash.*
4. Apparently a plant of the genus *Psoralea*; C. Leo Hitchcock and Arthur Cronquist, *Flora of the Pacific Northwest: An Illustrated Manual* (Seattle: Univ. of WA Press, 1973), 272, give bread-root as a colloquial name for the group.

Chapter VIII

1. Black Cottonwood.
2. The Malheur River flows from the Blue Mountains, running south and east into the Snake River at Ontario, Oregon. Although Townsend uses the name as a possessive, suggesting an eponymous individual, the name derives from *mal heur*, a French-Canadian idiom for misfortune used by Peter Skene Ogden in 1826 to identify the river because of the loss of furs and property; see McArthur, *Oregon Geographic Names*, 553.

Chapter IX

1. This is the Umatilla River, which flows northwest from the Blue Mountains into the Columbia River at the present town of Umatilla, Oregon. McArthur, *Oregon Geographic Names*, 857, discusses various forms the name has taken in early explorers' journals.
2. Fort Walla Walla was a Hudson's Bay Company fur and supply post at the junction of the Walla Walla River and the Columbia River, in present day southeastern Washington. See Howard McKinley Corning, ed., *Dictionary of Oregon History* (Portland, OR: Binford and Mort Publishing, 1956), 90.
3. For biographies of Pambrun, see Corning, *Dictionary of Oregon History*, 191, and Rich, *The Letters of John McLoughlin*, 351-52.
4. Much has been written about the life of John McLoughlin, an influential figure in Oregon History. For an overview, see Richard G. Montgomery, *The White-headed Eagle: John McLoughlin, Builder of an Empire* (New York: The Macmillan Company, 1935). Material illuminating McLoughlin's relationship with the Hudson's Bay Company is in Rich, *The Letters of John McLoughlin*.

Chapter X

1. See also *Oregon Historical Quarterly* 4 (1903), 399-402; Corning, *Dictionary of Oregon History*, 90; and Louis R. Caywood, "The Archeological Excavation of Fort Vancouver," *Oregon Historical Quarterly* 49 (1948), 99-116.

2. For more on Lee's Methodist mission, see Lee and Frost, *Ten Years in Oregon*; Brosnan, *Jason Lee: Prophet of the New Oregon*, 70ff; and Loewenberg, *Equality on the Oregon Frontier*.

3. Warrior Point is at the north end of Sauvie Island, Oregon; a large basaltic rock here provided a natural dock or wharf. Its name derives from an incident involving an encounter in 1792 bewteen members of George Vancouver's party and a party of Indians; see McArthur, *Oregon Geographic Names*, 886.

4. For the history of Kanakas, or Hawaiian Islanders, in the Pacific Northwest, see Janice K. Duncan, *Minority Without a Champion: Kanakas on the Pacific Coast, 1788-1850* (Portland: Oregon Historical Society, 1972), and Tom Koppel, *Kanaka: The Untold Story of Hawaiian Pioneers in British Columbia and the Pacific Northwest* (Vancouver, BC: Whitecap Books, 1995). Duncan and Koppel detail Wyeth's employment of Hawaiian Islanders on pp. 8-9 and 29-30, respectively. See Young, *Correspondence*, pp. 148-49 for Wyeth's description of the desertion of several islanders that were to accompany Captain Thing to Fort Hall.

5. Townsend's Wappatoo Island is now known as Sauvie Island. The older name derived from a plant, the wapato, or arrowhead, *Sagittaria latifolia*, which was a food source and trade item for the Chinookan Indians. For a description of Indian gathering and use of wapato, see Gary E. Moulton, ed., *The Journals of the Lewis & Clark Expedition*, X vols (Lincoln: University of Nebraska Press, 1990), 6:17, 44, 49-50, 142, 144.

6. Townsend's comments of collecting "several new species of birds" while residing on Wyeth's brig again suggests that the generally accepted type locality for many of his new species, Fort Vancouver, is not accurate and should instead be Sauvie Island. See also the introduction, note 37.

7. The nature of this affliction, which had a devestating effect on the Indian population of the lower Columbia River drainage, was debated by historians, but now is recognized as malaria. The disease, spread by mosquitoes, was brought to the area perhaps through visits of ships carrying infected sailors or through the arrival of traders or trappers that had become infected somewhere on their journey west. It first appeared in late summer or early fall of 1830, and continued causing epidemic loss of life throughout the decade. By the early 1840s, the loss of the native population had been over 90 percent. See Robert T. Boyd, "Another Look at the 'Fever and Ague' of Western Oregon," *Ethnohistory* 22 (1975): 139-42; Robert T. Boyd, "Demographic History, 1774-1874," in Wayne Suttles, ed., *Handbook of North Americam Indians: Northwest Coast* (Washington, D.C.: Smithsonian Institute, 1990), 139-40; and Herbert C. Taylor and Lester L. Hoaglin, Jr., "The 'Intermittent Fever' Epidemic of the 1830's on the Lower Columbia River," *Ethnohistory* 9 (1962): 167-73.

8. This matter is discussed by Wyeth in journal entries from November 10 through December 4, 1834, in Young, "Correspondence and Journals," 235-37; and in Duncan, "Minority Without a Champion," 8-9.

9. See Grace P. Morris, "Development of Astoria, 1811-1850," *Oregon Historical Quarterly*, 38 (1937), 413-19.

10. Peter Skene Ogden was a principle figure in the Hudson's Bay Company and a peripatetic explorer of the western fur lands. See T. C. Elliott, "Peter

Skene Ogden, Fur Trader," *Quarterly of the Oregon Historical Society*, 11 (1910), 229-78; and Corning, *Dictionary of Oregon History*, 178.

11. Pages 135-59 were deleted by Reuben Gold Thwaites in his 1905 reprint of the *Narrative*; see Thwaites, *Early Western Travels*, Vol. 8 (Cleveland, OH: Arthur H. Clark, 1905).

12. This could have been any of the three tropicbird species, but most likely was either the White-tailed Tropicbird, *Phaeton lepturus*, or the Red-tailed Tropicbird, *P. rubricauda*. Townsend's later description of tropicbirds seen on his voyage home, p. 196, are of Red-tailed Tropicbirds.

Chapter XI

1. Richard Charlton was British Consul and John C. Jones, Jr., was "Agent of the United States for Commerce and Seamen" (akin to a Consul) during Townsend's visit. William French, Eliab Grimes, and T. C. B. Rooke were merchants and traders. See Kuykendall, *The Hawaiian Kingdom, 1778-1854*, 80, 90, 95, 98, 180.

2. A description of Hiram Bingham and an account of his twenty-one years of missionary work in Hawaii, 1820-1841, is in Tabrah, *Hawaii: A Bicentennial History*, 37-48. Bingham is also discussed extensively in Bradford Smith, *Yankees in Paradise: The New England Impact on Hawaii* (Philadelphia: J. B. Lippincott Company, 1956). Bingham's own account is *A Residence of Twenty-one Years in the Sandwich Islands* (Hartford, CT: Hezekiah Huntington, 1847).

3. King Kamehameha III, or Kauikeaouli, became the ruler of Hawaii at the age of nine (under a regency) when his brother, King Kamehameha II, or Lihiliho, died in London of measles in 1824. Kamehameha's reign is discussed extensively in Kuykendall, *The Hawaiian Kingdom, 1778-1854*; and also in Tabrah, *Hawaii: A Bicentennial History*, 50-65.

4. This was the Nuuanu Pali, a high cliff, 2000 feet high, formed by erosion on the windward side of Oahu. For a brief discussion of its geological origins, see Joseph R. Morgan, *Hawaii: A Unique Geography* (Honolulu: Bess Press, 1996), 16; and Harold T. Stearns, *Geology of the State of Hawaii* (Palo Alto, CA: Pacific Books, 1966), 81-82.

Chapter XII

1. The Reverend Peter J. Gulick and his wife were Protestant missionaries on Kauai, on Hawaii, and on Oahu; see Smith, *Yankees in Paradise*, 168, 291, 342.

2. Townsend was the first naturalist to collect birds on Kauai (the only previous specimens from the island were of the Iiwi, *Vestiaria coccinea*, received in barter by members of Captain James Cook's 1778 visit to the island). Townsend's Kauai collection was broken up after Nuttall returned to the east, some going to the Academy of Natural Sciences of Philadelphia and some to Audubon, who in turn sold many to collectors in Europe. As a consequence, neither Townsend nor his Hawaiian collection received the attention they deserved. The Anianiau, *Hemignathus parvus*, was not named until 1887 from material collected in 1866 (Leonhard Stejneger, "Birds of Kauai Island, Hawaiian Archipelago, Collected by Mr. Valdemar Knudsen,

with Descriptions of New Species," *Proceedings of the United States National Museum* 10 (1887): 94-95), despite a Townsend specimen in the collection of the Smithsonian Institution, and noted by Stejneger. See David S. Medway, "The Contribution of Cook's Third Voyage to the Ornithology of the Hawaiian Islands," *Pacific Science* 35 (1981): 128-30; and Storrs L. Olson and Helen F. James, "A Chronology of Ornithological Exploration in the Hawaiian Islands, From Cook to Perkins," in Joseph R. Jehl, Jr. and Ned K. Johnson, eds., *A Century of Avifaunal Change in Western North America*, Studies in Avian Biology No. 15 (Lawrence, KS: Cooper Ornithological Society, 1994), 96.

3. Townsend's and Nuttall's shell collection was studied and published by J. W. Randall, "Catalogue of the Crustacea Brought by Thomas Nuttall and J. K. Townsend, from the West Coast of North America and the Sandwich Islands, with Descriptions of Such Species as are Apparently New, Among Which are Included Several Species of Different Localities, Previously Existing in the Collection of the Academy," *Journal of the Academy of Natural Sciences of Philadelphia* 8 (1839), 106-7.

4. It is not clear what species or group of birds Townsend means by *grallae*. In the Linnaean classification system, the Grallae was the fourth Order of birds, and included the herons, flamingoes, coots and rails, bustards and ostriches; see Alfred Newton and Hans Gadow, *A Dictionary of Birds* (London: Adam and Charles Black, 1893-1896), 379-80. As plovers and sandpipers were also members of this order, perhaps these are what Townsend meant. Another possibility, given that they are small birds on the open ocean, is that the *grallae* might be one of several species of storm-petrels.

Chapter XIII

1. Oak Point is about 40 miles inland from the mouth of the Columbia River on the south bank. It is about 30 miles downriver from Warrior Point at the northern end of Sauvie Island; see McArthur, *Oregon Geographic Names*, 628-29.

2. Wyeth's hardships can be followed in his correspondence to family, friends, and associates in the east in Young, "Correspondence and Journals." See in particular Wyeth to Friend Weld, April 3, 1835, pp. 148-49.

3. Of the warbler species discovered by Townsend in the northwest, only the Black-throated Gray Warbler, *Dendroica nigriscens*, is recognized as having Fort William, on Sauvie Island, as its type locality, the other species being identified as from Fort Vancouver. Townsend's statement here, while residing on the brig *May Dacre*, anchored on the north end of Sauvie Island, suggests that Sauvie Island is a more plausible type locality for these species. See also the introduction, note 37.

4. Nathaniel Wyeth built Fort William, which was to serve as his base and trading post, on the southwest side of Sauvie Island (what Townsend called Wappatoo Island), on the Willamette Slough, about 5 1/2 miles south of the present town of Scappoose. However, Fort William lasted only about one year. When Wyeth returned to the east, his Columbia Fishing and Trading Company a financial failure, the site was acquired by the Hudson Bay Company as a dairy. See J. Neilson Barry, *Fort William, 1835* (Portland, OR: Hill Miltary Academy, n.d.), not paginated; Spencer, *The Story of*

Sauvies Island, 41-44; and Cleaver, *Island Origins: Trappers, Traders & Settlers*, 9, 12, 21.

5. The Kalapuyans were here at the northern end of their Willamette Valley territory; the division Townsend encountered on the Clackamas River near present day Portland was presumably the Tualatin dialectic group. The population of the Kalapuyans declined catastrophically in the early 1830s because of malaria; see discussion in chapter 14, note 1; and Henry B. Zenk, "Kalapuyans," in Suttles, ed., *Handbook of North American Indians: Northwest Coast*, 548, 551. (Boyd 1975?)

6. The Chinook Jargon was a widespread trading language in the Northwest which probably pre-dated white contact with native speakers, but later incorporated elements of English and French; see Melville Jacobs, "Notes on the Structure of Chinook Jargon," *Language* 8 (1932): 27-28; Rena V. Grant, "Chinook Jargon," *International Journal of American Linguistics* 11 (1945): 225-27; Sarah Grey Thomason, "Chinook Jargon in Areal and Historical Context," *Language* 59 (1983): 859-67; and Laurence C. Thompson and M. Dale Kinkade, "Languages," in Suttles, ed., *Handbook of North American Indians: Northwest Coast*, 41. Richard Maxwell Brown's essay, "Language and Exploration: The Role of the Chinook Jargon," in Carlos Schwantes, ed., *Encounters with a Distant Land: Exploration and the Great Northwest* (Moscow, ID: University of Idaho Press, 1994), 86-101, shows the role Chinook Jargon played in several aspects—territorial, scientific, ethnographic, artistic—of exploration of the Northwest.

7. James L. Lambert, captain of Wyeth's brig, the *May Dacre*. Captain Lambert had been in command of Wyeth's first supply ship, the *Sultana*, which was to meet him during Wyeth's first overland trip to Oregon, in 1832. The *Sultana*, however, ran aground on a reef in the South Pacific. Lambert's command of the *May Dacre* was less eventful, though the experience was no more profitable for Wyeth. See Frances Fuller Victor, "Flotsom and Jetsom of the Pacific—the *Owyhee*, the *Sultana*, and the *May Dacre*," *Oregon Historical Quarterly* 2 (1901): 41-42, 53.

8. See introduction, note 42.

9. Regarding Gairdner, see Corning, *Dictionary of Oregon History*, 95; and A. G. Harvey, "Chief Concomly's Skull," *Oregon Historical Quarterly* 40 (1939), 163-66.

Chapter XIV

1. The population of the Northwest Coast Indians declined steadily from an aboriginal population of nearly 190,000 to about 75,000 by the mid 1830s. Aboriginal populations of groups Townsend had contact with—principally the Upper Chinookan groups of the Multnomah and Clackamas—were about 10,000 but arrival of Euro-Americans exposed the native populations to infectious diseases and the population declined in episodic fashion. On October 11, 1830, John McLoughlin wrote to his superiors in the Hudson Bay Company that three fourths of the Indian population in the vicinity of Fort Vancouver had died of the "Intermitting Fever," now believed to be malaria (see Chapter X, note 7). See John McLoughlin to The Govr. deputy Govr. and Committe Honble. Hudsons Bay Company, October 11, 1830, in Rich, *The Letters of John McLoughlin*, 88; Boyd, "Demographic History,

1774-1874," 136 (table 1), 137-39, 147; and Herbert C. Taylor, Jr.,
"Aboriginal Population of the Lower Northwest Coast," *Pacific Northwest Quarterly* 54 (1963): 164.

2. In a letter to his family, Townsend remarked that he felt deserted by Nuttall, and complained about Nuttall's lack of explanation for leaving; see Townsend to Charles Townsend, April 11, 1836, Townsend papers.

3. For a biography of Samuel Parker, see *Dictionary of American Biography* 14 (1934), 237-38. Parker's report was *Journal of an Exploring Tour Beyond the Rocky Mountains...* (Ithaca, NY: By the author, 1838); five American editions were published. See also the introduction, note 38.

4. For biographical sketches of William Fraser Tolmie, see Corning, *Dictionary of Oregon History*, 245-46; Johnson, "Early Medical Men in the Northwest," 214-17; Larsell, "An Outline of the History of Medicine," 483-85; and Howard T. Mitchell, "The Diarist," 1-10, *in* W. F. Tolmie, *The Journals of William Fraser Tolmie, Physician and Fur Trader* (Vancouver, BC: Mitchell Press Limited, 1963). Tolmie's diary unfortunately ended before his arrival at Fort Vancouver to relieve Townsend of the duties of surgeon. Townsend named the MacGillivaray's Warbler, *Opornis tolmiei*, after Tolmie (Townsend, "Description of a New Species of *Sylvia*," 150.

5. For discussion of Townsend"s treatment of Indians suffering from malaria, see Boyd, "Another Look at the 'Fever and Ague' of Western Oregon," 140-42.

6. Townsend here is unaware of the relatively recent arrival of malaria to the region; see Boyd, "Demographic History, 1774-1874," 139-40 for a chronology. Gunther, *Ethnobotany of Western Washington*, 42, discusses native use of dogwood as an emetic, laxative and physic.

7. This was probably the California Ground Squirrel, *Spermophilus beecheyi*.

8. Sharp-tailed Grouse, *Tympanuchus phasianellus*.

Chapter XV

1. Blue Grouse, *Dendragapus obscurus*.

2. For biographies of Marcus and Narcissa Whitman, Henry and Eliza Spalding, and William Gray, see Corning, *Dictionary of Oregon History*, 103, 229, 264; *Dictionary of American Biography* 20 (1936), 141-43; Clifford Merrill Drury, *Henry Harmon Spalding* (Caldwell, ID: The Caxton Printers, 1036); Drury, *Marcus Whitman, M.D.: Pioneer and Martyr* (Caldwell, ID: The Caxton Printers, 1937); and Nard Jones, *Marcus Whitman: The Great Command; the Story of Marcus and Narcissa Whitman and the Oregon Country Pioneers* (Portland, OR: Binfords and Mort, 1959).

3. Regarding James Birnie, see Thomas Nelson Strong, *Cathlamet on the Columbia* (Portland, OR: Metropolitan Press, 1930), 97-99; and Corning, *Dictionary of Oregon History*, 28.

Chapter XVI

1. Thwaites deleted all of the material from p. 197 to the end of the *Narrative*, including the scientific appendix, from his 1905 reprint.

2. Red-tailed Tropicbirds, *Phaeton rubricauda*. See also chapter 10, note 12.

3. A description of Nahienaena, and a brief account of her incestuous relationship with her brother, King Kamehameha III, and her death, is in Tabrah, *Hawaii: A Bicentennial History*, 49-51; and in Smith, *Yankees in Paradise*, 116, 181, 197.

4. Ferdinand Deppe, born in 1794, worked as a gardener for the Royal Gardens and was associated with the Zoological Museum of Berlin University, until selected to accompany Count von Sack to Mexico as a naturalist. Deppe collected birds, and other natural history objects, in Mexico from 1824 until 1826. Deppe returned to Berlin, then traveled again to Mexico where he worked as a merchants' commission agent. In 1836, when he appears in the *Narrative*, he was returning to Berlin again. He died in 1860. See Erwin Stresemann, "Ferdinand Deppe's travels in Mexico, 1824-1829," *Condor* 56 (1954): 86-88.

5. See introduction, note 44.

Chapter XVII

1. Dr. Dwight Baldwin, the Reverend Sheldon Dibble, and the Reverend Lorrin Andrews were missionaries and teachers on Maui, Andrews later receiving appointment as a Justice of the Superior Court. See Kuykendall, *The Hawaiian Kingdom, 177801854*, 111, 258, 264, 431.

2. Andrews's "A Vocabulary of Words in the Hawaiian Language" was published in 1836, and his dictionary first appeared in 1865; see Lorrin Andrews, *A Dictionary of the Hawaiian Language*, revised by Henry H. Parker (Honolulu: Board of Commissioners of Public Archives of the Territory of Hawaii, 1922), iii.

3. John Adams, known also by his Hawaiian name, Kuakini, was the brother of Kaahumanu, the favorite wife of Kamehameha I. Kaahumanu acted as regent during Kamehameha III's youth. During her regency she appointed Kuakini as acting Governor of Oahu. See Kuykendall, *The Hawaiian Kingdom, 1778-1854*, 125, 130; and Tabrah, *Hawaii: A Bicentennial History*, 32, 42.

4. Townsend's report that the Hawaiian Crow, *Corvus hawaiiensis*, was said to be "numerous at times" was supported also by Henshaw, *Birds of the Hawaiian Islands*, 36. However, The National Research Council, *Scientific Bases of the Preservation of the Hawaiian Crow* (Washington, DC: National Academy Press, 1992), 12-13, describe its range on the island of Hawai'i as restricted, and it is at present near extinction.

5. George Pritchard was a Protestant missionary and British consul in Tahiti, and Jacques Moerenhout, a Belgian, was United States Consul during Townsend's visit (later French Consul). Pritchard and Moerenhout were rivals, both in their trading activities and in missionary interests by the Protestants (represented by Pritchard) and Catholics (supported by Moerenhout). During Pritchard's absence from Tahiti in 1842, Moerenhout helped arrange a Tahitian request for protection by France, a step towards French annexation in 1843. See Colin Newbury, *Tahiti Nui: Change and Survival in French Polynesia, 1767-1945* (Honolulu: The University Press of Hawaii, 1980), 77, 78, 93, 95-98, 106-10.

6. Townsend's collecting activities in Tahiti are hinted at in Deignan, "Type Specimens of Birds," 105.

Chapter XVIII

1. For a discussion of the Chile-Peru conflict of the late 1830s, and the kidnapping and assassination of Diego Portales, see Robert N. Burr, *By Reason or Force: Chile and the Balancing of Power in South America, 1830-1905* (Berkeley: University of California Press, 1965), 33-57.
2. Although Townsend makes no mention of collecting birds after leaving Chili, see Deignan, "Type Specimens of Birds," 638.

Appendix

1. The scientific appendix was deleted by Thwaites, *Early Western Travels*, and was not included in the Ye Galleon Press and Bison Books reprints of Thwaites' abridgment. It has been reprinted separately in Keir B. Sterling, ed., *Early Nineteenth-Century Studies and Surveys* (New York: Arno Press, 1974), with the appendix's original pagination.

   Readers should be aware that Townsend's use of the term "Territory of the Oregon" preceding both the mammal and bird lists in the appendix is geographically broad, encompassing essentially all of the country traversed by the Wyeth party west of the Mississippi River. I have discussed this elsewhere in Jobanek, "Dubious Records in the Early Oregon Bird Literature," 3.

   The scientific appendix is also antiquated both in its systematics and its nomenclature. I have not attempted here to update the lists to current standards.
2. Townsend's mammal accounts are based on three articles by John Bachman: Bachman, "Observations on the Different Species of Hares (Genus *Lepus*) inhabiting the United States and Canada," *Journal of the Academy of Natural Sciences of Philadelphia* 7, part 2 (1837): 282-361, 403; Bachman, "Description of Several New Species of Quadrupeds," *Journal of the Academy of Natural Sciences of Philadelphia* 8, part 1 (1838): 57-74; and Bachman, "Additional Remarks on the Genus *Lepus*, with Corrections of a Former Paper and Descriptions of Quadrupeds Found in North America," *Journal of the Academy of Natural Sciences of Philadelphia* 8, part 1 (1840): 75-105.
3. For this and many of the following species, see also Townsend, "Description of Twelve New Species," 187-93.
4. See also Townsend, "Description of a New Species of *Sylvia*," 149-50; and Townsend, "Note on *Sylvia* Tolmoei," 159.
5. See also Townsend, "Description of a New Species of *Cypcelus*," 148.